7

RACE
AND
THE MAKING
OF AMERICAN
LIBERALISM

This cover illustration from an 1879 edition of *Harper's Weekly* illustrates both the complexity and fluidity of racial categories and their relationship to critical social, economic, and political developments of the day.

RACE

AND

THE MAKING

OF AMERICAN

LIBERALISM

Carol A. Horton

OXFORD
UNIVERSITY PRESS

2005

OXFORD

UNIVERSITY PRESS

Oxford University Press, Inc., publishes works that further
Oxford University's objective of excellence
in research, scholarship, and education.

Oxford   New York
Auckland   Cape Town   Dar es Salaam   Hong Kong   Karachi
Kuala Lumpur   Madrid   Melbourne   Mexico City   Nairobi
New Delhi   Shanghai   Taipei   Toronto

With offices in
Argentina   Austria   Brazil   Chile   Czech Republic   France   Greece
Guatemala   Hungary   Italy   Japan   Poland   Portugal   Singapore
South Korea   Switzerland   Thailand   Turkey   Ukraine   Vietnam

Copyright © 2005 by Oxford University Press

Published by Oxford University Press, Inc.
198 Madison Avenue, New York, New York 10016

www.oup.com

Library of Congress Cataloging-in-Publication Data
Horton, Carol A.
Race and the making of American liberalism / by Carol A. Horton.
    p. cm.
Includes bibliographical references.
ISBN-13 978-0-19-514348-5
ISBN 0-19-514348-5
1. United States—Race relations—Political aspects—History.
2. Racism—Political aspects—United States—History.
3. Social classes—Political aspects—United States—History.
4. Liberalism—United States—History.   5. United States—
Politics and government.   6.   United States—Social conditions.
7. Civil rights—United States—History.   I. Title.
E184.A1H656 2005
320.51'3'0973—dc22   2004024156

9 8 7 6 5 4 3 2 1
Printed in the United States of America
on acid-free paper

To Gary, Luke, and James

Acknowledgments

I have worked on this book on and off for longer than I care to state. It's correspondingly hard to find words that describe how I feel to be at the point where I can formally thank all of the individuals and organizations that have assisted and supported me along the way. But I am grateful, and there are many to thank.

Way back long ago in graduate school at the University of Chicago, I was fortunate enough to study and work with the late J. David Greenstone. His work on liberalism and American political thought set me on a path of inquiry that has sustained me throughout the course of writing this book. David exerted a formative influence on my intellectual development and I am grateful for it.

While it would require too long a list to acknowledge all of the individuals who influenced my thinking about race and American politics while at the University of Chicago, I would like to once again thank John Comaroff, Michael Dawson, Gary Orfield, and Cass Sunstein for serving on my dissertation committee and providing me with such varied and exciting examples of politically relevant scholarship. I would also like to specially thank Cass

Sunstein for his continued support as I took on the project of turning my dissertation into a book. I feel very fortunate to have had the opportunity to connect with such a brilliant and socially engaged scholar.

After leaving the University of Chicago, I had the good fortune to join the faculty of Macalester College in St. Paul, Minnesota. Macalester provided me with an environment that valued excellent pedagogy, intellectual creativity, and civic engagement. I learned much while I was there and grew as both a scholar and a person. I would particularly like to thank Chuck Green and David Blaney for being such supportive colleagues, Peter Rachleff for deepening my knowledge of the American labor movement, and my many wonderful students for inspiring me with their talent, energy, and ideas.

In 1997, I made the difficult decision to leave academia so that I could live in the same city as my husband and start a family. Back once more in Chicago, the Center for the Study of Race, Politics, and Culture at the University of Chicago generously provided me with temporary office space to work on what would eventually become this book. Thanks to Evalyn Tennant for helping me out with this arrangement and for her comradeship throughout the years.

In 1999, while living with my husband and young son in Göttingen, Germany, the Soziologisches Forschungsinstitut (SOFI) provided me with an office in which I could once again work on this manuscript. Officials at the Georg-August-Universität Göttingen also agreed to provide access to their library, which, to my good fortune, had an excellent collection of English-language social science materials. Many thanks are due to Professor Dr. Volker Wittke, Professor Dr. Michael Schumann, and Professor Dr. Martin Baethge for their generosity in extending these resources to me. I would also like to thank Ulrich Voskamp and Beate Henschel for their friendship and support, and Eva Bojemski for her help in taking care of Luke and for the opportunity to develop a relationship that crossed a formidable language barrier.

Upon returning from Germany, I was fortunate to be able to secure a book contract with Oxford University Press and to have Dedi Felman as my editor. Dedi and several anonymous reviewers provided me with wonderfully constructive criticism and insightful suggestions that enabled me to improve this book tremendously. I am particularly grateful to them for insisting that I develop my own voice and present my ideas as clearly and directly as possible. I am also indebted to Dedi for her patience and understanding through the course of an on-again, off-again writing process that had to be balanced with the birth of my second child and the development of a second career.

I would like to thank David Ericson, Tony Pinn, David Roediger, Rogers Smith, and Rick Valelly for reading and commenting on work that would eventuate in this book. Special thanks are due to Kelly Kleinman for helping me with my book proposal and for her friendship over the past seven years. Although they did not engage with me directly on this project, I would like to thank Marcia Kingslow and Robert Halpern for their friendship, collegiality, and support. The applied research that I have done with each of them on issues ranging from the building of women's health coalitions to the assessment of an after-school program initiative in Baltimore broadened my horizons and had an important impact on how I thought about the issues addressed in this book.

I would additionally like to thank my mother, Phyllis Horton, and my sister, Marion Horton, for their love and support over the years. Marion also helped me with my book proposal and provided needed assistance with child care at critical junctures in the writing process.

Words once again fail me when I try to think of a way to thank my husband, Gary Herrigel, for his love and support in the course of not simply writing this book, but living our lives and creating our family. We have been blessed with two amazing children, Luke and James. The love that we experience as a family has immeasurably deepened my experience of and appreciation for life. I am most grateful because I know that we share what words cannot express.

Contents

RACE
AND
THE MAKING
OF AMERICAN
LIBERALISM

INTRODUCTION

Race and American Liberalism

What is the best way to understand the relationship between race and liberalism in American political development? Has the historical experience of racial inequality been a troubling exception to a generally liberal rule of equal rights and opportunities? Or, has racial oppression constituted a basic component of American liberalism—albeit one that has been imperfectly masked by cultural pieties of individualism and equality? Has liberalism, in other words, functioned primarily as a progressive engine for racial equity or as an oppressive tool of racial injustice?

The American experience would be much easier to comprehend if such questions could be given simple answers. If liberalism could be neatly categorized as either a positive or negative force with regard to the nation's racial history, it would be easy to judge. This would be ethically and politically comforting, as we could rest secure in our estimation of the nation's primary political creed. The historical record, however, has been vexingly variable and complex. Viewed dispassionately, it cannot affirm that liberalism has played a consistently positive or negative role in whatever movement the nation has made toward the realization of racial justice.

Powerful variants of American liberalism have endorsed the maintenance of racial hierarchy while asserting fidelity to the principle of equal rights under the law. Alternative constructions of liberalism have combined the goals of nondiscrimination and social equity to produce exceptionally radical visions of American democracy. Viewed across a broad historical expanse, both more racially equalitarian and hierarchical forms of liberalism have played significant roles in the nation's political development. Consequently, it is impossible to issue a verdict regarding the fundamental nature of liberal politics with regard to issues of racial justice.

This does not mean that the relationship between race and liberalism has been inconsequential. When considered as a complex and variable dynamic, rather than as a singular set of substantive positions, this relationship has embodied an important set of historical patterns. Most notably, it demonstrates the long-standing significance of liberalism as the primary language of American politics, the pivotal importance of race in constructing different varieties of liberalism, and the tendency of racial politics to cement the dominance of forms of liberalism that erase socioeconomic factors from the calculation of civic equity in the United States.

Viewed from this perspective, race has played a primary role in the making of American liberalism. This has been a complex and double-edged phenomenon. On the one hand, race has been instrumental in creating some of the nation's most radically democratic forms of liberal politics, which emphasize the inclusion of the disfranchised, the importance of socioeconomic equity, and, more recently, the value of cultural diversity. On the other, it has reinforced the dominance of relatively inequitable forms of liberalism, which use the equation of equal rights and free markets to legitimate grossly unequal distributions of wealth, power, and status. As such, the story of race and liberalism in the United States is not one that simply concerns the racially disfranchised. On the contrary, it includes the entire nation and the dominant vision of civic equity that it embodies.

Multiple Liberalisms

Many, if not most, students of American politics would likely view the claim that liberalism is capable of encompassing positions with either an emancipatory or an oppressive relationship to racial justice as unacceptably broad. With regard to basic equity issues, liberalism tends to be viewed in all-or-nothing terms. Scholars with generally positive attitudes toward liberalism typically define it in ways that exclude the possibility of its support of ascriptive social categories or group-based discrimination.[1] The minority that holds a more negative view of liberalism follows a more Marxian-influenced line of argument, holding that it necessarily produces such inequities and exclusions.[2] Consequently, the claim that liberalism is flexible enough to have historically represented both racially progressive and retrogressive positions (as well as a variety of intermediate options whose ethical weight is more open to debate) is generally either not considered or dismissed as overly broad or illogical.[3]

Treating liberalism as a variegated, flexible, and politically contested discourse is in keeping, however, with widely accepted theories of cultural practice. Following the historical and linguistic turns in the social sciences, it is reasonable to examine American liberalism as a historically embedded, socially constructed discourse that has been of long-standing importance in American political development, even while it has remained open to continual contestation and change.[4] While liberalism can be defined as representing a core set of political commitments, these are large and indeterminate enough to be understood in a wide variety of ways. Viewed from this perspective, liberalism represents an evolving political language that has encompassed a variety of particular and often competing formulations. What it means in practice has necessarily varied substantially across time and among competing groups of political actors.[5]

For the purposes of this book, *American liberalism* may be defined as a framework for the fundamentals of political life that prioritizes the value of individual rights and liberties, limited and representative government, private property and free markets, and constitutionalism and the rule of law. Although these are broad categories whose precise meanings are open to interpretation, they represent principles that are by no means shared by all varieties of political thought. As decades of historical work have demonstrated, Americans have subscribed to a wide range of nonliberal political beliefs, including civic republicanism, anarchism, socialism, communism, religious fundamentalism, radical feminism, and varieties of black and white nationalism, among others. Lacking an essential commitment to political individualism, free-market capitalism, or constitutional government, such traditions cannot be considered part of an even broadly defined liberalism.[6]

Such cases have been used to discredit the idea of a singular liberal "consensus," in which all Americans share the same set of substantive political beliefs.[7] Following the popular demise of civic republicanism in the late eighteenth century, however, such nonliberal positions have generally occupied a relatively small corner of the American political landscape.[8] When liberalism is considered as a variegated discourse rather than as a monolithic consensus, the case for its historical dominance remains strong. The breadth and depth of liberalism in the United States has enabled it to encompass positions that are strongly opposed to one another: support for laissez-faire economics versus the welfare state, abolition of the income tax versus progressive taxation, unrestricted trade versus industrial planning, traditional gender roles versus feminism, Christian morality versus secular humanism, color-blindness versus affirmative action, and so on. The fact that both self-styled conservatives and social democrats have spoken the language of American liberalism attests to its long-standing and wide-ranging importance in American political development.[9]

Race and Liberalism

Since the abolition of slavery in 1863, there has been an extremely wide range of responses to the question of what it would take to establish racial equity in the United States, particularly with regard to the African-American population. As the following chapters demonstrate, these have included liberal positions that alternately endorsed or rejected racial hierarchy, race-based discrimination, and a more equitable distribution of social or economic resources. Although nonliberal positions that have advocated an alternative path to racial justice have also existed, these have not occupied nearly as important a position in the mainstream (read: white-dominated) political environment. The most influential nonliberal racial ideologies have in fact existed on the far right of the political spectrum, representing an extreme form of white nationalism that would deny even the most elemental rights to the black population.

Racial politics in the United States has of course encompassed many other groups besides African Americans. Few would deny, however, that black Americans have represented the nation's most politically consequential racial group. With notable exceptions, racial politics in America has largely turned on issues associated with Africans who were enslaved during the first two centuries of European habitation in North America and their descendants. This is not to deny the importance of other racially defined groups or the significance of their particular histories. All represent an important part of American history and political development. The culturally dominant understanding of race that developed in the United States has remained, however, fundamentally structured by a black-white dichotomy. As such, it has played a particularly important role in the evolving relationship between race and American liberalism.

If this dichotomy has remained central to American racial politics, the socially dominant understanding of "race" has in many other respects been fluid. *Race*, like liberalism, can be understood as a historically embedded discourse whose substantive meaning has varied across time and among groups.[10] Although it presents itself culturally as a simple and self-evident category, race is a complex social construct with several important dimensions. Most basically, the concept of race encompasses different understandings of the origins of racial categories: what some take for granted as biological fact, others understand to be social fiction. As the recent explosion of "whiteness" studies has demonstrated, the boundaries of particular racial designations have changed substantially over time, with groups such as the Irish, Italians, and Jews shifting from being defined as races to being understood as ethnic groups, or simply as whites.[11]

Different understandings of race also embody different ideas about the structure of social relations, particularly with regard to issues of inequality. Currently, for example, different explanations of why the black population remains disproportionately poor hinge on competing conceptions of race, which alternately emphasize its significance as a discriminatory barrier, proxy for class, or marker of cultural deficiency. Such different understandings of race are logically connected to different perceptions of what the legitimate role of government and the law should be with regard to issues of civil rights and racial justice. Those who believe that race represents a discriminatory barrier, for example, tend to favor affirmative action. Those who believe that it is a proxy for class are more concerned with universal strategies to mitigate poverty. If race is viewed as a marker of cultural deficiency, government-sponsored attempts to leverage increased opportunity are likely to be viewed with skepticism or hostility. In this sense, different understandings of the meaning of race have a direct impact on alternative constructions of liberalism.[12]

Race and Social Equity

Race is a particularly important construct in the United States because it plays a pivotal role in structuring perceptions of equity issues more broadly. Within the academy, this phenomenon is typically discussed in terms of the relationship between race and class. The literature on American exceptionalism in particular has frequently argued that race in the United States has served to mystify class relations while keeping the poor and working class politically divided. This line of argument differs from the one presented in this book to the extent that it is influenced by the traditional Marxian position that class represents an objective category of social relations that is determined by the economic system.[13] Such an approach, in essence, treats class as a fact that is obscured by the fiction of race. The constructivist approach taken in this analysis, in contrast, assumes that both class and race are contingent social categories whose existence depends upon historically embedded patterns of cultural and social practice. From this perspective, it is misleading to assert that race obscures the reality of class, as this assumes that class is something that must be recognized rather than invented.[14]

An alternative way to conceptualize this relationship is that race has severely constrained the development of class as a meaningful social category in the United States. At first glance, this may seem to represent little more than a hairsplitting difference with the traditional exceptionalist position. When considered more carefully, however, it rests on very different assumptions about the nature of human beings and social relations. For example, it does not assume the existence of a universal structure of rationality that would cause people to agree that their primary social and political identities are determined by their relative position in the structure of economic relations (if only they could be roused out of the mystification produced by the ruling class and its cultural machinery). Instead, it proceeds from the hypothesis that humans have an innate need to locate themselves in a meaningful structure of individual identity and social relations. These structures of meaning are created and recreated through sociohistorical processes of cultural formation that may alternately assign a greater significance to tribal, religious, materialist, or other understandings of the world. Consequently, there is no reason to assume that class, as understood in traditional Western terms, has a privileged status as a more objective way of understanding individual or group identity.

This type of constructivist approach also presents a very different understanding of the real and potential relationship between liberalism and capitalism. If capitalism is similarly considered as a flexible, nondetermined system with a variety of forms that have been constructed by particular cultural and social practices, then the possibility that significantly different varieties of liberalism may exist widens considerably. Most pointedly, if the market economies that are a part of a liberal political order may dramatically increase social exploitation and inequality, they may also be structured to minimize such outcomes, while supporting both social flexibility and innovation, and individual freedom and self-determination. From this perspective, even "free" markets have been necessarily structured by the law and government regulations in the context of large, complex industrial or postindustrial societies.

The question at issue is therefore not the presence or absence of politics in markets, but rather the particular goals, structures, and social organization of market economies.[15]

This, in turn, points to the possibility of significantly different conceptions of moral economy existing within a common liberal framework. American liberalism has historically contained significant strands of political thought that have been dedicated to the proposition that both individual rights and liberties and the civic virtue of the nation as a whole are threatened by the existence of huge disparities in wealth and social standing among the population.[16] Along the same lines, it has embodied a moral tradition dedicated to a distribution of social and economic resources deemed to be sufficient to provide every citizen with a meaningful opportunity to develop her full range of individual talents and capacities.[17] Other, more conservative traditions of American liberalism have of course rejected such equalitarian commitments as wrong-headed, arguing that individual morality and social virtue flourish best under conditions of unrestrained market competition, regardless of the inequities produced. Inequality, in fact, has been in many cases considered to be a vital feature of a desirable social order, as social hierarchy is assumed to be the necessary product of different and inherently unequal individual and group capacities that will naturally manifest themselves in a free society.[18]

The Limits of American Liberalism

In this sense, race has a broad impact on the structure of liberalism that goes substantially beyond the scope of formally defined racial issues such as nondiscrimination or affirmative action. In order to develop a form of liberalism that prioritizes goals such as structuring markets to promote equity, it is necessary to have a working conception of the social structure that includes but extends beyond divisions created by race. It must include race because it has always been a fundamental part of the structure of inequality in the United States. It should also extend beyond race, however, because at no time in American history could inequality be reduced simply to race. It should, in other words, include some conception of class, even if that term is not explicitly used. The politics of race in the United States, however, has made such group-based conceptions of structural inequality very difficult to create and sustain.

Movements to increase race and class equity in the United States have been repeatedly (although by no means consistently) disassociated or even in conflict with one another. On the one hand, efforts to secure basic standards of nondiscrimination and equal treatment for racially disadvantaged groups have had no necessary connection to a broader commitment to social equity, whether liberal or otherwise. (Although the predominant pattern within the African-American political tradition has been to oppose racial discrimination and support increased social equity, this has not held true more broadly.)[19] In some cases, strong antidiscrimination positions have served to legitimize continued racial and social inequality, as it was argued that the market system would inevitably produce fair (if unequal) outcomes once all discriminatory barriers were removed. At other times, the struggle to achieve basic antidiscrimination guarantees simply did not leave sufficient time or energy to pursue broader issues. And, in some instances, a commitment to increased social equity has been understood in purely racial terms, with support for racially targeted redistribution but not for universal laws and policies.

On the other hand, movements for increased social equity have not necessarily included racial minorities or addressed issues of immediate importance to them. In some cases, this was the product of a racially discriminatory world view, which was committed to greater equity for whites but not for racial minorities. In others, it was a matter of priorities: while racial equity was supported in principle, it was considered to be too difficult and divisive to pursue in practice. Either way, racial issues proved to be too deeply rooted in the social fabric to remain hidden forever. Sooner or later, suppressed racial divisions erupted that disrupted and discredited the form of politics that these movements represented.

In some cases, movements for greater social equity have tried to take on both racially specific dimensions of inequality and its broader societal form. This has required attempting to address both racially specific concerns, such as discrimination, and more universal issues, such as the structure of the labor market. Pursuing such an ambitious goal has necessarily involved attempting to transform the meaning of race in order to bridge racial divisions, while at the same time developing some functional understanding of class. It has necessitated attempting to create political solidarity across racially divided groups, trying to convince racial minorities to put their faith in those that have mistreated them and attempting to persuade members of the white majority to identify themselves with the racially stigmatized.

The creative tensions generated by these demands have produced forms of American liberalism characterized by radical visions of democratic inclusiveness. Such versions of liberalism have had a broad impact on American political development, particularly by inspiring other movements dedicated to the full political and cultural enfranchisement of socially marginalized groups. In this sense, American liberalism has contained variants that have significantly influenced and expanded the scope of traditional left-of-center politics, which has overwhelmingly focused on an implicitly male and racially homogeneous conception of class. Most historians would agree, for example, that recent social movements dedicated to achieving greater equality for women, sexual minorities, the disabled, and other marginalized groups were directly inspired by the Civil Rights movement of the 1950s–1960s.[20]

Within this proliferation of social equity movements, however, those dedicated to the simultaneous pursuit of racial and class equity have experienced relatively little success. This has been particularly true with regard to institutionalizing the broad goals of such movements in the government arena and achieving lasting structural reforms. In both the late nineteenth and late twentieth centuries, popular mobilizations geared around equity issues have been overwhelmed by the strength of racially charged countermobilizations. In short, although race has helped to create exceptionally democratic visions of American liberalism, it has also reinforced the dominance of comparatively inequalitarian forms of liberal politics in the United States.

Reconsidering the First and Second Reconstructions

The following eight chapters provide a historical examination of how multiple forms of racial and liberal discourse have intersected with one another to form competing understandings of civic equity. Focusing on the periods 1865–1896 and 1945–1980, this analysis centers around the epochs commonly referred to as the "first and second Reconstructions" and their aftermaths. Although many important racial developments occurred outside of these periods, any historical narrative that focuses on the evolving relationship between race and liberalism in the United States must include them as central building blocks of the larger story. Consequently, while this book cannot claim to be comprehensive, it does lay a foundation for broader efforts.

Chapter 1 describes the substantive content and political dynamics of what is here referred to as "anti-caste liberalism." Developed by Radical Republicans and their allies during the late 1860s, anti-caste liberals claimed that the Reconstruction amendments had placed the principle of racial equality at the pinnacle of the American constitutional order, charging the federal government with the responsibility to take action against the continued maintenance of racial caste. This position was quite radical for its time, as it insisted on the political imperative of a strong standard against racial discrimination. It was essentially conservative, however, with regard to economic issues, as it assumed that antidiscrimination measures would be sufficient to eradicate racial caste and establish a full measure of civic equality throughout the nation. This indifference to the economic bases of citizenship stood sharply opposed to the views of both the vast majority of the freedpeople themselves and the nascent labor and agrarian movements— which, as discussed in chapter 3, argued that the growing inequality of the postbellum era threatened the foundations of republican government.

Chapter 2 examines the highly influential position of Darwinian liberalism, which represented the primary counter to the anti-caste position during the 1870s. During that time, Darwinian liberals argued in favor of a minimalist conception of black citizenship rights. This position, however, was coupled with an insistence that equal rights could not and should not be expected to produce "social equality" between the races. In the context of a free-market order, Darwinian liberals claimed, the innate superiority of the white race ensured that it would forever dominate the black. The fact that this insistence on racial hierarchy was linked to a commitment to a minimal standard of black rights made it a politically moderate position in the context of the 1870s. By the turn of the century, however, this commitment had largely eroded, as Darwinian liberals forged an even more exclusive conception of white supremacy in reaction to the labor and agrarian movements of the 1880s–1890s.

Chapters 3 and 4 examine the rise and fall of these movements, which were commonly organized around the ideology of "producer republicanism." In contrast to both anti-caste and Darwinian liberals, producer republicans prioritized the economic foundations of citizenship. The extremes of wealth and poverty that had developed in conjunction with the rise of corporate capitalism, they argued, had effectively nullified the rights of millions of citizens and threatened the integrity of American government. In keeping with this position, republican activists attempted to organize a broad constituency of workers and farmers around the common identity of "producers," arguing that their interests and values stood opposed to those of the "nonproducing classes." Forging such an identity, however, required bridging racial divisions between not only whites and blacks, but between nativeborn whites and the rapidly growing population of Southern and Eastern European immigrants. While both movements made significant progress on this front, the subsequent force of racially charged reaction proved overwhelming. Following the denouement of this struggle, which was marked by the election of 1896, the nation entered the twentieth century with a highly exclusive conception of citizenship, which championed the necessity of both racial and class hierarchy, securely instated as the dominant cultural norm.

Although the political order inaugurated by the election of 1896 underwent significant reforms during the Progressive Era and was eventually overturned by the New Deal, no politically consequential opposition to racial discrimination emerged until the post–World War II period. Chapter 5 examines the content and context of what is here referred to as "postwar liberalism," which coupled a new commitment to antidiscrimination with a rejection of the more class-conscious and social democratic orientation of the New Deal. While representing a historic advance against deeply embedded norms of white supremacy, postwar liberals failed to recognize the immense significance of growing patterns of racial inequality that did not fit into their ideological frame.

As chapter 6 demonstrates, the early Civil Rights movement radicalized the postwar liberal agenda by infusing it with much more expansive conceptions of both racial equity and social justice. While postwar liberalism remained focused on the problem of Jim Crow in the South, the movement also emphasized problems of segregation and discrimination in the rest of the nation. At the same time, it encouraged the development of a new form of racial consciousness, particularly a more positive and empowered sense of black identity. The movement also advocated an essentially social democratic agenda, whose primary goal was to increase social and economic equity among all Americans. By the early 1960s, these commitments had created a pronounced rift between "white liberals," who favored the more moderate politics of postwar liberalism, and black activists, who supported the new form of social liberalism developed by the Civil Rights movement.

Chapter 7 focuses on the meteoric rise and fall of social liberalism during the mid- to late 1960s. In 1964, movement activists and their allies optimistically believed that they could form a new coalition of minorities, labor unionists, left-of-center liberals, and low-income voters that would have the political muscle to move the Democratic party substantially to the left in order to pursue the ambitious agenda of eliminating both poverty and racial injustice. By 1968, however, these hopes had been crushed. As the social and political turmoil growing out of racial politics and the Vietnam War engulfed the nation, a growing conservative "backlash" gained momentum. Although the election of President Richard Nixon in that year did not inaugurate the sort of extreme reactionary regime that some hoped for and others feared, it was widely taken to mark the beginning of a new, more conservative era.

Chapter 8 analyzes the development of the contemporary conservative movement from the late 1960s through the 1980s. In the 1970s, the neoconservative movement played a particularly important role in fashioning a new brand of racial conservatism with a powerful cultural resonance. Framed in the liberal language of nondiscrimination and equal rights, this position denounced race-conscious policies and equalitarian politics more broadly as politically illegitimate and socially destructive. During the same period, veteran conservative activists regrouped to organize the New Right, which combined a powerful appeal to the intertwined racial and class identities of working-class whites with innovative and effective techniques of political organizing. Together, the neoconservatives and the New Right laid the foundations for a new conservative political establishment with the organizational muscle to systematically market conservative ideas, engineer a conservative takeover of the Republican party, leverage a more conservative federal judiciary, and mobilize grassroots support for conservative causes. While encompassing a wide range of issues, a central—and ultimately successful—goal of the movement was to banish socioeconomic equity issues from the forum of legitimate political discussion.

Placing the contemporary weakness of equalitarian liberalism within a broader historical perspective enables a deeper understanding of the fundamental political dynamics at issue. The problem of developing a strong constituency dedicated to addressing growing socioeconomic inequality in a society that has been powerfully structured and deeply scarred by racial divisions is not new. Similarly, the tendency to justify entrenched racial inequality as the natural product of a competitive free-market system has deep roots. Yet, it is also true that simple formulas that prioritize class over race or equate racial inequality with discrimination do not work. Nor is it a simple matter of "good" forms of liberalism that promote civic equity and "bad" forms that negate it.

The interplay of race and class and the many competing understandings of liberal equality have been too variegated and complex to reduce to a single dynamic. Still, certain patterns are particularly striking. American liberalism has proven capable of generating inspiring visions of civic equality. Some have been deeply committed to the goal of a racially equalitarian society. Others have focused on the universal ideal of a nation in which all citizens possess the socioeconomic resources necessary to participate fully and to develop their innate human potential. Still others have understood these dreams as necessarily intertwined. All of these equalitarian conceptions of American liberalism have, however, proven extremely difficult to sustain—and even more difficult to realize concretely. Although there can be no single explanation of why this has been the case, race has consistently played a central role in undermining the strength of more equalitarian conceptions of liberalism. For this reason, developing a more nuanced understanding of the complex politics of race allows us to gain deeper insight into the strengths and limitations of American liberalism.

Our Constitution is colorblind, and neither knows nor tolerates classes among citizens. In respect of civil rights, all citizens are equal before the law.

—Justice John Marshall Harlan, Plessy v. Ferguson, 1896

1

Anti-Caste Liberalism

Justice Harlan's dissent in the Supreme Court case of *Plessy v. Ferguson*, which sanctioned racial segregation under the auspices of the "separate but equal" doctrine, represents one of the most famous statements, as well as one of the most infamous cases, in the history of American constitutional law. This was not always true: at the time it was decided, neither Harlan's dissent nor the case itself generated any notable public reaction.[1] By 1896, the battle over the legality of racial discrimination and segregation had already been effectively decided. Although there had been a long and determined effort to prohibit these practices in the spheres of government action and public accommodations, this movement had lost its political and legal strength in conjunction with the larger abandonment of the racially equalitarian experiments of Reconstruction. Rather than a powerful affirmation of a strong civil rights tradition, Harlan's dissent—laudable as it was—represented only a weak shadow of a formerly robust position.

This chapter relocates the Harlan dissent within this larger position, here referred to as "anti-caste liberalism."[2] From the mid-1860s to the mid-1880s, anti-caste liberalism represented an important current of radical thought and activism with regard to both racial and constitutional issues. All anti-caste liberals strongly opposed racial discrimination and segregation. A majority affirmed the then-radical proposition that there were no essential differences between the black and white races, except those imposed by slavery and its legacy. In support of these racial commitments, anti-caste liberals advanced a radical theory of constitutional government based on a highly equalitarian reading of the Thirteenth and Fourteenth amendments. These amendments, they argued, had been passed in the wake of the Civil War to create a new standard of national citizenship. Most critically, the federal government was required to take action to prevent conduct that would perpetuate the legacy of slavery by creating new systems of racial caste. As required by this responsibility, the power of the federal government had been significantly expanded, while the corresponding authority of the state governments had been sharply curtailed. In this sense, the Reconstruction amendments had recalibrated the entire system of government, creating a "new" constitutional order to replace a failed model that had been unfaithful to the fundamental principle of equal rights under the law.

Although anti-caste liberals took a radically equalitarian position on racial and constitutional issues, they were silent with regard to economic concerns. After a brief period during the mid-1860s when they championed the losing cause of land redistribution to provide the newly freed black population with homesteads, leading figures in the anti-caste movement disassociated economics from their understanding of both the rights of citizenship and the requirements of racial equality. Adopting the laissez-faire assumptions that came to dominate the Republican party by the 1870s, anti-caste liberals—both white and black alike—argued that the former slave population needed only to be protected from discrimination to have an equal opportunity to find their fortunes within a free-market order. In pursuit of this goal, they focused their energies on the passage of the Civil Rights Act of 1875, which prohibited discrimination in places of public accommodation. Although the battle for the passage of this legislation was eventually won, the law rapidly became a dead letter under the rule of an overwhelmingly hostile, white-dominated public sphere and judicial system. By the time of the *Plessy* decision, anti-caste liberalism was a relic of the past.

Despite its practical failure, the case of anti-caste liberalism is instructive for both what it did and did not represent. On the one hand, it demonstrates that mid- to late nineteenth-century liberalism was capable of supporting what was for its time a remarkably radical commitment against racial discrimination. This issue was deemed so important by a small, but nonetheless prominent political coalition that it succeeded in developing a coherent theory of constitutional interpretation that was correspondingly radical in its own right. Although only briefly upheld as the law of the land, anti-caste constitutionalism continued to find expression in legal arguments, books, speeches, and political meetings into the 1880s. On the other hand, anti-caste liberalism represented an essentially conservative position on economic issues. Particularly given the growing economic divisions and class antagonisms of the time, this combination of economic conservatism and racial, political, and legal radicalism illustrates the tremendous disjuncture that existed between the struggle against racial discrimination and the battle for economic justice in late nineteenth-century America.

Land and the Foundations of Citizenship

Anti-caste liberalism was a product of the historical period known as Reconstruction. Reconstruction began in the wake of the Civil War when the Republican party, representing the forces of the victorious North, used its dominance of the federal government to attempt to build a new social and political order in the South. The central challenge of Reconstruction was coping with the question of how best to incorporate almost four million former slaves into the social fabric of the nation. In sharp contrast to the Democrats who overwhelmingly dominated the white South, Republicans were commonly committed to the formal abolition of slavery. They divided, however, over the issue of what the consequent civil status of the ex-slave population should be.

With the commencement of the more radically reformist stage of congressionally directed Reconstruction in 1867, two competing positions dominated Republican debate over this issue. The majority position held that the freedpeople should be guaranteed basic rights of property and contract. These rights, it was argued, would allow them to compete on an equal basis in the free-market system that was claimed to now encompass the South. A small but vocal minority, however, held that the peculiarities of the southern situation required a redistribution of land to the former slaves. This was necessary, it was argued, to provide them with the economic foundation necessary for the effective extension of these and other citizenship rights.[3]

The most important figures in the minority contingent of Radical Republicans promoting land reform were Senator Charles Sumner of Massachusetts and Representative Thaddeus Stevens of Pennsylvania.[4] In March 1867, Sumner argued before the Senate that the "principles of justice and morality which constitute the foundation of republican government" demanded not only the extension of the ballot, but the provision of education and a homestead to the freedmen.[5] Congress, he maintained, should confiscate the land of former Confederates, "whose crimes had forfeited all their rights." This land should be redistributed so that "each liberated slave who is a male adult, or the head of a family" would have "a homestead of forty acres of land," along with $100 with which "to build a dwelling." Pointing out that the freedpeople and their ancestors had "toiled, not for years, but for ages, without one farthing of recompense," Stevens argued that "they have earned from their masters this very land and much more." These "disloyal" landowners, Sumner argued, should be prevented from continuing to appropriate the fruits of their former slaves' toil.[6]

In keeping with a long tradition of Jeffersonian thought, Stevens argued that land redistribution represented the necessary foundation of equal citizenship for the freedpeople. Stevens recognized that without some basis for economic independence, their widespread lack of education, skills, and resources left them far too defenseless against exploitation. The freedpeople would, Stevens warned, become "the servants and victims of others unless they are made in some measure independent of their wiser neighbors." Consequently, homesteads were "far more valuable" to them than even the right to vote—although, Stevens added, "both are their due."[7]

Certainly, the redistribution of land for the provision of homesteads constituted the first priority of the vast majority of the freedpeople themselves. Southern blacks considered the achievement of both individual and community autonomy to be a vital component of their newly won freedom and viewed landownership as a precondition of that goal.[8] Similarly, land was widely understood to represent the economic foundation necessary for any meaningful extension of legal and political rights. As one Charleston resident succinctly explained to a northern journalist in 1865: "without land, the old masters can hire or starve us, as they please."[9]

Black residents of Edisto Island elaborated on this theme. This group of freedpeople had settled upon abandoned plantation lands with the initial support of the Freedmen's Bureau, fully expecting to be given title to forty-acre plots. Upon learning that the government now planned to restore the land to its former owners, they formed a committee to write collective letters of protest to President Andrew Johnson and General O. O. Howard, commissioner of the Freedmen's Bureau. "General we want Homesteads; we were promised Homesteads by the government," they asserted. If the government reneged upon this promise, "we are left In a more unpleasant condition than our former . . . at the mercy of those who are combined to prevent us from getting land enough to lay our Fathers bones upon." Despite owning "property In Horses, cattle, carriages, & articles of furniture," being "landless and Homeless" rendered them once again subject to the will of their former owners. "We can not resist It In any way without being driven out Homeless upon the road," they explained. "You will see this Is not the condition of really freemen."[10]

Despite such protests, the few small-scale efforts at land redistribution that were attempted were quickly aborted. By 1870, it was clear that the entire issue was dead. The key reason for this failure was that the central power bloc in the Republican party was made up of northerners who were strong advocates of, and often investors in, a newly emerging system of corporate capitalism that could now be more easily extended into the South. Land redistribution posed a potentially serious threat to their economic interests. While other, similarly disruptive measures championed by the Radical wing of the party, such as the extension of suffrage to the freedmen, offered potentially significant gains (in the case of suffrage, for example, the chance to consistently win southern elections with the support of the black vote), land reform offered only potential costs. In all probability, such a move would drastically reduce the already slim chances of building any base of white support for the party in the South. At the same time, it would lessen opportunities for profitable northern investment in, trade with, and export to that region. In principle, it also set a potentially dangerous precedent for the abrogation of vested property rights.

Despite the practical failure of land redistribution, the larger political vision that it represented remained vital—at least outside of the realm of institutional party politics—throughout the remaining decades of the nineteenth century. Although many black political leaders, particularly those involved in mainstream party politics, increasingly took on a more moderate posture in the face of an ever more conservative political climate, many other African Americans turned toward either the resurgent black nationalism of the late 1870s–1880s or the radical labor and agrarian movements of the 1880s–1890s.[11] In the latter case, blacks joined with majority-white movements whose insistence that effective citizenship rights required a solid socioeconomic foundation very much paralleled the ideological structure of the earlier land reform movement.

The Rise of Laissez-Faire

Within the realm of institutionalized party politics, the defeat of the land reform issue coincided with the development of a new laissez-faire ideology that was embraced by radical, moderate, and conservative Republicans alike.[12] Basic laissez-faire principles, which held that the integrity of the free-market system depended on its protection from governmental intrusion, had been a central element of Republican political thought during the antebellum and Civil War periods. During that time, however, they were very much a part of what Foner termed the "free labor" ideology.[13] This position had been based on the faith that if markets were allowed to operate freely and were shielded from the inherent biases of government regulation, they would necessarily support the Jeffersonian goal of a citizenry composed of economically independent, and therefore politically virtuous, small-scale property owners. According to this perspective, the growth of "wage labor" (i.e., employees working for wages, as opposed to independent operators working for themselves) that was accompanying the development of a more technologically sophisticated industrial base would provide the opportunity for more individuals to acquire the capital necessary to become independent small businesspeople, artisans, or farmers.[14] There was, in other words, no need to worry that this new economic order might produce forms of social stratification that posed a threat to the Jeffersonian vision.

This perspective could not long survive the tremendous economic changes of the postbellum era. By the early 1870s, the free labor paradigm was unraveling into its two distinct and increasingly opposed components of laissez-faire capitalism and Jeffersonian equalitarianism. The decisive turning point in this process was the Panic of 1873, a credit crisis that instigated a sixty-five-month-long economic contraction. The subsequent economic malaise lasted, with some interruptions, almost until the turn of the century. Representing the "first great crisis of industrial capitalism" in the United States, this event powerfully undermined free labor assumptions, raised the labor issue to the forefront of social thought, changed the balance of power between the two major parties, and set the stage for the emergence of a new generation of industrial leaders.[15]

This pivotal event deepened already existing divisions that were cutting through the network of political alliances that formed the Republican coalition. Northern business interests, which were strongly represented in the Republican party, wanted to end the racial strife associated with Reconstruction in order to pursue profitable investment in the South. This put them into conflict with both the Radical wing of the party, which was committed to the cause of black civil rights, and the Stalwart faction, which wanted to "wave the bloody shirt" (i.e., invoke the horrors of the Civil War and the treason of the Confederate South) in an attempt to further their political fortunes. At the same time, as the largely northern labor movement grew increasingly better organized and more militant, it came into increasing conflict both with the conservative, business-oriented wing of the party and with the factions that remained focused on southern race issues. These rifts significantly deepened the alienation of labor advocates—always relatively tenuous members of the Republican coalition—from the party.[16]

The commitments to laissez-faire capitalism and Jeffersonian equalitarianism that had been united by the free labor paradigm soon broke sharply apart. The economic dislocations that followed the Panic of 1873 made it clear that unfettered market competition was not going to produce a harmonious society of virtuous small property holders. Instead, corporate wealth and power were expanding, while workers and farmers faced mushrooming poverty, wage cuts, and unemployment.[17] At the same time, deepening factional divisions made it clear that former political allies had extremely different interests in the face of such changed circumstances. Consequently, advocates of laissez-faire largely jettisoned the ideal of Jeffersonian equalitarianism, replacing it with a celebration of unrestricted economic development and societal competition.[18] Conversely, advocates of Jeffersonian equalitarianism attacked the dominant model of laissez-faire as unsuited to the new age of corporate capitalism, insisting that it be replaced with a new regime of politically structured market activity designed to maximize the public good.

The relative dominance of northern business interests within the Republican coalition helped to ensure that the party would go down the laissez-faire road. Strongly reinforcing this choice of direction was the fact that the line that divided Radicals and reformists from conservatives and moderates in the party had always been one of race, not class. The roots of radicalism in the Republican party were very much in the abolitionist movement, which had largely dismissed the labor movement as an unwarranted distraction from the central problem of slavery.[19] This lack of interest had been mutual: no part of the northern labor movement had ever been a consistent supporter of any sort of racially progressive agenda.[20] As a result, members of the Radical wing of the Republican party had no tradition of economic thought and no set of strong political alliances that would encourage them to attempt to block the shift from the free labor paradigm to a more aggressively laissez-faire position.[21]

The defeat of the land redistribution issue consequently caused the Radical faction to shift from a more socioeconomic to a more narrowly legal conception of what further reforms were needed to complete the racially equalitarian agenda of Reconstruction. Lacking a larger economic program that could sustain itself following the defeat of the land issue, Radical Republicans and their supporters dropped all references to the economic bases of citizenship and turned instead to focus exclusively on questions of legal rights. Subsequently, by the 1870s, they were consistently making the argument that the freedmen were entitled to equal legal and political rights and nothing more, as this represented the full measure of citizenship accorded to all enfranchised Americans.

Anti-Caste Liberalism

Nowhere was this shift more apparent than in the arguments made by Radical Republicans and their supporters in favor of the series of bills that would eventuate in the Civil Rights Act of 1875.[22] First proposed to the Senate by Charles Sumner in May 1870, this law prohibited racial discrimination in places of public accommodation such as restaurants, inns, and theaters, as well as in public transportation and jury selection. (Notably, the original version of the bill had also prohibited racial segregation in the public schools, churches, and cemeteries. The school clause in particular was extremely controversial, however, and was eventually dropped in a compromise agreement.) During the long battle to secure passage of the legislation, Sumner and other supporters of the measure repeatedly characterized it as the "capstone" needed to "crown and complete the great work of Reconstruction."[23] By presenting the civil rights bill in this way, they abandoned any claim that the establishment of racial justice would require some restructuring of economic relations in the South. In so doing, they relied on the classic laissez-faire argument that the provision of equal rights under the law was both the necessary and sufficient condition needed to guarantee social—or, in this case, racial—justice.

"This bill when enacted, it is believed, will be a finality, removing from legislation, from politics, and from society, an injurious agitation, and securing to every citizen that proud equality which our nation declares to be his right," proclaimed Senator Frederick T. Frelinghuysen of New Jersey. Holding that it "is the friction created by discrimination among citizens in the administration of law that disturbs the harmony of government," Frelinghuysen exhorted his colleagues to "take away the foreign substance." "We know we have proven that equality is the true principle on which to run society; give it full play with no obstruction, and the machine will run noiselessly and without a jar."[24] Similarly, Representative James A. Garfield of Ohio emphasized:

> I have never asked for [the black man] one thing beyond this: that he should be placed under the equal protection of the laws, with

the equal right to all the blessings which our laws confer . . . and that the negro, guaranteed an equal chance in the struggle of life, may work out for himself whatever fortune his own merit will win.[25]

"In the name of Christianity; in the name of the Declaration; in the name of the Constitution; by the voice of this bill," Senator Timothy O. Howe of Wisconsin intoned, "I invoke the angel of equal rights to remove the last obstruction from the pathway to equal fortune."[26]

Three of the seven black congressmen who participated in the debates over the civil rights bill made similar statements, and none of the other four contradicted them.[27] Representative Joseph H. Rainey of South Carolina asked his colleagues to "deprive us of no rights belonging to us as citizens; give us an equal opportunity in life; then if we fail we will be content if driven to the wall."[28] During the same debate, another black representative from South Carolina, Richard H. Cain, made an almost identical appeal: "Let the laws of the country be just; let the laws of the country be equitable; that is all we ask, and we will take our chances under the laws in this land. . . . Place all citizens upon one broad platform; and *if the negro is not qualified to hoe his row in this contest of life, then let him go down.*"[29] Representative John Roy Lynch of Mississippi asked the House to "pass this bill as it passed the Senate, and there will be nothing more for the colored people to ask or expect in the way of civil rights."[30]

This vision of an intrinsically fair free-market order that would run like clockwork if only the disturbance of racial discrimination were removed represented a conservative shift away from the more radical position that equal rights require an economic foundation to be meaningful. Nonetheless, the version of liberalism advanced by the supporters of the civil rights bill remained remarkably radical in two interrelated ways. First, it asserted the doctrine of human universalism, rejecting the then-common belief in the inherent superiority and inferiority of different races.[31] Second, it developed a highly equalitarian interpretation of American constitutional government, holding that the Reconstruction amendments had fundamentally altered both the nature of American citizenship and the balance of power within the federal system.

Anti-caste liberals commonly made the argument that "God is no respecter of persons, and that he made of one blood all nations of men to dwell on the face of the earth."[32] Direct connections were regularly made between the principle of humanist universalism, the substance of Christian values, and the nature of American nationalism. Senator Henry Wilson of Massachusetts, for example, attacked the civil rights bill's opponents by stating that "this talk about superiority of race, about these distinctions in this Christian and democratic land, should pass away and pass away forever. . . . All that is high and noble and pure in the country is against recognizing these unchristian, inhumane, and undemocratic theories."[33] Senator Samuel C. Pomeroy of Kansas, objecting to remarks of another senator, who had previously spoken "about races of men and races of women," remarked that he "thought we had got beyond that question long ago":

> I know of the human race, but I do not know anything about races of men. . . . I learned in my childhood that man was made but a little lower than the angels, not that there were any races of men. I hold that every individual, the poorest and the weakest, is a man notwithstanding, allied to immortality, and that in no sense can it be said that one is superior to the other: certainly not in his origin; certainly not in his destiny, and, if anything, only in his attainments, only in the circumstances that have surrounded him.[34]

Similarly, Senator Daniel D. Pratt of Indiana tied the equalitarianism of the Declaration of Independence to the Christian belief "that God was the creator of mankind. I believe what our fathers who laid the foundations of our political edifice taught, that all men are created equal."[35]

Anti-caste liberals further made the sociological claim that the differences that separated the races were essentially the result of the forced imposition of racial hierarchy by whites against blacks in the South. (Proponents of the Civil Rights Act never extended their analysis of the social bases of racial inequality to consider the position of blacks outside of the South.) Senator Howe, for example, argued that racial prejudice "is not a law of nature," but rather a belief that is taught and learned in particular environments. "We have but one creator and that is God, and he makes but one kind of men," he asserted. "Diverse culture has occasioned diverse conditions. Those unequal conditions are an impeachment of society, not of creation."[36]

The logical way to address such problems was to prohibit the discriminatory practices that perpetuated them. Representative William J. Purman of Florida argued, "Color is no crime, and the sacrilegious hands that would make it so . . . must be stayed by just and firm legislation." "It was well remarked by Rousseau," Purman added, "that 'It is precisely because the force of things tends always to destroy equality that the force of legislation should always tend to maintain it.'"[37] In the same vein, Senator George S. Boutwell of Massachusetts argued that while families could not be expected to teach children the "theory of human equality," it could and should be taught in the public schools, "where children of all classes and conditions are brought together." Such instruction, he believed, represented "the chief means of securing the perpetuity of republican institutions."[38]

Senator Charles Sumner, the primary sponsor of the civil rights bill and its most prominent and indefatigable advocate up until the time of his death in 1874,[39] repeatedly claimed that the equalitarian spirit represented by the Declaration of Independence constituted the soul of republican government.[40] "Why is the Declaration of Independence our Magna Charta?" Sumner queried the Senate in 1872. It was, he claimed, "because it announces the lofty truth that all are equal in rights, and, as natural consequence, that just government stands only on the consent of the governed—all of which is held to be self-evident." This essential truth, Sumner argued, constituted "the soul of republican institutions, without which the Republic is a failure, a name and nothing more."[41]

Sumner, as well as a few other congressmen, went so far as to "insist that the National Constitution must be interpreted by the National Declaration." The Declaration of Independence, claimed Sumner, "is of equal and coordinate authority with the Constitution itself." "Show me any words in the Constitution applicable to human rights," he argued, "and I invoke at once the great truths of the Declaration as the absolute guide to their meaning." Holding that "every word in the Constitution must be interpreted so that Liberty and Equality shall not fail," Sumner and his supporters elevated equalitarian principles to the pinnacle of the constitutional order.[42]

The Reconstruction Amendments

This interpretation of the Constitution was supported by a distinctly radical interpretation of the Thirteenth and Fourteenth amendments, which had been respectively passed in 1865 and 1868 to provide the constitutional authority for abolition and Reconstruction.[43] (The Thirteenth Amendment prohibited slavery, and the Fourteenth, most notably, established the principle of "equal protection" of the law.) Proponents of the Civil Rights Act argued that the primary purpose of these amendments had been to eradicate slavery fully and completely from American life. In so doing, they had necessarily altered both the nature of U.S. citizenship and the structure of American constitutional government. This was true for two reasons. First, it was argued, the scope of the Thirteenth Amendment extended beyond the simple prohibition of slavery to include a broad prohibition on any continued manifestation of racial caste. Second, the Fourteenth Amendment had nationalized the rights of citizenship and provided the federal government with the power, authority, and responsibility to enforce those rights. Consequently, the effect of these amendments had been to radically expand the duties and powers of the federal government, while substantially reducing the autonomy of the states. Given this cross-reinforcing interpretation of the amendments, advocates argued that the pending Civil Rights Act was not only constitutional, but a clear constitutional requirement.[44]

This argument was supported by a highly moralistic reading of the Civil War, which claimed that it had been fought over the issue of human—and, more particularly, racial—equality. According to this interpretation, the war was the logical outcome of a flawed constitutional structure that had demanded repair in the form of the Reconstruction amendments. Prior to the war, Sumner claimed, the Constitution "was interpreted always, in every clause and line and word, for Human Slavery. Thank God," he added, "it is all changed now! There is another rule, and the National Constitution, from beginning to end, speaks always for the Rights of Man."[45] Similarly, Representative Charles G. Williams of Wisconsin argued that at the close of the Civil War, the country had assumed that the principle of the "equal rights of all men before the law" had been "settled and secured." Today, he claimed, that principle "is the cornerstone of a reconstructed Republic." To fail to pass the civil rights bill would "leave a flaw" in the new constitutional foundation that could once again threaten the stability of the nation.[46]

Repeated contrasts were drawn between the "new" and "old" Constitutions, the latter of which, as Senator John Sherman of Ohio argued, "had not the word 'rights' in it."[47] The "Fourteenth Amendment goes much further than the old Constitution," explained Senator Frelinghuysen, as it "makes United States citizenship primary, and State citizenship derivative."[48] In the same vein, Representative Robert S. Hale of New York stated that while he had originally opposed the Fourteenth Amendment, he believed that Congress had the power and the duty to pass the civil rights bill under the dictates of the "new" Constitution.[49] Senator Howe applauded this newly established power of the federal government to uphold the rights of citizenship, which, in his view, had been horribly abused when left to the protection of the states. This fundamental shift, he suggested, represented common knowledge: "The Constitution has been changed, you may have heard, sir."[50]

Racial segregation, it was argued, represented an unconstitutional manifestation of racial caste under the Thirteenth Amendment and a violation of the rights of black citizens under the Fourteenth. The scope of prohibited discrimination, Senator Morton explained, was broad enough to include "all unjust discriminations against the negroes as a class," including those that occurred in privately owned enterprises that served the general public.[51] The federal government, Senator George F. Edmunds of Vermont argued, had the duty to protect citizens from "caste prejudice" regardless of whether particular state governments wanted it to do so or not.[52]

This position rejected what would come to be known as the "state action" doctrine, which held that the Fourteenth Amendment prohibited racial discrimination only on the part of government, as opposed to individuals or private enterprises.[53] Proponents of the Civil Rights Act argued against this doctrine in two distinct, if frequently overlapping, ways. Their more radical claim was that the Fourteenth Amendment acted directly against individuals, groups, and private establishments, as well as the state.[54] "Men may concede that public sentiment, and not law, is the cause of the discrimination of which we justly complain," argued Representative Josiah T. Walls, a black congressman from Florida. "If this be so, then such public sentiment needs penal correction, and should be regulated by law."[55] The more moderate, although still legally powerful, position was that since all businesses had to be licensed and regulated by the state, they represented "legal institutions" subject to government regulation, including antidiscrimination laws.[56]

Racial and Constitutional Radicalism

Such radical positions on constitutional issues were strongly related to what were for the time similarly radical positions on racial equality. As detailed in tables 1.1 and 1.2, an analysis of the constitutional and racial positions represented by each of the thirty-five congressmen who argued in favor of the civil rights bill demonstrates that a solid majority held radical positions on both issues and that these were highly correlated with one another. Both the larger historical context and specific positions argued suggest that racial attitudes played a primary role in shaping the theories of constitutional law and liberal government espoused by the supporters of the civil rights bill.

Table 1.1 details the number of congressmen whose statements indicated either a strong or moderate endorsement of the principles of constitutional radicalism and racial equalitarianism described above. Specifically, "strong" statements of constitutional radicalism were coded as those that asserted that the Reconstruction amendments had fundamentally changed the basic constitutional structure or that the Fourteenth Amendment represented a broad antidiscrimination principle. "Moderate" statements, in contrast, simply

Table 1.1.
Positions Represented by Congressional Supporters of the Civil Rights Act of 1875 (N=35)

	N	% Total
Constitutional Radicalism		
Strong	23	66%
Moderate	7	20%
No position stated	5	14%
Racial Equalitarianism		
Strong	20	57%
Moderate	10	29%
No position stated	5	14%

For sources of these data, see chapter 1, note 22.

Table 1.2.
Cross-Tabulation of Supporters' Positions (N=25)

	Radical Equalitarianism	
	Strong	Moderate
Constitutional Radicalism		
Strong	15	4
	(60%)	(16%)
Moderate	2	4
	(8%)	(16%)

For sources of these data, see chapter 1, note 22.

held that the civil rights bill was constitutional in that it established equal rights under the law. Similarly, "strong" statements of racial equalitarianism claimed either that the races were inherently equal or that racism was fundamentally wrong. "Moderate" statements asserted that "every man has the right to become the equal of any other man if he can" or that racial segregation was wrong because it was a manifestation of the legacy of slavery and degrading to blacks.

As can be seen in table 1.1, 86 percent of the thirty-five congressmen made either a strong or a moderate endorsement of both the constitutionally radical and racially equalitarian positions. The vast majority in both cases took the strong, rather than the moderate position, with 66 percent taking a strong position on constitutional radicalism and 57 percent taking a strong position on racial equalitarianism. Table 1.2 analyzes how these different positions correlated with one another in the statements made by the subset of twenty-five congressmen (71 percent) who took a clear position on both constitutional and racial issues. Sixty percent took a radical position in both cases, which exceeds the combined total of the three other alternatives by 20 percent.

The Road to *Plessy*

Strongly adhered to only by a minority of Republicans and their largely black constituencies, the political fortunes of the anti-caste position declined rapidly in conjunction with the demise of Reconstruction. By the time that the Civil Rights Act was passed in 1875, it was evident that the power of the Radical Republican faction that had used this position to spearhead the bill's passage would soon be eclipsed. Since the late 1860s, the racially equalitarian policies of Reconstruction had been rapidly losing ground in the face of white southern militancy, northern business hostility, and general disillusionment with a presidential administration that was widely viewed as exceptionally corrupt. The Republican coalition that had been formed during the antebellum and Civil War periods was breaking apart. The formerly powerful Radical faction increasingly looked like a relic of the past, while the similarly pro-Reconstruction Stalwart faction was losing its ability to affect national party strategy.[57]

The decision by President Rutherford B. Hayes to abandon Reconstruction and pursue sectional reconciliation in 1877 marked the ascension of conservative forces in the Republican party to a position of virtually unassailable dominance. Consequently, anti-caste liberalism remained in a politically powerless position throughout the remainder of the nineteenth century. It did not, however, disappear entirely. Most notably, it appeared on the losing side of court cases and in statements made by politically marginalized white radicals and black activists.

The *Civil Rights Cases* of 1883, for example, revisited the arguments that had been presented in Congress during the debates over the Civil Rights Act of 1875.[58] These important cases held that the sections of the Civil Rights Act of 1875 that prohibited racial discrimination in public accommodations and transportation were unconstitutional. In so doing, the cases gave constitutional sanction to the position that had been championed by conservative opponents of the law during the debates over its passage. The two government briefs filed in these cases, however—one in 1879 and the other in 1882—forcefully reasserted the arguments that had been made by the Civil Rights Act's supporters.

The initial government brief, written by Attorney General Charles Devens and Assistant Attorney General Edwin B. Smith, explicitly invoked earlier congressional debates, holding that the "meaning and purpose" of the Reconstruction amendments "must be gathered from 'the history of the times.'"[59] Quoting extensively from the original transcripts, this brief reasserted the argument that the Reconstruction amendments had changed the constitutional structure by nationalizing the rights of U.S. citizenship, establishing a broad antidiscrimination principle, giving Congress the power to enforce these standards by legislation, and shifting the balance of power between the states and the federal government. The first object of government, Devens and Smith emphasized, was to protect an expansive standard of individual rights. The federal system, they reasoned, was a tool that should be adapted as necessary to achieve that end.[60] According to this viewpoint, the Civil Rights Act of 1875 was unquestionably constitutional. Quoting from the remarks of Senator Frelinghuysen during the 1874 congressional debates, they insisted, "[F]reedom from discrimination is one of the rights of United States citizenship."[61]

Although this brief also reiterated the anti-caste argument against the state-action doctrine, it spent relatively little time developing this point.[62] The subsequent government brief, however, filed by Solicitor General S. F. Phillips in 1882, developed an extensive argument against it. Phillips's central claim was that the prohibition of racial segregation mandated by the Civil Rights Act was constitutional not simply because of the "quasi-public" nature of the businesses covered, but also because the systematic practice of segregation in such establishments would create a social institution similar to slavery. Pointing out that the "involuntary servitude" prohibited by the Thirteenth Amendment was an "*institution . . . not* mere scattered trespasses against liberty committed by private persons," Phillips argued that racial discrimination on the part of individuals such as innkeepers and passenger carriers "testifies to, and at the same [time] tends to enlarge, a particular current in *public opinion*, and this in its turn is fruitful of *public, i.e. State*, institutions." Such discrimination, Phillips held, did not simply represent the "private views" of such individuals, but rather "the views of whole communities of citizens, upon whom their history has naturally imposed these views."[63] Consequently, the 1875 Civil Rights Act was simply the logical "sequel" of the Thirteenth and Fourteenth amendments. All three, he maintained, shared the common premise that "every rootlet of slavery has an individual vitality, and, to its minutest hair, should be anxiously followed and plucked up."[64]

Justice John Marshall Harlan—the lone dissenter in the later *Plessy* case—strongly supported the government's position, filing the sole dissenting opinion in the *Civil Rights Cases*. Under the Thirteenth Amendment, he argued, Congress had the power to "enact laws to protect people against the deprivation, *because of their race*, of any civil rights granted to other freemen in the same State." The scope of such legislation could legitimately extend to include both government agents and "such individuals and corporations as exercise public functions and wield power and authority under the State."[65] The same held true of the Fourteenth Amendment. At the time of its passage, Harlan maintained, "it was perfectly well known that the great danger to the equal enjoyment by citizens of their rights, as citizens, was to be apprehended not altogether from unfriendly state legislation, but from the hostile action of corporations and individuals in the States." Consequently, it should be presumed that the amendment was intended "to clothe Congress with power and authority to meet that danger." In short, the power of Congress under the Fourteenth Amendment extended to cover all discrimination that would harm the "civil rights which are fundamental in *citizenship* in a republican government."[66]

The anti-caste position articulated in the government's briefs and Harlan's dissent echoed across the country following the Supreme Court's ruling. Widely considered to be important and controversial, the decision in the *Civil Rights Cases* "precipitated pages of news reports, hundreds of editorials, indignant rallies, congressional bills, a Senate report, and much general debate."[67] The tide of mainstream public opinion, however, ran strongly in favor of the decision. Most (white) Americans, perceiving the *Civil Rights Cases* as a validation of the Compromise of 1877 and a rejection of the abandoned policies of Reconstruction, applauded the decision as a beneficial measure that would heal the wounds of the past by promoting sectional reconciliation.[68]

The decision in the *Civil Rights Cases* produced significantly more public commentary and active opposition than the now much more well known *Plessy* case, which occurred thirteen years later.[69] Many Republican leaders strongly disapproved of the Court's ruling. Republican congressmen introduced five bills, including a proposed constitutional amendment, to replace the lost provisions of the Civil Rights Act. Senator James Falconer Wilson of Iowa, for example, offered a joint resolution to amend the Constitution, arguing that "if the doctrine of the *Civil Rights Cases* is to remain the law of the land . . . the most flagrant violation of the rights of citizens may be a constant practice."[70] Lacking the support of President Chester Arthur, however, opponents of the decision were unable to pass a countermeasure.[71]

Members of the African-American community also voiced forceful denunciations of the *Civil Rights Cases*. The black press was virtually unanimous in its condemnation of the decision, interpreting it as a direct attack on the civil rights of people of African descent. Protests were widely voiced in the black churches, and public meetings were held in numerous cities.[72] Prominent African-American leaders such as Frederick Douglass and Bishop Henry M. Turner made speeches protesting the decision, attacking it as a clear violation of both the Reconstruction amendments and basic morality.[73] Such protests once again rearticulated the anti-caste liberal position. Bishop Turner, for example, argued in 1889 that the purpose of the Reconstruction amendments had been "to entirely free, not to partly liberate" the former slave population. The Thirteenth Amendment, he claimed, sanctioned the Civil Rights Act of 1875 because it was intended to eradicate "not simply . . . the institution of slavery" but also its "badges and incidents."[74]

In 1889, a group calling itself the Brotherhood of Liberty attacked the decision in the *Civil Rights Cases* in a lengthy book entitled *Justice and Jurisprudence*.[75] This book once again asserted that the Fourteenth Amendment had fundamentally altered the shape of American constitutional government by establishing a broad prohibition against racial discrimination.[76] The state-action doctrine upheld by the *Civil Rights Cases* constituted a move by "color-caste constructionists" to nullify this original intent. "The all-absorbing, vital, and important question," wrote the Brotherhood, "is *whether or not the individuals of the State* can be constitutionally inhibited by congressional legislation under the Fourteenth Amendment." If private citizens could "violate this solemn constitutional compact," the authors reasoned, "the framers of the Fourteenth Amendment, who also framed the Civil Rights bill, have labored in vain."[77]

Six years later, these arguments were restated by attorneys James C. Walker and Albion W. Tourgee in their brief submitted on behalf of plaintiff Homer A. Plessy in *Plessy v. Ferguson*. The "object of the Thirteenth Amendment," Walker and Tourgee argued, was not only "to abolish the legal form of chattelism" but also "to undo all that slavery had done in establishing race discrimination and collective as well as personal control of the enslaved race." The statute at issue in the case, which required "equal but separate" accommodations for black and white railway passengers within the state of Louisiana, represented "a perpetuation of the essential features of slavery" and was unconstitutional under the Thirteenth Amendment. "A law assorting the citizens of a State in the enjoyment of a public franchise on the basis of race," they insisted, "is obnoxious to the spirit of republican institutions because it is a legitimation of *caste*."[78]

The purpose of the Civil War, they argued, had not been simply to end slavery. Its goal had also been to establish a new standard of national citizenship that would abolish the failed constitutional system of state control over individual rights.[79] The Fourteenth Amendment had consequently made the rights of "national citizenship expressly *paramount and universal*" and the rights of state citizenship "expressly *subordinate and incidental*." In the process, state governments had been "ousted of *all control over citizenship*." An entirely new standard had been created, "embracing new rights, privileges, and immunities, derivable in a *new* manner, controlled by a *new* authority, having a *new* scope and extent, dependent on national authority for its existence and looking to national power for its preservation."[80] This standard of national citizenship, they argued, was "in strict accord with the Declaration of Independence, which is not a fable as some of our modern theorists would have us believe, but the all embracing formula of personal rights on which our government is based." As a result of the Civil War, the Declaration had fittingly "become the controlling genius of the American people" that "must always be taken into account in construing any expression of the sovereign will, more especially a constitutional provision which more closely reflects the popular mind."[81]

Justice Harlan filed the sole dissent against the majority opinion that upheld the constitutionality of state-mandated segregation under the separate-but-equal doctrine. Although this dissent has come to hold a canonical position in American political and legal history, it represented only a very muted version of what had been a much more radical tradition of liberal thought. Harlan's opinion in *Plessy* did not, for example, fully articulate the view that the Thirteenth and Fourteenth amendments represented a broad prohibition against racial caste and discrimination, whether perpetuated by individuals, groups, businesses, or the state. Consequently, it did not explicitly attack the state-action doctrine. It did not stress the equalitarianism of the Declaration of Independence nor present an unambiguous endorsement of the principles of human universalism and racial equality. Finally, it did not claim that the shape of American constitutional government had been radically restructured by the enactment of the Reconstruction amendments. Harlan's dissent was nonetheless part of the larger tradition that had been built around each of these claims. Commonly read in isolation from this larger historical narrative, however, its ideological roots have remained almost completely obscured.

The Limits of Racial Radicalism

Approximately one hundred years later, Harlan's dissent became an important feature of a new conservative attack on affirmative action and other race-conscious policies. Beginning in the 1980s, conservative activists argued that Harlan's position represented a "color-blind" principle that had historically been at the heart of American liberalism. "Modern liberals perpetuate the *Plessy* decision by replacing the notion of 'reasonable' racial classifications with the concept of 'benign' discrimination," charged Bolick in a *New York Times* editorial marking the hundredth anniversary of the *Plessy* case. "As Justice Harlan recognized, no middle ground exists. The Government will either have the power to classify and discriminate or it won't."[82] If Americans "continue to view group-oriented social issues as civil rights issues and to pursue color-conscious solutions," admonished Assistant Attorney General William Bradford Reynolds during the height of the Reagan era, we "could well find ourselves in 1996 in a racially ordered society similar to that approved by the *Plessy* Court in 1896."[83]

In principle, such contemporary appropriations of the Harlan dissent run counter to the commitments of the larger anti-caste tradition of which it was a part. In asserting a constitutional mandate to take federal action against social practices that serve to perpetuate racial caste, this tradition is in fact remarkably consonant with contemporary policies that seek to use government power to break up entrenched patterns of racial hierarchy.[84] Affirmative action, for example, is intended to break up social patterns that are held to prevent racial minorities from having equal access to a full range of public goods and individual opportunities. For its supporters, it could reasonably be said to represent a modern-day extension of the anti-caste position. In this sense, contemporary conservatives have got the significance of the Harlan dissent backward: rather than representing a commitment to color-blind individualism, it stands for a larger tradition of anti-caste, and therefore color-conscious, constitutionalism.

Of course, the anti-caste liberals of the nineteenth century also insisted that the simple prohibition of racial discrimination would be sufficient to ensure that African Americans would stand on an equal footing with their fellow citizens in the "race of life." Unlike their twentieth-century counterparts, their faith that these measures would set up a racially fair social structure never had the chance to be put to the test. The fact that the most prominent anti-caste leaders had been supporters of the earlier land redistribution movement suggests that they were not opposed to at least selected instances of racially targeted redistribution. Given the importance of landownership in what was at the time a largely agricultural regional economy, this support for land redistribution represented an attempt to establish a more equitable foundation for the operation of a market economy. Despite its racial radicalism, however, this commitment reflected an essentially conservative economic position, as it was disconnected from any thought that the larger structure of economic relations might need to be reexamined in light of the values and requirements of republican government.

The adoption of the Fourteenth Amendment could not make Anglo-Saxons out of Africans. It was unjust to the negro to force him to play a role for which by the forces of nature he was unfitted.... It is one of the fundamental precepts of political science today that only those people in a community can participate equally in its civil, social, and political life who are conscious of a common origin, share a common idealism, and look forward to a common destiny.

—Charles W. Collins, "The Fourteenth Amendment and the Negro Race Question," American Law Review, 1911

2

Darwinian Liberalism

During Reconstruction and its aftermath, conservative opponents of anti-caste liberalism converged around an alternative position here referred to as *Darwinian liberalism.*[1] Most centrally, this ideology combined a minimalist conception of citizenship rights with a fierce commitment to both laissez-faire and white supremacy. To contemporary ears, this sounds incoherent, as we assume that a commitment to racial hierarchy cannot be squared with either equal rights or free-market principles. In the context of late nineteenth-century America, however, this was decidedly not the case. On the contrary, a majority of political elites, as well as the mainstream of educated opinion very much supported the presumption that the extension of equal rights to an inferior race in the context of a free-market system could logically do nothing other than produce and maintain racial hierarchy.[2]

From the time of Reconstruction through the end of the nineteenth century, Darwinian liberals argued that the full extension of citizenship rights to African Americans would do nothing to disrupt the natural system of racial hierarchy that put whites in an authoritative position of social dominance and control. This position was considered politically moderate for its time, particularly (although by no means exclusively) in the white South. In contrast to other, more extreme elements, Darwinian liberals accepted the legitimacy of the Reconstruction amendments and the principle of equal citizenship for African Americans. White nationalists, in contrast, rejected both in their entirety and advocated the use of terrorist tactics to achieve their ends. Consequently, the Darwinian liberal position represented some modicum of protection to black citizens—although its ostensibly temperate advocates were usually willing to violate these minimal guarantees when they believed that political expediency demanded it.

By the end of the nineteenth century, however, the political commitment to even such a minimalist and contingent conception of black citizenship had largely eroded. Although the abolition of slavery as a legal institution remained accepted as a primary outcome of the Civil War, the decision to enfranchise the freedpeople by the extension of citizenship rights became widely viewed in respectable circles as a historic mistake. This was particularly true with regard to the Fifteenth Amendment, which had extended the right of suffrage to black men. Respected jurists argued that the experience of Reconstruction had proved that African Americans were incapable of assuming the rights and responsibilities of citizenship in a democratic republic. In order to maintain the integrity of the Constitution, they urged that most of the Fourteenth Amendment and all of the Fifteenth Amendment be repealed. This wholesale rejection of even the most basic rights of black citizens once again illustrates the relative moderation of Darwinian liberalism for its time. In the context of late nineteenth-century America, providing the most minimal rights to African Americans remained controversial, even when accompanied by assurances of eternal white domination and racial hierarchy.

The Necessity of Racial Hierarchy

Like anti-caste liberalism, the Darwinian construction of citizenship began with the premise that the establishment of equal legal and political rights constituted the singularly legitimate way of establishing civic equality, which was equated with the provision of equal opportunity to compete in the "race of life." Similarly, both agreed that the purpose of the Reconstruction amendments had been to extend the full rights of citizenship to black Americans, and both accepted their legitimacy as constitutional principles. Even staunch opponents of the Civil Rights Act of 1875, such as Representative John M. Glover, a Democrat from Missouri, held that the Fourteenth and

Fifteenth amendments "have brought the colored race of this country upon the same plane with the white race, and there the two races should be left, the individuals of each to work out their own destiny."[3] As Representative Charles A. Eldredge, a Democrat from Wisconsin, argued: "So far as the law is concerned, the black man is in all respects the equal of the white. He stands and may make the race of life upon terms of perfect equality with the most favored citizen."[4]

From this common beginning point, however, the two positions diverged dramatically. While the anti-caste position viewed racial discrimination and segregation as illegitimate barriers to civic equality that should be prohibited by federal law, the Darwinian position viewed such practices as a natural part of a social order that incorporated two extremely different, and inherently unequal, racial groups. From this perspective, the civil rights bill represented a draconian attempt to use the power of the federal government to impose "social equality" between the races in violation of both natural and constitutional law.[5]

The line separating civic and social equality was deemed to be both sharp and unbridgeable. Representative Eppa Hunton, a Democrat from Virginia, argued, for example, that while "the white people of the South" were "willing and desirous" to extend equal rights to the freedpeople, they would "resist by all legal means every attempt, whether in or out of Congress, to establish social equality between the races."[6] Echoing this sentiment, Representative William S. Herndon, a Democrat from Texas, stated that while he would "go as far toward securing equal protection in all political rights before the law" to the black man, he was "unwilling to legislate him into our social system on terms of equality with the white race."[7] "We have already by our Constitution and by the laws of the several States conferred upon the colored man equal political and civil rights. He stands the equal of the white man before the law," argued Representative William E. Finck, a Democrat from Ohio. "But you seek by this bill to say there shall be social equality between the races. You cannot invade that domain. You cannot by law compel social equality."[8]

White supremacy was presented as the natural bedrock of the natural order. "God himself has set His seal of distinctive difference between the two races, and no human legislation can overrule the Divine decree," Representative Milton I. Southard, a Democrat from Ohio, asserted. "Legislate as we may, the race passions and prejudices, the social tastes and inclinations, will remain, and forever keep the two classes upon terms of actual inequality."[9] Representative Glover similarly argued that "any legislation to counteract natural principles or to repeal natural laws or obliterate natural distinctions is impotent for good." Waxing sarcastic, he queried: "Why does not some learned gentleman introduce a bill to regulate the rainfall and to provide for the movements of the wind and tides? It would belong to the same class."[10]

To follow the dictates of the natural order, leaving the hierarchy of white supremacy and black subordination undisturbed, was held to be the only means of securing progress and harmony in race relations. As Representative James C. Harper, a Conservative from North Carolina, argued, blacks and whites could live together for their mutual benefit—"side by side, in perfect peace, in perfect civil equality before the law, in the equal enjoyment of civil, moral, educational, and religious privileges"—as long as the prohibition against social equality was not violated:

> And so we should continue to live, each race helping the other, the whites teaching the blacks economy of time, improved methods of labor, and the cultivation of those qualities which give a man self-respect and the good will of his fellows. And the colored race, lending to the whites their strong arms and trained muscles, giving their labor for wages to support themselves and their families. Generations hence, should the negro exist that long, will see no change in the relations between the races, the whites acknowledging the civil equality of the blacks, and habituated to it; the blacks equally cognizant of and believing in their social and intellectual inferiority to the whites.[11]

To attempt to disturb this arrangement would inevitably generate violent white resistance and invite potentially disastrous social consequences. The only reason that blacks and whites were able to coexist in their current state of "concord and peace," Representative Hiram P. Bell, a Democrat from Georgia, explained, was that "the line of social distinction has been kept distinctly marked." Although, Bell claimed, the "colored people have never sought to cross or obliterate it," the civil rights bill "seeks to blot it out." Such a move, Bell emphasized, would never stand: "This attempt at its abolition invites the negro to take his position in the social scale with the whites. This will be resisted at the very threshold by all classes, and will never be submitted to or allowed, whatever consequences may result."[12]

Any attempt to legislate social equality was held to pose an equally dangerous threat to the integrity of American constitutional government. Rejecting the anti-caste argument that the Reconstruction amendments had altered the shape of the federal system by significantly expanding the power of the national government, the Darwinian position emphasized that the original system represented an indispensable bulwark against the growth of centralized power and despotic control. According to this perspective, the pending Civil Rights Act represented an illegitimate overextension of federal power that, once unleashed, would destroy the institutions of local self-government that formed the bedrock of the constitutional order.

Senator Orris S. Ferry, a Republican from Connecticut, castigated his opponents for their contention "that by the adoption of the three most recent amendments to the Constitution of the United States, our old system of Government has been subverted." Such a claim, Ferry argued, amounted to the idea that in order "to give all citizens the equal protection of the laws," Congress "may go into every city, town, borough, and hamlet in the United States and enact ordinary police laws, and put a Federal officer to keep guard over your streets." If "the construction which [Senator Sumner] and his associates have put upon the new amendments to the Constitution be received as the law of the country," he added, "we may bid farewell to our hopes of American liberty for the generations to come."[13]

Representative Finck argued that if Americans had "the wisdom and patriotism to preserve this [federal] system" in its original form, "we will exhibit to the world the best and freest system of government, and the most prosperous and happy people known in the history of mankind." If, on the other hand, "we overstep the well-defined boundaries of power and invade the just rights of the States," he warned:

> this well-balanced system of State and Federal Government will be placed in the utmost peril of being converted into a strong centralized power, whose history will be marked by oppression and despotism, and add one more to the long list of failures in the attempt to establish and perpetuate a free representative government.[14]

In keeping with this insistence on the imperative of maintaining the original constitutional limits on the distribution of governmental power, the Darwinian position championed a minimalist construction of the rights of national citizenship guaranteed by the Fourteenth Amendment. In contrast to the expansive reading of these rights characterized by the anti-caste position, Darwinian liberals insisted that they consisted simply, in the words of Senator George Vickers, a Democrat from Maryland, of "the right of personal security, the right of personal liberty, [and] the right of private property."[15] As Senator Lyman Trumbull, a Republican from Illinois, argued: "I understand by the term 'civil rights' rights appertaining to the individual as a free, independent citizen; and what are they? The right to go and come; the right to enforce contracts; the right to convey his property; the right to buy property—these general rights that belong to mankind everywhere."[16]

The anti-caste argument that the Fourteenth Amendment embodied a broad prohibition against racial discrimination was rejected as ludicrous nonsense. Representative Aylett Hanes Buckner, a Democrat from Missouri, argued that it was "inconceivable that the provisions of the Fourteenth Amendment should have any application to the pretended rights" represented by the pending civil rights bill. "The 'equal protection of the laws,'" Buckner continued, "could not have been designed for any such case. It could never have been contemplated that every citizen, male and female, black and white, foreign and native, should be accorded the enjoyment of every right in the same measure and in the same degree."[17] Senator Allen G. Thurman, a Democrat from Ohio, addressed the question of "whether the Constitution forbids [racial] discrimination while it permits all others." The proponents of the civil rights bill, Thurman noted, "admit that you may discriminate: you may discriminate against those who are ignorant of the English language, against those who are ignorant of their own language, against those who have not resided a particular time, [and] against a particular sect." At the same time, however, they contradictorily claimed that "the moment you discriminate on the grounds of race or color, that moment you transcend the Constitution of the United States and Congress is authorized to interfere." "Sir," Thurman countered, "there is not one word in the Constitution that authorizes any such argument."[18]

Using a logic remarkably similar to some of the more strident contemporary arguments fixated on the idea of "reverse discrimination," opponents of the civil rights bill held that to prohibit racial discrimination was to establish an illegitimate form of discriminatory legislation which both violated the rights of whites and diminished the motivation and self-respect of blacks. Arguing that "social prejudice is a social liberty that the law has no right to disturb," Representative Henry D. McHenry, a Democrat from Kentucky, charged that "the object of this bill is to abolish distinctions on account of 'race, color, or previous condition of servitude,' but it in fact makes a discrimination against the white man on account of his color."[19] Representative Glover described the civil rights bill as an "odious form of race and class legislation" which signaled to the black man "that he is the especial ward and pet of the nation, to whom forty millions of white men should pay tribute and admiration."[20] Representative Eldredge expanded upon this theme:

> To make the colored citizen feel that he is the pet, the especial favorite of the law will only feed and pander to that conceit and self-consequence which is now his weakest and perhaps most offensive characteristic. If he be made to feel that extraordinary pro-

visions of law are enacted in his favor because of his weakness or feebleness as a man, the very fact weakens and enfeebles him. The consciousness that there is necessity for such legislation and protection for him must necessarily humiliate and degrade him. Such laws, too, are a constant reminder to him that he is inferior to the white race.

The bottom line, Eldredge concluded, was that there could "be no peace, no harmony, no confidence, no mutual respect, no feeling of equality between two races living together and protected from the infringement of each other's rights by different laws and different penalties."[21]

Most objectionable was the fact that the civil rights bill, by proscribing racial discrimination in public accommodations and transportation, violated the property rights of the owners of these enterprises. Consistent with the contention that the right to property was one of the few fundamental rights of citizenship and that the power of the federal government should remain strictly curtailed, the Darwinian position held the rights of private property to be virtually absolute. As Representative J. Ambler Smith, a Democrat from Virginia, explained:

> [T]he right of property is so sacred that the Legislature of my State itself cannot dare to say to me, though one of her citizens, that I shall not decide for myself whom I shall admit and whom I shall exclude from *my* hotel. The assumption would be an impudent, unendurable usurpation and tyranny. . . . And so, sir, of my stage-coach, my steamboat, my theater—they are *my* property; and my State . . . cannot interfere with that property so long as I do not allow it to be a nuisance and to damage the public. If this be not so, then property, instead of being one of the great elements of society and a propulsion of honorable ambition and patriotic enterprise, would be a worthless bauble.[22]

Similarly, Representative Buckner characterized the bill as "such an interference with the rights of private property and the rules and regulations of society that no free people would tolerate such mischievous intermeddling."[23]

In contrast to the anti-caste position, which recognized a grey zone of privately owned enterprises that were quasi-public in nature, Darwinian liberalism posited a sharp divide between the public and private realms. This, in turn, allowed for a rigid commitment to the state-action doctrine, which held that antidiscrimination law was applicable only to government agents and not to private enterprises, social groups, or individuals. As Senator Thomas

F. Bayard, a Democrat from Delaware, asserted: "the Fourteenth Amendment is addressed entirely to the States and never to the people."[24]

Tables 2.1 and 2.2 summarize the ideological positions advanced by each of the fifty-four congressmen who argued against the civil rights bill, paralleling the analysis of the positions taken by its supporters provided in the previous chapter. Table 2.1 details the number of congressmen whose statements indicated either a strong or moderate endorsement of the ideologies of constitutional conservatism and white supremacism described above. "Strong" statements of constitutional conservatism were coded as those that clearly asserted that the civil rights bill was unconstitutional or that the rights of national citizenship guaranteed by the Fourteenth Amendment consisted simply of those of life, liberty, and property. "Moderate" statements, in contrast, were coded as those that asserted that the civil rights bill was probably unconstitutional or that it was simply not needed. Similarly, "strong" statements of white supremacism were coded as those that clearly asserted either that whites constituted a distinct race innately superior to blacks, that racial segregation was natural or ordained by God, or that blacks must never be allowed to exist on a level of social equality with whites. Alternatively, "moderate" statements were coded as those that simply asserted that blacks already had equal rights or that the separate-but-equal standard was constitutionally acceptable, if not necessarily naturally or divinely preordained.

As can be seen in table 2.1, 83 percent of the fifty-four congressmen analyzed made either a strong or a moderate endorsement of the constitutionally conservative position, while 85 percent made either a strong or a moderate endorsement of the white supremacist position. Notably, the vast majority in both cases took the strong, rather than the moderate position, with 78 percent taking a strong position on constitutional conservatism and 68 percent taking a strong position on white supremacism.

Table 2.2 provides an analysis of how these different positions were correlated with one another in the statements made by the subset of thirty-eight congressmen (70 percent of the total analyzed) who took a clear position on both constitutional and racial issues. Here it can be seen that a solid 71 percent majority took a strong position on both constitutional and racial issues, which exceeds the combined total of the three other alternatives by 42 percent.

Thus, while some congressmen made extensive constitutional arguments but made no explicit or extensive comments on race,[25] and others spoke extensively on race but not at all on constitutional issues,[26] the vast majority of congressmen who argued against the civil rights bill took positions on both racial and constitutional issues that fit the larger ideological patterns described above. There was clearly, then, a strong connection be-

Table 2.1.
**Positions Represented by Congressional Opponents
of the Civil Rights Act of 1875 (N=54)**

	N	% Total
Constitutional Conservatism		
Strong	42	78%
Moderate	3	5%
No position stated	9	17%
White Supremacism		
Strong	37	68%
Moderate	9	17%
No position stated	8	15%

For sources of these data, see chapter 1, note 22.

Table 2.2.
Cross-Tabulation of Opponents' Positions (N=38)

	White Supremacism	
	Strong	Moderate
Constitutional Conservatism		
Strong	27	9
	(71%)	(24%)
Moderate	2	0
	(5%)	(0%)

For sources of these data, see chapter 1, note 22.

tween the particular construction of liberal discourse represented by the conservative constitutional position and the ideology of white supremacy. These two ideological currents combined to form a minimalist definition of citizenship, which, when applied to black Americans, explicitly relegated them to a permanently subordinate place in a racially defined social hierarchy.

While the majority of the congressmen who articulated this position during the debates over the civil rights bill were members of the Democratic party, it did command some bipartisan support, with 16 percent of those who adhered to both its constitutional and racial components being Republicans. Furthermore, the explicit support voiced by these Republicans was almost certainly only the tip of the iceberg: party members cast 11 percent of the votes against the bill in the House and 23 percent in the Senate.[27] Many Republicans avoided taking a position at all by absenting themselves from the debates and abstaining from the final vote.[28] This weak Republican support for measures disruptive of the racial status quo was indicative of a growing trend, as widening rifts among traditional party constituencies were moving its center of gravity in a more and more conservative direction. As this shift took place, the paired ideologies of white supremacism and laissez-faire liberalism became increasingly dominant forces in the national political culture.

The Abandonment of Reconstruction

The full extent of this growing dissolution of the Republican coalition became even more apparent with the onset of the Panic of 1873, which marked the beginning of a severe and extended economic contraction, as well as a shift in national political attention away from issues of race and Reconstruction and toward questions of labor and class. This event had a major impact on the political ideologies associated with the Republican party, working to erode the standing of the free labor position while building support for the more conservative doctrine of laissez-faire. Significantly, this shift away from the free labor perspective and toward undiluted laissez-faire was accompanied by "a resurgence of overt racism" among northern Republicans. Increasingly, Reconstruction became widely viewed as an unmitigated failure based on what was now viewed as the demonstrably false premise that citizens of African descent could be treated as equal partners in a democratic project of self-governance.[29]

The resounding influence of *The Prostrate State: South Carolina under Negro Government* (1874) was emblematic of this pronounced shift in both northern and Republican opinion. This ostensible exposé of the horrors of black-dominated Reconstruction government was first published as a series of popular articles before being released as a book. Written by James S. Pike, a former antislavery crusader and lapsed Radical Republican employed as a reporter for the *New York Tribune*, *The Prostrate State* was suffused with the mixture of white supremacism and laissez-faire liberalism which comprised the Darwinian position.[30]

For Pike, the question of innate racial capacities had been definitively closed:

> [The] black is a child of vice and ignorance and superstition in
> South Carolina as well as in Africa. What he might have been ca-
> pable of, under different conditions than those in which he has
> ever existed, it is useless to inquire. Races of men exhibit the same
> general characteristics from age to age. The question which con-
> cerns us is not what might be, or what in some remote future may
> be, but what now is.[31]

As things stood, Pike asserted, the vast majority of African Americans could
accurately be described as "ignorant, narrow-minded, vicious, worthless ani-
mals." The "Sambos" who had taken over the state capitol were, in Pike's opinion, little better. Having brought about "the rule of ignorance and corruption,"
they represented nothing less than "barbarism overwhelming civilization."[32]

In Pike's view, this desperate situation was not simply a result of having
unqualified individuals in office or evidence of a governmental system in
need of reform. On the contrary, the root problem was definitively racial.
The black man, Pike explained, "is certainly not the kind of man, and his
race is not the race, for whom our political institutions were originally made;
and it is already a serious question whether he is the man, or his the race, for
which they are adapted." The power that African Americans wielded in
South Carolina was not a result of their own might or merit, but rather existed "by means of an alien and borrowed authority only," that is, "the com-
pulsive power of the Federal authority in Washington."[33]

In keeping with standard laissez-faire prescriptions, Pike asserted that
the end of such destructive governmental intrusion would permit "the forces
of civilization [to] readjust themselves and overturn the present artificial situation." The presence of blacks in a governing system that had been created
by and for whites was "a hybrid born of unnatural connections, offensive
alike to God and man."[34] If federal power were removed and the state allowed
to adjust to a free-market economy, both races would be better off:

> There seems to be no reason to doubt that an ample supply of
> faithful and steady laborers could be readily obtained by any man
> who would honestly undertake to farm in South Carolina . . .
> giving the negro such food and such shelter as the dictates of an
> enlightened self-interest and a humane spirit would prompt.

Such a system, Pike optimistically concluded, would particularly benefit
African Americans, as it "would pave the way for their social and moral elevation" and perhaps even lay "the foundation of a revolution in the character of the race."[35]

Darwinian Liberalism

Pike's analysis of the evils of black political power in South Carolina was widely repeated in the national press. Particularly popularized by the *Nation*, a rash of articles advocating an end to Reconstruction also appeared in popular magazines such as *Scribner's*, *Harper's*, and the *Atlantic Monthly*. Dissenting voices were extremely few: while the New York *Herald* criticized Pike for presenting a "less than cosmopolitan study," the book popularly succeeded in making South Carolina into a national symbol of government venality, the folly of Reconstruction, and blacks' incapacity for self-government.[36]

This perspective caused the leading lights of northern political opinion to embrace some of the key ideologies advocated by their former enemies in the South. In May 1874, for example, the *New York Times* editorialized that the manifest horrors of Reconstruction governments in states such as South Carolina should be enough to convince "any intelligent reader" that the doctrine of states' rights advocated by southern Democrats represented a foundational principle of American government. Reconstruction policies were, after all, only "experimental." Given their evident failures, the *Times* asked, "[C]an we wonder that people everywhere begin to ask how long the experiment is to last?"

> The negro has had a very fair amount of protection. It is important before going any further to find out what use he has made of the freedom given to him; in what way he has exercised the vast political powers with which he has been endowed; what sort of government he has helped to set up in States where he is most powerful; whether, in short, he at this moment stands in need of protection from the white man, or the white man stands in need of protection from him.[37]

Six months later, the *Times* took a harder line still. While acknowledging that some "dreadful crimes" had been perpetuated against southern blacks by white extremists determined to prevent them from voting, the paper maintained that there were nonetheless extremely good reasons to support the disfranchisement of blacks. The black man, the *Times* editorialized, "has incurred the hatred of his white fellow-citizen not only as a voter who was formerly a slave, but as a voter who is the sure support of thieves, the origin of the power for bad men, and almost incurably given over to clannish, ignorant, and brutal politics." States such as Louisiana ("where the negro has been long the ruler") had been forced to learn the hard way that "his partial and temporary supremacy—it can never be anything but partial and temporary—is purchased at great cost."[38]

Subsequent events quickly proved the *Times* right on one score: black political power in the South was indeed only "partial and temporary." Shortly after the highly contested presidential election of 1876, the Democratic and Republican parties forged a compromise agreement that brought Reconstruction to a close. As the last remaining federal troops were pulled out of the South (and, in a critical turn of events, immediately redeployed to put down an unprecedented wave of labor protests in the rest of the country), white supremacist rule quickly returned to the region. With an often ruthless deployment of force, black politicians and their white Republican allies were quickly ousted from any positions of power. In the process, the Democratic party, united behind a common commitment to white supremacy, established a lockhold on southern government.

White Supremacy and the New South

The collapse of Reconstruction inaugurated the reign of a faction of the Democratic party commonly referred to as the "Redeemers" in the South. Largely composed of the planter and business elite, the Redeemers (also known as Conservative Democrats) were on good terms with powerful political and economic forces in the North and well positioned to take the reins of power in their own region. Despite having cooperated with more reactionary forces during the violent struggle to overthrow Reconstruction, once its collapse ended the need for this alliance, the Redeemers were able to claim the mantle of the moderate center. As a central feature of this claim, they pledged to maintain the constitutional rights of black citizens in the South. In so doing, they explicitly rejected racial terrorism and advocated a return to the "paternalism" that had supposedly characterized race relations under slavery. Their stated goal was to establish a lawful form of racial reconciliation under the terms of an ostensibly benign and enlightened form of white supremacy. Using the terms of Darwinian liberalism, the Redeemers advocated a minimal standard of black citizenship rights under a rigid system of racial hierarchy.

Governor Wade Hampton of South Carolina was paradigmatic of the Redeemer movement. Elected in 1876, Hampton appealed to white voters as a racial moderate who would achieve social accommodation and harmony. At the same time, he courted black votes with the slogan of "free men, free schools, and free ballots."[39] Quickly emerging as a preeminent leader of southern conservatism, Hampton was subsequently elected senator in 1878.

In 1879, Hampton articulated his views on black citizenship in a panel discussion entitled "Ought the Negro to Be Disfranchised? Ought He to Have

Been Enfranchised?" This debate was published in the *North American Review*, one of the leading intellectual journals of the period.[40] Here, Hampton explained that the wisdom of extending the right of suffrage to the black man had been dubious at best, "ignorant and incompetent as he was to comprehend the high responsibility thrust upon him." Nonetheless, "the deed has been done and it is irrevocable." If African Americans were provided with proper educational training and moral guidance, Hampton argued, the new standard of black citizenship could be upheld without undue damage to the body politic. Contending that "as the negro becomes more intelligent, he naturally allies himself with the more conservative of whites," Hampton believed that "the inevitable tendency of things as they now stand in the South" was a controlled standard of black enfranchisement under the terms of white supremacy laid down by Conservative Democratic leadership.[41]

The Redeemers' racial ideology was directly bound up with an advocacy of laissez-faire through the much-touted conception of the "New South." The central claim of the New South position was that the future of the region lay in pursuing the same sort of industrial capitalism that had long been negatively associated with the crass, money-grubbing North. Self-consciously rejecting the anticapitalist ideals of the "Old South," New South advocates preached the virtues of unrestrained laissez-faire capitalism and embraced the money standard, profit seeking, and business acumen.[42]

New South boosters repeatedly reiterated the Darwinian liberal construction of citizenship. Henry W. Grady, for example—the man universally regarded as "the leading prophet of the 'New South'"[43]—pontificated in an 1887 speech, "No race has risen, or will rise, above its ordained place. Here is the pivotal fact of this great matter—two races made equal in law, and in political rights, between whom the caste of race has set an impassable gulf." The South "would not, if she could, cast this race back into the condition from which it was righteously raised" nor "deny its' [*sic*] smallest or abridge its' [*sic*] fullest privilege." Nonetheless, the region must continue to "walk in that integrity of race" which God "created in His wisdom." White supremacy, Grady explained, represented a divine decree that must be maintained forever:

> Standing in the presence of this multitude, sobered with the responsibility of the message I deliver to the young men of the South, I declare that the truth above all others to be worn unsullied and sacred in your hearts, to be surrendered to no force, sold for no price, compromised in no necessity, but cherished and defended as the covenant of your prosperity, and the pledge of peace

to your children, is that the white race must dominate forever in the South.[44]

Despite the melodramatic extremism of such statements, figures such as Grady and Hampton represented the centrist forces of political moderation in the South at the time. To contemporary ears, the Darwinian liberal claim to simultaneously uphold the standards of black citizenship and white supremacy sounds ludicrous. In the context of the times, however, simply to assert any, however minimal, standard of rights for African Americans was to adopt a centrist position. While this was, of course, particularly true in the South, it was also the case in the North. In this historical context, Darwinian liberalism was indeed liberal: at least on its own terms, it extended the rights of citizenship to all individuals regardless of race. While obviously not a form of liberalism that most contemporary Americans would want to embrace as a part of their historical heritage, it was, nonetheless, a prominent part of the American liberal tradition. Recognizing it as such demonstrates both the tremendous flexibility of liberal principles and the centrality of race in constructing politically consequential variants of them.

White Nationalism and "Redemption"

The relative centrism of Darwinian liberalism is best demonstrated by comparing it to the more extreme, but nonetheless widely prevalent position here referred to as *white nationalism*. Particularly prominent in the South, white nationalism distinguished itself from the more moderate position of Darwinian liberalism in two ways. First, white nationalism held that black people were not simply inferior to whites, but so fundamentally different that they represented a "lower" order of being that was unworthy of being accorded any rights whatsoever. Given this assertion, it followed that persons of African descent could not be considered citizens, even within a hierarchical system of white supremacy. As an 1868 article in the New Orleans *Times* succinctly explained: "No privilege can be secured to the negro to which his white neighbors do not consent."[45]

Such views were prevalent throughout the course of Reconstruction. Louisiana's 1865 Democratic party platform, for example, stated, "[W]e hold this to be a Government of white people, made to be perpetuated for the exclusive benefit of the white race. . . . people of African descent cannot be considered as citizens of the United States."[46] Similarly, a New Orleans newspaper complained that "wicked demagogues" from the North were corrupting blacks and stirring up potentially dangerous trouble by instilling them with inappropriate notions of "rights." "Negroes care nothing for 'rights.' They know intuitively that their place is in the field; their proper instruments of self-preservation, the shovel and the hoe. . . . Every real white man is sick of the negro, and the 'rights' of the negro."[47]

Observers of everyday life in the Reconstruction South verified the prevalence of such views. A Freedmen's Bureau agent stationed in Greenville, South Carolina, reported in 1866 that the "men that understand the Freedmen to have, or that they are entitled to any more rights than a horse are exceptions to the general rule."[48] In his widely read examination of the Ku Klux Klan, *The Invisible Empire* (1879), Albion W. Tourgee,[49] a well-known author, judge, and political activist, cited the following as "the best explanation" of the attitude of southern whites toward blacks "that has ever been attempted":

> In order that we may comprehend the disposition of the Southerners towards the blacks, let me use an illustration: Men do not hate dogs; on the contrary, there exists a strong friendship between master and brute. But if a dog attempts to get upon a man's table, and persists in his objectionable course, he is apt to be shot for his trouble, and we approve of the killing. . . . *Taught by the laws of caste to look upon himself and his class as alone entitled to exercise the prerogatives of citizenship*, he rested the disposition of the black man to claim his franchise about in the same spirit in which a man will shoot a dog which has climbed upon the table and will not [get] down.[50]

"In the view of the average Southern white," Tourgee reported, the "freedman is no less an inferior, no more a man . . . than was the slave."[51]

In contrast to Darwinian liberals, who (at least up until the political upheavals of the late 1890s) insisted on the constitutional authority of a minimalist construction of all of the Reconstruction amendments, white nationalists accepted a narrow reading of the Thirteenth Amendment only. If, they conceded, the formal abolition of slavery was an inevitable consequence of Confederate defeat in the Civil War, the subsequent enfranchisement of the freedpeople as citizens under the despotic regime of the Radical Republicans was neither legitimate nor binding. As white nationalist ideology equated constitutional integrity with racial purity, the Fourteenth and Fifteenth amendments were by definition outrageous corruptions of the constitutional order. Holding that the Confederacy had fought the Civil War not to maintain slavery per se, but rather to uphold the fundamental principles of the republic—which had coequally centered on both state sovereignty and white supremacy—Reconstruction was viewed not simply as a set of undesirable policies, but rather as a wholesale violation of constitutional principles.

As J. A. Minnis, a federal official stationed in Alabama in 1871, explained: "When the war was over, the Southern people had no idea, while they expected slavery to be abolished, that their slaves were to be made their political equals." Consequently, the subsequent "Reconstruction measures of Congress were regarded by the great body of the white people in the South as usurpations, unconstitutional, and void, and all who sustained them were bitterly denounced as enemies to the people."[52] Similarly, Tourgee explained:

> [The] average Southern man . . . believes most solemnly that he fought in a holy cause and in support of the true theory of constitutional liberty. He regards the North not only as having been the aggressor as regards the institution of Slavery, but also as having subverted and destroyed the Constitution which he fought to maintain and preserve in its original purity.[53]

White nationalist ideology was translated into practice by various terrorist organizations, which served as the self-appointed shock troops of the southern battle to defeat Reconstruction. The Oath of the Invisible Empire, for example, swore that the mission of the Ku Klux Klan was to "uphold and defend the Constitution of the United States as it was handed down by our forefathers in its original purity . . . and forever maintain and contend that intelligent white men shall govern this country."[54] Similarly, the Constitution and Ritual of the Knights of the White Camellia (1868) stated:

> [O]ur main and fundamental object is the MAINTENANCE OF THE SUPREMACY OF THE WHITE RACE in this Republic. . . . the government of our Republic was established by white men, for white men alone, and . . . it was never in the contemplation of its founders that it should fall into the hands of an inferior and degraded race. . . . It, then, becomes our solemn duty, as white men, to resist strenuously and persistently those attempts against our natural and constitutional rights, and to do everything in our power in order to maintain, in this Republic, the supremacy of the Caucasian race, and restrain the black or African race to that condition of social and political inferiority for which God has destined it.[55]

Under the guise of this supposed logic, unchecked violence and terrorism against both southern blacks and their white Republican allies became the most widespread practical expression of this "solemn duty." While the history of extralegal violence in the South during Reconstruction has been well documented and need not be reiterated here, several points related to this phenomenon require particular emphasis.[56] First, racial and political terrorism were inextricably intertwined and played an absolutely central role in the defeat of Reconstruction. Second, while the amount and intensity of terrorist activity varied from region to region, its general character was not random and haphazard, but rather systematic, organized, strategic, and targeted. Third, terrorist groups such as the Ku Klux Klan were not rogue operations but served as the quasi-underground, paramilitary arm of the mainstream Democratic party.[57] White nationalism was not, in other words, a marginal phenomenon, in either ideological or practical terms. Rather, it played a crucial role in southern politics, which in turn affected the rest of the nation.

Darwinian Liberalism and the Constitution

The dominant ideology represented by the bench and bar during the late nineteenth century was rooted in the same hybrid of laissez-faire liberalism and racial hierarchism articulated by the congressional opponents of the Civil Rights Act of 1875. Just as political elites in the Republican and Democratic parties, the national press, and northern public opinion converged on the common ground of laissez-faire liberalism and white supremacism during the 1870s–1880s before shifting further to the right in the 1890s, the courts and the legal profession generally adopted a steadily more antiblack position during this period, constructing an ever-narrowing definition of the meaning of black citizenship. Consequently, while the 1870s began with the Supreme Court making its first move to counter anti-caste liberalism by narrowing the meaning of the Fourteenth Amendment, by the turn of the century influential jurists were bluntly stating that the Fourteenth and Fifteenth amendments should be ignored or repealed.

Although the *Slaughterhouse Cases*, decided by the Supreme Court in 1873, did not deal directly with issues of racial equality, they were nonetheless important in this regard, as they addressed the meaning of the rights of citizenship under the Fourteenth Amendment. In these cases, the Court stressed that there was a sharp distinction between the rights of national and state citizenship and that the purpose of the Fourteenth Amendment had been simply to prevent states from violating these nationally guaranteed rights. In keeping with the Darwinian position, however, the rights of national citizenship as specified by the Court were exceedingly minimal, consisting simply of the rights to "free access to [national] seaports," federal protection "when on the high seas or within the jurisdiction of a foreign government," peaceful assembly, the "petition of redress of grievances," and "the writ of *habeas corpus*."[58] The Court insisted that the Reconstruction amendments had not wrought any significant changes in the constitutional structure. States retained primary control over matters of civil rights, while the federal government continued to have only minimal authority. While the balance of power in the federal system had been slightly adjusted, the essential nature of American federalism had not been changed.[59]

Ten years later, in the *Civil Rights Cases* of 1883, the Court addressed the issue of how the Thirteenth and Fourteenth amendments had affected the rights of black citizens in particular. To review, this decision held that the prohibition against racial discrimination in public accommodations and transportation effected by the Civil Rights Act of 1875 was unconstitutional. The 8–1 majority opinion in this case strongly reaffirmed the basic tenets of laissez-faire. Flatly rejecting the broad reading of the Reconstruction amendments advocated by the anti-caste position, Justice Joseph Bradley wrote that the "Thirteenth Amendment has respect, not to distinctions of race or class or color, but to slavery." As such, it had absolutely no bearing on the issue of racial discrimination: "It would be running the slavery argument into the ground to make it apply to every act of discrimination which a person may see fit to make as to the guests he will entertain, or as to the people he will take into his coach or cab or car, or admit to his concert or theater, or deal with in other matters of intercourse or business."[60] Similarly, the Court significantly narrowed the scope of the Fourteenth Amendment by holding that under the state-action doctrine, citizens were protected from discrimination only when effected by legislation or by an agent of the state. Defining the establishments covered by the Civil Rights Act—inns, theaters, railroads, and so on—as wholly private, discriminatory action by the managers of such enterprises constituted simply a nonactionable "individual invasion of individual rights," rather than part of a larger pattern of social practice that violated the rights of black citizens and perpetuated the legacy of slavery.[61]

Echoing the arguments made during the congressional debates that the proposed law would harm the black man by causing him to view himself as "the especial ward and pet of the nation," the Court held that the Civil Rights Act itself, as a species of racially targeted legislation, violated the principle of a nondiscriminatory standard of citizenship. "When a man has emerged from slavery, and by the aid of beneficent legislation has shaken off the inseparable concomitants of that state, there must be some stage in the progress of his elevation when he takes the rank of a mere citizen, and ceases to be the special favorite of the laws," sniffed the Court. According to this logic, to prohibit racial discrimination was itself discriminatory, as it established a form of class-specific legislation that did not apply equally to all citizens as individuals.[62]

Justice Bradley's opinion in the *Civil Rights Cases* was well in keeping with the dominant current of political opinion of the time. This was particularly true in the sense that it removed a contentious racial issue from the realm of national politics, while simultaneously asserting that it was protecting the rights of black citizens. The most influential newspapers in the country, including an important segment of the Republican-identified press, lauded the decision, hailing it as a beneficent move toward sectional reconciliation and away from the "dangerous centralizing tendencies" of the Reconstruction era.[63] The *Nation*, for example—one of the most influential journals of intellectual opinion and strongly associated with the conservative wing of the Republican party—approvingly noted that "the calm with which the country receives the news that the leading sections of the celebrated Civil Rights Act of 1875 have been pronounced unconstitutional by the Supreme Court, shows how completely the extravagant expectations as well as the fierce passions of the war have died out."[64]

The central point of Reconstruction, the *Nation* claimed, had been to secure "the ordinary civil rights of the freedmen against hostile or reactionary state legislation." In contrast, the "notion that the social equality of the colored people could be hastened by legislation sprang up later." The political weight of this wrong-headed idea, however, "was never strong enough to procure either the adoption of a Constitutional amendment or the passage of an act which anybody expected to be enforced." Noting that the arguments that had been used to support the Civil Rights Act of 1875 "have almost wholly passed away," the editorial went on to ridicule them as having amounted to little more than the clearly absurd idea that "the division of powers made by the Constitution between the States and the Union is not a proper one, and that the framers might have made a far better Government than the one they did make, if they had only tried."[65]

Given the national dominance of the laissez-faire understanding of citizenship and the white supremacist construction of race during the 1870s–1880s, it is not surprising that *Plessy* generated so little public attention by the time that it was decided in 1896.[66] The majority opinion in *Plessy* simply reiterated the basic themes of Darwinian liberalism that had been voiced during the congressional debates over the Civil Rights Act of 1875 during Reconstruction.[67] Although the purpose of the Fourteenth Amendment, the Court ruled:

was undoubtedly to enforce the absolute equality of the two races
before the law . . . in the nature of things it could not have been
intended to abolish distinctions based upon color, or to enforce
social, as distinguished from political, equality, or a commingling
of the two races upon terms unsatisfactory to either. . . . If one
race be inferior to the other socially, the Constitution of the
United States cannot put them upon the same plane.[68]

The *Plessy* case is popularly regarded today as a primary indicator of the
gravity of racial injustice in late nineteenth-century America.[69] The current
symbolic meaning of the decision is, however, highly misleading from a historical perspective. Rather than representing the extent to which the nation
had retreated from a more robust conception of the meaning of American
citizenship, the decision reaffirmed an understanding of the relationship between race and citizenship that was contemporaneous with the passage of
the Fourteenth Amendment itself. If anything, the symbolic prominence of
the *Plessy* decision serves to mask the virulence of racist ideology during the
late nineteenth and early twentieth centuries, when the Darwinian position
represented by the majority opinion was largely eclipsed by the even more
violent politics of white nationalism and racial terrorism.

To focus on the *Plessy* case similarly obscures the way in which the terms
of the larger universe of legal debate shifted during the late 1890s from the
question of how the Reconstruction amendments should be interpreted to
whether parts of the Fourteenth Amendment and all of the Fifteenth
Amendment should be repealed as dead letters that marred the integrity of
the Constitution. With the definitive defeat of the Lodge Bill to enforce fair
elections in 1892, the idea of actually enforcing the amendments, particularly
as they pertained to suffrage, was no longer seriously entertained by anybody
in a position of power. Some constitutional purists worried about the implications of this situation. The Honorable John S. Wise, for example, asked the
Ohio State Bar Association in 1903: "Are you not degraded—is not our
whole nation degraded—by this condition of the law, and this false pretense
of living under a Constitution which nobody respects and nobody obeys?"[70]

John R. Dos Passos—a highly prominent lawyer, businessman, and legal scholar—articulated what had become a well-established view in the legal profession in a 1903 *Yale Law Journal* article on "The Negro Question":[71]

The effort to change the intellectual and political character of this
race, not by the necessary and progressive processes of education
and culture, but by an artificial and unhealthy transformation
through the brute force of constitutional amendments is admitted

to be a dismal failure. . . . The history of the last thirty-six years illustrates very forcibly the futility and powerlessness of laws intended to operate against natural conditions.[72]

For the time being, Dos Passos argued, the best response to this situation
would be to repeal the second section of the Fourteenth Amendment and all
of the Fifteenth Amendment. "The suggestion is temporarily to deprive
[blacks] of suffrage, to put them upon probation, to quarantine them, until
such time as they demonstrate an ability to intelligently and honestly cast a
vote," he explained. "This means a retrograde movement in our constitutional history. It means we must retrace our steps and undo organic legislation which was hastily enacted after the rebellion; to take back that which was
given."[73]

Similarly, Charles Wallace Collins argued in a 1911 edition of the *American Law Review*:

[The] Republican party, which controlled all branches of the government after the War, might have made the negroes wards of the
nation, putting them into a position similar to that occupied by
the American Indians. . . . Under this system of sympathetic tutelage the African might have been led to develop whatever latent
powers that may be inherent in his race.[74]

According to this perspective, the very act of extending citizenship to black
Americans—even on the most minimal terms—had been a disservice to a
race that was naturally incapable of living up to the standards which this
required.

While the Darwinian construction of African-American citizenship
which had been dominant during the 1870s and 1880s had drawn a line in the
sand against any attempts to establish social equality between black and
white Americans, it had also insisted upon the maintenance of a standard of
ostensible legal and political equality that conformed to a very minimalist interpretation of the Reconstruction amendments. The more reactionary position that developed during the 1890s and became dominant around the
turn of the century, in contrast, rejected the idea of political equality as unworkable and abandoned that of legal equality as meaningless. As Collins explained in his closing remarks on "The Fourteenth Amendment and the Negro Race Question":

In conclusion we may ask what positive gain has the operation of
the Fourteenth Amendment been to the negro race? We can point
to nothing. All attempts at Federal intervention have been fruit-

less in permanent results. The operation of the Amendment in its relation to the negro race has in it all the irony of history. It is the perversion of a noble idealism that the lowest and most benighted element of the African race should in these enlightened days be the ones to rise up and claim the sacred heritage of Anglo-Saxon liberties which, through the fortune of circumstance, have become embodied in the supreme law of the land in the shape of the Fourteenth Amendment.[75]

Liberalism, in other words, had to be racially exclusive: the dictates of nature provided no other choice. At this point, the claims of a common American citizenship no longer had to be honored even in theory, let alone in practice.

Give a man all the liberty in the world, politically, and then leave him at the mercy

of mercenary speculators and their cunning, so that he may be reduced to the

condition of a pauper, and his political liberty is valueless, as he, by the force of his

necessities, becomes the slave of the controllers of money.

—National Economist: Official Organ of the Farmers' Alliance, *1889*

3

Race and the Emancipation of Labor

Late nineteenth-century American liberalism contained significantly different ideological variants, which represented very different understandings of the relationship between race and citizenship in the post-Emancipation era. With the collapse of Reconstruction, Darwinian liberalism, which embraced white supremacy both in ideology and practice, quickly achieved a dominant position in mainstream political discourse in both the North and the South. Although anti-caste liberalism, which was most distinctively marked by its racial equalitarianism, continued to present a distinct alternative, its articulation was increasingly limited to a dwindling minority of politicians, lawyers, intellectuals, and activists, who consistently found themselves on the losing side of important political and legal battles.

If the Darwinian and anti-caste positions were fundamentally opposed on issues concerning the so-called social equality of the races, they nonetheless shared the important assumption that an acceptable standard of civic equality otherwise existed in the rest of the nation. Their dispute, in other words, centered on the extremely important, but nonetheless particular, question of how best to incorporate the newly emancipated slave population into the existing body politic. Neither position, in this sense, questioned the legitimacy of the more general standard of citizenship that prevailed in the nation as a whole.

Anti-caste and Darwinian liberalism were not, however, the only important civic discourses in late nineteenth-century America. Another important alternative, here referred to as *producer republicanism*, attracted the support of millions of Americans during the 1880s–1890s, providing the ideological ballast for two major social movements and scores of related political initiatives.[1] The central claim of producer republicanism was that the new form of corporate capitalism that had developed in the wake of the Civil War had so undermined the economic bases of citizenship that it threatened to destroy the foundation of the American republic. The rapid growth of corporate capital, republicans asserted, had divided American society into two great classes marked by enormous disparities of wealth and power. Neither civic equality nor democratic rule, they warned, could be maintained under such conditions.

Consequently, republicans argued, it was imperative to establish the public power necessary to check the power of "monopoly capital." The economy, they insisted, needed to be restructured to ensure fairness and equity to the small producers and wage laborers who constituted the civic backbone of the nation. In the short run, producer republicans hoped to further this goal by means of legal and political reform. Over the long term, however, they hoped to achieve it through the development of alternative institutions and cultural mores, which would replace what they saw as an exploitative system of "wage labor" with a new "cooperative commonwealth." They desired, in other words, first to reform the existing political economy and then to transcend it.[2] In this sense, the ambitions of producer republicanism went beyond the boundaries of American liberalism, holding forth a vision of a society in which social cooperation would replace individual competition, both in the economic sphere and more broadly.[3]

The primary location of producer republicanism was in the great labor and agrarian movements of the 1880s–1890s. Within the labor movement, an organization known as the Knights of Labor represented its most powerful expression, particularly during the Knights' period of greatest strength in the early to mid-1880s.[4] Its most important counterpart in the agrarian sphere was the Populist movement, which reached its peak of influence a decade later, during the early to mid-1890s.[5] Although neither movement was able to attain national political power and implement the majority of the legal and policy reforms that they advocated, their size and prominence nonetheless made them an important part of late nineteenth-century American politics.

While the Knights focused on industrial laborers and the Populists on farmers and agricultural workers, both were dedicated to organizing the broad constituency of what they referred to as the "producing classes." Producer republicans commonly believed that the power of corporate capital had produced a deep and unhealthy schism between the producing classes, which were the true creators of wealth, and the nonproducing classes, which had rigged the economic system so that they could enjoy a monopoly of money and control. Members of the producing classes, according to this perspective, included industrial laborers, farmers, agricultural workers, artisans, and small businesspeople. Members of the nonproducing classes included lawyers, bankers, speculators, corporate businesspeople, and large planters. Both the Knights and the Populists, in other words, saw class as the central dividing line in American society and sought to organize popular movements on that basis.[6]

The demographic realities of late nineteenth-century American demanded, however, that they simultaneously grapple with the deeply divisive issue of race—a category which, at that time, included all of the groups which we would today refer to as "ethnic." (The distinction between "racial" and "ethnic" groups that we now take for granted did not exist in the late nineteenth century and did not become common until the 1940s.)[7] This was true for the simple reason that the American producing classes were tremendously diverse, incorporating not only native-born whites but also Asians and a rapidly growing number of Southern and Eastern European immigrants.[8] Consequently, organizing a broad-based social movement required building bridges between groups that would otherwise remain separated along racial lines.

Given the tremendous power of the negative racial stereotypes that were deeply embedded in American culture, as well as the concrete structural divisions which incorporated an important racial dimension, this was a formidable task. Attempting it required both reformulating the operative meaning of race among movement constituencies and implementing risky and often dangerous organizing techniques. Consequently, neither movement consistently pursed interracial organizing. (The Populist movement in particular had a widely varying record on racial matters, with only the most radical activists attempting to build interracial coalitions.) Race-bridging initiatives generally came from the more elite leadership of the two movements and were carried out with various degrees of success in different times and places. Nonetheless, both the Knights and the Populists pursued what were, for the time, exceptionally ambitious attempts to forge a common, class-based producer identity among deeply divided racial groups.

Understanding the significance of racial politics in these republican movements is important for several reasons. First, it demonstrates that even these class-based movements, which had no strong interest in issues of race or civil rights per se, had to grapple with racial issues on both ideological and practical levels. Race was so important, both culturally and structurally, that it simply could not be ignored. Second, it reveals important connections among different constructions of race, liberalism, and American democracy. Although these linkages were complex and did not follow a uniform pattern, there was nonetheless a clear, logical relationship between the movements' positions on racial matters and their broader political commitments. Finally, the cases of the Knights and the Populists illustrate the extent to which their attempts to forge a more equalitarian standard of American democracy hinged on their ability to develop a new form of racial politics capable of uniting constituencies that the existing political order kept divided. The fact that racial divisions were woven into the fabric of regional politics and the party system meant that this included not only bringing together different racial groups, but creating new regional alliances and alternatives within the electoral system. Although neither movement successfully realized this ambitious project, the fact that they got as far as they did demonstrates the tremendous appeal of producer republicanism for millions of citizens in late nineteenth-century America.

The Knights of Labor

Producer republicanism emerged out of the breakdown of the free labor ideology that began in the early 1870s. This highly influential political ideology had been characterized by its simultaneous endorsement of laissez-faire liberalism and Jeffersonian equalitarianism, holding that unregulated capitalist expansion would produce an overwhelmingly middle-class society dominated by small-scale property holders. The rapidly changing political economy of the postbellum period increasingly forced a disassociation of these two principles, however, as laissez-faire became more deeply wedded to the newly expanding power of the corporation, and the economic fortunes of the nation's citizenry increasingly diverged.

As new processes of industrialization and corporate consolidation gained unprecedented momentum, they caused severe economic dislocations and sparked a growing wave of labor unrest. Consequently, by the late 1870s, the central focus of national politics shifted decisively away from the racial and sectional issues of Reconstruction and toward what was commonly referred to as "the labor question." As the controlling elites of the two major parties moved toward the accommodation that would end Reconstruction, anti-caste liberalism became increasingly marginalized and Darwinian liberalism increasingly dominant. Consequently, during the 1880s and 1890s, the central contest within mainstream political culture was between a form of laissez-faire liberalism that explicitly embraced social hierarchy and a reconstructed republicanism that aggressively attacked class stratification.

Laissez-faire liberalism represented the dominant political language of the elite during this period. Producer republicanism represented the oppositional voice of large sectors of the public. While largely shut out of the Republican and Democratic parties, where various forms of laissez-faire prevailed, republicanism dominated the massive waves of radical social activism that rocked America during the 1880s and 1890s. Notably, this meant that the voices of republican protest often remained unrepresented in formal political institutions such as the legislatures and the courts. (This was particularly true at the federal level.) Republicanism nonetheless represented a powerful political force up through the mid-1890s.

During the 1880s, the Knights of Labor (KOL) served as the primary organizational vehicle through which this republican discourse was publicly articulated, developed, and promoted. Founded in 1869 as a small, secret labor organization in Philadelphia, the Knights emerged as an important political force in 1878, when, riding the wave of momentum generated by the Great Strike of 1877, the organization first began systematic national recruitment drives. During the next eight years, KOL membership skyrocketed with a rate of growth "unparalleled in the history of the labor movement," rising from an initial base of 20,151 in 1879 to its greatest height of close to one million in 1886.[9]

The membership of the Knights was both diverse and widespread, with local assemblies (LAs) organized in every type of community, "from mine patches and country crossroads to rural county seats; from small industrial towns to cities and metropolitan centers." Between 1869 and 1896, half of the 3,500 towns with populations of more than 1,000 had at least one LA, as did all but a dozen of the 400-plus cities that had populations of more than 8,000. All told, 15,000 LAs existed during this period. In 1887, fully half of these flourished at once. With an organized presence in every state in the Union, in nearly every Canadian province, and in several lands overseas, the

Knights of Labor represented a vital force in late nineteenth-century politics and culture.[10]

A brief consideration of the difficulties of working-class existence during the late nineteenth century helps to explain the widespread appeal of the Knights. By the late 1880s, roughly 40 percent of industrial workers lived below the poverty line—which at that time was $500 per year—while another 45 percent were just above it. On the job, workers commonly faced serious injury and even death from hazards such as molten steel at open hearths, toxic gases in coal mines, or fast-moving machinery with no protective shields. Basic social provisions such as disability pay, unemployment compensation, occupational health and safety standards, or a standard eight-hour day did not exist. Women and children were commonly forced to work in order to keep families at a subsistence level. They, too, were afforded no legal protection. At the same time, however, the great fortunes of the Gilded Age were being made, with leading businessmen, industrialists, and financiers acquiring the wealth that would turn them into household names for generations to come (e.g., Carnegie, Rockefeller, Stanford, and Morgan). By 1890, the accumulated inequities of the past quarter-century of industrial development had produced a situation in which the richest 1 percent of the population commanded more wealth than the remaining 99 percent combined.[11]

"The alarming development and aggressiveness of great capitalists and corporations, unless checked, will inevitably lead to the pauperization and hopeless degradation of the toiling masses," asserted the preamble to the Declaration of Principles of the Knights of Labor in 1878:

> The demand of the Knights is, then, that this development shall
> be checked, not only because of the danger to our institutions
> from the power of these great monopolists and monopolies, but
> because of the pauperization and degradation of the workers in
> consequence thereof. . . . It is true that the demands are revolu-
> tionary, as it is the purpose of the Order to establish a new and
> true standard of individual and national greatness.[12]

The Knights of Labor saw its mission not simply as improving the lot of the working class but as reestablishing the integrity of the American republic. "These extremes of wealth and poverty are threatening the existence of the government," wrote George E. McNeill, secretary-treasurer of the Knights of Labor, District 30, in his 1887 compendium, *The Labor Movement: The Problem of Today*.[13] "In light of these facts, we declare that there is an inevitable and irresistible conflict between the wage-system of labor and the republican system of government—the wage-laborer attempting to save the government, and the capitalist class ignorantly attempting to subvert it."[14]

In the view of producer republicans, the "wage-system of labor" gave employers despotic control over their employees, reducing wealth-producing citizens to the status of "wage slaves": "We are wholly in the hands of our employers—serfs of the mill, the workshop, and the mine—subjects of the railroad kings and the cotton lords." While laissez-faire liberals insisted that the right of free contract (that is, the right of each individual wage-earner to choose the terms of his employment) established a full measure of civic equity in the economic sphere, republicans insisted that the putative rights of citizenship meant nothing to those who lived in a state of economic thralldom. Further, such individuals could not be true citizens: lacking independence, education, health, time for reflection, and, often, moral cultivation, they were all too often reduced to a condition of "barbarism." Working hours needed to be reduced and wages increased in order to allow the working man to be one "upon whom the honors and duties of civilization can safely rest." In this sense, McNeill explained, the "labor problem is a question of civilization." Contrary to laissez-faire assumptions, with regard to the integrity of the republic, "extremes of wealth and poverty are curses, not benefits."[15]

Like anti-caste liberals, republican activists often argued that the Declaration of Independence represented a national commitment to equalitarian principles that should be translated into legal doctrine.[16] *John Swinton's Paper*, the leading labor journal of the 1880s,[17] for example, stated in its front-page declaration of purpose: "It is time to make a struggle for the Declaration of Independence, the self-evident and everlasting truths of which are being overwhelmed by the tides of plutocracy. It is time to proclaim again its true and original purposes, to apply them to institutions and legislation, to enforce them upon all men and every man."[18] While the anti-caste commitment to the Declaration was exclusively organized around issues of race, its republican counterpart was driven by questions of class. Notably, this meant that while producer republicanism was much more radical than anti-caste liberalism when it came to questions of economic equity, the reverse was true with regard to racially specific issues of segregation and discrimination. Although the Knights of Labor was committed to organizing black workers and achieved a high degree of success in that regard, it had no principled commitment to antidiscrimination as such—on the contrary, it was an avid supporter of Chinese exclusion, both within and without the movement. (Similarly, the Populists supported mainstream segregationist doctrine with regard to blacks.)

While anti-caste liberals argued that the Declaration had been made manifest in the Constitution by the passage of the Reconstruction amendments, producer republicans demanded that the Constitution be amended or reinterpreted in a way that would establish the public power necessary to tame the new menace of monopoly capital.[19] "A greater power than that of the State has arisen—'a State within a State'—a power that is quietly yet quickly sapping the foundations of the majority-rule," wrote McNeill. "The government has the right, and is bound in self-defense to protect the ability of the people to rule. It has the right to interfere against any organized or unorganized power that imperils or impairs this ability. . . . The foundation of the Republic is equality."[20] Like anti-caste liberals, producer republicans believed that the federal government should be given a constitutional mandate to intervene in both the public and private sectors in order to break up entrenched concentrations of power that violated the equalitarian promise of the Declaration of Independence. Again, however, while the former directed their challenge to questions of racial segregation and discrimination, the latter focused on class-based issues of wealth and power.

Specific legal and policy proposals championed by the Knights included the right to organize labor unions, set wages according to union scale, and toil reasonable hours. On the national level, the KOL demanded that primary commercial arteries of communication, transportation, and banking be placed under public ownership, so that they might be administered with a view toward the good of the many, rather than the wealth of the few. On the state level, the Knights sought the establishment of health and safety laws, the creation of bureaus of labor statistics, and the "abrogation of all laws that do not bear equally on capital and labor."[21]

Although never amassing enough political force to achieve these aims, some breakthroughs were made on the local level. Fink documents that at the height of its power in 1886, the Knights fielded labor tickets in at least 189 towns and cities, encompassing thirty-four (out of a total of thirty-eight) states, as well as four territories. (There were also, Fink adds, "scores of other cases where local elections were waged on the basis of allegiance or opposition to the aims of the labor movement.") Victories were achieved in approximately sixty of those races, including in Mobile, Alabama; Wilmington, Delaware; Boise, Idaho; Chicago, Illinois; Dubuque, Iowa; Kansas City, Kansas; Lynn, Massachusetts; Raleigh, North Carolina; Harrisburg, Pennsylvania; Richmond, Virginia; and Milwaukee, Wisconsin. During 1886–1888, certain local-level victories were achieved: Quincy, Massachusetts, for example, established a nine-hour maximum working day and a minimum wage.[22] Beyond the realm of law and policy, the Knights "built a dense network of alternative institutions and practices, including local assemblies, boycotts, reading rooms, bands, parades, lecture circuits, cooperatives, and labor parties."[23] Strong advocates of self-organization and self-help, the Knights' political efforts went far beyond the traditional governmental arena.

At its most ambitious, the republicanism of the Knights sought not simply to regulate but to transcend what were seen as the social and political failures of the existing capitalist economy. The long-term republican goal was to establish a cooperative commonwealth in which socioeconomic relations would be based on cooperation, rather than competition. As McNeill explained:

> At present, the chief efforts of organized labor are directed toward securing amelioration of the wage-system. Arbitration, a shorter working-day, restriction of the labor of children and married women, are the immediate demands. Beyond these a majority of workingmen have as yet no definite plan, save, as they hope, by limiting the competition for employment, to get better wages. The leaders of the co-operative movement go farther. . . . They assert that the arrangement by which profits are distributed—solely on the basis of capital, while labor, having no control of the means of production, is bought at the lowest market rates—is wrong.[24]

If, as McNeill suggested, the goal of the cooperative commonwealth was too abstract to engage the energies of the average worker, the repeated references to it in the primary literature demonstrate that it captured the imaginations of leading organizers and intellectuals. Substantively, the call for cooperation was most commonly linked to proposals to establish new forms of industrial organization and new systems of finance, distribution, and exchange. Concretely, a substantial number of cooperative or semi-cooperative enterprises were established.[25]

At its most idealistic, the republican vision of the cooperative commonwealth extended substantially beyond building alternative business and financial institutions. The rejection of competition in favor of cooperation was to extend to the whole of human relations. Refuting the Darwinian claim that the greatest good for both the individual and society came from a competitive struggle for the "survival of the fittest," republicans argued that both flourished best in a cooperative system structured around the commonality of the public good. As prominent social critic and labor advocate Henry Demarest Lloyd argued in 1884: "A rope cannot be made out of sand; a society cannot be made of competitive units."[26] In this sense, republicanism aspired to go well beyond the boundaries of American liberalism, rejecting the

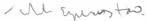

basic premises of a competitive market economy and an individualistic political ethos. Given, however, the fact that leading activists themselves acknowledged that this did not form the basis of the movement's popular appeal, the meaning of republicanism as understood by the millions of ordinary Americans who subscribed to it remains best described as a radical variant of American liberalism.

Organizing the Producing Classes

The goal of the Knights of Labor was, in the words of George McNeill, to organize "all laborers into one great solidarity."[27] Given that, by 1880, native-born white Americans constituted only about one-fourth of the industrial labor force, this required bridging deeply entrenched racial divides.[28] In the South, where African Americans made up a substantial portion of the working population, this primarily meant forging a cooperative movement between blacks and whites. In the rest of the country, where recent immigrants from Southern and Eastern Europe (whose racial status, as will be discussed below, was ambiguous) represented approximately 42 percent of those employed in mining and industry,[29] this primarily meant breaking down the barriers among different immigrant groups, as well as between immigrants and native-born whites.[30]

Both were very difficult projects. Racial divisions not only commanded a tremendous cultural force, but were structurally embedded in larger regional divides, party politics, and economic arrangements. Opponents of the labor movement exploited these divisions by manipulating racial fears and resentments in what would prove to be a successful effort to discredit and divide it. Nonetheless, KOL organizers worked hard to overcome racial barriers and succeeded, for a time, in building a remarkably inclusive movement.[31] This was done by a combined process of ideological and organizational innovation, in which the meaning of race was reformulated to support the growth of a common, class-based producer identity, while a variety of culturally appropriate organizing methods was deployed.

Despite what was, for the time, a truly remarkable feat of interracial organizing, the KOL was not, as noted above, uniformly committed to basic antidiscrimination principles as such. The organization's treatment of the Chinese represented by far the most dramatic evidence of this, with Chinese workers being commonly denounced as racial inferiors and barred from union membership. The Knights of Labor was a proud supporter of the Chinese Exclusion Act of 1882, which barred further Chinese immigration on explicitly racist terms, and actively lobbied on its behalf. As will be discussed below, however, this negative stereotyping of the Chinese was done in a way that supported the Knights' larger republican ideology. Arguably, it also played an important role in the success of the KOL's broader organizing initiatives.

The Knights of Labor consequently presents a fascinating example of the malleability of racial meanings, their relationship to larger political principles, and the complexity of racial politics within class-based progressive movements. The Knights of Labor reinterpreted familiar symbols such as the Constitution and the Declaration in ways that not only promoted a radically equalitarian politics but, in so doing, pointed beyond the dominant liberalism of the larger political culture. This republican ideology incorporated different constructions of race, some of which were similarly equalitarian, and others of which were not. Dedicated to class rather than racial equity, the critical question for the Knights was who should be included in the organization of the producing classes. As the Chinese were placed outside of this group, there was no sense that they merited equal treatment. In short, while there was a logical connection between the Knights' republicanism and its racial politics, it was based on class expediency and did not include a consistent opposition to racial discrimination.

The Racial Status Quo

Anti-African racism was an extremely powerful component of late nineteenth-century American politics and culture. The small minority of whites who supported basic antidiscrimination principles wielded negligible influence following the collapse of Reconstruction. The vast majority, both in the North and the South, embraced the belief that people of African descent constituted a distinct group located at the bottom of the racial totem pole (whites, of course, being at the top). In the context of the times, whites who simply supported discrimination and segregation and left it at that were considered racial moderates. Many others insisted that blacks be dehumanized completely, exempted from even the most basic protections of life, liberty, and property. Racial terrorism was rampant and accepted, with the torture and lynching of African Americans (most often men, but also women and children) commonly treated as a spectator sport. (The number of recorded lynchings peaked at 156 in 1892. They continued, however, with some frequency through the 1940s.)[32]

Beyond the overt brutality of the racial caste system, the division between whites and blacks constituted an important part of the larger social structure. In particular, it was a critical (although by no means determinate) factor in the structure of the dominant two-party system and the shape of the national economy. This meant that attempting to change the racial status quo by building an interracial alliance between white and black workers involved much more than taking on the already formidable challenge of white racism, pure and simple. Pursuing such a project also meant confronting extremely powerful political and economic interests that had a stake in preserving the racial accord that had been forged at the end of Reconstruction. In addition, it involved overcoming the loyalties that other, less-powerful people had to their party or region—which were, once again, partially understood in racial terms.

The basic political orientations of both the Republican and Democratic parties had been established in conjunction with the collapse of Reconstruction. The Radical wing of the Republican party, which was defined by its dedication to establishing equal citizenship rights for the former slave population, lost its political influence at that time. Consequently, an increasingly powerful set of northern business interests assumed a dominant position within the national party. Dedicated to the laissez-faire proposition that government should minimize its interference in the free play of the market economy, the Republicans had no sympathy for the growing wave of working-class protest represented by the Knights of Labor. When faced with the need to reach out to the common citizen, the primary tactic of the party was to "wave the bloody shirt," or attempt to stir up the old passions and loyalties of the Civil War. This largely cynical appeal to sectional loyalty was calculated to scare off potential defectors from the party by threatening to label them as unpatriotic sympathizers with the former "rebels."[33]

Although the lingering northern loyalty to the Union cause was only loosely related to racial concepts (the important issue having been, for most white northerners, the preservation of the Union, rather than the abolition of slavery), the southern commitment to the Democratic party was overwhelmingly racial in nature. The Democratic lockhold on the post-Reconstruction South was primarily maintained by the party's constant championing of the cause of white supremacy, which ostensibly stood to protect the region from a return to the Reconstruction era horrors of "Negro domination."[34] For the average white southerner, even to consider a break with the Democratic party was to run the risk of being labeled a traitor to the white race—a charge which was never to be taken lightly, as it carried with it very real threats of social ostracism and even retaliatory violence. In this way, the Democrats managed to hold onto the vast majority of white voters, despite the fact that, when it came to the economic issues which vitally concerned the vast majority of ordinary citizens, they, like the Republicans, had nothing to offer.

The strong ties of economic interest between the elites of the New South and the Northeast ensured that this would remain the case. Both understood that the continued vitality of large-scale plantation agriculture in the South hinged on maintaining a high degree of control over the black labor force. The agricultural economy of the South, in turn, affected the more industrial economy of the North in that it constituted a good source of inexpensive raw materials, a limitless supply of cheap labor, and a prime market for manufactured goods. Consequently, the powerful elites that dominated both parties shared a common economic agenda that was supported by the racial status quo.

This arrangement was further strengthened by the fact that while the western states were dominated by small farmers who might have formed an alternative alliance based on common economic problems with their counterparts in the South, they were more responsive to the divisive politics of the "bloody shirt" than to calls for agrarian unity. This meant that the West split along lines determined by the North-South divide, rather than establishing an independent political force of its own. Consequently, the political and economic accord between southern and northeastern elites set the agenda for the two major parties, keeping both immune to the temptation of responding to the burgeoning labor movement. (The Populist movement would later attempt to break this dynamic by establishing a new alliance of the producing classes along the lines of a strong West/South agrarian axis.)[35]

Wage Slavery

All of this meant that if the Knights were to organize an interracial alliance in the South—which was necessary if it was to build a broad alliance of the producing classes—it had to overcome the barriers of not only raw white racism, but also the racially charged pull of regional and party loyalties and the often fierce opposition of wealthy planters and industrialists.[36] One way in which the Knights attempted to do this was by reconfiguring the meaning of race as it applied to black and white workers in the context of the post-Emancipation South. This was done by restructuring the long-standing conception of "wage slavery" in a way that described both party politics, regional loyalties, and anti-African prejudice as divisive tools that were manipulated by and for the interests of monopoly capital. White and black workers in the

South, KOL organizers argued, must learn to see through these ploys and unite on the basis of their common interests as members of the producing classes.

The metaphorical use of the term *slavery* to denote the denial of individual freedom had played a central role in American political discourse since the colonial period. In this conception, legally bonded, chattel slavery was simply the most extreme manifestation of the much larger and more general phenomenon of being subject to "the arbitrary will and pleasure of another." This was, it had been widely believed, the condition that afflicted the vast majority of humanity that lived under despotic governments. America, however, was supposed to be different, as it was founded on the principle of rule by and for the people. The term *wage slavery* consequently came into popular usage during the early to mid-nineteenth century, when labor radicals argued that the form of waged work that was developing at that time was so exploitative that it entailed such a loss of freedom and independence.[37]

Rather than representing a source of racial solidarity, however, the concept of wage slavery during the antebellum period was used to advance the claim that the white worker, who had been born to be a free and independent citizen, should not be reduced to the degraded status of the black slave.[38] The discourse of the American labor movement during this time was, in fact, thoroughly saturated with negative constructions of blacks, who served as a "negative reference group" against which to pit contrastingly positive constructions of the white worker.[39] With some notable exceptions, white racial identity was a primary means by which the labor movement advanced the causes of the "abolition of wage slavery" and the "emancipation of labor" during the early to mid-nineteenth century.[40]

The Knights reconfigured these key symbols by claiming that the outcome of the Civil War—itself an extremely potent cultural reference at the time—had represented a critical first step toward the wholesale emancipation of labor. "The 'War for the Union,'" wrote Swinton, "grew out of the Labor Question, and was waged over it: Shall the working population of our country, or any part of it, be held in slavery?"

> Stupendous sacrifices were then made to secure the emancipation
> of the black laborer, and the old chattel system was overthrown at
> a price that has not yet been paid. We had to abolish this system
> before we could grapple with any of the other wrongs which must
> be done away with. Since that time a question of even greater
> magnitude, and yet more revolutionary, has been brought to the

front—one which is often summed up in the phrase, "the rights of labor."[41]

The eradication of chattel slavery, in other words, had been a necessary precursor of the abolition of wage slavery. According to this reasoning, the primary significance of Emancipation was not that it extended existing rights to a disfranchised group. Rather, it was that it destroyed an exploitative system of labor-capital relations that had formed an important part of the socioeconomic structure of the nation.

"There still remains a battle to be fought for the establishment of universal freedom," proclaimed William H. Mullen, the chief KOL organizer in Richmond, in an 1885 speech. "Can those who are now the slaves of monopoly and oppression be liberated as easily as was the African race in America? Yea, even more easily!"[42] The Knights of Labor sought to inspire a sense of optimism and historical destiny among its constituencies by arguing that the enormity of the change that had been effected in the nation's political economy by the outcome of the Civil War demonstrated both the rightness and attainability of its goals. "The propositions that all men are free and equal, that slavery is wrong, that one man is as good as another before the law, were all opposed, and those who advocated them were looked upon in their time as agitators, dreamers, doctrinaires," a labor advocate writing in an 1886 edition of the *North American Review* reminded his readers. "So will those be now regarded and resisted who advocate a better industrial system, by which labor shall have more of the wealth it produces."[43] The labor movement, in other words, had history on its side and would be similarly proven right in the end.

This parallel between the successful battle to abolish chattel slavery and the then-current battle to eradicate wage slavery was used to encourage both blacks and whites, and northerners and southerners to overcome the artificial divisions that separated them. An organizer at an 1886 meeting of the Blue and Grey Association (an affiliated group designed to reconcile former Union and Confederate soldiers) in Cleveland, for example, explained to the assembled veterans that the "war gave one kind of masters for another, and [the] wealth once owned by the masters of the South has been transferred to the monopolist of the North and multiplied a hundred-fold in power, and is now enslaving more than the war liberated." "We therefore urge the men of both armies to shun the politician who seeks to create sectional animosity," he concluded, "and to turn away from all such as the agents of those who would blind you to existing evils and make you tenants at will in your native country."[44] "The politicians have kept the white and black men of the South apart, while crushing both," stated Terence Powderly, the grand master work-man (i.e., executive director) of the Knights in a speech given in Richmond in 1885. "Our aim shall be to educate both and elevate them by bringing them together."[45] "No Mason and Dixon's line, no color-tests divide North, South, East and West; wherever laborers congregate . . . one chord of sympathy unites them all," proclaimed McNeill in 1887. "No demagogue's cant of race or creed will hold them from their purpose to be free."[46]

All of this meant that the black worker now had to be regarded by his white colleague as a fellow citizen and producer. "The negro is free; he is here, and he is here to stay," argued Powderly in a speech first delivered in Richmond in 1884 and subsequently reprinted in the Richmond *Dispatch* in 1886:

> His labor and that of the white man will be thrown upon the mar-ket side by side, and no human eye can detect a difference be-tween the article manufactured by the black mechanic and that manufactured by the white mechanic. Both claim an equal share of the protection afforded to American labor, and both mechanics must sink their differences or fall a prey to the slave labor now being imported to this country.[47]

(As will be seen below, this reference to "slave labor" was directed at the Chi-nese and carried with it all of the negative associations that had formerly been ascribed primarily to blacks.)

In the African-American community, the Knights' attempt to secure black support met with considerable controversy.[48] Many African-American leaders had long been wary of the labor movement and feared that the Knights simply wanted to use blacks as a means of advancing what was es-sentially a white movement. The highly influential black press, however, was generally strongly supportive of the KOL and encouraged black workers to develop a class-based identity and recognize their common cause with white labor. "It should have been the easiest thing in the world to have foreseen that upon the lines laid down by the moulders [*sic*] of the Reconstruction policy that chattel slavery would certainly be followed by industrial slavery, no less galling and degrading to the enfranchised class and far more profitable to the employers of labor," stated the well-known African-American newspaper the *New York Freeman* in 1886.[49] "The colored people of the South are gradually, as a class, sinking deeper and deeper in to the cesspool of industrial slavery."[50] Another article published in the same year concluded: "Nothing short of a potential [power] like the Knights of Labor can ever force Southern capital-ists to give their wage workers a fair percentage of the results of their labor."[51]

Despite its support from the black community, the Knights did not enforce an antidiscrimination standard within the union. Instead, its policy was that the members of every local assembly could decide whether they wished to be organized on a racially inclusive or exclusive basis. While the national office encouraged the formation of interracial locals, there was no strict policy that forbade the establishment of segregated assemblies. In practice, this meant that while many white Knights were willing to accept blacks as members of the larger union, they refused to include them as members of their own local organizations. While this discrimination was strongly resented by most black workers, there was nonetheless a prevailing sense that the Knights represented an important progressive force that merited their support.[52] In some areas where the Knights were particularly strong, such as Richmond, black activists advocated the formation of all-black locals as a means of building a stronger and more independent position within the movement.[53] Further, as will be discussed in the next chapter, some LAs were so deeply committed to an antidiscrimination principle, both within the movement and more broadly, that they were not only willing but eager to provoke dramatic and even dangerous confrontations with supporters of the Jim Crow South.

Despite these complexities, the Knights' campaign to form an interracial movement met with what was, for the time, astounding success, particularly during 1885–1886, when black membership skyrocketed in conjunction with the growth of the union at large. By 1886, there were an estimated 60–95,000 African-American Knights nationwide; in the South, they constituted between one-third and one-half of the total. Black workers were best organized in Richmond, where they claimed 3,125 members in twenty-one LAs plus a separate black district assembly. Black LAs existed in every major southern city, including Atlanta, Memphis, New Orleans, Louisville, Charleston, Houston, and Birmingham, and in many smaller cities and towns. Black LAs were also formed outside of the South, including in such diverse locales as Ohio, Texas, Indiana, Michigan, Nebraska, Massachusetts, Rhode Island, Maryland, New York, New Jersey, and even Montana. At the same time, many other "mixed," or racially integrated LAs existed across the country.[54]

In sum, while the Knights did not enforce a strict nondiscrimination standard with regard to the integration of African Americans into the union, it was nonetheless dedicated to building a strong interracial movement and achieved considerable success in that endeavor. Although the bonds which had been forged between white and black workers remained highly vulnerable to the force of a stepped-up oppositional assault, the Knights successfully demonstrated that racial and class identities could be changed substantially, even under the pressure of extremely difficult and often dangerous circumstances.

The New European Immigrants

By the early 1880s, a rapidly increasing influx of new European immigrants, primarily from Italy, Austria-Hungary, the Balkans, and Russia, was dramatically changing the composition of the national labor force. In communities that attracted large numbers of immigrants, native-born whites quickly became a minority of the working-class population. By 1890, for example, immigrants and their children constituted 90 percent of the workforce in Milwaukee,[55] while native-born whites constituted only 14 percent of the working-class population in Detroit.[56] Overcoming the widespread divisions between the immigrants and the native-born, as well as among the various immigrant groups themselves, was consequently critical to the Knights' project of organizing a powerful alliance of the producing classes.

This could not be accomplished, however, without creating a new political identity capable of uniting existing ethnic identities into a common class-based paradigm. Numerous cross-reinforcing barriers made this difficult, including the multiplicity of languages involved, religious divisions between the largely Protestant native-born and predominantly Catholic immigrants, differing political orientations rooted in different national histories, and the fact that native-born workers tended to be more highly skilled than their immigrant counterparts. Particularly during 1883–1886, all of these long-standing structural barriers were further exacerbated by the impact of intensified economic contraction and dislocation in the industrial sectors. Native-born workers feared that their growing campaign to improve their working and living conditions would be sabotaged by a flood of "cheap labor" drawn from lands where the accepted standard of living was far below that of the United States. Consequently, nativist sentiment easily blended with labor militancy to produce great hostility against new immigrants among the native-born.[57]

Race, too, played a role in these divisions, although not in a way which would be familiar to us today. Up through the mid-1880s, the racial status of the new European immigrants was relatively ambiguous (the Haymarket Affair of 1886, as will be discussed in the next chapter, was a critical turning point in this regard). As Higham explains, "the very concept of race had not yet attained its later fixity and definitiveness," as it remained rooted more in political and literary concepts than in what would later be regarded as the precision and certainty of (a so-called) biological science. Although this had, of course, been more than enough to set up a rigid distinction between the "black" and "white" races, it nonetheless left substantial room for play with regard to the new immigrants from Southern and Eastern Europe. Since the concept of "ethnicity" did not yet exist to draw a distinction between groups deemed more or less different from the reigning Anglo-Saxon norm, the term *race* was regularly invoked to denote the differences among various European national groups.[58] Although this relatively high degree of openness with regard to the racial status of the new immigrants made the task of organizing them across these lines substantially easier than in the case of African Americans, it also left the door open for hostile attacks on the racial integrity of any part of the labor movement which welcomed them into its ranks.

Although the general policy of the Knights of Labor was to reach out to the new European immigrants as important members of the producing classes, the range of statements which leading activists made regarding them indicates both the ambiguity of their racial status and the extent to which it hinged upon the perception of whether they would help or hinder the cause of the labor movement. McNeill, for example, argued that while the racial stock of the impoverished and exploited European worker might well be lower than that of the native-born American, this gap would be closed within the course of a generation:

> The physical transformation of races under the influences and opportunities of republican institutions is marked, and can be read of all men. The poor, over-wrought worker of the Old World, stunted in growth, with marked physical characteristics of expression, and of almost physical deformity, and made a subject because of this, to caricature and ridicule, finds under our institutions such opportunities of development as shall cause his children to be born, not only under better opportunities, but under better physical conditions, until the wonderful transformation of a generation shall witness the glistening eye, the well-formed mouth and chin, as the result of the change in habits, thoughts and actions, consequent upon his environment.[59]

In 1884, however, Powderly published the following denunciation of Hungarian workers in the Scranton *Truth*:

> If it were possible to make good and useful citizens of these men, I would never raise my voice against them. But that seems impos-

sible. They will not adopt our manners and customs, except in rare instances. I have seen nine of them—eight men and one woman—occupying two small rooms. . . . Show me an American who will live like that, and I will show you a being who was born in vain. He may be fit to work, but so is a mule. . . . I believe that this country was intended for a race of freemen, and, believing that, I will always oppose the introduction of such men as are not capable of enjoying, appreciating, defending and perpetuating the blessings of good government.[60]

An immigrant group's racial status was, in other words, dependent on the extent to which it was perceived to support, rather than erode, the cause of the American working man.

Despite such ambiguities, the dominant approach of the Knights to the new European immigrants was to attempt to absorb them into the mutually reinforcing constructions of working-class militancy and American patriotism. Fink, for example, in a detailed case study of the growth and decline of the KOL in Milwaukee, argues that the Knights' creed of "common-denominational Americanism" was key to its success in organizing native-born whites together with Irish, German, and Polish immigrants.[61] Similarly, Oestreicher, in an examination of the growth and decline of working-class consciousness in late nineteenth-century Detroit, concludes that the exceptional success of the Knights of Labor in creating a "subculture of opposition" was directly tied to the inclusiveness and breadth of its ideological appeal.[62]

Stressing the necessity of organizing all workers regardless of nationality, the KOL leadership reached out to the new immigrants by translating union literature into the appropriate languages, recruiting organizers who could speak to them in their native tongues, and forming both single- and mixed-nationality LAs. By 1885, for example, KOL national headquarters had translated its literature into French, German, and various Scandinavian dialects and was working on requests for Spanish, Italian, Hungarian, Bohemian, Yiddish, and other translations. Translators were secured as needed for multilingual meetings, while tutors were at times hired to teach interested members to speak English. During the same period, a polyglot of ethnic locals formed across the country, including Cuban locals in Florida, French locals in Michigan, Italian locals in Connecticut, and Jewish locals in Chicago, New York, and St. Louis. In Illinois and New Jersey, over 50 percent of KOL members were foreign-born.[63]

Chinese Exclusion

If the general record of the Knights of Labor with regard to the inclusion of blacks and immigrants was quite impressive, its history with regard to the Chinese was not. In 1879, the Knights not only excluded the Chinese from membership, but asserted that they were inherently unfit to live in the United States. Over the next several years, KOL leaders worked to pass legislation restricting Chinese immigration on both the state and national levels, while regularly denouncing them in unabashedly racist terms. The Knights boasted of the important role that it played in the passage of the Chinese Exclusion Act of 1882, which prohibited all further immigration from China to the United States. Even after this law was passed, the KOL leadership continued to agitate against them, calling for the expulsion of the approximately 100,000 Chinese workers who remained in the country.[64]

Both the Knights and the American labor movement more broadly regularly vilified the Chinese as, in the words of John Swinton, "a submissive, obedient, tractable, yielding, servile race" of "depraved and debased blood."[65] "Every writer conversant with the habits and customs of the race," warned McNeill in 1887, "and every experiment of their settlements had proved that this people were moral and spiritual lepers." The Chinese, asserted W. W. Stone, secretary of the KOL California District Assembly, had the mentality of "the brute slave, without the first instincts of the freeman."[66] As such, they were deemed inherently incapable of assuming the rights and responsibilities of American citizenship. Most dangerously, if allowed to immigrate in sufficient numbers, they threatened to sabotage any hope of securing the legitimate rights that the producing classes were struggling to obtain.

"That Chinese labor comprehends a system of slavery," continued Stone, "is a fact that it is idle to deny; and to invite immigration is only to welcome a repetition of our past experience."[67] The Chinese, it was regularly argued, were the willing pawns of the forces of monopoly capital, which sought to drown the labor movement in a flood of cheap labor. "The Chinese labor element is calculated to produce, and has actually set on foot, a destructive social change. It is a change similar to that wrought by slavery," wrote labor advocate John H. Durst in an 1884 edition of the *North American Review*. "This immigration threatens to destroy the democratic constitution of our society, to diminish, if not to obliterate, the middle class, and to hopelessly degrade the laboring class."[68] The forces of monopoly capital, in other words, sought to turn history backward by using the Chinese to reestablish a system of labor exploitation that would be the functional equivalent of chattel slavery. Given the Knights' contention that abolition had been the necessary precursor to the battle to abolish wage slavery, this meant that the labor movement would be defeated if this new system of slave labor were established.

If the Knights responded to the threat of African and immigrant European labor being manipulated by the forces of monopoly capital by trying to organize them into a common alliance of the producing classes, why didn't they attempt the same thing with the Chinese? This question is particularly intriguing given the fact that the actual number of Chinese immigrants outside of the West was quite small. In 1870, there were only 368 Chinese living outside of that region, and by 1880, their numbers had only increased to 3,663.[69] With such small numbers, one would imagine that it would be relatively easy to organize them—or, if not going that far, at least to ignore them. Yet, the Knights were actively involved in anti-Chinese activities on a national scale. ("The men of the West must not be allowed to fight the battle [against Chinese immigration] single handed and alone," Powderly assured Stone in 1887. "The Order must act as a unit on this matter.")[70] How to best explain this phenomenon, particularly given the KOL's exceptional degree of inclusiveness with regard to European immigrants and blacks?

Saxton argues that the Chinese constituted an "indispensable enemy" for the burgeoning labor movement (including but not limited to the KOL) in California during the late 1870s and 1880s, as they provided a common negative focal point for an otherwise diverse working population to define themselves against.[71] California was, by all accounts, the hotbed of anti-Chinese agitation, undoubtedly because it was the state in which they constituted by far the largest percentage of the working population. (In 1870, approximately 50,000 Chinese workers represented 25 percent of the waged labor force in the state. Native-born whites accounted for another 40 percent, and the new European immigrants formed the remaining 35 percent. The number of Chinese Californians rose to 75,000 in 1880, peaked in 1882, and entered a long period of decline following the Chinese Exclusion Act of 1882.)[72] Saxton's work does not explain, however, why the Knights would adopt the anti-Chinese cause on a national basis.

Although further research needs to be done on this issue, a good conjecture is that the Chinese played a similar role for the Knights on a national level to the one that Saxton describes for the labor movement in California. Incorporating the negative symbol of the Chinese into its larger ideological framework presumably helped the Knights to draw a clear line between those who should be considered legitimate members of a producers' alliance and those who should not. At the same time, the negative racialization of the

Chinese seems to have been an important way of channeling the deeply embedded power of negative racial stereotypes in a direction that would not hurt the KOL's cause: unlike both blacks and European immigrants, the Chinese simply did not have the numbers to represent a crucial part of the desired coalition of the producing classes. In this sense, the negative racialization of the Chinese may have served as a means of promoting an otherwise exceptionally inclusive construction of class.[73]

Bracketing the question of why the Knights adopted such an aggressive anti-Chinese posture, it remains true that its negative racialization of the Chinese was directly linked to its larger republican ideology. Most notably, these stigmatizing racial images went hand in hand with negative representations of corporate power. As the Knights portrayed it, the fact that the Chinese submitted to being the serfs of monopoly capital proved their racial inferiority. This observation is not meant to legitimize the KOL's racism. Rather, the point is that the Knights' varying conceptions of race were closely bound up with its determination to organize an alliance of the producing classes and the larger republican agenda of which this was a part.

The Populist Movement

Despite the success of the Knights of Labor in organizing a broad alliance of the producing classes, its strength and numbers declined precipitously in the wake of the Haymarket riot of 1886. Although the Knights continued to exist as a national organization and maintained a significant presence in a variety of communities across the country, its opponents ceased to fear the KOL as a potentially disruptive force after 1886. If the decline of the Knights marked the end of a strong republican presence within the labor movement, however, republicanism found an even more powerful vehicle with the rise of the Populist movement in the early 1890s.

The culmination of years of steadily building economic distress and political discontent among small farmers and agricultural workers, Populism represented a powerful insurgent movement that posed the last major challenge to the system of corporate capitalism that had been expanding since the end of the Civil War. During its period of greatest strength in the early to mid-1890s, it represented a formidable political force, particularly in its strongholds of the South, Great Plains, and Rocky Mountain West. Although Populism fell apart after the election of 1896, it amassed enough momentum up to that point to pose an unprecedented challenge to the dominant political and economic arrangements of the postbellum period.

The status of small farmers and agricultural workers had been worsening steadily throughout the 1870s–1880s. Small farmers were saddled with debt and stood in constant risk of losing the little land that they had. Many did so, and the number of landless tenant farmers rose from 25 percent in 1880 to 28 percent in 1890.[74] Conditions were particularly bad in the South, which, as the most heavily populated agrarian region in the country, represented the heart of the Populist movement. In the wake of the Civil War, southern agriculture had become dominated by what is referred to as the *crop lien* system. Under this arrangement, small farmers and sharecroppers (i.e., tenant farmers) were required to grow cash crops (generally cotton and tobacco) in order to receive credit from local merchants, who supplied the everyday necessities of life. These merchants, however, charged exorbitant rates, in terms of both goods and interest. Harvested crops had to be immediately turned over to the merchant in exchange for what was always only a partial reduction of accumulated debt. Making matters worse, commodity prices dropped and the costs of railway transportation increased throughout the 1880s. Consequently, by the early 1890s, southern agricultural workers had been reduced to a state of bare subsistence.[75]

During the 1880s, numerous voluntary associations dedicated to bettering the condition of the small farmer sprang up throughout the South, Great Plains, and Rocky Mountain West. These included the Grange, the Agricultural Wheel, the Farmers' Alliance, and the rural arm of the Knights of Labor. Of these, the Farmers' Alliance was the largest and most important. By 1890, it consisted of three affiliated organizations: the Northern Alliance (no membership figures available); the Southern Alliance, representing approximately 3 million members; and the Colored Farmers' Alliance, representing an estimated 1.25 million blacks.[76] (The Southern Alliance had refused to admit blacks during the 1880s, resulting in the formation of a separate Colored Farmers' Alliance in 1886.)[77] Beginning in 1890, various activists associated with the Farmers' Alliance and other like-minded organizations began to discuss the possibility of joining forces to create a national movement capable of fielding an independent third party. The Populist movement consequently emerged, with the People's party running its first candidates in 1892.

The political thought of the Populist movement was rooted in the same tradition of producer republicanism that had animated the Knights. "The fruits of the toil of millions are boldly stolen to build up colossal fortunes unprecedented in the history of mankind, and the possessors of these in turn despise the Republic and endanger liberty," charged the Declaration of Industrial Independence adopted by the combined forces of the Knights of Labor and the Farmers' Alliance at an important 1892 Populist conference. (Although the

Knights of Labor cooperated with the Populist movement throughout the 1890s, it did not by that time represent a powerful political force.) "From the same prolific womb of governmental injustice we breed the two great classes—paupers and millionaires. In this crisis of human affairs," the document continued, "the intelligent working people and producers of the United States have come together in the name of peace, order, and society to defend liberty, property, and justice."[78]

The Populists, like the Knights of Labor before them, believed that the government had been taken over by the forces of monopoly capital. This situation, they warned, endangered the health of the republic. "The spread of corporations and the triumph of monopoly evidence the entrance of the plutocrat into politics and the control of the state by the wealthy class," charged the *National Economist*, the "official organ of the Farmers' Alliance," in 1889:[79]

> The United States Senate has become the property of this class, and is virtually closed against all who do not belong to and serve it. The elections are decided by money. The sources of legislation are corrupted, as is evidenced by thousands of instances, both State and National. . . . The courts—the very fountains of justice—are corrupted and tainted, and great corporations can sometimes buy decisions and immunities. The individual citizen has no chance, justice is made a mockery.

"If thus a few wealthy men are to control all the affairs of the Nation, and the balance are to be dependent on them," the article concluded, "although the form of republican government may survive, yet the essence, the spirit is dead."[80]

Like the Knights of Labor, the Populists maintained that the Constitution was meant to uphold the equalitarian promise of the Declaration of Independence and must be amended as necessary to check the power of monopoly capital. "We have a written Constitution," wrote Populist leader James Weaver in his 1892 work, *A Call to Action*, "but the slave power claimed it for its own. Of late corporations have taken refuge behind it. It will be the dawning of a glorious day when the monopoly-ridden people shall be able to use it as their own shield and buckler." As the "Constitution is the Declaration enacted into law," Weaver continued, it "should enable the citizen to strike down . . . the internal foes of social order and personal liberty" represented by the forces of "monopoly capital." "If it be not capable of such translation," Weaver concluded, "it is a broken reed and the most stupendous failure of the Century."[81]

While united by this republican philosophy, the specific politics of Populism varied widely from state to state. Although the movement existed in every southern state and throughout the West and Midwest, its strength in different regions varied widely. Populism was quite strong in Georgia, Alabama, Texas, Kansas, Arkansas, and North Carolina. It was relatively weak, however, in Tennessee, Florida, Virginia, South Carolina, and Louisiana. Similarly, the radicalism of Populist politics varied among states. At their most radical, Populists insisted upon the full slew of antimonopoly demands represented by the 1892 National People's Party Platform. These included the establishment of a subtreasury system designed to provide low-interest loans to small producers; currency reform; the establishment of a graduated income tax; government ownership of the railroad, telephone, and telegraph systems; government reclamation and redistribution of railroad and corporate land holdings; national legislation of an eight-hour workday; and the abolition of the Pinkerton guards (a force that was instrumental in the suppression of industrial strikes).[82] At its least radical, however, Populism narrowed its focus to the single issue of "free silver"—that is, putting silver coinage into circulation along with gold in order to increase the money supply.[83]

The degree of movement radicalism corresponded directly with the different political strategies that Populists pursued in their attempt to gain political power. Generally speaking, Populists who focused on the free-silver issue favored the strategy of fusion with one of the two major parties. More radical activists, however, insisted that the People's party remain an independent force, as they believed that neither the Republicans nor the Democrats would ever accept the demands of the 1892 platform. "So great has become the power of corporations over every department of human effort and so subservient to them are political parties and politicians," charged *The People's Party and the Present Political Contest* (1896), "that our government for many years has been a government of corporations, for corporations, and by corporations."[84] "The People's Party," asserted *The People's Party Campaign Book* (1892), "is the protest of the plundered against the plunderers—of the victims against the robbers."[85]

Racial Barriers to Radicalism

Racial politics posed the single most formidable obstacle to Populists who wished to pursue a more radical politics by going the third-party route. This was particularly true given the fact that the heart of the movement—as well as the center of its radicalism—was in the South. This region contained the

greatest concentration of agricultural workers, who lived under the most difficult, poverty-stricken, and repressive conditions in the country. Racial politics was very much a part of this dismal picture. As discussed above, race
constituted a key structural element of the economy, the party system, and
the strong cultural and political divides which separated the producing
classes of the North, South, and West. While these structures affected the
country at large, extending the scope of southern racial politics to the rest
of the nation, it was in the South that their racial component took its most
direct and brutal form.[86]

"The professional politicians of both parties, both North and South,
who have devoted their lives so assiduously to the promotion of corporate
interests, recognize that this union of the two sections is the great danger that
threatens the power of monopoly," charged the *Farmers' Advocate* in 1890.
Consequently, it continued, politicians worked assiduously to maintain regional divisions.[87] For both the Republicans and the Democrats, the key
means of manipulating "sectional prejudices" was through appeals to highly
racialized symbols. It was, as W. Scott Morgan noted in the *History of the
Wheel and Alliance, and the Impending Revolution* (1891), the "'bloody shirt'
and 'rebellion' on the one side, and 'Reconstruction' and 'Negro domination'
on the other."[88] "Do you ask for what purpose is this ceaseless arraignment
of the North against the South, and the South against the North, kept up?"
wrote the Honorable B. H. Clover, a Kansas congressman and vice president
of the National Farmers' Alliance in 1891:

> Gentle reader, let me ask: Could any other thing have kept the
> people so blinded to their interest, that, having the ballot in their
> hands, they would have allowed the soul-and-body destroying,
> monopolistic influences to wrap their slimy folds around each
> and every industry, and send the honest toiler shivering to a
> hovel, and elegant idleness to a palace?[89]

By 1892, disgust with the two major parties (if most immediately with
the Democrats, who overwhelmingly dominated the South) was sufficiently
strong that a People's party ticket had been organized in every southern state.
The central dilemma facing the new party was how to negotiate the dangerous racial politics of the region. The white population, of course, harbored
a deep anti-African racism and identified strongly with the "party of white
supremacy." African Americans, for their part, were highly constrained by
the Democrats, who used manipulation backed by force to ensure that the
black vote would go their way. Whites who dared to defect from Democratic
rule faced social ostracism and physical violence. Blacks risked violence and

even death. Electoral fraud was rampant and virtually impossible to police, being perpetuated by the same political forces that controlled the region at large. The vast majority of mainstream newspapers and other organs of public opinion also supported Democratic rule and white supremacy.

The extraordinarily difficult racial politics facing the People's party in the South were further compounded by the fact that as long as African-American men were still voting in large numbers—which they would be up until the collapse of the movement in 1896—the Populists had to have their support in order to win elections.[90] This was true whether the People's party sought to win as an independent force or through fusion with the Republicans or Democrats. The reason for this was that if the white vote split—as it inevitably would with a strong Populist presence—blacks suddenly represented the decisive swing vote.[91] This meant that whites had to be willing to give their support to an insurgent movement that—if it were to build the strength that it needed—would be strongly associated with blacks. Such a crossing of entrenched racial divisions was extremely difficult to achieve, particularly as Conservative Democrats would inevitably charge that such voters were traitors to the cause of white supremacy and might return the region to the supposed Reconstruction era horrors of "Negro domination."

Considering the circumstances, it should come as no surprise that only the most radical Populist leaders seriously attempted to form an interracial alliance of the producing classes. White Populists were themselves a product of their time and place, and shared the racial prejudices that so dramatically shaped the everyday realities of life in the South. Even the most outspoken advocates of interracial politics in the movement underscored their support for white supremacy and their rejection of social equality. The more progressive Populists did, however, modify these positions to allow for an unqualified defense of black political rights and opposition to such racially oppressive practices as lynching and the convict-lease system.[92] Given the harsh realities of African-American life at the time, this was enough to create a significant level of black support for the movement in those areas in which it occurred.

Populist leaders in Texas and Georgia pushed hardest for an interracial alliance. These states were also where the movement provided the strongest support of black rights and had the highest levels of black participation. (Kansas, Arkansas, Louisiana, North Carolina, and Virginia also had lesser, but still substantial African-American involvement.) Not coincidentally, these states were also the strongest bases of Populism nationwide, as well as the places in which the movement achieved its most radical incarnation. Of these, Georgia represents the most interesting and important case. In that state, Tom Watson, the most innovative and accomplished radical Populist leader, made the movement's strongest bid to establish a powerful third-party presence that would break the interlocking chains of racial and class oppression that secured the dominant political and economic structures of the late nineteenth-century South.[93]

In 1890, when Watson was the most well known supporter of the Farmers' Alliance in the state, he was elected to Congress to represent Georgia's Tenth District on the Democratic party ticket. Watson soon broke with the Democrats to organize the People's party, consequently becoming the new party's official leader in the House. In 1891, he started the *People's Party Paper*, which received national attention. In 1892, he published the *People's Party Campaign Book: Not a Revolt, It Is a Revolution*, which attracted a wide audience and caused a considerable stir in the halls of Congress.[94]

Watson correctly believed that the People's party could only succeed on the basis of an interracial, class-based coalition. Consequently, in 1892, he launched an all-out drive to break the lockhold of the Democratic party in the South by appealing to the poor of both races to recognize their common interests and join the Populist movement. The result was a nationally watched campaign of unparalleled intensity, which was widely taken to represent "a barometer of the third party's future in the deep South."[95]

Watson's strategy centered on a series of interrelated assumptions: that the black and white poor shared common enemies, that these enemies were in control of the Democratic and Republican parties, and that both parties systematically played on racial divisions in order to maintain their power and exploit the poor of both races. He also believed that both blacks and whites could be brought to recognize these facts. Consequently, they would abandon their old political loyalties and join the People's party. It was, after all, in their interest to do so, and "self-interest," Watson maintained, "*always* controls." As he explained in his 1892 article, "The Negro Question in the South":

> The white tenant lives adjoining the colored tenant. Their houses are equally destitute of comforts. Their living is confined to bare necessities. They are equally burdened with heavy taxes. They pay the same rent for gullied and impoverished land. They pay the same enormous prices for farm supplies. Christmas finds them both without any satisfactory return for a year's toil. Dull and heavy and unhappy, they both start the plows again when "New Year's" passes.
>
> Now the People's Party says to these two men, "You are kept apart that you may be separately fleeced of your earnings. You are

made to hate each other because upon that hatred is rested the key-stone of the arch of financial despotism which enslaves you both. You are deceived and blinded that you may not see how this race antagonism perpetuates a monetary system which beggars both."

This is so obviously true it is no wonder both these unhappy laborers stop to listen.[96]

"The People's Party," Watson optimistically predicted:

will settle the race question. First, by enacting the Australian [or "official"] ballot system.[97] Second, by offering to white and black a rallying point which is free from the odium of former discords and strife. Third, by presenting a platform immensely beneficial to both races and injurious to neither. Fourth, by making it to the *interest* of both races to act together for the success of the platform.[98]

True to his word, Watson succeeded in rallying an extraordinary level of support for the People's party during the campaigns of 1892 and 1894. As Woodward notes, however, the key reason for this was not that Watson was a charismatic leader (although this was certainly the case), but rather that the people of Georgia were so poor that they were desperate enough to take enormous risks once they had been given some hope of change. Many small farmers, as well as agricultural and factory workers, faced homelessness and even starvation. In 1892, the Atlanta *Journal*, investigating the conditions of mill workers just outside of the city, reported that "famine and pestilence are to-day making worse ravages than among the serfs of Russia." With an average wage of thirty-six cents a day for a family of four, people were literally dying of want. The paper reported on "rooms wherein eight and ten members of one family are stricken down, where pneumonia and fever and measles are attacking their emaciated bodies; where there is no sanitation, no help or protection from the city, no medicine, no food, no fire, no nurses—nothing but torturing hunger and death."[99]

Watson's campaign rallied such people, both white and black. In 1892, the *Washington Post* reported that "all over the State . . . the People's Party element have been meeting twice a month, on Saturday afternoon, in school-houses, for two years, and signal fires are on every hilltop. They are imbued with the spirit of turning things upside down."[100] After Watson was defeated in that election, people simply rallied for the next in 1894. As Woodward documents, the "contemporary accounts of the enthusiasm evoked by the speeches of Watson border on the incredible":

Throngs of three to ten thousand people crowded into cross-roads villages from the countryside of a twenty-mile radius. Riding through the open country from town to town, Watson and his party not infrequently met with such experiences as the following: "When within four miles of Sylvania (at six in the morning) we found the road blocked with vehicles of every description. The rumbling, muffled sound of wheels, ploughing through the sand, sounded like the roar of an army wagon train. The atmosphere loaded with dust and cheers. . . . At least 6,000 people were in hearing of his voice, while at least a thousand more wandered around loosely unable to hear a word."

All told, during the 1894 campaign, Watson visited thirty-seven counties and addressed an estimated 150,000 people.[101] The percentage of votes cast for the People's party in Georgia rose from 19.17 in 1892 to 44.46 in 1894.[102]

Needless to say, the state's Democratic party machinery did not take this lying down. An intensive campaign of race-baiting, bribery, intimidation, violence, and fraud was launched in an effort to quell the new movement and restore Democratic hegemony in Georgia. Race, as Watson and other local movement leaders recognized, was the central principle around which such oppositional efforts were organized and legitimated. "The Democratic State Central Committee met in Atlanta last week and decided to take to the warpath," reported the *People's Party Paper* in 1892:

Reports of the members from every section disclosed the unwelcome fact that the People's Party was gaining strength daily and everything pointed to a complete overthrow of the old political rings in every county in the State. The committee spent many hours in anxious consultation and finally came to the conclusion to try to put a cheerful face on the matter and appear not to be too badly scared and to get their biggest men into the field at once, cry "nigger supremacy," and try and rally their failing fortunes.[103]

Watson succinctly summed up this reactionary phenomenon in an 1892 editorial: "The argument against the independent political movement in the South may be boiled down into one word—NIGGER!"[104]

Watson recognized the power of such race-baiting tactics to manipulate the white public and sought to counteract it through both education and ridicule. His 1892 article, "The Negro Question in the South," lamented the unwarranted vulnerability of the poor white to calculated racial appeals:

You might beseech a Southern white tenant to listen to you upon questions of finance, taxation, and transportation; you might demonstrate with mathematical precision that herein lay his way out of poverty into comfort; you might have him almost persuaded to the truth, but if the merchant who furnished his farm supplies (at tremendous usury) or the town politician (who never spoke to him excepting at election times) came along and cried "Negro rule!" the entire fabric of reason and common sense which you had patiently constructed would fall, and the poor tenant would joyously hug the chains of an actual wretchedness rather than do any experimenting on a question of mere sentiment.[105]

Watson also adopted the less-admirable tactic of attempting to belittle the Democrats' fear-mongering tactics by asserting his belief in white supremacy. "I yield to no man in my pride of race," thundered Watson in an 1893 speech. "I believe the Anglo-Saxon is stronger, in the glorious strength of conception and achievement, than any race of created men. But from my very pride of race springs my intense scorn of that phantasm, manufactured by the political boss, and called 'Negro domination!'"[106]

Like all other white Populists, Watson vowed, "Never in my life have I advocated social equality." "Let the blacks stay to themselves in their own social life and have peace and happiness," he exhorted in an 1894 Atlanta speech. "Let the whites dwell to themselves and have peace and happiness."[107] In keeping with other Populist leaders throughout the South—including the most radical and well-educated—Watson supported racial segregation and did not favor extending jury duty to blacks. In this sense, the Populists, despite their economic radicalism, were very much in line with the Conservative Democrats on the issue of black citizenship: while willing to support a minimal standard of legal and political rights, they remained staunch supporters of white supremacy and segregation.[108]

Given this position, it is difficult to see, from the contemporary perspective, both why blacks might support the Populist movement and how race-baiting tactics could be used against it. Understanding this requires an appreciation of the extremity of racial politics in the late nineteenth-century South. The "paternalist" politics of the Conservative Democrats represented a moderate position compared to the extremism of the radical, white nationalist right. In a climate where lynching represented an everyday danger, segregation was nowhere near the greatest evil that black people faced. If the People's party could make a credible case that it represented the only chance for whites and blacks to free themselves from the economic exploitation that locked them both into a never-ending cycle of poverty, it was able to attract substantial black support.

Further, despite his support for white supremacy and opposition to social equality, Watson made what was, for the time, a strong defense of black citizenship rights. When giving speeches, for example, he would regularly ask his white listeners to hold up their hands and pledge to support the rights of African Americans established by the Constitution.[109] He also sought to include blacks in the party and assured them of its commitment to their interests. "I pledge you my word and honor that if you stand up for your rights and for your manhood, if you stand shoulder to shoulder with us in this fight, you shall have fair play and fair treatment as men and as citizens, irrespective of your color," Watson promised his African-American constituents in an 1892 campaign speech. "My friends, this campaign will decide whether or not your people and ours can daily meet in harmony, and work for law, and order, and morality, and wipe out the color line and put every man on his citizenship irrespective of color."[110]

Georgia blacks responded to Watson's message with great enthusiasm. Thousands attended his political rallies. Many played important roles as political organizers. Several held high offices in the People's party. This level of black support was particularly impressive given the fact that those who did openly side with the Populists had to live under the constant threat of retaliation from movement adversaries. African Americans who actively campaigned for Watson or other Populist candidates in Georgia literally did so at risk of their lives. In the course of the 1892 election, Democratic forces murdered at least fifteen black Populist activists.[111]

Writing in the late 1930s, C. Vann Woodward looked back on this period of Georgia Populism as an exceptional and tragically brief moment in the region's history. "Never before or since have the two races in the South come so close together politically," Woodward concluded.[112] The intensity of the countermovement that Watson and others like him generated, combined with the larger defeat of Populism nationwide, ushered in a new era marked by an even more intensive and all-encompassing level of white supremacist racism, in both the South and the nation at large. The defeat of the republican challenge to laissez-faire liberalism, which was sealed by the outcome of the fiercely contested presidential election of 1896, was the turning point in this shift. The intensification of white supremacism and the defeat of producer republicanism, in other words, were not only concurrent but highly interrelated phenomena.

While the law [of competition] may be sometimes hard for the individual, it is best

for the race, because it insures the survival of the fittest in every department.

We accept and welcome, therefore, as conditions to which we must accommodate

ourselves, great inequality of environment; the concentration of business, industrial

and commercial, in the hands of a few; and the law of competition between these,

as not only beneficial, but essential to the future progress of the race.

—*Andrew Carnegie, "The Gospel of Wealth," 1889*

4

Inequality and White Supremacy

Conservative advocates of laissez-faire were horrified and alarmed by the waves of labor unrest that swept the country beginning in the late 1870s. In response to the labor movement's growing demands for protective legislation and government regulation, conservative leaders—drawn primarily from the ranks of Eastern elites, mainstream politicians, corporate businessmen, social scientists, journalists, lawyers, and judges—began preaching an intensified version of laissez-faire. This position claimed that the labor movement was attempting to interfere with the "law of competition" and, consequently, turn back the clock of civilization's advance. "Socialism," as such conservatives sweepingly labeled all forms of progressive dissent, was depicted as a retrograde and un-American doctrine that threatened to sabotage the achievements of late nineteenth-century capitalism by forcibly attempting to establish equality where none naturally existed. The rich were rich because they were more able, Darwinian liberals asserted. The poor were poor because they lacked talent, intelligence, and drive. The law of competition dictated that only the most talented and able members of society would survive and prosper. Socialism represented a perversion of this natural arrangement in that it sought to place social power in the hands of those who were inherently unsuited to hold it.

Such arguments blended easily with a newly expansive and more severely hierarchical conception of race. Socialism, it was increasingly claimed, was attractive to members of inferior racial groups, who naturally gravitated to more primitive social philosophies. Conversely, opposition to socialism was designated to be the mark of a "true American," who was increasingly described as a member of a superior "Anglo-Saxon race." During the 1880s–1890s, this prototypical distinction between the politically conservative, white American citizen and his radical, racially inferior, and un-American counterpart became increasingly common. According to this construction of race, whites were generally conceived of as native-born Americans of Northern or Western European descent. The rapidly growing population of immigrants from Southern and Eastern Europe, in contrast, was categorized as comprising the lowest stratum of the "European races." Through this conflation of political radicalism and racial inferiority, Italians, Poles, Hungarians, Slavs, Bohemians, and so on were commonly blamed for the increased prominence of socialism in America.[1]

This division of Americans of European descent into a hierarchy of racial groups hurt the labor movement by dividing its constituency and discrediting its philosophy. This was especially true of the Knights of Labor. Dedicated to organizing all members of the producing classes into "one great solidarity," the Knights had achieved considerable success with its determined outreach to various immigrant groups. The KOL was irreparably damaged, however, by the virulent conservative reaction to the Haymarket riot of 1886, which blamed it for stirring up the uncivilized passions of "inferior races" by preaching un-American socialist doctrines. This combination of political denunciation and racial stigma packed a powerful punch in a political culture steeped in racial thinking and unnerved by economic dislocation, labor unrest, and rapid demographic change. Providing an easy explanation for a frightening outburst of violence and social disorder, this conservative position helped to delegitimize the Knights' political program while dividing its constituents along racial and cultural lines.

Anti-African racism played an even more powerful role in destroying the Knights of Labor in the South and, roughly ten years later, sabotaging the Populist movement. The Conservative Democrats who controlled the postbellum South were willing to take whatever action they deemed necessary to contain the threats of labor and agrarian radicalism represented by these movements. Consequently, beginning in the late 1880s, there was a dramatic upsurge in antiblack rhetoric and political race-baiting, as well as widespread violence and fraud, which, while centering most heavily on the black population, affected poor whites as well. This period of political terror was followed in the mid- to late 1890s by an intensification of existing patterns of segregation and disfranchisement, producing the edifice of Jim Crow laws countenanced by *Plessy* and the effective elimination of the African-American vote.

The presidential election of 1896 marked the collapse of Populism and, consequently, the final defeat of producer republicanism. After deciding to cast its lot with Democratic presidential nominee William Jennings Bryan, the Populist movement fell apart after he lost what was an exceptionally rabid and controversial election. This critical election marked an important turning point in American political development. In particular, it supported the development of three institutional arrangements that played a primary role in creating a more unequal society and a more constricted political universe: (1) the dominance of the highly conservative American Federation of Labor (AFL) within the labor movement, (2) the establishment of Jim Crow segregation and the "solid South," and (3) the dramatic reduction of electoral participation, particularly among lower-income groups. Through these primary mechanisms, the scope and aspirations of American liberalism were dramatically contracted. Although the ensuing Progressive Era would achieve some important reforms, this triumph of Darwinian liberalism reinforced the cultural and political dominance of a newly differentiated form of racial hierarchy, a broad endorsement of social and economic inequality, and a narrow and exclusionary conception of citizenship.

The Great Strike of 1877

The roots of this shift toward the advocacy of social inequality and a more elaborate system of racial hierarchy can be traced back to the Great Strike of 1877. Coming immediately on the heels of the Compromise of 1877, the Great Strike played a central role in shifting national political attention away from the racial issues of Reconstruction and toward the newly emerging economic conflicts of the Gilded Age. Representing "one of the most widespread and militant strikes" in U.S. history,[2] the Great Strike signaled the beginning of a period of unprecedented labor activism and industrial strife. In so doing, it marked the onset of a newly reconfigured pattern of national political and cultural conflicts.[3]

The roots of the Great Strike were in the Panic of 1873, which had set off a long period of economic contraction and brought labor issues to the forefront of national attention for the first time. Railway workers, like millions of others, had been severely affected by this prolonged recession. By 1877, they were ripe for revolt. Consequently, what began as a small, localized protest in West Virginia over a wage cut by the Baltimore and Ohio Railroad quickly spread to railway lines in Maryland, Pennsylvania, New York, New Jersey, Kentucky, Ohio, Illinois, Missouri, and California. Given widespread worker discontent, as well as general public resentment against what were widely perceived as gouging railway companies, the rapidly growing strike generated substantial public support. In the end, after eighteen days, the Great Strike "left more than a hundred dead, millions of dollars of property destroyed, and a toughened company and government stand against unions."[4]

Sending shock waves across the entire country, the Great Strike immediately became a pivotal symbolic marker, sharply dividing those who sympathized with striker grievances from those who viewed the labor movement as a menace to society.[5] While sparking the growth of many labor unions (including the KOL), the Great Strike also marked the beginning of what would, over the course of the next two decades, become an increasingly common distinction between the un-American political radicalism promulgated by the "lower orders" of the working population and the authentically American political quiescence of their ostensibly superior counterparts.

Journalists and writers who reported on the strike regularly made such distinctions. This was true even among many of those who had some sympathy for the strikers' cause. In the *Annals of the Great Strikes* (1877), for example, J. A. Dacus wrote, "American workingmen are not thieves, incendiaries, and murderers, but honest, true men, as a class, who were engaged in an effort to redress certain wrongs, of which they believed themselves to be the victims." Although initially happy to welcome all who would support their cause into their ranks, "when they saw the deeds of the Communists and roughs in Baltimore and Philadelphia . . . they were disgusted, felt themselves outraged, and dishonored by the association." Consequently, American workers "were ready to assist anybody representing the ideas of social order and political stability, to put down the howling mobs wherever they might appear."[6]

Others condemned the strikers more broadly, suggesting that the formerly admirable American worker had been fatally infected with such contemptible ideas and behavior. "The fact is clearly manifest," stated the *National Republican* of Washington, DC, on the day after the Baltimore strike, "that communistic ideas are very widely entertained in America by the workmen employed in mines and factories and by the railroads. This poison was introduced into our social system by European laborers." The Great Strike, the paper concluded, "is nothing less than communism in its worst form . . . not only unlawful and revolutionary, but anti-American."[7]

Beyond this sort of simple nativism, at least one prominent voice of opposition to the strike—that of E. L. Godkin's *Nation*—suggested that the anti-American proclivities of these "European laborers" stemmed from a biological, or racial, source.[8] The key problem, the magazine explained, was that "the well-to-do and intelligent classes of the population" had not been sufficiently aware of

> the profound changes which have during the last thirty years been wrought in the composition and character of the population, especially in the great cities. Vast additions have been made to it within that period, to whom American political and social ideals appeal but faintly, if at all, and *who carry in their very blood* traditions which give universal suffrage an air of menace to many of the things which civilized men hold most dear. . . .
>
> Some of the talk about the laborer and his rights that we have listened to on the platform and in literature during the last fifteen years . . . has been enough, considering the sort of ears on which it now falls . . . [to] put our very civilization in peril. . . . Our superiority to the Ashantees or the Kurds is not due to right thinking or right feeling only, but to the determined fight which the more enlightened part of the community has waged from generation to generation against the ignorance and brutality, now of one class and now of another.[9]

The *Nation* and other prominent periodicals, such as the *Galaxy* and *Harper's Weekly*, called for the establishment of a larger standing army to prevent such uprisings in the future. Such warnings were heeded, as most states subsequently reorganized their National Guards to be more effective in riot control. The majority of northern cities constructed new armories. While generally financed with public funds, they also received financial support from the new tycoons of the Gilded Age, such as the Vanderbilts, Astors, Lenoxes, and Morgans.[10]

Inequality: A Prerequisite for Civilization?

Coming only six years after the Paris Commune of 1870–1871, the Great Strike had a profound effect on Americans who feared the onset of what they viewed as a similarly destructive form of political radicalism in the United

States.[11] Certain segments of the elite classes—particularly conservative writers and academics, corporate businessmen, and members of the bench and bar—suddenly began to take the threat of lower-class insurgency extremely seriously.[12] Having long believed that America was immune to the class conflicts that had traditionally plagued Europe, this fear came as a shock. This was particularly true because it overturned what had been for many a deeply cherished, but formerly taken-for-granted ideal of the nation.

While progressive forces viewed the rise of class conflict as a legitimate response to an increasingly unequal and brutally competitive society, conservatives condemned it as an unwarranted outbreak of unpatriotic agitation. Such conservatives served as the driving force behind the development of a more broadly aggressive form of Darwinian liberalism, which held that the combination of civic equality and a free-market order would naturally produce social hierarchy, particularly along racial lines. Breaking with the long-standing practice of embedding questions of political economy within a larger tradition of moral philosophy, conservative writers and academics began to propound new forms of social science, which, they claimed, had identified the inexorable "laws" of societal development.[13] Conveniently, one of the most important of these laws dictated that the growth of social and economic inequality necessarily accompanied the process of civilization's advancement. Although the resultant system of social stratification was at first discussed in relatively vague terms, it increasingly became coupled with a newly elaborate conception of racial hierarchy. First emerging during the 1880s–1890s, this pattern would continue to maintain its political and cultural prominence through the first two decades of the twentieth century.

Herbert Spencer, a well-known English writer and social theorist, and William Graham Sumner, a professor of political and social science at Yale, were the two most prominent intellectual progenitors of this revised Darwinian position. Many of the nation's most successful businessmen and entrepreneurs, such as Andrew Carnegie and John D. Rockefeller, promulgated more popularized versions of Spencer's and Sumner's ideas. Carnegie, for example, enthusiastically spread the good news of "The Gospel of Wealth."[14] Legal professionals also embraced this current of thought, as the majority of lawyers and judges began to interpret such tenets as "freedom of contract" in ways that allowed them to invalidate virtually any legislation that might restrict corporate power in the name of the common good.[15]

Carnegie's Gospel of Wealth encapsulated a perspective that had become increasingly influential since the collapse of Reconstruction.[16] His central contention was that civilization could only be advanced in a society that understood and accepted the eternal verities of a naturally ordained law of competition. As a result of this law, Carnegie argued,

> The Socialist or Anarchist who seeks to overturn present conditions is to be regarded as attacking the foundation upon which civilization itself rests, for civilization took its start from the day when the capable, industrious workman said to his incompetent and lazy fellow, "If thou dost not sow, thou shalt not reap," and thus ended primitive Communism by separating the drones from the bees.[17]

"Let it be understood," wrote Sumner during the 1880s, "that we cannot go outside of this alternative: liberty, inequality, survival of the fittest; not-liberty, equality, survival of the unfittest." (Notably, Sumner's views, which were instrumental in laying the basis for the newly invented "science" of sociology, were crystallized by his "heated reaction to the violent railroad strikes of 1877.")[18] "The former," he continued, "carries society forward and favors all its best members; the latter carries society downwards and favors all its worst members."[19] Giving free rein to the law of competition was not, in other words, simply a matter of allowing individual talents to flourish, although this was certainly one of its most important achievements. Rather, it was a matter of civilization's advancement or, as Carnegie put it, "the future progress of the race."[20]

From this formulation, it followed that societies that elected to embrace the law of competition would advance, while those that did not would stagnate. Such divergent patterns of social development divided humanity into more- and less-civilized groups, which were generally presented in terms of racial categories. Both Carnegie and Sumner, for example, presented Native Americans as a prime example of a socially and racially inferior group. As Sumner explained:

> [T]he Digger Indian is a specimen of that part of the race which withdrew from the competition clear back at the beginning and has consequently never made any advance beyond the first superiority of man to beasts. . . . If you want equality you must not look forward for it on the path of advancing civilization. You may go back to the mode of life of the American Indian, and, although you will not then reach equality, you will escape those glaring inequalities of wealth and poverty by coming down to a comparative equality, that is, to a status in which all are equally miserable.[21]

Carnegie noted that among the Sioux there was only a "trifling difference" between "the wigwam of the chief . . . and those of the poorest of his braves." Just as such equality demonstrated their lack of advancement, the growing inequality of the larger American society demonstrated civilization's growth. "The contrast between the palace of the millionaire and the cottage of the laborer with us today measures the change which has come with civilization."[22]

Both Sumner and Carnegie recognized that the industrial revolution had dramatically changed the course and pace of development within American society. "A century ago," noted Sumner, "there were very few wealthy men except owners of land." Changes such as the "extension of commerce, manufactures, and mining, the introduction of the factory system and machinery, the opening of new countries, and the great discoveries and inventions" had, however, created an unprecedented situation in which "the chance of acquiring capital . . . has opened up before classes which formerly passed their lives in a dull round of ignorance and drudgery." Consequently, "those who were wise and able to profit by the chance succeeded grandly; those who were negligent or unable to profit by it suffered proportionately. The result has been wide inequalities of wealth within the industrial classes."[23] "Millionaires," in other words, were "a product of natural selection," since, as Carnegie noted, "able men soon create capital."[24]

Socialists of all stripes, it was charged, tried to deny these realities. Refusing to accept that inequality was both natural and beneficial, they hoped to ameliorate it by crafting an alternative political economy. This was not simply wrong, but potentially dangerous and destructive. "Every scheme of theirs for securing equality has destroyed liberty," wrote Sumner. "Equality of possession or of rights and equality before the law are diametrically opposed to each other." By stirring up the "malice and envy" of those unable to compete successfully in the new capitalist order, socialist thought encouraged the formation of dangerous "mobs" with "the most savage and senseless disposition to burn and destroy what they cannot enjoy." The most vital political project of the age was to beat back the danger posed by socialist thought and the mob action that it inspired. "Institutions must now be devised to guard civil liberty against popular majorities," warned Sumner, "and this necessity arises first in regard to the protection of property, the first and greatest function of government and element in civil liberty."[25]

Radical Politics: A Mark of Racial Inferiority?

The next major wave of labor unrest, commonly referred to as the Great Up-heaval of 1883–1886, significantly intensified this trajectory of conservative thought. In 1886, approximately 700,000 workers went on strike during the peak of the labor movement's agitation for the establishment of a standard eight-hour working day.[26] The Knights of Labor reached its peak of strength with more than 700,000 members.[27] By the close of that year, however, its numbers began what was to be a huge and irreversible decline. At the same time, the cause of labor as a whole suffered a similar reversal of momentum. The key event sparking this change of fortune was what is commonly re-ferred to as the Haymarket Affair of 1886. This critical event sent shock waves throughout the entire nation and generated a ferocious and powerful con-servative response.

The Haymarket Affair occurred on May 4, 1886, when about 3,000 peo-ple gathered at Haymarket Square in Chicago to protest a lockout at the lo-cal McCormick Harvester plant. The rally had been instigated by a group of anarchists—primarily composed of German immigrants—and was being heavily monitored by the police. Toward the end of the protest, a bomb ex-ploded. Police began firing into the crowd, and a riot ensued. Subsequently, eight local anarchists were arrested and convicted, and four were eventually hanged. There was, however, not a shred of evidence that directly linked the anarchists to the bombing.[28]

Haymarket, like the Great Strike before it, was immediately established as a key symbol dividing opposing views of the labor movement. The con-servative reaction to Haymarket revitalized and intensified the movement to bifurcate the working class into its ostensibly American and un-American counterparts, while injecting a much stronger and more consistent racial di-mension into both categories. Once again, the propensity toward anar-chism—or un-American radicalism in general—was constructed as a racial trait to which the Anglo-Saxon worker, no matter how exploited or abused, was immune. As the business periodical *Age of Steel* explained in an article entitled "Anarchy as a Blood Disease":

> The instinct of fair play is dominant in the ruling race. The En-glish laborer came through centuries of oppression and has borne the brunt of a grand struggle without a taint of anarchy in his bones. . . . I am no race worshipper, but am not blind to the dan-ger of certain blood predominances in this republic. . . . if the master race of this continent is subordinated to or overrun with

the communistic and revolutionary races, it will be in grave danger of social disaster.[29]

"Such foreign savages, with their dynamite bombs and anarchic purposes, are as much apart from the rest of the people of this country as the Apaches of the plains are," ranted the *New York Sun*. "Workingmen who are citizens of the Republic and understand its institutions, utterly detest them and their teachings, and would have the law forbid them land on our shores, as they would keep out an invasion of venomous reptiles."[30] "These aliens, driven out of Germany and Bohemia," charged the *Chicago Tribune*, "have swarmed over into this country of extreme toleration and have most flagrantly abused its hospitality. . . . These serpents have been warmed and nourished in the sunshine of toleration until at last they have been emboldened to strike at society, law, order, and government."[31] "Labor trouble, with its concomitants of socialism, communism, outrage, murder, red flags, and petards," explained an article in the 1886 compendium *The Labor Problem: Plain Questions and Practical Answers*, had brought the issue of "race influence" to the forefront of public concern:

> It would indicate if not establish the danger that the hot-blooded races, emotional, savage, and clannish, would submerge in a sea of kerosene the old Saxon solidity and granite. . . . The constituents of these labor importations, mostly from Southern Europe, are soaked through and through with ignorance and superstition, and are festering yet in body and soul with filth and clannishness, a blister on the social body and a check on its advancement.[32]

Such racial typecasting had a powerful cultural appeal. "There has been of late considerable abuse of the foreigner," noted a more moderate editorial in the *Age of Steel* several months after the bombing. "He has suddenly become a monster, a menace, and an anaconda coiling around the continent. We charge him with the criminals that pack our penitentiaries and the social heresies that vitiate public citizenship. We are," the paper cautioned, "going to extremes in this matter." Advocating a more temperate approach, it concluded that while "we should have restricted paupers and anarchists long ago," native-born, "Saxon" Americans should "be just to the foreign element and not endeavor to prove that all of our evils are ladled out of one pot."[33]

Such admonitions did not, however, prevent widespread accusations that the Knights of Labor were "responsible for bringing about the condition of affairs that make it possible for the socialists to unfurl their red flags and fire dynamite bombs into the ranks of the guardians of the peace in Chicago," as the *Wisconsin State Journal* put it.[34] The Knights had "roused and angered the American people," accused the *Atlantic Monthly*, by encouraging the growth of imported socialist doctrines that were "utterly opposed to our form, or to any form, of civilization." "Framed in direct opposition to natural law" and rejecting "the doctrine of the survival of the fittest," such socialist projects promised the impossible, destroyed liberty, and encouraged "the sacrifice of excellence, faithfulness, ambition, and individualism":

> The socialist theory of a paternal state system which provides everybody with work and wages is a mischievous fallacy. It simply encourages indolence and dependence. . . . No regulation of the hours of labor, no increase in wages, no monopoly of work, no trades-union rules, however cunningly contrived, can change the laws of nature. While the world lasts there will be fit and unfit men, and the former will prosper and the latter will fail—because they are not adapted to their environment.[35]

"The demands of the Knights and their sympathizers," wrote one participant in a symposium on "The Labor Crisis" published in the *North American Review* in 1886, "are so utterly revolutionary of the inalienable rights of the citizen and so completely subversive of the social order, that the whole community has come to a firm conclusion that these pretensions must be resisted to the last extremity of endurance and authority." Having "sacrificed the sympathy which lately was entertained for them," he continued, "they stand discredited and distrusted before the community at large as impracticable, unjust, and reckless." As a consequence, "their cause is gone and their organization doomed to failure."[36] "If Grand Master Powderly and the honest men he has associated with him in the management of the labor question wish to benefit their fellow workmen," admonished another writer in the same symposium, "they should disband the present order, and start anew with an organization to be known as the Knights of Labor of the United States of America—admitting none to membership who are not American citizens, and ready to uphold to the uttermost the principles of freedom upon which our government is founded."[37]

The membership of the Knights declined rapidly in the wake of Haymarket. By 1887, it had dropped to approximately 511,000 from its height of more than 700,000 in 1886. By 1888, it had been reduced to 220,000.[38] A number of factors contributed to this abrupt shift, including the loss of an important strike against Jay Gould's railway in the Southwest, intensified opposition from the business community, and growing antagonisms with the trade unions. The political fallout surrounding the Haymarket riot, however, was one of the most important causes of this decline. While Haymarket stigmatized the entire labor movement by smearing it with the potent image of anti-American radicalism brought on by a foreign influx of inferior races, it was especially important in eroding the popular legitimacy of the Knights of Labor. Apart from the anarchists themselves, the KOL was the organization most strongly linked to the riot.[39] Haymarket also brought on a new wave of state-sponsored labor repression, which similarly affected both the labor movement at large and the Knights in particular.[40]

The fact that ethnic divisions within the KOL became much more pronounced around 1886 suggests that the negative racialization of a major part of the Knights' constituency significantly reinforced internal processes of fragmentation.[41] This is particularly likely given that the KOL leadership, rather than attempting to combat this divisive construction of race, frantically sought to distance themselves from the negative image of the bomb-throwing anarchist. Although this effort primarily consisted of proclaiming the republican hostility toward anarchism, it also at times included an antiforeign, quasi-race-baiting element.[42] Middle-class leaders in some immigrant communities insisted that anti-American radicalism had no place among their constituents.[43] Although more research needs to be done on the issue, it appears that such responses caused significant cleavages within the Knights along both political and racial lines, further contributing to its suddenly snowballing decline.[44]

The significance of the Haymarket Affair, however, goes far beyond the issue of the demise of the Knights of Labor. There is something of a scholarly consensus that Haymarket was the single most important incident in the history of late nineteenth-century nativism, which became a significant force in American life only after that time.[45] Its connection to larger patterns of racial discourse, however, has rarely been considered, either theoretically or empirically.[46] Making this connection provides a reinterpretation of its political and cultural significance. Haymarket was important because it cemented the cultural connection between negatively coded political and racial attributes. This, in turn, accelerated the growth and influence of Darwinian liberalism, while elevating the importance of a more exclusionary—and politically scripted—construction of white racial identity.

Maintaining the Color Line in the South

Only four months after the Haymarket debacle, a similarly racially charged incident occurred in the South that unleashed a flood of conservative reaction that was highly damaging to the Knights of Labor. In this case, however, the KOL itself provoked this event. Members of the New York delegation to the annual convention of the General Assembly of the Knights of Labor in Richmond, Virginia, deliberately crossed the color line. As a result of this racial defiance, the KOL was once again attacked as an organization that pursued destructively radical politics, while encouraging agitation among racially inferior groups. As in the case of Haymarket, these attacks were effective in discrediting the organization among much of the white public. Throughout the South, white membership plummeted in the wake of this controversial incident, never to regain its former strength.[47]

The chain of events leading up to what would quickly become a nationally celebrated event began when District 49 of New York learned that the Richmond hotel designated for convention delegates would not accept the one black member of their sixty-man delegation, Frank J. Ferrell. Unanimously resolving not to stay at any hotel that discriminated on the basis of "color, creed, or nationality," District 49 delegates arrived in Richmond prepared to sleep in tents that they carried with them. Determined, as the *New York Times* reported, to uphold "what they claim is a fundamental principle of their order—that the black man is the equal of the white socially as well as politically, and that all races stand upon an equal footing in all respects,"[48] District 49 persuaded Terence Powderly to have Ferrell play a prominent role in the convention by having him introduce the grand master workman immediately following the opening remarks of Virginia governor Fitzhugh Lee.[49]

The situation blew up into a national controversy when Ferrell, accompanied by eighty-five of his white colleagues, attended a performance of *Hamlet* at the traditionally segregated Mozart Academy of Music. As Powderly later recounted in *Thirty Years of Labor*:

> When it became known that a colored man was admitted to one
> of the choicest seats in the theater, all interest in the play was lost,
> and many left the building vowing vengeance on the intruder who
> had so recklessly defied one of the rules of Richmond life. The
> next evening the attendance at the theater was very slim, many
> theater-goers having determined to boycott it. . . . Outside the
> building an angry mob assembled, armed with revolvers and
> other weapons. . . . The excitement ran high for many days,
> and on several occasions, men who claimed to be residents of
> Richmond, appeared at the hotel where the general officers
> were stopping, and threatened to do violence to some of the
> delegates.[50]

This crossing of the color line of social equality was extensively commented on by the Democratic, Republican, and independent press nationwide.[51] In the South, the solidly Democratic press loudly denounced the Knights, predicting that the order would quickly fail in the region if it did not immediately change its behavior. The *Atlanta Constitution*, for example, wrote that the "conduct of the Knights of Labor delegates from District 49 . . . cannot be too strongly condemned":

> This agitation over the color question is a side issue, but it is big
> enough to wreck the Knights of Labor. The Southern members of
> the order are not likely to submit to the insufferable conduct of a
> gang of radical cranks. . . . if the other Northern delegates stand
> by them, the only thing left for the Southern delegates is to secede.

The Augusta, Georgia, *News* opined: "If the Knights of Labor intend to make the social equality of the races part of their creed they will gain little strength in the South. The white working man has as little taste for that as anybody and understands very clearly that social intermixture is the first and longest step toward miscegenation, which means mongrelization."[52]

In an effort to calm things down, Powderly wrote a long statement explaining his views on the issue and submitted it to the Richmond *Dispatch* for publication.[53] Assuring white residents that "there need be no further cause for alarm," Powderly bowed to social convention and promised that "the colored representatives to this Convention will not intrude where they are not wanted, and the time-honored laws of social equality will be allowed to slumber on undisturbed." At the same time, however, Powderly more defiantly insisted:

> We have not done a thing since coming to this city that is not
> countenanced by the laws and Constitution of our country. . . . In
> the field of labor and American citizenship we recognize no line
> of race, creed, politics, or color. The demagogue may distort, for a
> purpose, the words of others, and for a time the noise of the vocal
> boss may silence reason, but that which is right and true will be-
> come known when the former has passed to rest and the sound of
> the latter's voice has forever died away.[54]

Although the convention closed on an upbeat note, with a parade and a picnic that represented "the largest black-white affair in Richmond's history," the strength of white southern reaction to the Ferrell incident had a decidedly negative effect.[55] Not only did it fuel the fires of anti-African racism among white workers, but it provided an important new source of ammunition for antilabor forces threatened by the growing strength of the union in the South. As racial divisions and mistrust intensified, what had been an exceptionally vibrant biracial reform movement, rooted in but expanding beyond the KOL, collapsed in Richmond.[56] This pattern was replicated throughout the South, as racial divisions overwhelmed the Knights' efforts to maintain class-based solidarity.

As white southerners began leaving the organization in droves, blacks, who had been positively impressed by the Richmond incident, began to join in increasing numbers. Consequently, within the course of the next year, the southern wing of the Knights of Labor became a largely black union. (Indicative of the general situation was the comment by one black Knight in 1887 that "Nigger and Knight have become synonymous terms" throughout the South.)[57] Bereft of white support, the newly reconstituted movement lacked any real political power. It also had no allies when white planters and large farmers, alarmed by the increased organization of the black labor force, began a series of violent antilabor reprisals.[58] After the KOL national office failed to respond to black requests either to aid their fight against violent repression or to sanction white racism within the organization, black membership also began to decline precipitously. Consequently, by 1890, the KOL, for all practical purposes, had died in the South.[59]

As early as 1887, however—less than a year after Haymarket and Richmond—conservative commentators were celebrating both the decline of the Knights of Labor and what they saw as the concurrent dissipation of socialist politics in general. "The Socialistic movement," the *Contemporary Review* approvingly explained, "appears to be burning itself out":

> A year ago, a very large proportion of our thoughtful writers were inclined to take it for granted that the wage-workers had a grievance that could, in some way, be corrected. The opinion was very general, that of the abounding and exuberant prosperity of the country, the masses of people did not receive their fair share. But those who have been most emphatic in their complaints have utterly failed. . . . It is coming to be seen that the great accumulations of certain individual men . . . are the inevitable consequence of opportunity on the one hand, and liberty on the other.

"The same general drift of public opinion," the article noted, "shows itself in its attitude toward that vast organization from which so much was expected, the Knights of Labor."[60] Similarly, another journalist happily pointed to the disintegration of the KOL as evidence that "reason is resuming her sway among American workingmen. The only wonder is that the madness lasted so long."[61]

Race and the Collapse of Populism

Although such predictions of the end of socialist politics were premature, it was true that a critical turning point had been reached. Like the 1880s, the 1890s would be marked by intense political protest against the tremendous economic inequalities that continued to accompany the growth of corporate capitalism. In particular, the flowering of the agrarian-based Populist movement in the early years of that decade would maintain the politics of producer republicanism as a vital part of American civic life. Yet the Populists, like the Knights of Labor, would prove to be highly vulnerable to racially charged attacks. Once again, a powerful social movement organized around a primary, if tenuously developing, class identity would be irreparably damaged by its opponents' manipulation and intensification of existing racial divisions. This, of course, was particularly true in the South, where the racial hysteria whipped up to defeat the movement produced a tidal wave of antiblack discrimination and violence that reached its peak around the turn of the century.[62] (During the 1890s, for example, an average of 138 persons were lynched in the South each year, commonly in highly public spectacles. Roughly 75 percent of these victims were African American.)[63]

The Populist movement had a complicated and inconsistent relationship with African Americans in the South. Only the most radical Populist leaders—such as, most notably, Tom Watson of Georgia—were willing to take on the formidable task of attempting to build a strong interracial alliance. Nonetheless, historians largely agree that the most important factor explaining the collapse of Populism in the mid-1890s was that "conservative whites were successful in convincing poor whites that a vote for Populism was racial treason and that the fate of all Anglo-Saxons depended upon white solidarity within the Democratic Party."[64] This successful push to rally whites with conflicting economic interests around the flag of white supremacy was not accomplished by a simple appeal to racial prejudice, however. Rather, vicious race-baiting was accompanied by repeated campaigns of violence, intimidation, bribery, and fraud. Using these means, Conservative Democrats managed to sabotage the growing strength of the People's party. This, in turn, created the conditions that caused the most radical, southern wing of the movement to pursue fusion with the Democratic party and reduce its political demands to the establishment of free silver.[65]

The black vote was of critical importance to the balance of electoral power in the South. The viability of the two-party system depended on it, as only the continued loyalty of the black electorate allowed the Republican party to be a meaningful contender in the region. Similarly, the success of the People's party—or any other third-party movement—was highly dependent on the racial balance of power. If the white vote were significantly split, blacks became the critical bloc of swing voters. Consequently, the battle to attract—or control—the black vote mounted in conjunction with the defection of white Democrats into the People's party.[66]

By 1892, the Populists had achieved a significant electoral presence in the majority of southern states. Votes for the People's party, or for the fusion of Populists with either the Democrats or the Republicans, constituted 36.6 percent of the total in Alabama, 16.06 percent in Florida, 19.17 percent in Georgia, 19.42 percent in Mississippi, 15.94 percent in North Carolina, and 23.64 percent in Texas. Showings of between 3 and 9 percent were also achieved in Arkansas, Kentucky, Louisiana, Missouri, South Carolina, and Tennessee. These numbers went up even higher in the subsequent election of 1894, when the corresponding figures were over 50 percent in North Carolina, over 40 percent in Alabama and Georgia, over 30 percent in South Carolina and Texas, close to 20 percent in Florida and Arkansas, and over 8 percent in Missouri and Tennessee. (Figures for Kentucky, Louisiana, and Mississippi are not available.)[67] While the relationship between white Populists and black voters varied enormously from state to state, the overall impact of this newfound Populist strength was to make the issue of black political power in the South more salient than it had been since the end of Reconstruction.[68]

Nowhere was this more true than in Georgia, where the battle between the People's party and the Democrats was attracting national attention. "The first question asked by everyone when the probabilities of the South are considered is, 'What are Watson's chances?'" reported the *National Watchman* in 1892. "Mr. Watson is now a national character and there is not a single congressional contest going on in the nation that is being looked upon with as much interest as the one in his district." Powerful business interests in Georgia capitalized upon this situation by appealing to their northern connections to make contributions to defeat Watson, warning that he was "a sworn enemy of capital, and that his defeat was a matter of importance to every investor in the country." Such entreaties produced a significant response. "Insurance and railway companies responded liberally," reported the

New York *Tribune*, "so that $40,000 was in hand for use, in addition to the local funds."[69]

Both in 1892 and 1894, however, the key weapons used to ensure Watson's defeat were race-baiting, fraud, and violence. Populist leaders were accused of being traitors to the white race, dangerous radicals who would turn the state over to "Negro rule." (This campaign was additionally reinforced in the 1892 election by drumming up white hysteria surrounding the pending Lodge Bill, a congressional Republican proposal for federal monitoring of national elections in the South. This "Force Bill," southern Democrats warned, would result in a return to "Negro domination" of the region.) At the same time, the Democratic party shamelessly manipulated and coerced the black vote. "I remember," recounted one resident of Watson's district:

> seeing the wagonloads of negroes brought into the wagon yards,
> the equivalent of our parking lots, the night before the election.
> There was whiskey there for them, and all night many drank, sang
> and fought. But the next morning they were herded to the polls
> and openly paid in cash, a dollar bill for each man as he handed in
> his ballot.[70]

Other black voters were, the *People's Party Paper* reported, "bulldozed, intimidated, driven from the polls, and in some instances, shot for attempting to exercise the right of citizenship."[71] Relatively elite blacks were subjected to a combination of promises and threats in an effort to convince them that they had much more to gain by an alliance with the upper-class whites of the Democratic party than with the lower-class Populists. Although many African Americans remained skeptical of the People's party and a few actually wanted to vote Democratic, their votes were rarely a simple matter of choice.[72]

Nor were violence and fraud practiced solely against blacks. "The leaders and newspapers of the Democratic party have touched a depth of infamy in this campaign which is almost incredible," charged the *People's Party Paper* in 1892. "They have intimidated the voter, assaulted the voter, murdered the voter. They have bought votes, forced votes and stolen votes. They have incited lawless men to a frenzy that threatens anarchy . . . and put lives in danger."[73] In 1894, Populists in Wilkes County reported that "here human life is as valueless as corn cobs. We are in a reign of terror."[74] Historians confirm that such accounts were not mere hyperbole. Violence, intimidation, bribery, ballot-box stuffing, and false counts were ubiquitous not only in Georgia, but throughout the lower South. In short, the elections of both 1892 and 1894 were wholesale frauds.[75]

Not surprisingly, these experiences weakened the Populists' commitment to attempting to gain political power by means of an independent third party. Consequently, the alternative strategy of attempting to gain electoral strength through fusion with the Democrats gathered steam. While Watson led the charge against this strategy, denouncing it as "a trap, a pitfall, a snare, a menace, a fraud" that would kill the movement by stripping it of its radical potential, his efforts proved to be unsuccessful.[76] By 1896, a series of heavily contested state, regional, and national Populist conventions produced the decision to pursue fusion with the Democrats under the banner of free silver. What remained of the badly demoralized movement was absorbed into the campaign to elect Democratic presidential nominee William Jennings Bryan in the upcoming election. Although Bryan's consequent defeat is commonly taken to mark the death of Populism, it had been essentially rendered lifeless beforehand. With its radicalism gone and its independent momentum lost, all that remained was the hollow shell of a formerly vital movement.[77]

The Limits of Progressive Politics

The successive collapses of the Knights of Labor and the Populist movement during the 1880s–1890s marked an important turning point of American political development. With the election of 1896, the political movements that had sustained the republican challenge to the dominance of Darwinian liberalism reached a dead end. Although the subsequent wave of reformist politics represented by the Progressive movement had some important continuities with late nineteenth-century republicanism, it nonetheless represented a severe contraction of the scope of American political life. Three developments were particularly important in this regard: (1) the consolidation of the "solid South," (2) the establishment of the American Federation of Labor (AFL) as the dominant force within the labor movement, and (3) the contraction of the popular bases of electoral politics. Although the causal factors behind each of these developments were complex and continue to be a subject of scholarly debate, it can be said with relative certainty that all were directly connected to the final collapse of republican politics, which was marked by the election of 1896—and, consequently, to the politics of race.

The Solid South

In the South, the force of the successful conservative crusade against Populism merged with the popular reaction to its defeat to produce a violent, reactionary, and rigidly conformist political order organized around the principle of white supremacism. By the turn of the twentieth century, the South was locked into a new system of social, political, and economic relations that was significantly more oppressive than that of the earlier postbellum period.

One of the most important features of this new system was the political disfranchisement of most blacks and many poor whites. As Kousser argues, the wave of legal devices designed to restrict suffrage which swept over the South during 1889–1908—poll taxes, literacy tests, property requirements, "grandfather" clauses, and so on—was primarily driven by elite Conservative Democrats (particularly from the "black belt" counties) who were determined to consolidate their political control in the face of the Populist threat of the 1890s. The logic driving this campaign was quite simple: if most blacks, as well as many lower-class whites, were barred from voting, the possibility of a class-based political insurgency was eliminated.[78]

Tragically if ironically, this conservative-led disfranchisement campaign achieved the success that it did only because it was able to enlist a crucial margin of support from formerly radical whites, who blamed the defeat of Populism on the manipulation of the black vote. Those in favor of disfranchisement argued that the elimination of the black vote would bring an end to corrupt elections by removing an ignorant and easily manipulated class of voters, allowing the white vote to split freely and improving race relations by relegating blacks to their proper place. By framing the issue in this way, the campaign for disfranchisement merged into the larger discourse of Progressive reform and was perversely presented as a "good government" measure. What disfranchisement accomplished, however, was the establishment of a reactionary one-party system that relentlessly repressed the consideration of virtually all important political issues in the name of white racial solidarity while cementing the rule of a small cadre of conservative elites.[79]

This elite crusade for absolute political control constituted the driving force behind the establishment of segregation. Although segregationist practices existed long before the 1890s, they had been nowhere near as systematic—either physically or ideologically—as they would now become. (Remarkably, the term *segregation* itself, as used to indicate a strict system of racial separation, was not in common usage in the United States until after 1890.) The new Jim Crow[80] system spread extremely quickly after 1896, however. By 1915, it had a monolithic grip over almost every imaginable arena of social, political, and economic life in the South. Segregation, like disfranchisement, reinforced the dominance of conservative elites by crushing all politically salient divisions among whites under the overwhelming weight of racial hierarchy. As Cell argues, the "principal function of the segregationist ideology was to soften class and ethnic antagonisms among whites, subordinating internal conflicts to the unifying conception of race."[81] In tandem with disfranchisement and Republican abandonment of the region, Jim Crow cemented a lockhold of conservative Democrats on the South that would not be broken until the mid-1960s.[82]

This situation produced what is commonly referred to as the *solid South*: a one-party system under the firm control of conservative elites. Beyond its regional significance, this development had a profound effect on the shape of national politics. As the Democratic party became dominated by southern conservatives, a de facto arrangement was established whereby the Republican party—which had, in the wake of the 1896 election, become similarly dominated by conservative elites (in this case, large northern business interests)—was acceded control of the presidency as long as the Democrats maintained absolute dominance in the South.[83] In Congress, southern Democrats who were reelected term after term in the absence of any real electoral competition progressively accrued a disproportionate amount of power under the seniority system. The power of this socially conservative southern bloc would subsequently prove to be a major obstacle to progressive reforms during both the New Deal and Great Society eras.

The Politics of Labor

The retrenchment of racial divisions that attended the collapse of republicanism also restricted the scope of political thought and action outside of the South. The deradicalization of the labor movement that took place during this period was particularly significant in this regard. By the turn of the century, an increasingly conservative American Federation of Labor (AFL) rose to a position of unquestioned organizational dominance within the labor movement.[84] In contrast to the Knights, the AFL, by this point in its history, regularly endorsed and practiced systematic racial discrimination.[85] At the same time, it pursed economic and labor market strategies designed to benefit its members exclusively, while rejecting all forms of government regulation over the economy. These polices represented a stunning reversal of the republican politics of the Knights of Labor, which had been dedicated to transforming the national political economy in a way that would help the producing classes as a whole.

By the late 1890s, the AFL not only regularly excluded blacks, Asians, and the new European immigrants from union membership, but justified this policy in terms that mimicked the intensifying racial nationalism of the dominant Darwinian discourse.[86] AFL leaders regularly contrasted the "sturdy, intelligent and liberty-loving races of Northern and Western Europe" with the "servile and degraded hordes of Southern and Eastern Europe." The latter, they argued, were "beaten men of beaten races" with an un-American inclination toward "radical doctrines" that made them undesirable union members.[87] Always rabidly anti-Asian, in 1902 AFL president Samuel Gompers published *Some Reasons for Chinese Exclusion: Meat vs. Rice: American Manhood against Asiatic Coolieism, Which Shall Survive?* This pamphlet explained that "the Yellow Man found it natural to lie, cheat and murder." "Ninety-nine out of every one hundred Chinese are gamblers," Gompers charged. As a race, they lived happily in "vice, filth, and an atmosphere of horror." (This work proved to be so popular that it was reissued in 1908.) In 1906, the AFL argued that Southern and Eastern Europeans and the Chinese should be barred from immigration, as the "maintenance of the nation depended upon [the] maintenance of racial purity" and the barring of "cheap labor that could not be Americanized."[88] Although AFL policy toward blacks was originally more enlightened, by the turn of the century the organization endorsed Jim Crow segregation both within its ranks and more broadly.[89]

This embrace of racial exclusion was matched by a correspondingly conservative commitment to the principles of voluntarism, which rejected virtually all forms of government regulation of the labor market or control over the economy, including protection for collective bargaining, medical and unemployment insurance, and minimum-wage and maximum-hours laws.[90] Consequently, while the AFL became powerful enough to successfully bargain for good working conditions for its members, it opposed any political program that might help workers outside of its ranks.[91] This, in turn, helped to reinforce the development of highly racialized patterns of labor-market segmentation and economic stratification.[92] The ranks of skilled workers were largely limited to native-born white Americans. African Americans and Southern and Eastern European immigrants generally took the less desirable, unskilled positions. During 1890–1914, the wages of skilled workers increased by 74 percent, while those of unskilled workers rose by only 31 percent.[93] Both in the North and in the South, African-American workers faced particularly intense discrimination, as they were forced out of skilled occupations, denied entrance to apprenticeship and training programs, and relegated by organized labor to lower-tier seniority tracks in union contracts.[94]

Electoral Politics

It is commonly agreed that the level of voter participation in national elections declined significantly sometime around the turn of the century. The question of why this decline occurred, however, has been a matter of long-standing controversy. This controversy has centered on the work of Burnham, who argues that the failure of the election of 1896 to establish a winning class-based coalition inaugurated a dramatic shift toward an elite-dominated political system, most prominently characterized by the cultural and material hegemony of corporate capitalism and exceptionally low rates of poor and working-class participation.[95] The most prominent critics of the Burnham thesis—Converse and Rusk—argue, in contrast, that this drop-off in popular participation was due to electoral reforms, such as the introduction of the Australian Ballot and the personal registration system. (The Australian or "official" ballot was issued by the government, rather than by a political party, and listed all candidates together, rather than only those of the issuing party. The personal registration system required that individuals register to vote prior to election day, which allowed their status as voters to be more systematically verified and tracked.) These reforms, they argue, reduced voter turnout by eliminating the corruption, coercion, and fraud that had been previously endemic to late nineteenth-century politics. In so doing, they also established the reign of the more aware and responsible voter, who was willing and able to meet new registration requirements and vote on a more independent and informed basis. (Notably, this argument applies only outside of the South, which both Burnham and his critics view as an exceptional case.)[96]

Although Burnham agrees that these electoral reforms had important effects, he does not believe that they account for the preponderance of the drop-off in voting nor that they were purely beneficial initiatives designed to strengthen the democratic process. Even after the distortions associated with electoral corruption are accounted for, he argues, the full decline in participation which occurred—dropping, for example, from a nonsouthern participation rate of 87.6 percent in the election of 1880 to one of 56.3 percent in 1920—can only be explained in terms of a profound shift that increased popular alienation from the electoral system, lessened party competition, and legitimated the establishment of a significantly contracted political universe.[97] Furthermore, Burnham suggests that this shift, while not simply the product of an elite "conspiracy," was at the same time not wholly unintended: the most powerful forces of Progressive reform were anxious to restrict and control the potential political power of what were seen as the dangerously untutored and volatile masses.

Ironically, Rusk's refutation of the Burnham thesis very much embraces the same sort of elitist assumptions that Burnham critically attributes to the Progressive reformers. Asserting that only the "unenlightened" segment of the electorate dropped out of the system, Rusk contends that the exceptionally low rates of popular participation in twentieth-century American politics are best interpreted as a sign of a healthier and more intelligent democracy. Aside from its elitism, this assertion is impossible to verify, as it would require precisely identifying this group of nonvoters and establishing that the vast majority of them were inherently lazy, corrupt, or otherwise objectionably noncivic-minded.

Regardless of its accuracy in this particular case, this dispute over the meaning of a significantly restricted electoral universe is also one of differing political values. Is it preferable to restrict the power to make electoral decisions to a relatively small group of more elite (but arguably more responsible) voters, or to have it extend to include as much of the adult citizenry as possible? The rise of Progressivism and demise of producer republicanism represented the triumph of the former perspective over the latter. As such, it entailed a significant narrowing of both the aspirations and practices of American liberal democracy.

Race, Class, and Citizenship

These three institutional developments—the creation of the "system of 1896," the expansion of segregation and disfranchisement in the South, and the establishment of the AFL as the key representative of organized labor— effected a dramatic contraction of the scope of American political life, as much of the poor and working classes, as well as most people of color, were effectively shut out of the major centers of political power. In keeping with this development, the cutting edge of reform politics dramatically shifted its primary social location from that of the poor and working classes (which included most people of color) to the middle and professional classes (which were predominantly composed of native-born WASPs) during the opening years of the twentieth century. The significance of this shift is particularly evident when looked at in a comparative perspective: precisely at the time when the foundations of twentieth-century social democracy were being laid in many of the countries of Western Europe, the United States moved decisively toward establishing an elite-dominated politics that would remain essentially closed to comparable political movements.[98]

Although the harshest edges of late nineteenth-century laissez-faire would be significantly sanded down during the subsequent course of the Progressive Era, the variety of racial nationalism which had been established earlier would continue to exert a powerful influence. Although key parts of the Progressive reform movement—such as, in particular, the commitment

to taming the excesses of corporate power through increased public regulation—had important continuities with producer republicanism, the major
political developments of that era nonetheless represented a crucial impov-
erishment of this earlier civic vision. Furthermore, the fact that these developments were consistently charged with a newly intensified current of racial
nationalism meant that if the Darwinian liberalism of the 1880s–1890s had
been in certain respects modified and restrained, its fundamental logic had
been in other ways reinforced. In particular, racial discourse continued to be
constructed in a manner that naturalized the existence of deeply entrenched
patterns of social, economic, and political inequality. Consequently, a relatively narrow definition of citizenship, which endorsed a comparatively high
degree of societal inequality, was even more securely instated as the dominant national norm.

The American Creed represents the national conscience.... From the point of view

of the American Creed the status accorded the Negro in America represents

nothing more and nothing less than a century-long lag of public morals.

—*Gunnar Myrdal,* An American Dilemma, *1944*

5

Postwar Liberalism

The reconfiguration of liberalism and race that occurred in the wake of World War II represented a fundamental shift from the paradigm that had dominated the first Reconstruction and its aftermath. During the 1940s, a new understanding of American liberalism was consolidated that centrally featured a strong, principled stand against racial discrimination. Best exemplified by Gunnar Myrdal's 1944 work, *An American Dilemma*, this position held that such discrimination stood in profound conflict with the most cherished ideals of the American polity. As such, it constituted a landmark rejection of the Darwinian liberalism that had so dominated American racial discourse during the 1870s–1890s. Rather than contending that a supposedly natural system of racial hierarchy dictated the necessity of discrimination and segregation, it argued that such practices violated fundamental American political values. When the national Democratic party embraced this position in the late 1940s (despite intense opposition from its southern wing), it marked the first time that a major political party had taken an antidiscrimination stance since Reconstruction.

Although presenting itself as articulating a long-standing truth, this paradigm in fact represented an important reconfiguration of the meanings of both liberalism and race. With regard to liberalism, this new position maintained the New Deal commitment to an expanded federal role in regulating social and economic activities for what was seen as the common good. Although the push for greater federal involvement in civil rights issues was new, it was in keeping with this larger allegiance to a more activist national government. At the same time, however, postwar liberalism rejected the social democratic interpretations of New Deal liberalism that had been prevalent in the 1930s in favor of a new position that prioritized Cold War anti-Communism and consumer-oriented economic growth. As in the case of nineteenth-century anti-caste liberalism, this meant that its commitment to antidiscrimination was uncoupled from any conception of the more economic dimensions of racial inequality, as well as from any form of class analysis more broadly.

With regard to race, postwar liberalism emphasized a newly simplified black-white binary in conjunction with its strong antidiscrimination stance. In contrast to the belief in a hierarchy of white races and the strong anti-Asian racism that had dominated the late nineteenth and early twentieth centuries, this understanding of race posited a singular white identity and focused almost exclusively on the problem of anti-African racism, particularly as epitomized by the Jim Crow South. This view of race was embedded in the "American dilemma" paradigm, which held that the white majority shared both enduring political values and deeply ingrained anti-African prejudices. Given the claim that these values were logically opposed to discrimination, the case of the "Negro American" was presented as a historical aberration. Race, in this sense, became reduced to the relatively simple and static problem of white prejudice against black Americans.[1]

While inspiring and motivational in many respects, the fact that racial inequality was presented as an issue that plagued the white moral conscience tended to place undue emphasis on the strictly formal aspects of racial discrimination and the ethical intentions of white Americans. In the process, equally important aspects of the problem were written out of consideration. These most notably included (1) the disproportionately negative impact of deindustrialization and labor-market segmentation on the African-American population, (2) the importance of complex discriminatory forces outside of the South and their role in building the walls of the new postwar ghetto, and (3) the beginnings of what would become a politically pivotal reaction against the racial commitments of postwar liberalism among the working- and lower middle-class "white ethnics" of the urban North. Particularly given the rejection of social democratic politics that characterized the larger postwar liberal position, these more structural, class-rooted developments were simply off the radar screen of the postwar liberal mind.

With the benefit of hindsight, it can be seen that postwar liberalism contained an internal contradiction that would sabotage its credibility and potential over time. By making a dramatic, controversial, and highly public commitment to resolving the American dilemma, postwar liberals promoted a vision of American democracy that would prove immensely more difficult to approximate than they realized at the time. Although their concrete commitment was restricted to the simple removal of evident discriminatory barriers (no mean feat in the context of the times), the majesty of their rhetoric promised the achievement of an ethically rejuvenated nation, which would finally be purged of the racial injustices that had blighted even its finest achievements. When, however, the eventual passage of historic antidiscrimination laws instead ushered in a new era of racial division and conflict, the unprepared forces of progressive liberalism went into a tailspin from which they have yet to recover.

The American Dilemma

During the course of the New Deal (roughly 1932–1941), attacks on racial hierarchism became an increasingly important—if still, compared to the postwar period, relatively marginal—part of the political and cultural landscape. Two broad sets of factors were primarily responsible for this change. First, by the mid-1930s, the Great Migration of huge numbers of African Americans from the rural South to the urban North (which had begun in conjunction with World War I) had achieved sufficient mass to provide the northern black population with an unprecedented measure of political clout. Although the vast majority of blacks living in the South remained disfranchised, those in the rest of the country could not only vote, but were increasingly concentrated in areas of strategic importance for national party politics. The newfound significance of the black vote first became evident in the presidential election of 1936, when 76 percent of African Americans abandoned their historic allegiance to the Republican party to support the reelection of Franklin Delano Roosevelt. As the two major parties consequently began to compete for this suddenly important bloc of support, the political climate became more receptive to ideas of racially equalitarian reform.[2]

Broad currents of social thought were also slowly moving in a direction conducive to a shift in mainstream racial ideology. In the intellectual world, a social scientific assault on biological conceptions of racial hierarchy had become relatively well established by the late 1920s, and it continued to grow steadily more influential thereafter. (Notably, scholars who were members of the European immigrant groups that had been themselves widely attacked as racial inferiors largely spearheaded this movement.) At the same time, the devastating experience of the Great Depression powerfully undermined the belief that social status was naturally determined, which indirectly worked to erode previously sacrosanct notions of racial hierarchy.[3]

These broad political and cultural trends intensified during World War II and the immediate postwar years. During the course of the 1940s, the number of African Americans living outside the South jumped from 2.36 million to 4.6 million, an increase of almost 100 percent. This demographic shift increased the power of the black vote, which proved critical to Democratic victories in the presidential elections of 1944 and 1948. At the same time, the onset of the war-generated economic boom and the resultant labor shortage increased the general level of affluence among a significant percentage of the black population. The resultant increase in resources available for political action, combined with the geographic proximity produced by urbanization, enhanced both the existing and potential clout of the African-American community.[4]

Culturally, the widespread reaction against the genocidal anti-Semitism of Nazi Germany further discredited the legitimacy of biological racism. Both in Europe and the United States, this horrifying encounter with extreme racism caused many political, cultural, and intellectual leaders, as well as ordinary citizens, to reject the formerly acceptable view that racial hierarchy was both natural and desirable. The onset of the Cold War in the late 1940s provided another powerful impetus away from ideologies of racial hierarchism, as the Soviet propaganda mill began churning out embarrassingly accurate portraits of state-sanctioned racial discrimination in the self-proclaimed home of freedom and democracy. With the international spotlight now fixed upon the United States as a uniquely wealthy and powerful nation, such attacks found a wide global audience. Not surprisingly, many American political and intellectual leaders came to believe that the nation's racial situation represented a significant political liability in the new postwar world order.[5]

Against this backdrop, the publication of *An American Dilemma* in 1944 marked an important political and cultural development of its own. Appearing at an exceptionally receptive historical moment, Myrdal's book provided a new framework for understanding racial issues that quickly became a defining feature of a newly emerging postwar liberal position. As Myrdal explained in his opening chapter, his central claim was that the "American Negro problem is a problem in the heart of the American":

Though our study includes economic, social, and political race relations, *at bottom our problem is the moral dilemma of the American.* . . . The "American Dilemma," referred to in the title of this book, is the ever-raging conflict between, on the one hand, the valuations preserved on the general plane which we shall call the "American Creed" . . . and, on the other hand, the valuations on specific planes of individual and group living. . . . The subordinate position of Negroes is perhaps the most glaring conflict in the American conscience and the greatest unsolved task for American democracy.

"The liberal Creed," Myrdal proclaimed, "is adhered to by every American."[6] Consequently, Myrdal argued, the most effective way to solve the American dilemma was to expose the moral gap between America's liberal precepts and racial practices and thereby inspire the nation to take corrective action.

In the years following the publication of *An American Dilemma*, its thesis was popularized by a variety of influential elites. Northern journalists and writers received the book warmly and enhanced its prominence by publishing numerous favorable reviews in national magazines and major regional newspapers.[7] Some of the most influential public intellectuals of the time similarly endorsed Myrdal's position. For example, *The Vital Center* (1949)—a widely acclaimed work by Arthur Schlesinger, Jr.—asserted that the "sin of racial pride still represents the most basic challenge to the American conscience. We cannot dodge this challenge without renouncing our highest moral principles."[8]

As this new racial position gathered cultural momentum and moved further into the political mainstream, it became attached to an important new set of proposed reforms that promised to disrupt the racial status quo in a way that had not been seriously contemplated by powerful white elites since the days of Reconstruction. This new institutional agenda began to consolidate in 1946 when President Harry Truman established a special Committee on Civil Rights that included a number of prominent business, labor, political, and civic leaders. The following year, this committee issued a book-length report, *To Secure These Rights*, which recommended that the federal government prohibit racial discrimination and segregation in public education, employment, voting, housing, the military, public accommodations, and interstate transportation. In February 1948, Truman sent a special civil rights message to Congress endorsing these recommendations and requesting immediate action to abolish the poll tax, establish lynching as a federal crime, reduce discrimination in employment, and prohibit segregation in interstate commerce. Soon afterward, the reformist wing of the Democratic party—after a bitter fight with the militantly hostile southern faction and a group of cowed moderates led by Truman himself—succeeded in inserting a strong civil rights plank into the Democratic platform in the presidential election of 1948. With this development, it was evident that an important new form of racial ideology had emerged as a major presence in mainstream American politics.[9]

Concrete proposals for racial reform were regularly framed in terms of the moralistic position symbolized by *An American Dilemma*. *To Secure These Rights*, for example, stated:

> We need no further justification for a broad and immediate [civil rights] program than the need to reaffirm our faith in the traditional American morality. The pervasive gap between our aims and what we actually do is creating a kind of moral dry rot which eats away at the emotional and rational bases of democratic beliefs. . . . *The United States can no longer countenance these burdens on its common conscience, these inroads on its moral fiber.*[10]

President Truman repeated this injunction in his 1948 message to Congress, stating that "there is a serious gap between our ideals and some of our practices. This gap must be closed."[11] Similarly, a review of *To Secure These Rights* published in the *New Republic* in 1947 endorsed its recommendations by proclaiming: "For those who cherish liberty, freedom and forbearance . . . here is a noble reaffirmation of the principles that made America."[12]

The Rejection of Class Politics

This newfound dedication to eradicating racial discrimination from American life represented a defining characteristic of postwar liberalism. This novel form of liberal discourse was also marked, however, by another set of commitments that constituted a distinct break with the left-liberal politics of the 1930s and early 1940s. Most prominently, these included a fierce opposition to Communism and a corresponding mistrust of class-based politics and rejection of social democratic interpretations of the New Deal legacy. (*Social democracy* is here used to refer to the belief that a primary role of government is to counteract the socioeconomic inequities created by a capitalist economy.) Although it was not recognized at the time, these closely related tendencies played an important role in both creating and obscuring important socioeconomic developments that had a disproportionately negative effect on the African-American population.

From the 1930s through the early 1940s, the main currents of left-of-center liberalism had differed significantly from this postwar model. Issues of racial equity were not emphasized, as it was widely believed that such matters were best handled indirectly, by means of the universal benefits of New Deal policies for lower-income groups.[13] At the same time, broad questions of political economy had remained contested. Many public intellectuals, including John Dewey, and leaders of the newly powerful labor movement urged moving beyond the New Deal to some indigenous form of social democracy. Many political observers interpreted FDR's 1936 reelection campaign, which railed against "economic royalists" and the disgrace of "one-third of a nation ill-housed, ill-clothed, and ill-fed," as a sign that the New Deal was moving in just such a direction. This tendency seemed to be further reinforced by the formation of the Congress of Industrial Organizations (CIO) that same year. Representing a powerful new alternative to the relatively conservative AFL, the leadership of the CIO was also strongly oriented toward social democracy.[14]

During the late 1940s, however, this vision of a more social democratic form of New Deal politics was eclipsed. Four factors most powerfully account for this change: (1) the power of the conservative congressional bloc that had emerged in the mid-1930s, (2) the failure of the CIO to expand its political influence during the mid- to late 1940s, (3) the emergence of the Cold War, and (4) the political and cultural effects of the postwar economic boom. Notably, racial politics played a decisive role in the first two of these factors. As such, race represented an important, although by no means determinative, role in producing the shift from a more broadly social democratic to a more narrowly reformist form of left-of-center liberal politics.

The conservative congressional bloc that emerged in the mid-1930s was composed of two groups: southern Democrats who opposed any extension of federal power capable of disrupting the white supremacist status quo and conservative Republicans who opposed a strong federal government both as a matter of long-standing principle and because of its potentially negative effects on big business. (Notably, this alliance paralleled the basic political arrangement that had emerged with the collapse of Reconstruction.) This powerful coalition was successful in blocking or severely circumscribing proposed social programs favorable to labor, small farmers, low-income urban dwellers, and blacks during the late 1930s. In addition, it was able to roll back important New Deal social reforms during and immediately after World War II.[15]

At the same time, southern racial politics posed an enormous obstacle to the further expansion and strengthening of the labor movement. In mid-1946, the CIO, hoping to break the power of the southern Democrats, launched Operation Dixie, an all-out drive to unionize the South. Despite some initial gains during 1946–1947, however, Operation Dixie was not able to overcome the formidable combination of a vociferously opposed white power structure and a racially divided working class, and it quickly proved to be a complete failure.[16] Coming on the heels of the defeat of the Full Employment Bill of 1945 and the passage of the Taft-Hartley Act in 1947, this represented a tremendous political setback for the CIO and worked to push the labor movement in an increasingly conservative direction.

During the same period, the onset of the Cold War drove a sharp wedge between New Deal liberals, who became intensely committed to a strong anti-Communist position, and other left-of-center forces with whom they had formerly been allied. From the mid-1930s through the mid-1940s, the politics of the Popular Front, which was dedicated to maintaining a progressive alliance against fascism, had allowed for an exceptional degree of cooperation among Communists, liberals, and social democrats. By 1946, however, growing tensions between the United States and the U.S.S.R. were creating a rift within this alliance. By 1948, this division mushroomed into an open contest between liberals, who refused to have anything further to do with Communists, and other progressives, who favored maintaining the old Popular Front position. In that year's presidential election, Popular Front loyalists broke with the Democratic party to support Progressive party candidate Henry Wallace. His predictable defeat in favor of Harry S. Truman signaled the consolidation of a new form of liberalism that remained committed to New Deal reformism but rejected its more radical, social democratic interpretations.[17]

The final factor that reinforced the political standing of this new position was the newfound affluence of the postwar period. Growing prosperity widely discredited the progressive position that it was important to have socially directed governmental interference in the capitalist market.[18] During the late 1940s, it became clear that much of the American population was enjoying a tremendous jump in socioeconomic status. In 1936, for example, 68 percent of the overall population had been poor, while only 13 percent qualified as middle class. By 1947, however, those numbers had shifted to 37 percent poor and 29 percent middle class. (By 1960, the trend went further to 23 percent poor and 47 percent middle class.) Given this historic expansion of the middle class, politics and policies that prioritized reducing economic inequities by improving the situation of lower-income Americans seemed to many postwar liberals to be simply unnecessary.[19]

Hidden Costs of Postwar Liberalism

This wholesale rejection of a social democratic orientation to the New Deal was implicated in a number of highly problematic social developments that were not recognized at the time. Most critically, it inadvertently helped to create the conditions under which the lower to middle classes became increasingly divided into a securely employed, well-paid, and widely unionized sector, on the one hand, and a much more marginally employed, poorly paid, and nonunionized sector on the other. Not surprisingly, African Americans (and other marginalized populations, such as small farmers and members of female-headed households) were disproportionately represented in the latter group.

Although the shift from an industrial economy dominated by manufacturing jobs to a postindustrial economy dominated by service sector employment is commonly thought to have begun during the 1970s, historical analysis demonstrates that it can be dated back to the 1950s. Sugrue, for example, calculates that between 1947 and 1963, Detroit lost 134,000 manufacturing jobs, despite an increase in the number of working-aged men and women living there. African Americans were particularly hard hit by this development. By 1960, for example, 15.9 percent of blacks, compared to 5.8 percent of whites, were out of work in that city.[20] Although few political commentators remarked on it at the time, a new class of discouraged workers, disproportionately composed of African-American men suffering from the effects of long-term unemployment, was becoming a permanent fixture of life in American cities.[21]

The negative effects of deindustrialization on the more vulnerable segments of the working and lower classes were reinforced by concurrent developments in the labor movement. Beginning in the mid-1940s, American labor lost its broad social democratic vision, beginning instead to pursue a much more narrow form of interest-group politics.[22] As organized labor entered into an era of accommodation with major American corporations (which would last until the mid-1970s), it abandoned its ambition of leveraging national economic planning to achieve social goals in favor of the narrower project of securing high wages and good benefits for union members. In the process, key social welfare provisions, such as pensions and health insurance, became privatized goods available only to those fortunate enough to have the right sort of job. Consequently, American labor became increasingly divided into an elite, unionized class that (for a time) enjoyed a high level of wages and social provisions and a larger substratum that lacked such benefits and protections.[23]

The new direction for federal policy adopted by postwar liberals further exacerbated the growing socioeconomic divisions produced by deindustrialization and labor-market segmentation. As noted above, the onset of the Cold War had precipitated a fierce anti-Communist reaction, breaking the wartime alliance between liberals and other left-of-center forces. To a large extent, this development represented a wholly justified response to the horrors of Stalinist totalitarianism and the antidemocratic proclivities of Communists at home. At the same time, however, it all too easily turned into an undifferentiated hostility toward anything that smacked of left-wing radicalism, including forms of class-based and social democratic politics that were not incompatible with an expansive conception of liberalism.[24]

In the realm of public policy, these tendencies most notably manifested themselves in the shift from what Skocpol refers to as social to commercial Keynesianism.[25] While the former prioritized the attainment of full employment and the integration of macroeconomic planning and social welfare goals, the latter was committed to promoting national prosperity via policies designed to spur mass production and mass consumption. The achievement of a booming consumer economy, in other words, replaced the vision of a more equitable society. Political attention was consequently directed away from the growing problems affecting the lower- to working-class populations—including its African-American members—caused by the onset of deindustrialization in an increasingly divided labor market. Coming on top of the establishment of a two-tiered social welfare system that similarly had a disproportionately negative impact on blacks, this development substantially reinforced the socioeconomic bases of racial inequality during the postwar period.[26]

The Postwar Ghetto

In addition to being disproportionately hard hit by these socioeconomic trends, African Americans were also targeted by a wide array of discriminatory practices. The interactive effects of employment discrimination and residential segregation were particularly damaging to this population. The black ghettos created in the 1950s were the largest and most racially isolated and contained the highest concentrations of poverty in American history. Because they were primarily located in the urban centers of the North and West—far away from the Jim Crow South that represented the American dilemma in the eyes of postwar liberals—these ghettos remained outside of the purview of national political attention until the eruption of the Watts riots in 1965.

Rampant employment discrimination contributed tremendously to the development of the postwar ghetto by exponentially intensifying the broader problems of deindustrialization and labor-market segmentation. Although such practices would eventually be greatly ameliorated by the passage of the Civil Rights Act of 1964, they remained largely unconstrained (despite the passage of numerous state-level antidiscrimination laws outside of the South) up to that time. A 1961 study of employment practices in the Chicago metropolitan area conducted by the Urban League, for example, found that the types of jobs that blacks were allowed to perform in those industries that employed large numbers of nonwhites were "severely restricted." Similarly, a survey conducted by the Bureau of Jewish Employment Problems of Chicago during that same year reported that "98 percent of the white collar job orders received from over 5,000 companies were not available to qualified Negroes." Industries judged to "seriously limit" the employment of nonwhites included banking and finance, insurance, air transport, electrical equipment manufacturing, printing and publishing, chemicals and petroleum, railroads and trucking, medical and health services, and construction.[27]

In his study of postwar Detroit, Sugrue documents the many processes through which African Americans were overwhelmingly confined to "the meanest and dirtiest jobs."[28] Discrimination was rampant in all of the city's major employment sectors, including the automotive, steel, chemical, machine tool, and brewing industries; municipal employment; retail sales; the building trades; and the casual labor market. Sugrue emphasizes that while this discrimination was at times the product of simple, intentional racial animosity, it was more commonly the result of much more complex processes involving such diverse factors as hiring procedures, apprenticeship systems, seniority rules, employer cost cutting, employee kinship and friendship networks, the desire to maximize worker camaraderie, and union procedures.[29] The postwar liberal understanding of racial discrimination as a simple case of intentional wrongdoing was not equipped to perceive the complexity of this problem.

This was even more true with regard to what was quickly becoming the greatest obstacle to the achievement of racial equity in American society, that is, the institutionalization of the inner-city ghetto. While many ethnic and racial groups had experienced ghettoization in the past, the postwar African-American ghetto was a new phenomenon. In particular, its high levels of racial segregation and economic marginalization made it different from all comparable predecessors. The postwar ghetto was significantly more racially homogeneous, for example, than ethnic neighborhoods composed of European immigrants had ever been.[30] At the same time, the loss of good working-class jobs in the nation's central cities coupled with ghetto residents' inability to follow new employment opportunities out to the suburbs to create a growing class of working-aged men with little or no connection to the mainstream labor market.[31]

The racial makeup of the nation's metropolitan areas was changing dramatically during the 1950s. Most critically, the suburbs were rapidly expanding and becoming largely white, while the central cities were declining and becoming increasingly black. Social forces encouraging suburbanization included the onset of the postwar baby boom, the tremendous growth of the (largely white) middle class, the construction of the federal highway system, the decentralization of business and industry prompted by deindustrialization, and the increased affordability of mortgages provided by the Federal Housing Administration (FHA) and Veterans Administration (VA) programs. In 1940, only one-third of metropolitan residents were suburbanites. By 1970, they numbered over 50 percent.[32]

Concurrently, during the 1950s–1960s, the percentage of African Americans living in large northern cities more than doubled, growing from 14 to 33 percent in Chicago; 16 to 38 percent in Cleveland; 16 to 44 percent in Detroit; and 18 to 34 percent in Philadelphia. All in all, 1.5 million blacks left the South during the 1950s, with another 1.4 million following during the 1960s. Given, however, the intensity of discriminatory forces, the overwhelming majority of these northern migrants were forced into existing African-American ghettos, which quickly became overcrowded to the point where they were literally bursting at the seams. This in turn set off a process of rapid neighborhood transformation, as blacks sought better housing in less overstressed areas, and panicked whites—spurred on by unscrupulous real estate dealers looking to buy low, sell or rent high, and make a quick buck—fled the neighborhood. In the process, the levels of African-American racial isolation (that is, the percentage of blacks in a given city who lived in racially homogeneous neighborhoods) increased dramatically in northern cities, rising, on average, from 32 percent in 1930 to 74 percent in 1970.[33]

This growth of residential segregation was not the result of freely made choices on the part of blacks, who have consistently indicated a preference for racially integrated neighborhoods in public opinion polls. On the contrary, a combination of both public and private forces propelled this development. Redlining, which officially designated nonwhite or racially changing neighborhoods as poor mortgage risks, represented one of the most devastating government-supported factors, as it deprived black families of the financing necessary to achieve homeownership. From its beginning in the 1930s under the auspices of the Home Owner's Loan Corporation

(HOLC), federal redlining continued to shape the lending practices of the FHA and VA programs during the 1940s and 1950s. To make matters worse, these federal procedures were widely followed by private banks, which consequently refused to invest in black neighborhoods. It is no exaggeration to say that the federal government shut African Americans out of the historic suburban housing boom—while encouraging the deterioration of urban black neighborhoods—by depriving them of the opportunity to become homeowners.[34]

During the 1940s–1950s, federally sponsored "urban renewal" programs also played a major role in the development of the postwar ghetto. Although this was not the intention of the federal bureaucrats who designed these programs—many were deeply committed to the achievement of a more equitable housing market—it was the most common result, as local political forces channeled federal monies into projects that reinforced the racial status quo. In Chicago, for example, the combined forces of white city residents determined to keep blacks out of their neighborhoods, powerful business interests who wanted to move them out of the way of downtown expansion, and university administrators dedicated to holding back the expanding ghetto from their campus turned the Chicago Housing Authority into an active promoter of residential segregation. Urban renewal initiatives were consequently perverted into disastrous developments, such as the building of the Robert Taylor Homes, which crammed 27,000 low-income blacks into twenty-eight identical sixteen-story "projects" intentionally isolated from the rest of the city by their location next to railroad tracks and a major expressway.[35]

The violent resistance of white urban residents to any influx of blacks into their neighborhoods represented one of the most powerful private forces contributing to the development of the postwar ghetto. These violent incidents were generally not publicized in the mainstream newspapers of that time. (Black papers had much more extensive coverage.) As a result, they were not common public knowledge. Historical research has demonstrated, however, that they were frequent occurrences. Hirsch, for example, documents that during the late 1940s, one racially motivated bombing or arson attack occurred every twenty days in Chicago.

In contrast to the now-familiar images of black urban rioters (from Watts in 1965 to Los Angeles in 1992), these violent incidents consistently involved white attacks on black people and their property. All members of the white community were involved. While young males were predictably at the forefront of the physical violence, older men and women of all ages actively supported them. Mostly children and grandchildren of the Southern and Eastern European immigrants of the late nineteenth century, these predominately Catholic, working-class residents of racially threatened urban neighborhoods either could not afford to flee to the suburbs or did not want to, given the tightly knit nature of their ethnically based communities. Consequently, in contrast to most WASPs and Jews, they stood their ground and fought to defend what they saw as their rights, way of life, and bases of economic security.[36]

With ever-increasing numbers of poor black migrants from the South confined to racially segregated neighborhoods, largely excluded from sources of capital investment, and steadily losing their most lucrative sources of employment, ghetto conditions deteriorated further. Those with the means, talent, or luck to escape increasingly did so, taking their resources, skills, and sense of personal optimism with them. Black communities became more and more internally segregated by class, as the more affluent sought to protect themselves and their families from the growing problems of the ghetto by establishing their own, economically exclusive enclaves.[37] As a result, the economic marginalization of ghetto residents intensified further. By the early 1960s, many young people in cities such as Detroit were angry, alienated, and increasingly ready to turn to criminal activity as a replacement for legitimate work.[38] A downward spiral had begun in which the forces of deindustrialization and discrimination produced a reaction that intensified the marginality of ghetto communities further. It would only get worse during the coming decades.

Race, Class, and Ethnicity

Postwar liberals were oblivious to the existence, let alone the significance, of these urban developments. African Americans, they believed, would follow the pattern of previous generations of European immigrants and move quickly into the social, political, and economic mainstream once obvious discriminatory barriers were removed. Despite good intentions, they remained ignorant of the more complex discriminatory forces that were creating a nationwide ghetto system, whose unprecedented degree of segregation and economic marginalization would prove to be a seemingly insurmountable obstacle to this assimilationist goal. Similarly, they were not aware that the increased presence of African Americans in northern cities was generating a tremendous political reaction in many white, working-class neighborhoods, where residents were literally fighting to keep them out. Although it was not evident at the time, this development would prove central to the later demise of postwar liberalism, as it represented the beginnings of the "white backlash" that would, beginning in the late 1960s, serve as the linchpin for the undoing of the historic New Deal coalition, which had successfully united small farmers, labor unions, African Americans, white ethnics,[39] and business interests supportive of Keynesian economic policies.[40]

As noted above, violent reaction to the influx of black residents was primarily located in white, working-class Catholic neighborhoods, whose residents were the children and grandchildren of the Southern and Eastern European immigrants of the late nineteenth century. These immigrants had themselves experienced racial animosity in the past, being derided and discriminated against by native-born whites who labeled them as members of inferior races. This negative racial designation faded, however, during the 1930s–1940s. (By the 1950s, it had been effectively erased from the common national memory.) In this process, members of these groups became rechristened as "ethnics"—or, more simply, as "whites." Although the causal factors that account for this change have yet to be adequately theorized, contributing factors most likely include the reduction in Southern and Eastern European immigration produced by the Johnson-Reed Act of 1924, the rise in northern black political leverage that helped to propel the black civil rights issue forward, the postwar reaction against biological racism, and the improved political and social standing of these former immigrant groups occasioned by New Deal policies and the postwar economic boom.[41]

In the urban working-class neighborhoods that were engaged in systematic antiblack warfare, the designation "white" was proudly and forcefully claimed. Adopting the same equation between whiteness and Americanness that had formerly been used to exclude their parents and grandparents from a full measure of citizenship, members of these communities asserted their rights as respectable white citizens against the presumed degeneracy of blacks. "White people built this area [and] we want no part of this race mixing," stated one community newspaper in Chicago during the 1950s. "Race pride has come to the fore as a new set of values." The immigrant experience was held up as an example that blacks should emulate. "The foreigners . . . built this country," stated another article, "making it what it is through their many varied experiences. They are not tearing down—they raise families, buy homes, beautify their little neighborhood[s]. Can the negro compare with that?"[42]

The newly established whiteness of these former immigrant groups was a complex matter, however. To a significant extent, it was true that a common white identity had supplanted the European national identities of their past. Certainly, this new identity was highly evident in the urban racial confrontations of the mid-1940s to mid-1950s, which consistently pitted a unified front of diverse ethnic groups against what was seen as a common African-American enemy.[43] At the same time, however, these freshly minted white ethnics continued to occupy a different social position from the WASPs, whose ancestors had labeled their forbearers as racial inferiors.

Most significantly, white ethnics remained in a relatively precarious social and economic position. As new entrants into the stable working or lower-middle classes, most had poured all of their available income into buying and improving modest homes, and had no other resources to fall back on. While less hard hit by the impact of the early phases of deindustrialization than were blacks, they were similarly vulnerable to the loss of good working-class jobs that it entailed. As a result, their racial identity, while framed in the nationalistic language of Americanness, in fact had a sharp class edge. Their animosity toward blacks was heavily fueled by the fear of losing their anchor in respectable society and falling back into their former status as stigmatized and impoverished foreigners.

Both economically and ideologically, the homes of these white ethnic groups represented the measure of two or three generations of hard work and achievement. As such, their drive to protect them was fierce. Further, given the larger social and economic dynamics at play, their fears that racial transition would drastically reduce the value of their homes were realistic: it happened many times in many such neighborhoods across the country. While well-crafted public policies could have arguably intervened in this process and encouraged the growth of more economically stable, racially integrated neighborhoods, no such policies were in place. Instead, working- and lower middle-class white ethnics commonly blamed blacks for both the real and imagined problems that were threatening their security. In the process, old tropes of racial hatred and stigmatization were infused with yet another set of meanings.

Although many whites of all social stations openly supported residential segregation, their views were sharply divided along class lines. A 1951 survey of white residents of Detroit, for example, found that 85 percent of poor and working-class whites supported residential segregation. These numbers declined to 56 percent of middle-income and 42 percent of upper-income whites.[44] To the extent that lower- and upper-status whites were aware of such differences in racial opinion, they explained them in mutually unsympathetic terms. Battles over "urban renewal" in Chicago during the 1950s, for example, demonstrated that white elites commonly derided the working-class whites who violently opposed neighborhood racial change as "irrational," "ignorant," or "dupes of bigots." White ethnics, in turn, dismissed these elites as "so-called intellectuals" who were "sick in mind and spirit," or "perverted people" who were impervious to reason.[45]

Different ideological commitments and social positions supported such name calling. Postwar liberals believed that anti-African discrimination represented the preeminent moral dilemma facing the nation, as it conflicted with the fundamental principles of American liberalism. As they assumed that all citizens shared these political values, they reasoned that discriminatory attitudes could be eradicated with sufficient rousing of the latent white moral conscience. While in many respects a force for progressive racial change, such an understanding of the dynamics of racial division had profound blind spots as well. Certainly, it did not allow for the very real possibility that other Americans did not share the same understanding of liberal values that it pronounced. Even more problematically, it failed to consider how more impersonal, social structural forces could encourage the development of different conceptions of the "race problem." Particularly given that all forms of class analysis had been abandoned back in the 1940s, postwar liberals were ideologically unequipped to perceive the world view of the working-class white ethnics, who would increasingly come to despise them.

This ideological divide was reinforced by the different social positions that these two groups occupied. The liberals who were the strongest advocates of antidiscrimination measures were disproportionately members of the professional class. As such, they generally lived in prosperous and secure neighborhoods far from the problems of the expanding black ghetto. Working- and lower middle-class white ethnics, in contrast, commonly lived in much more economically precarious enclaves that were very close, if not adjacent, to it. Consequently, they quite justifiably believed that these liberal elites would not be adversely affected by the enactment of the antidiscrimination policies that they advocated. White ethnics resented the fact that while they had to cope with the day-to-day problems produced by living in close proximity to the growing social problems of the ghetto, the elites who were pushing antidiscrimination laws did not. This disparity was the source of tremendous class-based hostility and resentment.

The Coming Crisis of Postwar Liberalism

The new form of liberalism that emerged during the immediate post–World War II period was centrally defined by its commitments to solving the American dilemma through the establishment of federal antidiscrimination laws and to promoting the prosperity of the nation via Keynesian policies designed to stimulate a robust consumer economy.[46] While its strong stance against racial discrimination represented a tremendously important political development—the likes of which had not been seen in a major political party since the time of Reconstruction—it also embodied certain critical blind spots that would, in time, prove enormously problematic. In particular, postwar liberals were overwhelmingly oblivious to (1) the ways in which labor-market segmentation and deindustrialization were contributing to the development of new forms of socioeconomic inequality, which had a particularly negative impact on the black population, (2) the importance of complex forms of discrimination outside of the South, particularly with regard to employment and housing, (3) the development of a system of ghettoization in the urban North unprecedented in scope and intensity, and (4) the fierce reaction of the newly christened white ethnics to the threat of black entry into their neighborhoods and the growing class-based resentment against liberal elites that this entailed.

The cultural and political commitments of postwar liberals prevented them from even beginning to grasp the importance of these trends. While conceiving of racial discrimination as a problem of the white moral conscience undoubtedly provided many liberals with an important sense of urgency and legitimacy, it also concentrated attention on purely intentional forms of discrimination, rather than those that emerged out of the convergence of more impersonal, social structural factors. This tendency to ignore the structural aspects of racial inequality was reinforced by the rejection of class-based politics, including the influential social democratic interpretations of the New Deal that had existed from the mid-1930s to the mid-1940s. This blindness with regard to the interactive dynamics of race, class, and related social structural developments provided postwar liberals with no lens through which they could understand the growing patterns of racial stratification and class division that were transforming the country. This conceptual void allowed postwar liberals to develop tremendous optimism regarding what the enactment of basic antidiscrimination laws would accomplish. Those who did not revise their views were left wholly unprepared for the new forms of racial politics that would explode into crisis beginning in the mid-1960s.

A dream of equality of opportunity, of privilege and property widely distributed; a dream of a land where men will not take necessities from the many to give luxuries to the few; a dream of a land where men will not argue that the color of a man's skin determines the content of his character; a dream of a nation where all our gifts and resources are held not for ourselves alone but as instruments of service for the rest of humanity; the dream of a country where every man will respect the dignity and worth of human personality—that is the dream.

—Martin Luther King, Jr., "If the Negro Wins, Labor Wins," 1961

6

Race, Class, and the Civil Rights Movement

In contrast to postwar liberalism, whose racial agenda was limited to the relatively simple program of prohibiting overt discrimination in critical areas such as education and employment, the Civil Rights movement embodied a highly ambitious, even visionary political agenda, which reached far beyond this important but far from all-encompassing goal. This was true from even the earliest days of the movement, which are commonly defined as spanning the years between the beginning of the Montgomery bus boycott in 1955 to the passage of the Civil Rights acts of 1964–1965. Although the practical activities of the movement during this period remained targeted on the immediate problem of ending the reign of Jim Crow segregation in the South, the larger political program that it articulated aimed at nothing less than the realization of a more truly democratic America. The twin pillars of this program were an extensive attack on specific problems of racial inequality and a commitment to a broader set of social democratic policies designed to improve the position of all lower- and middle-income Americans.[1] These two goals were considered inseparable, as movement leaders recognized that many of the most serious problems facing the African-American population were fundamentally economic in nature. The repercussions of what was commonly referred to as "automation," they believed, while affecting the black population most severely, were having a negative impact on lower-income Americans as a whole.[2]

Movement activists held that a positive transformation of the personal and political consciousness of ordinary African Americans was the necessary first step in building a viable political movement capable of realizing these goals. After generations of racist assault, they believed, African Americans were all too often unable to embrace their racial identity with a healthy sense of self-worth. Reversing this damaging situation, it was hoped, would spur a parallel transformation of white consciousness, prompting the common realization that racism limited the development of the full humanity of its perpetuators, as well as its targets. This, in turn, would allow the movement to expand its scope of influence and serve as the driving force behind the creation of a newly powerful progressive coalition. This coalition, in turn, would provide the momentum necessary to leverage the achievement of an unprecedented measure of racial and class equity in the United States.[3]

In contrast to the presumptions of postwar liberalism, activists involved with the early Civil Rights movement believed that segregation and discrimination were not simply southern problems but were prevalent throughout the nation. These problems were viewed as being so entrenched in mainstream society and varied and complex in their forms that their simple legal prohibition—while certainly extremely important—would prove insufficient to address them. Consequently, movement leaders proposed a variety of compensatory race-conscious policies, including, quite commonly, affirmative action, particularly with regard to employment opportunities. Although the vast majority of movement leaders supported the goal of affirmative action, some—such as, most notably, Bayard Rustin—opposed it on the grounds that it would impede the movement's ability to develop a strong interracial coalition.

By the time of the passage of the Civil Rights Act of 1964, both the ambitious policy agenda and transformative vision of the Civil Rights movement were generating substantial controversy among outside observers. Postwar liberals believed that the legal prohibition of discrimination would be sufficient to address problems of racial inequality and were unaware of the importance of more complex factors, such as diminishing employment opportunities and ghettoization. Consequently, when it became clear that the Civil Rights movement was pursuing a significantly more expansive agenda, a rift began to develop between the more radical liberals, who supported it, and the more moderate ones, who did not. Commonly described at the time as a new and growing split between "white liberals" and the "Negro movement," this division represented a fundamental disagreement over whether it was better to stick with the individualistic legalism of the postwar liberal position or to adopt the new forms of race and class consciousness represented by the Civil Rights movement. There was, in other words, a basic split between the political world view of the movement and that of more mainstream liberals, who supported an end to Jim Crow but rejected the call for a more transformative democratic agenda.

The "New Negro"

Today, it is commonly claimed that the early Civil Rights movement was committed to a "color-blind" position that rejected all considerations of racial consciousness as inherently reactionary and un-American.[4] This perception is grossly oversimplistic and essentially incorrect. Although it is certainly true that the movement rejected both the ideology and practice of white supremacy and embraced a racially transcendent vision of democratic community, issues of racial identity nonetheless played a centrally important role in both its generation and development. This section focuses on the importance of such issues in developing the sense of political empowerment that made the movement possible; subsequent sections focus on their significance in the development of its more substantive political agenda.

The Civil Rights movement could never have gotten off the ground if a widespread sense of political empowerment had not been rekindled among ordinary black people in the South.[5] Issues of racial consciousness and identity were critically important to the early movement, which understood that the goal of empowering blacks as individuals was inseparably linked to that of empowering them as a group.[6] This is not to say that the movement rejected the classically liberal goal of individual emancipation, favored a racially separatist agenda, or embraced an ideology of racial essentialism. On the contrary, it was clearly committed to liberal individualism, racial integration, and the self-directed transformation of racially defined groups. The key point, however, is that these goals were furthered, rather than contradicted, by the development of new forms of African-American identity.

During the mid- to late 1950s, issues of racial consciousness were symbolically encapsulated in the term "the new Negro."[7] To take the most notable example, Dr. Martin Luther King, Jr.—widely acknowledged as the preeminent leader of the Civil Rights movement—regularly reiterated that neither the meaning nor significance of the movement could be understood without recognizing the transformation in black consciousness that it embodied. In a speech delivered to the NAACP Legal Defense and Education Fund in 1956, King asserted that the "tension which we are witnessing in race relations in the South today is to be explained in part by the revolutionary change in the Negro's evaluation of himself. . . . You cannot understand the bus protest in Montgomery without understanding that there is a New Negro in the South."[8] Similarly, in an article published in *Liberation* in 1956, he wrote:

> *We Negroes have replaced self-pity with self-respect and self-depreciation with dignity.* . . . our nonviolent protest in Montgomery is important because it is demonstrating to the Negro, North and South, that many of the stereotypes he has held about himself and other Negroes are not valid. Montgomery has broken the spell and is ushering in concrete manifestations of the thinking and action of the new Negro.[9]

Likewise, King's *Stride toward Freedom: The Montgomery Story* (1958) asserted that "growing self-respect has inspired the Negro with a new determination to struggle and sacrifice until first-class citizenship becomes a reality. This is the true meaning of the Montgomery Story."[10]

Such assertions of a transformed "Negro" identity were not casually made. On the contrary, as Morris documents, they were representative of a larger, deliberate strategy on the part of the Southern Christian Leadership Conference (SCLC)[11] to change the consciousness and therefore the political efficacy of ordinary black people in the South. One internal SCLC document written in 1958 explained that the organization aimed to be "penetrating each community, reaching the man on the streets . . . to break through the oppressive system of discrimination and oppression, change his surroundings and his oppressors, and make a new person." Another SCLC document written in 1959 stated:

> [M]any Negroes of the South have developed, not simply an indifference or apathy toward voting, but a strong fear and a deep antipathy toward having anything to do with politics. These fears and misconceptions of the Negro in regards to politics must be overcome. . . . his thought patterns must be changed by an effective crusade to inform, impress and recondition his thinking and feeling.[12]

Activists involved in the early Civil Rights movement, like many outside observers at the time, believed that the historical experience of racial oppression had significantly damaged the black psyche. In contrast to the vast

majority of white commentators, however, the movement operated according to the premise that the best means of overcoming this damage was not by
eliminating all black-identified cultural traits, but rather by finding ways to
reconfigure African-American cultural patterns to enable a positive transformation of deeply entrenched racial identities. Pointedly, this did not mean
simply assimilating into the white middle-class cultural mainstream. Rather,
it involved a reassertion of the positive aspects of the black experience, which,
while developed under conditions of oppression, was never entirely defined
by them.

Although this orientation did not crystallize into an explicit ideological
position until the early 1960s, it was clearly articulated from at least the mid-
1950s onward. In 1956, for example, Bayard Rustin—a prominent labor and
civil rights activist since the 1930s and one of King's closest advisors[13]—published an article in *Liberation* that critically assessed the widespread tendency
of African Americans both to denigrate and to disassociate from the beau-
ties and strengths of their own culture:

> Negro children tend to develop early a basic lack of self-respect.
> They may show this, for example, by their shameful rejection of
> such aspects of their cultural heritage as Negro spirituals. A
> prominent Negro singer has been met several times before high
> school concerts by committees of Negro children who ask him
> not to sing spirituals. "They remind white folks of our past slav-
> ery, and we don't like it," one teenager explained. In the year 1956
> it is almost impossible to mention Africa to Negro boys and girls
> in school without provoking embarrassed laughter. Even African
> students studying in America are sometimes affected in the same
> way. One such student, looking at African sculpture in a New
> York apartment, laughed wryly at their "crudity" and said "My
> people have a long way to come," oblivious to the rare beauty of
> the work.[14]

By the early 1960s, the force of the movement had already sparked a widespread rejection of such internalized cultural prejudices among a significant
portion of the black public.

The most powerful way in which the movement reconfigured African-
American cultural resources to promote a positive transformation in black
consciousness was not, however, through abstract analysis and intellectual
indoctrination. Rather, it was through actively reappropriating some of the
most deeply resonant cultural symbols of the southern black community
and turning them into vehicles for building the movement. As Morris points

out, the central locus of this activity was the black church, which contained by far the most powerful set of organized practical and symbolic resources in the community.[15]

One of the most important examples of this sort of cultural reconfiguration was the transformation of the traditional music of the southern black church into a powerful repertoire of "freedom songs." As one black minister who had been the preeminent leader of the movement in his local community later noted: "The songs that we sang had more influence than anything else in enabling us to endure what the white people put on us. . . . It linked us with our past, it gave us a bridge from which to move during our present, and it hooked us onto the future."[16] Similarly, Bernice Reagon, recalling her days as a student activist with the Student Nonviolent Coordinating Committee (SNCC) during the Albany, Georgia, campaign of 1961–1962, explained in a 1989 interview, "The song-singing I heard in Albany I'd never heard before in my life, in spite of the fact that I was from that congregational singing culture. The only difference was that in Albany, Georgia, black people were doing some stuff around being black people."[17] Likewise, in another interview, conducted in 1979, Reagon explained:

> The mass meetings had a level of music that we could recognize
> from other times in our lives. And that level of expression, that
> level of cultural power present in an everyday situation, gave a
> more practical or functional meaning to the music than when it
> was sung in church on Sunday. The music was a group statement.
> If you look at the music and the words that came out of the
> Movement, you will find the analysis that the masses had about
> what they were doing.[18]

The oratorical tradition of the southern black church was similarly adapted to function as a means of bringing people together, changing their personal and political awareness, and strengthening their resolve to engage in direct action. The following excerpt of a speech given by King to a small church during the Albany campaign illustrates the ways in which movement orators utilized indigenous cultural resources such as religious symbolism, the call-and-response form, and rhythmic speech patterns (words in brackets indicate the audience's responses):

> There is nothing in this world more powerful than the power of
> the human soul, and if we will mobilize this soul force right here
> in Albany, Georgia, we will be able to transform this community
> [Yes. Well.] and we will see something *new* and powerful. And

we'll be eatin' where we couldn't eat before. We will be marchin' where we couldn't march before. We will be doin' things that we couldn't do before. And so let's get our marchin' shoes ready . . . [Yeah. shouts, applause]. For we are goin' [drowned out by applause] . . . For we are goin' to Albany's March to the Sea. And we're goin' to see great things happen.

In the same speech, King drew upon the collective memory of his black audience and used it in a way that affirmed their cultural heritage, strengthened a positive sense of group identity, and reinforced a feeling of political empowerment:

> For centuries we worked here without wages. We made cotton king. We built our homes and homes for our masters, enduring injustice and humiliation at every point. And yet, out of a bottomless vitality, we continued to live and grow. If the inexpressible cruelties of slavery could not stop us, certainly the opposition that we now face cannot stop us. [pandemonium] We go on with this faith knowing that we are right [Amen], that we will win [Amen].[19]

By the early 1960s, references to the "new Negro" on the part of movement activists were being increasingly replaced by assertions that, while similarly stressing the importance of developing an empowered black consciousness, were significantly more strident in terms of their explicit rejection of the middle-class, white mainstream norm. In an article published in *Harper's* in 1961, Charles Sherrod—then a well-known student activist involved in leading the sit-in movement in Richmond, Virginia—explained his political motivations by asserting: "We are *not* the puppets of the white man. We want a different world where *we* can speak, where *we* can communicate."[20] Similarly, in 1963, James Bevel, then a staff member of the SCLC, emphasized to an interviewer that "we don't want to end up aping the white man's ways. We want to develop a new spirit."[21]

During the same period, movement activists worked deliberately to change the sort of cultural perceptions that Rustin had identified as contributing to low self-esteem. One woman interviewed by Beardslee, for example—who had grown up with little education and in extreme poverty in the rural South—described her experience with a SNCC activist who boarded with her in 1964 as follows:

> She'd sit and talk to us for hours. She told us the history of black people. She told us exciting stories about ourselves. I didn't know

anything about the history of black folks. I never related it to Africa on any terms because all we saw was the jungle movies— the folks going "booga, booga booga"—and we didn't want to be a part of that. We learned that there was something more. She explained how we have our own culture . . . and that we don't have to be like white people.[22]

This sort of interaction had a profound effect, which manifested itself in ways ranging from a newfound commitment to political activism to the mundane—if, in this case, politically charged—aspects of everyday life. Mrs. Washington, for example, subsequently decided, after "about a year and a half," to stop having her hair "fixed" (i.e., chemically processed to straighten out its natural kinks and therefore look more like "white hair"). At the time, this was a notable break with the familiar norm. "Everybody looked," she recounted.

"Now," however, she continued, "you walk around here and you're just liable to see hair fixed or not fixed." Seemingly a minor detail, this sort of cultural change was in fact extremely important in that it signaled a newfound comfort with, as well as pride in, a distinctive African-American identity. People who experienced it at the time understood it as highly significant: Mrs. Washington, for example, described it as a "breakthrough." Most important, this breakthrough was occurring on a mass scale. As John Lewis— a prominent activist in the sit-ins and freedom rides of 1961 and chairman of SNCC from 1963 to 1966—explained in an interview conducted in the spring of 1964: "There's been a radical change in our people since 1960; the way they dress, the music they listen to, their natural hairdos—all of them want to go to Africa."[23]

This assessment of an important change in the black public consciousness was shared by outside observers. In January 1964, *Time* magazine published a cover story on "Negro Revolt," featuring Martin Luther King, Jr., as Man of the Year. "The most striking aspect of the revolt," *Time* reported, "is the change in the Negroes themselves." There was, the magazine explained, "a new pride" in African roots and identity:

Where most Negroes once deliberately ignored their African beginnings and looked down on the blacks of that continent, many now identify strongly with Africa . . . and take pride in the emergence of the new nations there. Some Negro women are affecting African style hairdos; Negroes are decorating their homes with paintings and sculpture that reflect interest in African culture. There has been a decline in sales of "whitening" creams, hair straighteners and pomades, which for years found a big market among Negroes obsessed with ridding themselves of their racial identity.[24]

Given the cultural intensity of anti-African racism in American history, the importance of such a change was profound, extending far beyond the realm of fashion or personal taste. Some external observers of the movement understood this at least as early as 1962. In that year, Harold Isaacs, a professor of international studies at MIT, published an article in the influential political journal *Commentary* which argued: "What is new is that today's 'New Negroes' are appearing in a situation where for the first time the odds are with them; their newness, their militancy, and their self-assertion are bound at last to pay off." This, he predicted, portended enormous changes for American society as a whole. As more and more blacks moved from "no-bodiness" to "somebodiness," Isaacs wrote:

> All the elements of group identity, e.g., name, color, nationality, origins, will have to acquire new shape and new content. All the choices—alienation, assimilation, integration—will have to be redefined. Out of the recombining of all of these elements in a new environment, a new Negro group identity will begin to be formed, and so too will the new shape of American society.[25]

Racial Transformation and Democratic Renewal

In the highly optimistic, even utopian vision of the early Civil Rights movement, the transformation of African-American consciousness was to be the spark of a larger process that would transform the consciousness of white America as well and, consequently, set the entire country on the road toward democratic renewal. This meant that while the most immediate and overriding priority of the movement was winning the fight against Jim Crow in the South, the political beliefs that animated it extended far beyond the simple elimination of such overt discriminatory barriers.[26] "Eventually our society must abide by the Constitution and not permit any local law or custom to hinder freedom or justice," wrote James Lawson, one of the most influential founders and early leaders of SNCC, in 1960. "But such a society lives by more than law. In the same respect the sit-in movement is not trying to create a legal battle, but points to that which is more than law."[27]

As King explained in *Stride toward Freedom*, the goal of the Civil Rights movement was not the simple elimination of formal discriminatory barriers, but the creation of a new form of democratic community based on mutual communication, interaction, and respect:

> Court orders and federal enforcement agencies will be of inestimable value in achieving desegregation. But desegregation is only a partial, though necessary, step toward the ultimate goal which we seek to realize. Desegregation will break down the legal barriers, and bring men together physically. But something must happen to touch the hearts and souls of men that they will come together, not because the law says it, but because it is natural and right. In other words, our ultimate goal is integration, which is genuine intergroup and interpersonal living.

Notably, this was a national, not simply a regional, goal. "There is a pressing need," King continued, "for a liberalism in the North which is truly liberal, that firmly believes in integration in its own community as well as in the Deep South."[28]

By forcing not only the white South but the nation at large to confront the inhumanity of segregation, movement activists hoped to provoke a change in white consciousness that would in certain respects parallel the transformation in black consciousness that had occurred. Most centrally, whites would come to understand that the full realization of their own humanity was being impeded by the existence of oppressive racial divisions—just as much as, although in very different ways from, the full humanity of blacks was being constrained. With this realization, a common desire to come together in a political community dedicated to realizing the full potential of all human beings would animate a decisive majority of Americans, and a project of national democratic renewal could begin.[29]

For King and many others, this optimistic vision was rooted in religious faith. "The Christian favors the breaking down of racial barriers because the redeemed community of which he is already a citizen recognizes no barriers dividing humanity," explained Lawson in 1960. "We are pointing to the viciousness of racial segregation and prejudice and calling it evil or sin. The matter is not legal, sociological or racial, it is moral and spiritual."[30] The universality of such religious faith undergirded the optimistic belief that whites, as well as blacks, possessed an innate yearning to be freed of the oppressive restrictions that racism placed on their humanity. As the Reverend Fred Shuttlesworth, a prominent civil rights leader who was extremely active in both the Alabama Christian Movement for Human Rights (ACMHR) and the SCLC, preached to an enthusiastic audience during the Albany campaign of 1963:

We are goin' into court hopin' that the God of this universe will stand by His children who stood up for Him. [Yes, yes.] For when we stand up for Him [Amen], we are standin' up for each other [Amen]. And when the Negro stands up for the Negro, he is in effect standin' up for the white man. [applause; dissonant shout: Yeah, brother.] He is not free as long as we are not free [applause, shouts].[31]

If such religiosity permeated the early movement, however, civil rights activists also expressed the same democratic vision in secular language. "By and large, this feeling that they have a destined date with freedom, was not limited to a drive for personal freedom, or even freedom for the Negro in the South," wrote Ella Baker—a leading civil rights activist since the 1930s, who served as executive director of the SCLC and spearheaded the formation of SNCC—in a 1960 report on a student leadership conference aptly entitled "Bigger than a Hamburger." "Repeatedly it was emphasized that the movement was concerned with the moral implications of racial discrimination for the 'whole world' and the 'Human Race.'"[32] Similarly, James Baldwin explained to the nation in an article published in the *New York Times* in 1961 that "the goal of the student movement" was not "the consumption of overcooked hamburgers and tasteless coffee at various sleazy lunch counters," but rather "nothing less than the liberation of the entire country from its most crippling attitudes and habits."[33]

The initial stirrings of the white student movement in the early 1960s were taken as a sign that this hoped-for shift in white consciousness was beginning to occur. King, for example, wrote in 1961:

Not long ago the Negro collegian imitated the white collegian. In attire, in athletics, in social life, imitation was the rule. For the future, he looked to a professional life cast in the image of the middle-class white professional. He imitated with such energy that Gunnar Myrdal described the ambitious Negro as "an exaggerated American."

Today the imitation has ceased. The Negro collegian now initiates. Groping for unique forms of protest, he created the sit-ins and freedom rides. Overnight his white fellow students began to imitate him. As the movement took hold, a revival of social awareness spread across campuses from Cambridge to California. It spilled over the boundaries of the single issue of desegregation and encompassed questions of peace, civil liberties, capital punishment and others.[34]

During the next few years, movement leaders increasingly pushed white student activists to commit to a program of fundamental political change. Vincent Harding posed the following challenge to white student volunteers whom he was training for participation in SNCC's 1964 "Freedom Summer" campaign:

> Are you going . . . as "In" members of the society to pull the "Outs" in with you? Or are we all "Outs"? Are you going to bring the Negroes of Mississippi into the doubtful pleasures of middle-class existence, or to seek to build a new kind of existence in which words like "middle-class" may no longer be relevant? Are we trying to make liberal readjustments or basic change?[35]

The situation of black America, in other words, could not be changed without changing that of white America as well. The promises of American democracy could not be realized simply by removing the formal barriers to the assimilation of one, exceptionally disfranchised racial group. Rather, movement leaders insisted, the basic orientation of American political life would have to be dramatically redirected.

The Economic Bases of Citizenship

Although it is commonly believed today that the early Civil Rights movement restricted itself to a relatively minimalist conception of civil rights based on the simple premise that all individuals should be treated equally under the law, it was in fact fundamentally concerned with broad questions of political economy that affected not only African Americans, but the nation as a whole. Like both the African-American public during Reconstruction and the producer republicans of the late nineteenth century, leaders of the early Civil Rights movement believed that the goal of establishing equal legal and political rights could be realized only under conditions of socioeconomic equity. Movement activists operated very much within the social democratic tradition, believing that a primary role of government was to promote social and economic equity by means of policies designed to counteract the divisions created by a market economy. During the late 1950s and early 1960s, this commitment was primarily expressed in terms of their concern with the effects of automation (or what we would today term deindustrialization) on lower-income Americans.

As early as 1956, Bayard Rustin was stressing the central importance of macroeconomic issues in plotting the long-term political strategy of the nascent Civil Rights movement:

In his political thinking about strategy today the Negro must take cognizance of two dangers. The first is that the industrial revolution of the South may make him less important economically. . . . The second danger is that when the present economic boom slackens, the Negro will be the hardest hit by unemployment and will be further displaced from the land. . . . Under the shadows of these two dangers the Negro people must move carefully but swiftly while the initiative is theirs, or they may discover that they and the democratic impulses for which they stand are on the defensive or even forced to retreat.[36]

"All this does not mean," Rustin continued, "that the Negro can or should struggle alone to achieve freedom for himself":

The mass of Negroes are farmers or workers, and their interests are fundamentally allied to those of other farmers and workers. The role of the Negro is unique only in that his especially demeaned position and, consequently, unprecedented new drive for dignity and self-respect lend him a momentum and initiative lacked by Southern white workers. The Negro is, therefore, pivotal to the resolution of the major problems confronting all classes in the South.[37]

Although Martin Luther King, Jr., clearly had a significantly less class-conscious orientation than did Rustin, whose politics grew directly out of the socialist tradition, *Stride toward Freedom* and a number of King's other early writings and speeches contained a similarly strong endorsement of socio-economic equalitarianism and interracial, class-based coalitions. In *Stride toward Freedom*, King wrote that "the Negro has been a perpetual victim of economic exploitation," which "continues down to the present day." At the same time, he emphasized:

Both Negro and white workers are equally oppressed. For both, the living standards need to be raised to levels consistent with our national resources. Not logic but a hollow social distinction has separated the races. The economically depressed white accepts his poverty by telling himself that, if in no other respect, at least socially he is above the Negro. For this empty pride in a racial myth he has paid the crushing price of insecurity, hunger, ignorance, and hopelessness for himself and his children.

Strong ties must be made between those whites and Negroes who have problems in common. . . . The organized labor movement, which has contributed so much to the economic security and well-being of millions, must concentrate its powerful forces on bringing economic emancipation to white and Negro by organizing them together in social equality.[38]

Although the parallel was not noted at the time, such words are eerily reminiscent of those of Populist leader Tom Watson in 1892.

Movement leaders, as well as many rank-and-file participants, understood the infamous confrontation that took place between black protesters and the white power structure in Birmingham, Alabama, in April 1963 as effecting a decisive turning point in the evolution of the movement.[39] As explicated by Rustin in "The Meaning of Birmingham," this new spirit of black protest was characterized by a grassroots determination to broaden the scope of the struggle on a national level. In "city after city where the spirit of Birmingham has spread," Rustin asserted, "Negroes are demanding fundamental social, political and economic changes." Repeating the same basic claims that he made back in 1956—this time, however, expanding his focus from the South to the nation at large—Rustin argued that the next "great battle" which "the black population is now prepared to wage" was "the battle for jobs":

> Negroes are finally beginning to realize that the age of automation and industrialization presents them with peculiar problems. There is less and less of a market where the unskilled can sell his labor. Inadequate, segregated schools increase the problem. The negative attitude of the trade unions compounds it further. The Cold War economy, geared to armaments production (perhaps the most automated of all industries) is throwing millions out of work, but the minority groups are being hit hardest. For every white person unemployed, there are close to three Negroes without jobs.

Here again, this view was coupled with the belief that the black population's new sense of political empowerment would galvanize a parallel transformation among a similarly aggrieved, if less holistically oppressed, white population. By the same token, Rustin predicted that the race-centered struggle for social justice would logically expand into a class-conscious movement:

> In general, the unemployed, whether white or black, are not yet prepared to take radical action to demand jobs now. However, unemployed black people are prepared to move in conjunction with

the rest of the black community and its many white supporters, within the context of the broad civil rights upheaval. Since their most immediate ends are economic, their banner will be "Dignity of work with equal pay and equal opportunity."

"This agitation on the part of Negroes for jobs," Rustin concluded, "is bound to stimulate unemployed white workers to increased militancy."[40]

A few months after Birmingham, A. Philip Randolph—an exceptionally important labor and civil rights activist since the 1910s and founder and president of the Negro American Labor Council (NALC)—appointed Rustin to be the key organizer of the March on Washington (MOW), which took place in August 1963. As originally envisioned by Rustin and Randolph, the MOW was to be primarily economic in focus, with the central demand of full employment. "In their historical nonviolent revolt for freedom, the Negro people are demanding the right to decent jobs," stated an early call for participation in the march. "There is no way for Negroes to win and hold jobs unless the problems of automation, a stagnant economy, and discrimination are solved; therefore, the Federal Government must establish a massive works program to train and employ all Americans at decent wages and at meaningful and dignified labor."[41]

After President John F. Kennedy's introduction of an omnibus civil rights bill to the Congress in June 1963, the focus of the MOW was broadened to include both economic and more traditional civil rights issues in an attempt to pressure the government into passing the legislation. At the same time (and in large part because of this new focus), the number of groups officially sponsoring the march grew from the original Big Six civil rights organizations—the NALC, the National Association for the Advancement of Colored People (NAACP), the National Urban League (NUL), the SCLC, the SNCC, and the Congress of Racial Equality (CORE)—to include religious groups and labor unions, such as, most notably, the National Council of Churches, the American Jewish Congress, the National Catholic Conference for Interracial Justice, and the United Auto Workers (UAW). (Notably, the AFL-CIO chose not to officially endorse the march.) As many of the white liberal religious groups disagreed with some of the more radical economic demands being advocated by Randolph and Rustin (for example, doubling the minimum wage), the focus of the MOW shifted further to a more pronounced legalistic emphasis. Finally, when the march actually occurred, the mass media coverage largely ignored the economic issues that it still, if less forcefully, continued to represent.[42]

Nonetheless, in the opening remarks which he delivered as the official chairman of the march, A. Philip Randolph explicitly linked the economic and legal demands that it represented. "Yes, we want all public accommodations open to all citizens, but those accommodations will mean little to those who cannot afford them," Randolph argued. "Yes, we want a Fair Employment Practices Act, but what good will it do if profits geared to automation destroy the jobs of millions of workers, black and white?"[43] Shortly after the event, Rustin published an article, "The Meaning of the March on Washington," which predicted: "Historically, the significance of the March will be seen to have less to do with civil rights than with economic rights: the demand for jobs."[44]

Confronting Discrimination and Segregation

The broad economic problems that confronted the poor of both races, movement leaders argued, were tremendously exacerbated among the black population due to the racially specific problems of segregation and discrimination. Although, of course, all of the major battles against segregation and discrimination up until the passage of the Civil Rights Act of 1964 were being waged in the South, movement leaders began emphasizing the importance of these problems in the rest of the country in the early 1960s. In his 1962 article "The Case against 'Tokenism,'" King argued, "Segregation may exist in the South in overt and glaring forms, but it exists in the North in hidden and subtle ways. Discrimination in housing and employment is often as bad in the North as it is anywhere. The racial issue confronting America is not a sectional issue but a national problem."[45] Similarly, a 1961 NUL report warned, in the words of the *New York Times*, that "a rapidly growing Negro population hampered by inferior opportunities in employment, housing, and education is a major race problem."[46]

Given these cross-reinforcing emphases on the macroeconomic dimensions of social inequality, on the one hand, and the race-specific problems of discrimination and segregation, on the other, it is not surprising that some civil rights leaders began to warn against the fallacies of relying on any sort of simple, legalistic solution to the problems of racial injustice well before President Kennedy introduced the first of the series of bills that would eventuate in the passage of the Civil Rights Act of 1964. In 1961, for example, Whitney Young predicted at the annual conference of the NUL (one month before he became that organization's executive director), "Negroes in America will face a battle against 'hidden' prejudice and discrimination after they win their fight for equal rights." As reported by the *New York Times*, Young went on to explain:

> Outward signs of discrimination will disappear, "conversation will become polite," laws or voluntary action will make mandatory the elimination of racial discrimination in employment, education, housing, health, and people will insist that all doors are open to the highly qualified and exceptional Negro citizen. . . . However, he said, the real problem will be to keep society aware of the subtle prejudices, and to prevent society from forgetting that the Negro still bears the scars of generations of prejudice and is not yet starting out on an equal footing.[47]

Similarly, in 1962, Young asserted at the NUL's national conference that while the "Negro is on the verge today of winning rights and respect long denied, rights and respect are empty symbols unless they can be translated into tangible social, economic, and cultural gains."[48]

At a 1963 address to the AFL-CIO, Randolph emphasized that "long ago—during Reconstruction—the Negro learned the cruel lesson that social and political freedom cannot be sustained in the midst of economic insecurity and exploitation. . . . Freedom requires a material foundation."[49] Similarly, King in *Why We Can't Wait* (1964) explained, "Many white Americans of good will have never connected bigotry with economic exploitation. They have deplored prejudice, but tolerated or ignored economic injustice. But the Negro knows that these two evils have a malignant kinship."[50]

A 1963 survey conducted by the Fund for the Republic supported the claim that northern blacks were much more concerned about finding good employment than with the problems of segregation and overt discrimination. As reported by the *New York Times*, the conclusion of the researcher who conducted the survey was that the "real problem" of the northern black "is not racial discrimination per se but the fact that he is becoming permanently unemployed." Unskilled and semiskilled workers, the study noted, were being increasingly replaced by machinery. Given the new demand for well-educated workers, many low-income blacks were so poorly educated that they simply never moved far enough along in the job process even to experience overt discrimination.[51]

As the movement's commitment to socioeconomic equity became more explicit, its existing emphasis on the devastating interaction between racial discrimination and segregation and a changing economy marked by increasingly entrenched class divisions became more pronounced. Randolph expressed this position exceptionally well in his 1963 address to the AFL-CIO:

> Automation is destroying tens of thousands of the unskilled and semi-skilled jobs to which Negroes have traditionally been relegated. Meanwhile, centuries of discrimination and exploitation have deprived Negro workers of the education and training required by the new skilled jobs opening up. Thus, we find that approximately 25 percent of the long-term unemployed are black American[s]. As unemployment becomes increasingly structural, the Negro is increasingly rendered economically useless.[52]

This situation, Randolph warned, was in danger of creating an "underclass" in American society. Similarly, King in *Why We Can't Wait* wrote that the "livelihood of millions has dwindled down to a frightening fraction because the unskilled and semi-skilled jobs they filled have disappeared under the magic of automation. In that separate culture of poverty where the half-educated Negro lives, an economic depression rages today."[53] Likewise, Herbert Hill, the labor secretary of the NAACP, warned in 1964 of "the social dangers that could arise should a permanently unemployed Negro population emerge because of automation. Unless the problem is solved, Negroes, in desperation, may abandon their legalistic approach and challenge the fundamental structure and values of American society."[54]

While it was widely thought that this developing underclass would be disproportionately black due to the factors identified above, it was also believed that, as Randolph put it, "the Negro is not alone. Many white workers also find themselves caught short by the profound transformations our economy is undergoing."[55] Consequently, movement leaders believed that there were practical as well as moral reasons for many whites, and particularly those within the white-dominated ranks of organized labor, to support the further progress of the civil rights revolution. "The Negro's increasing political strength and success are crystallizing public opinion in favor of action to meet the nation's pressing problems, and may well be responsible for major social reforms in the whole society," wrote Whitney Young in *To Be Equal*, published in the summer of 1964. "The Negro, therefore, is going to pull up with him other disadvantaged Americans, including the poor whites."[56] Or, as Randolph succinctly put it: "To discuss the civil rights revolution is therefore to write the agenda of labor's unfinished revolution."[57]

Civil rights leaders aspired to build a stronger coalition among blacks, progressive liberals, and organized labor on the basis of a new, radicalized political agenda centering around such common concerns as the negative impact of automation on lower-income workers. This coalition would, it was hoped, be powerful enough to leverage the Democratic party into a more social democratic position and, consequently, transform it into an engine of needed social change.[58] During 1963–1964, various policy proposals were presented as potential prototypes for a new Democratic agenda. In June 1963, for example, the NUL formally issued its Domestic Marshall Plan proposal, which advocated an intensive program of public, private, and philanthropic interventions designed to help black ghetto residents in particular advance quickly in the key areas of education, employment, housing, and health.[59] Similarly, although with a significantly more pronounced universalist emphasis, Rustin advocated the following "five point program" in May 1964: "full employment, national economic planning, worker training, federal subsidies for education, and a $30 billion works program to help absorb unskilled Negro labor."[60] Likewise, King in *Why We Can't Wait* endorsed the NUL's Domestic Marshall Plan and additionally proposed "a broad-based and gigantic Bill of Rights for the Disadvantaged."[61]

Calls for compensatory programs and preferential policies targeted specifically on the black population began as early as 1961. At that year's annual NUL conference, President Whitney Young insisted: "I contend, over many protests, that as the Negro for over 300 years has been given the special consideration of *exclusion*, he must now be given by society special treatment, through services and opportunities, that will insure his inclusion as a citizen able to compete equally with others."[62] Similarly, the following year, in an address to the Third Annual Negro American Labor Council Convention, Young argued that the "disappearance of old barriers and the establishment of new laws . . . will not in and of themselves, substantially erase the 300 years of deprivation . . . unless something special happens":

> I have insisted that if those who make the decisions in this country are really sincere about closing the gaps, then we must go further than fine impartiality. We must have, in fact, special consideration if we are to compensate for the scars left by 300 years of deprivation, which actually represented special consideration of another type. Equality for a while, therefore, is not enough. We must have better schools, better teachers, better facilities, and all else being equal the Negro should be given special priority in employment.[63]

Likewise, in March 1962, Coretta Scott King, wife of Martin Luther King, Jr., addressing an "overflow crowd" at the Abyssinian Baptist Church in New York, argued that the Negroes "at the bottom of the economic scale" should be given "better than equal opportunities."[64] That same year, Loren Miller—a prominent civil rights attorney and vice president of the NAACP—published an article in the *Nation* observing:

> There is a growing cynicism about the current stress being laid on absolute fairness in public and private employment and in political appointments—beginning as of today. The Negro wants a little more than that. One hundred years of racial discrimination have produced a wide gap between him and white Americans. The Negro wants that gap closed in political appointments, in civil service, in schools and in private industry. He sees no way to close it unless he gets preferential treatment.[65]

With the notable exception of Bayard Rustin, all of the most prominent leaders of the Civil Rights movement supported—albeit to significantly greater and lesser degrees—the idea of preferential treatment for blacks. Young, generally considered to be the most politically conservative member of this group, was preferential treatment's most forceful and consistent advocate.[66] King gave the idea a strong endorsement in *Why We Can't Wait*.[67] Roy Wilkins, Loren Miller, and Jack Greenberg of the NAACP all supported it, as did James Farmer of CORE.[68] Randolph felt that the whole question would be rendered moot with the adoption of full-employment policies, which, in his view, constituted an inestimably higher priority.[69] Rustin, on the other hand, opposed preferential treatment because he felt that it would make too many whites feel threatened that blacks would deprive them of their jobs, and therefore sabotage the development of a strong, interracial labor alliance—which would, in turn, destroy the movement.[70]

No one, including Rustin, however, expressed the view that preferential policies should be opposed because they violated liberal principles of individual rights and legal neutrality. On the contrary, preferential policies were generally seen as part of a much larger program of social reforms that would make the attainment of meaningful civil rights for all American citizens a reality. Those that opposed them did so not because they were too radical. On the contrary, they were against them because they were not seen as an effective means of achieving much more ambitious goals for dramatic social change.

This is not to say that proposals such as preferential treatment were not extremely controversial. They were. Their opponents, however, were generally not directly involved in the Civil Rights movement. Rather, they either opposed the movement or—more significantly—supported the movement but believed that it should represent a different, and more limited, set of goals.

White Liberals and Black Activists

By 1963, numerous articles were appearing that discussed the increasingly marked divergence between black activists and their ostensible "white liberal" allies. Although not so clearly differentiated at the time, in retrospect two parallel sets of developments can be traced. First, there was increasing cynicism regarding the extent to which the white liberals who had been so supportive of the movement's efforts to overturn Jim Crow in the South were willing to accept similar changes in the racial status quo when it would affect them where they lived, in other parts of the country. Second, on a more philosophical level, there was a growing split between those white liberals who accepted the redefinition of racial equity developed by the movement and those who rejected it as incompatible with the individualist ethic of American liberalism. These two developments were clearly related, in the sense that both had to do with the growing white realization that the Civil Rights movement was not simply about overturning Jim Crow in the South, but had much larger ambitions that would, if implemented, dramatically affect the nation as a whole. At the same time, however, these two different developments must be kept distinct, since while the first boiled down to a cynical dismissal of the integrity of the white liberals' commitment to racial justice, the second pointed to the importance of truly different conceptions of the boundaries and possibilities of American liberalism.

An article published in the January 1963 issue of the *Atlantic*—tellingly entitled "The White Liberal's Retreat"—pointed out that the same white liberals who strongly supported the movement to abolish Jim Crow in the South were simultaneously trying to physically separate themselves from the growing black populations of the central cities of the North and West. While working to pass laws abolishing racial discrimination in housing and education, the article noted, white liberals were also moving to the suburbs and placing their children in private or racially segregated public schools in record numbers. Consequently, the growing realization that the Civil Rights movement wanted to do more than simply eliminate Jim Crow laws in the South was generating increased hostility and resentment: "In the final analysis, a liberal, white, middle-class society wants to have change, but without trouble."[71]

The summer 1963 issue of *Dissent* echoed this assessment in an article entitled "The Black Man's Burden: The White Liberal." "The honeymoon between white liberals and the Negroes is over," it proclaimed. "This break has been growing almost in proportion to successes in integration and direct-action movements." "White liberals," it went on to explain, suffered "from one of those tenacious liberal illusions: that, contrary evidence notwithstanding, they could achieve integration at no cost or inconvenience to themselves (always having been better prepared for integration in the South than next door up North)":

> They expected to achieve equality for all Americans without pain
> or strain, and then emerge as innocent as they began. But now,
> with the stumbling translation of the moral principle into a real-
> ity, they are discovering that it's going to cost and that they're
> going to have to pay too. And so the liberals are restive. . . . Liber-
> als are showing signs of being just like everyone else when it's
> their neighborhood that is integrated.[72]

The term *white backlash* was coined that same summer. [73]

The October 1963 cover story of *Newsweek*, "What the White Man Thinks of the Negro Revolt," featured a Jules Feiffer cartoon that sardonically portrayed the white liberal disgruntlement with increased black assertiveness: "[C]ivil rights," a representative liberal groused, "used to be so much more tolerable before Negroes got into it." The issue's feature article pointed out that while white support for legal equality was reasonably strong—80 percent of whites nationwide believed that the law should prohibit racial discrimination in employment, and 63 percent favored the passage of the pending civil rights bill—whites were also clearly uncomfortable with the pace and direction of racial change. Seventy-four percent, for example, believed that "Negroes are moving too fast," while 97 percent opposed the idea that "Negroes should get preference in job openings to make up for discrimination." In addition, racial stereotypes remained strong, with 69 percent of whites believing that "Negroes have looser morals," 50 percent believing that "Negroes have less native intelligence," 49 percent believing that "Negroes want to live off the handout," and 36 percent believing simply that "Negroes are inferior to whites."[74]

Dramatic evidence of the growing momentum of the white backlash appeared with the results of the Democratic primaries in the spring of 1964, when presidential candidate George Wallace—the former governor of Alabama famous for his die-hard defense of southern segregation—received 43 percent of the vote in Maryland, 35 percent in Wisconsin, and 30 percent in Indiana. The strength of the Wallace vote was widely associated with urban white working-class reaction against a rising tide of black protest that, it seemed, threatened the insularity and security of their homes, jobs, and schools.[75] At the same time, however, pollster Lou Harris believed that white middle-class suburbanites were equally reactive to black demands for change.

"Fundamentally," Harris wrote, "more than half the suburbanites felt that Negroes must be kept in their place. Yet they protest vigorously against Southern attitudes and claim they are moderate on all things, including civil rights." Suburban whites, Harris continued:

> reflect the mood and tenor of the gentleman's agreement as applied to the Negro revolution. Most resent being called bigots and claim they have no sympathy for Governor Wallace—and even for Barry Goldwater because of his civil rights views. But suburbanites are the strong silent partner to overt anti-Negro sentiment, and could be aroused this summer and at the polls next November.[76]

By the time of the passage of the Civil Rights Act of 1964, it was widely acknowledged that the rift between white expectations and black demands had grown very wide and would be extremely difficult to bridge. In a popular and widely noted book published that summer, *Crisis in Black and White*, author Charles Silberman flatly stated, "Myrdal was wrong. The tragedy of race relations in the United States is that there is no American Dilemma":

> White Americans are not torn and tortured by the conflict between their devotion to the American creed and their actual behavior. They are upset by the current state of race relations, to be sure. But what troubles them is not that justice is being denied but that their peace is being shattered and their business interrupted. . . . Nothing less than a radical reconstruction of American society is required if the Negro is to be able to take his rightful place in American life.[77]

Similarly, David Danzig, the associate director of the American Jewish Committee and a lecturer at the Columbia University School of Social Work, wrote in the August 1964 issue of *Commentary* that "in 1964, the year of the Civil Rights Act, the Negro is more exposed to social reaction within the white communities than he has been at any time since Reconstruction."[78]

As this backlash was taking place among the general public, a reaction against the new understanding of racial equity developed by the Civil Rights movement was also occurring in more rarefied circles. By early 1964, it had become clear to white intellectuals, activists, and other observers of the movement that there was a fundamental clash between the understandings of "civil rights" adhered to by white liberals and the "Negro movement." "What we have here, in effect, is a radical departure from the traditional conception of civil rights as the rights of individuals," wrote Danzig in a widely noted article in the February issue of *Commentary*. "This departure lies at the heart of the 'Negro Revolution,' and may, indeed, almost be said to *be* that revolution":

> The Negro has made us forcefully aware that the rights and privileges of an individual rest upon the status attained by the group to which he belongs—that is to say, by the power it controls and can use. What is now perceived as the "revolt of the Negro," amounts to this: the solitary Negro seeking admission into the white world through unusual achievement has been replaced by the organized Negro insisting upon a legitimate share for his group of the goods of American society. The white liberal, in turn, who—whether or not he has been fully conscious of it—has generally conceived of progress in race relations as the one-by-one assimilation of deserving Negroes into the larger society, finds himself confused and threatened by suddenly having to come to terms with an aggressive Negro community that wishes to enter it en masse. . . . Liberal opinion, in the North and the South, thus continues to stand upon its traditions of gradualism . . . and to reject the idea that to help the Negro it must help the Negro community. *Yet the fact is that the Negro belongs to an economic as well as a racial group.*[79]

The following month, *Commentary* published an acrimonious "round-table discussion" among Norman Podhoretz, Nathan Glazer, Sidney Hook, Gunnar Myrdal, and James Baldwin on the subject of "Liberalism and the Negro" that picked up on Danzig's major themes. Podhoretz began the discussion by explaining:

> I think it may be fair to say that American liberals are by now divided into two schools of thought on what is often called the Negro problem. . . . On the one side, we have those liberals whose ultimate perspective on race relations . . . envisions the gradual absorption of deserving Negroes one by one into white society. . . . Over the past two or three years, however, a new school of liberal (or perhaps it should be called radical) thought has been developing which is based on the premise . . . that "the rights and privileges of an individual rest upon the status attained by the group to which he belongs." From this premise certain points follow that are apparently proving repugnant to the traditional liberal mentality . . . [which] conceives of society as being made up not of

competing economic classes and ethnic groups, but rather of competing *individuals* who confront a neutral body of law and a neutral institutional complex.

This division, Podhoretz noted, could lead—or, perhaps, already had led—"to a widening split between the Negro movement and the white liberal community."[80]

Given this situation, key movement activists, as well as some of its most committed outside supporters, were seriously concerned that the progressive thrust of the movement would founder on the shoals of white reaction and, simultaneously, break apart through its inability to contain the anger and disappointment of increasing numbers of alienated and frustrated blacks. In the summer 1964 issue of *Dissent*, Bayard Rustin, Tom Kahn (Rustin's chief assistant in the MOW), Norman Hill (national program director of CORE), Irving Howe (founder and editor of *Dissent*), and Michael Harrington (author of *The Other America*) discussed these concerns and what could be done to address them. All agreed that because "the demand for Negro rights is deeply related to problems of the economic structure" that affected not only blacks but society at large, the crucial project was to develop a broad-based, interracial movement committed to a social democratic agenda—"questions," as Rustin put it, "like total employment, limited planning, work training within planning, and a public works program."[81]

The stakes, all agreed, were enormously high. Kahn contended:

[T]he consequences of failure of the Negro movement would really be catastrophic. If you take automation and technological change into account, and if the rate of Negro displacement through automation continues, you get a picture of a class-color society. This will provide the basis for all kinds of extremely reactionary political developments.

Similarly, Harrington stated that "we're not talking about the Negro question, we're talking about the American question":

If the American labor movement continues to take the John L. Lewis approach to automation, that is, to bid farewell to the workers who are kicked out, to re-form their organizations on a narrow but highly-skilled, fairly well-paid base, to accept a smaller role in the society but to keep their structure intact on that base, then you can say that instead of an alliance there will probably be a war between white and black at the bottom of American society. Second, if the American labor movement does that . . . neither [it] nor any force for social change will be able to answer *any* of the questions, the automation question, the school question, the hospital question, the whole shooting match.

Even more broadly, as Kahn perceptively argued: "The liberal ideology spreads over the country but at the same time, underneath, certain regressive trends are going on that clash with it. . . . it is bad to have so much activity without visible results, because *the democratic ethic may suffer from the disillusionment*."[82]

Despite such concerns, the level of optimism among those committed to the further expansion of the Civil Rights movement remained fairly strong. Harrington, for example, believed that "the trade-union movement, out of its self-interest more than concern for the Negro, will be forced to start doing some things that will move it into a position of alliance with the Negroes." Similarly, Rustin and others believed that the movement had generated the political momentum necessary to allow for the effective organization of a broad coalition of blacks, progressive trade unionists, white liberals, religious leaders, students, and the poor around issues such as full employment.[83] As Danzig put it, "[T]he Negro movement today provides the only likely center around which a new coalition might be created to fill the current political vacuum."[84]

Civil Rights and Social Justice

By the early 1960s, it was widely recognized that there was a deep and growing rift between the black-led movement for social change and the white majority's commitment to maintaining the racial status quo outside of the Jim Crow South. At the same time, it was similarly recognized that very different understandings of the meaning of liberal politics had emerged and come into open conflict with one another. Although these realizations crystallized during the 1963–1964 period, it would be a mistake to view them as indicators that the Civil Rights movement had suddenly taken on a radically new direction or broken decisively with its earlier orientation. All of the major factors that contributed to the movement's race- and class-conscious politics—the commitment to an empowered African-American identity, the vision of a truly integrated society, the analysis of the combined effects of automation and racial discrimination outside of the South, and the advocacy of a broad social democratic agenda—had been articulated by movement leaders since the mid-1950s. Given the movement's day-to-day absorption in the battle to defeat Jim Crow in the South, however, its larger aspirations did not become evident to outside observers until it achieved a higher degree of national prominence following the Birmingham campaign and the March on Washington in 1963.

This is not to say that the politics of the movement did not evolve over time. Of course, they did. Movement leaders' promotion of preferential or affirmative action policies, for example, did not begin until 1961. Such developments can be seen, however, as logical outgrowths of a broader set of political commitments, which centered around the interrelated goals of racial and class equity. The general outlines of the movement's transformative democratic vision were apparent from the beginning, at least to those who took the time to look beyond the scope of immediate events to consider the larger structure of political thought that permeated the public statements of key activists and leaders. While the precise contours of the movement's goals changed over time, they never entailed a break with the broader political vision that had animated it since its inception.

If a society is interested in stability, it should either not make promises

or it should keep them.

—Bayard Rustin, "A Way Out of the Exploding Ghetto," 1967

7

The Broken Promise of Liberal Revolution

During the fleeting historical moment of 1964–1965, there was a fairly widespread and quite palpable hope that the forces of mainstream liberal reformism could join together with those of the Civil Rights movement to form a strong political coalition capable of propelling America into a new era of racial equality and social justice. Although public discussion of a growing rift between white liberals and black activists was well established by 1964, President Lyndon B. Johnson's landslide victory that November, combined with his highly publicized call for a national commitment to ending poverty and racial inequality, suggested that a reinvigorated Democratic party could lead the country toward the new vision of social liberalism inspired by the Civil Rights movement.[1] During this short period, the promise of a peaceful, progressive liberal revolution, in which America would transform itself in order to fully realize its innate potential, was repeatedly made to an apparently receptive public by the highest political authority in the land.

It quickly became apparent, however, that this liberal revolution had been promised without any sense of how difficult it would be to achieve.

Shortly after the War on Poverty was launched, it was criticized as being far too timid to achieve the changes that it had promised (a charge that all students of the subject have since agreed was correct). Even as government officials were attempting to expand the War on Poverty, and other, more radical proposals were being made, it quickly became evident that even the less-than-adequate programs that existed were rapidly losing political support.

A number of factors rapidly emerged that dramatically changed the prevailing political climate. First, the eruption of the Watts riot in August 1965 abruptly wrenched the focus of racial issues from the Jim Crow South to the urban ghettos in the rest of the country. While forcing a hurried government response, this and the many other urban disorders of the next several years intensified an already existing white backlash and caused moderates to pull back from civil rights issues. Second, the rapid escalation of the Vietnam War that began in 1965 not only drained attention and funds from domestic issues, but created deep divisions among social liberals while fiercely radicalizing the New Left. Finally, the sudden intensification of radical politics represented by the increasingly "revolutionary" New Left and the newly emergent Black Power movement reinforced a growing public desire for the restoration of "law and order," while subjecting both Civil Rights movement leaders and their Democratic supporters to incendiary attacks.

Hemorrhaging support from the middle while being denounced by the Left, the formerly optimistic forces of social liberalism found themselves in a state of tremendous anxiety and uncertainty. By 1967, it was clear that a new American dilemma had emerged which dwarfed the old Myrdalian paradigm of the 1940s. On the one hand, it was widely believed that the political ante had been permanently raised: nothing less than the dual abolition of poverty and racial discrimination, it was insisted, could resolve the nation's racial problems. On the other hand, it had become equally clear that the political tide was turning away from any serious attempt to fulfill such an ambitious promise. Consequently, social liberals turned to an apocalyptic jeremiad that counterposed a continued commitment to their agenda against an impending threat of democratic collapse. If America did not make good on its promises now, it was repeatedly claimed, then the liberal values that constituted the heart of the nation's political culture would be tragically violated and perhaps even destroyed.

The events of 1968—which included the assassinations of Martin Luther King, Jr., and Senator Robert F. Kennedy, an intensified wave of ghetto riots, the radicalization of the New Left and Black Power movements, and street fighting at the Democratic National Convention in Chicago—deepened this sense of jeopardy. Many social liberals (among others) believed that the country was polarizing between the Right and the Left, and that if this dynamic were not soon arrested, a dangerous tide of political reaction would undoubtedly sweep the nation. Although no such extreme outcome occurred— the United States did not, as many feared (and some radical elements hoped), turn to either racial warfare, revolution, or fascism—the election of President Richard Nixon was widely perceived as a decisive shift to the right. Consequently, while many advocates of social liberalism continued to hold the course, there was a newfound and growing perception that they represented an agenda that had, depending on the perspective, either been defeated or been proven wrong—but one which, in any event, had failed to pass successfully through a particularly crucial political juncture.

Although important elements of the old agenda survived, albeit in a modified and truncated form (most commonly, shifting to the elite world of the courts and bureaucracies, where controversial initiatives were shielded from electoral politics), the sense of expansive optimism that had existed in 1964 had been lost by 1968. Although other, equally important political movements would develop during the next several years—women's liberation, gay rights, and a variety of racial and ethnic identity movements—the specific variety of social liberalism that had been developed by the Civil Rights movement and to a significant extent embraced by the Johnson administration had lost its momentum. Consequently, while many important political and legal reforms were pursued in a variety of other, often-related arenas, the central goals of dismantling de facto segregation and eradicating poverty had been essentially defeated in the realm of national electoral politics. Both had become bound up with a newly potent form of racial politics that would, beginning with the 1968 election, play an increasingly important role in leveraging a more and more conservative Republican party into the White House and, more broadly, creating the conditions under which a powerful new conservative movement could emerge.

The Promise of Liberal Revolution

During the brief period sandwiched between President Johnson's landslide victory in 1964 and the congressional elections of 1966, the prospect of uniting the forces represented by the Civil Rights movement, the labor movement, social liberals, and the social democratic Left in a powerful coalition capable of progressively transforming American politics appeared to be exceptionally bright. The trajectories of the Civil Rights movement and the reformist wing of the Democratic party appeared to be, if not merging together, at least converging to the point where a symbiotic transformation of both could be envisioned. The movement, it was thought, could gain direct access to institutional power, while the party, finally freed from the constricting influence of the southern Democrats, would realign itself to represent a broader constituency including not only labor and liberals, but also minorities, the poor, and the non-Communist Left. With such a development, it was imagined, the social liberal agenda could begin a concentrated process of implementation.

Two key statements made in 1965 best encapsulate this significant, if short-lived, moment in American politics. These are Bayard Rustin's "From Protest to Politics," published in *Commentary* in February, and President Johnson's Howard University speech, delivered in June of that year. Widely read and discussed at the time, both were commonly recognized as signature statements that symbolized the hope that an ambitious period of political reform was about to begin.

The central significance of "From Protest to Politics" lay in its confident announcement that just as the Civil Rights movement had shifted into a new, more complicated, and ambitious phase, so America at large had turned the corner to find itself confronting a new era of political challenge and opportunity. After Birmingham, Rustin wrote, it was clear that the movement was not only committed to "the concept of collective struggle over individual advancement," but that "the single-issue demands" of the movement's earlier "classical stage" had given way to the "package deal": "No longer were Negroes satisfied with integrating lunch counters. They now sought advances in employment, housing, school integration, police protection, and so forth" throughout the nation, not simply in the South.[2]

Of course, Rustin's argument that the Civil Rights movement needed to insist that issues of "social and economic welfare are inextricably entangled with Civil Rights" did not represent a substantively new position, as both he and other movement leaders had been making similar claims since at least the mid-1950s. By 1965, however, it appeared that the time was ripe to assert that the movement had exited its intital stage, when it had focused on the battle to destroy Jim Crow, and entered a distinctively new political era.[3] The passage of the Civil Rights Act of 1964 had been a historic turning point, effectively abolishing de jure segregation and tremendously expanding the power of the federal government to prosecute discriminatory activity in both the public and private sectors.[4] Although what would soon become the equally historic Voting Rights Act of 1965 had not yet been introduced in Congress (Johnson would do so on March 17), the SCLC, under King's leadership, had begun the Selma, Alabama, campaign to force the issue forward. Further, the political climate in Congress remained exceptionally favorable to the passage of new civil rights legislation.

"The 1964 election," Rustin wrote, "marked a turning point in American politics."[5] The sweeping Democratic victories that occurred at both the presidential and congressional levels, he argued, represented a "majority liberal consensus" whose strength could be expanded if the party seized the opportunity to move further to the left, which would enable it to form a new coalition including previously marginalized and inactive low-income voters. Such a coalition, Rustin claimed, would be more stable than the one that elected Johnson, since it would drive both Dixiecrats and transient refugees from the specter of Goldwaterism out of the party ("Big Business being the major example"). This refashioned Democratic party, Rustin claimed, would have the strength and vision to "set fundamental changes in motion" aimed at nothing less than "a refashioning of our political economy" around objectives such as "full employment, abolition of slums, the reconstruction of our educational system, [and] new definitions of work and leisure." "The Negro's struggle for equality in America is essentially revolutionary," Rustin approvingly noted, as it required "the qualitative transformation of fundamental institutions, more or less rapidly, to the point where the social and economic structure which they comprised can no longer be said to be the same."[6]

President Johnson's Howard University speech employed similar language of revolutionary transformation.[7] "Nothing is more freighted with meaning for our own destiny than the revolution of the Negro American," stated Johnson. *Revolution*, in Johnson's terms, referred to a process by which "men charged with hope . . . reach for the newest of weapons to realize the oldest of dreams; that each may walk in freedom and pride, stretching his talents, enjoying the fruits of the earth." Whereas Rustin spoke strategically of forming a political coalition capable of carrying this revolution forward, Johnson—in keeping with the logic of the Myrdalian paradigm—suggested that the common conscience of the nation, once aroused, would not rest until this vision was realized. "The voice of the Negro was the call to action," the president stated. "But it is a tribute to America that, once aroused, the courts and the Congress, the President and most of the people, have been the allies of progress."[8]

The Civil Rights movement, in other words, had succeeded in invoking a common ideal that demanded to resolve the one great contradiction of the nation, that is, the discriminatory treatment historically accorded the African-American minority. Johnson concluded his speech with the following exhortation:

From the first, this has been a land of towering expectations. It was to be a nation where each man could be ruled by the common consent of all—enshrined in law, given life by institutions, guided by men themselves subject to its rule. And all—all of every station and origin—would be touched equally in obligation and in liberty. . . . This is American justice. We have pursued it faithfully to the edge of our imperfections. And we have failed to find it for the American Negro.

It is the glorious opportunity of this generation to end the one huge wrong of the American Nation and, in so doing, to find America for ourselves, with the same immense thrill of discovery which gripped those who first began to realize that here, at last, was a home for freedom.[9]

The president's expansive rhetoric in this speech matched that of his earlier announcements of his vision of the Great Society, as well as what would quickly become its most controversial component, the War on Poverty. "The Great Society," Johnson explained to University of Michigan students in 1964, "rests on abundance and liberty for all. It demands an end to poverty and racial injustice, to which we are totally committed in our time. But this is just the beginning":

The Great Society is a place where every child can find knowledge to enrich his mind and enlarge his talents. . . . It is a place where man can renew contact with nature. . . . It is a place where men are more concerned with the quality of their goals than the quantity of their goods. But most of all, the Great Society is not a safe harbor, a resting place, a final objective, a finished work. It is a challenge constantly renewed, beckoning us toward a destiny where the meaning of our lives matches the marvelous products of our labor.

"For better or for worse," Johnson concluded, "your generation has been appointed by history to deal with those problems and to lead America toward a new age. You have the chance never before afforded to any people in any age. You can help build a society where the demands of morality, and the needs of the spirit, can be realized in the life of the nation."[10]

Whatever their specific substantive differences, both Rustin and Johnson forcefully projected a powerful image of a peaceful, progressive, and, above all, *liberal* revolution. This revolution would simultaneously liberate a historically oppressed group; uplift other, similarly disadvantaged Americans; and establish the quintessentially liberal right of every individual, as Johnson put it, "to be treated in every part of our national life as a person equal in dignity and promise to all others."[11] In this optimistic moment, there was no perceived contradiction in proposing a political agenda that prominently featured policies targeted to benefit a particular racial group, reforms designed to help all disadvantaged Americans, pragmatic coalition building, and fundamental American values. American liberalism, in other words, could commit itself to addressing inequities of both race and poverty and still flourish and prosper politically.

(Under)Estimating the Costs of Liberal Reform

While the Civil Rights movement had long seen the goals of eradicating poverty and racial inequality as inextricably linked, the more mainstream perspective of postwar liberalism traditionally understood them as separate. Even in 1964, when the policy foundations for the War on Poverty were first being laid, racial inequality was widely seen as a peculiarly southern problem,[12] and poverty as an issue that had no strong connection with race.[13] This perspective began to change rapidly, however, during the period immediately following the passage of the Civil Rights Act of 1964. As it became increasingly clear that even such monumental legislation was not going to solve the problem of racial inequality and that the most pressing problems facing African Americans had at least as much to do with matters of education, poverty, employment, and housing as with matters of de jure segregation and discrimination, the formerly separable issues of race and poverty began to overlap and merge.

Johnson's Howard University speech was a milestone in this evolution. Like Rustin, Johnson portrayed the ongoing struggle to achieve a true measure of civic equality for black citizens as having entered a new phase that would require a direct attack on entrenched patterns of socioeconomic inequality. Using words that would later become touchstones in controversies over the legitimacy of a variety of civil rights–related initiatives (alternatively characterized as an inspiring imperative toward racial justice or a disastrous departure from true liberal principles), Johnson stated:

> You do not take a person who, for years, has been hobbled by chains and liberate him, bring him up to the starting line of a race and then say, "you are free to compete with all the others," and still justly believe that you have been completely fair. . . . This is

the next and more profound stage of the battle for Civil Rights. We seek not just freedom but opportunity—not just legal equity but human ability—not just equality as a right and a theory but equality as a fact and as a result.[14]

Stating that major obstacles were preventing this more-expansive conception of civic equality from being realized, Johnson went on to detail the ways in which the socioeconomic status of the majority of the black population (which stood outside of the growing, yet relatively minute black middle class) was, contrary to all expectations, actually declining.[15] While, the president stated, the full complex of factors that explained this development remained unknown, the two most central were clear. One was that a large number of blacks—like many others—were "trapped in inherited, gateless poverty." The other, he asserted, was the unique set of problems that afflicted the black community due to the "devastating heritage of long years of slavery; and a century of oppression, hatred and injustice." Here, while Johnson pointed to such things as the erosion of hope and the pain inflicted by racism, he added that perhaps "the most important" problem was "the breakdown of the Negro family structure."[16]

The first factor cited by Johnson reflected the belief, then dominant among postwar liberals, that the reason that certain segments of the population (poor whites in Appalachia being the favorite example during the early 1960s) had not benefited from the postwar boom was that they lived in a socially isolated "culture of poverty" that prevented them from gaining the skills, habits, and attitudes needed to achieve economic success. The second point regarding the specificity of black poverty was part of what would soon become the infamous Moynihan report ("The Negro Family: The Case for National Action").[17] Together, they represented the view that the best way to eradicate poverty and racial inequality in America was to supplement the already established War on Poverty program with specific initiatives designed to strengthen the structure of the black family.

At first, this new policy position seemed to dovetail quite well with the agenda of the Civil Rights movement. The White House had sought and obtained approval of the Howard speech from Martin Luther King, Jr., Roy Wilkins, and Whitney Young before it was delivered. The initial reactions of these and other prominent movement leaders to the speech had been consistently positive.[18] Around the middle of 1965, however, it started to become clear that the movement and the administration were at odds on the key questions of what the central causes of poverty were and what it would cost the government to eradicate it.

The dominant view within the administration was that poverty was primarily a problem of human capital development.[19] If certain groups were unnecessarily trapped in a self-perpetuating culture of poverty, it was believed, this vicious cycle could be broken by providing additional education, job training, and counseling, which would equip the poor with the confidence and skills needed to compete successfully in the labor market. Correspondingly, the policy initiatives that constituted the War on Poverty legislation were built around a service strategy of human capital development, rather than direct job creation or income-maintenance programs.[20]

In contrast, both prominent Civil Rights movement leaders and social democratic intellectuals tended to see poverty as a structural problem. Not only did the labor market not provide enough good jobs to lift the entire able-bodied population out of poverty, they believed, but other structural barriers, such as discrimination and inadequate education, kept the poor from being able to take full advantage of the jobs that were there. Consequently, these figures largely tended to advocate alternative policies, such as an expansion of public sector jobs and a guaranteed minimum income.[21]

In keeping with this basic difference of opinion regarding the causes of poverty, the Johnson administration and the Civil Rights movement leadership were also divided over the question of the magnitude of public resources that would have to be dedicated to the War on Poverty if it were to be won. When the program was initially launched in 1964, Johnson and other key government players had assumed that "winning" would be relatively easy; correspondingly, they believed that it would not cost a great deal of money. This perspective was exemplified by the early publication of such self-confident tracts as "We Can Win the War on Poverty" and "Why the Poverty Program Is a Low-Cost Program."[22]

Two interrelated factors best explain this sort of now-inconceivable confidence. First, the nation was in the midst of the golden age of postwar affluence, and it seemed that it could well afford to be boldly experimental and generously idealistic. In a time when the federal government had surplus funds even as it cut taxes, it appeared that the United States could certainly manage to eradicate what was regarded as a few remaining vestiges of poverty.[23] Second, faith in the ability of social scientists and policymakers to enact successful reforms was at an all-time high. The triumph of Keynesianism seemed permanent; the economy, the cognoscenti believed, could now be managed to produce a steady state of growth. If economists had succeeded in solving such a world-historical puzzle as how to control the boom-and-bust cycles of modern capitalism, then, many assumed, surely social scientists could solve the seemingly archaic problem of residual poverty.[24]

Prominent social democratic intellectuals such as Michael Harrington, however, were quick to charge that the War on Poverty was both inadequately conceived and underfunded. The editor of one collection of critical essays published in 1965 offered the following anecdote to illustrate the differences at issue:

> Harrington delights in telling the story of his first visit to Sargent Shriver after the latter had been designated chief of the War on Poverty. Shriver asked Harrington what he thought of the assignment. Said Harrington, "It's nickels and dimes in the poverty program." Shriver stared at him. "Mr. Harrington," he replied, "perhaps you've spent a billion dollars before, but this is my first time around." . . . Yet Harrington's wry response cannot be gainsaid, for public assistance alone accounts for some $5–6 billion, while OASDI [old age, survivors, and disability insurance; the official name for Social Security] and unemployment insurance require about $18 billion of outlays. One can hardly expect that a billion dollars a year will cure wounds for which band-aid treatment has cost more than twenty times that much.[25]

Although poverty warriors such as Shriver quickly came to agree with this assessment, realizing that their goals were much more daunting than had been originally supposed, additional funding proved difficult to come by, primarily due to the escalating costs of the Vietnam War and the increasingly conservative climate within Congress.[26]

Leading Civil Rights movement figures were quick to propose much more costly and ambitious alternatives to the War on Poverty. In late 1965, A. Philip Randolph called for a "Freedom Budget" of $100 billion to address problems of poverty and unemployment; one year later, a detailed proposal was submitted to the White House. Insisting that the problem of poverty had to be understood "in terms of the national economy, and not only in terms of the personal characteristics of the poor,"[27] the Freedom Budget prioritized the goal of full employment through extensive government planning and called for federal expenditures of $18.5 billion a year for the next ten years. (Although hearings were held on the proposal in Congress, it was never taken seriously by the federal government and was consequently ignored.)[28]

If significant differences existed among members of the erstwhile social liberal coalition regarding the question of the nature of poverty and how best to combat it, however, they paled in comparison to the furor that broke out over the Moynihan report, which had provided the basis for Johnson's proposal to attempt to strengthen the black family in his Howard University speech.[29] Written by Assistant Secretary of Labor Daniel Patrick Moynihan in March 1965,[30] the primary purpose of the report was to persuade government officials that civil rights laws were an insufficient means of addressing the problem of racial inequality and that an intensive, long-term commitment to improving conditions in the urban ghetto should be a national policy priority.[31] Although in this sense fully in line with the basic social liberal agenda, the report quickly came to be considered a reactionary ruse designed to block further progress and was resoundingly denounced by left-of-center forces, including, most notably, the Civil Rights movement leadership and other prominent black political figures.

As Rainwater and Yancey demonstrate, a combination of political ineptitude and combustible circumstances caused the report to become coded as a new conservative manifesto that claimed that the problems of the urban ghetto were caused, purely and simply, by the "pathological" culture of lower-class blacks.[32] As national attention suddenly became riveted on the black ghetto as a result of the Watts riot in August 1965, prominent conservatives adopted the report and used it as a vehicle to advance their own, quite particular interpretations of it. In one especially influential newspaper column, political commentators Roland Evans and Robert Novak wrote:

> Weeks before the Negro ghetto of Los Angeles erupted in violence, intense debate over how to handle such racial powder kegs was under way deep inside the Johnson administration. The pivot of this debate: The Moynihan Report, a much-suppressed, much-leaked Labor Department document which strips away the usual equivocations and exposes the ugly truth about the big-city Negro's plight. . . . [Moynihan] wondered, for instance, why in a time of decreasing unemployment, the plight of the urban Negro was getting worse—not better. His answer . . . the breakdown of the Negro family.

In conclusion, they darkly warned that "preferential treatment" for African Americans loomed on the horizon ("a solution far afield from the American dream") since, unlike Jews, blacks did not have the capacity to move ahead in society once discriminatory barriers were removed.[33]

Such statements served to spread the erroneous claim that the official government explanation for the Watts riot was the cultural deficiency of the black family. The original report had, in fact, stressed that unemployment, poverty, discrimination, and an inadequate wage structure formed the "economic roots of the problem." The Johnson administration did absolutely nothing, however, to counter the building mischaracterization of the report.

This inaction reinforced the belief that the conservative construction of the report was in fact an accurate portrait of the administration's position.[34]

Consequently, by the fall of 1965, prominent black activists and intellectuals began to attack the report. In a widely read article published in the *Nation*, for example, CORE activist William Ryan warned that the Moynihan report was providing "fat fodder" for a "new racist ideology." "Unemployment, the new ideologists tell us, results from the breakdown of Negro family life; poor education of Negroes results from 'cultural deprivation'; the slum conditions endured by so many Negro families is the result of lack of 'acculturation' of Southern rural migrants." Similarly, former CORE president James Farmer editorialized that the report "has been specifically hailed by the American right wing and is currently being used to 'explain away' the Negro Revolution as the hysterical outburst of a mentally unbalanced subculture."[35]

The report's implicit assumption that, as CORE director Floyd McKissick put it, "middle class American values are the correct ones for everyone in America" was roundly attacked. Farmer, for example, scathingly noted: "Nowhere does Moynihan suggest that there may be something wrong in an 'orderly and normal' white family structure that is weaned on race hatred and passes the word 'nigger' from generation to generation." Similarly, Whitney Young insisted that "one can't talk about the pathologies of Negroes without talking about the pathologies of white society. If Negroes are sick socially, then whites are sick morally." Even staunch coalitionists such as Rustin joined in, arguing that "what may seem to be a disease to the white middle class may be a healthy adaptation to the Negro lower class."[36]

In this acrimonious climate, the Johnson administration and Civil Rights movement leadership, in conjunction with a variety of academic, business, and labor notables, were attempting to plan a special White House conference, "To Fulfill These Rights," which would lay out a blueprint for achieving the goals outlined in the Howard speech. When the conference occurred in June 1966, however—exactly one year after it had been announced in what seemed to be such promising terms—it proved to be a total flop. Many who attended stridently denounced the whole exercise as a farce, and even its supporters felt demoralized by the experience.[37]

While the poisonous climate that had come to surround the Moynihan report played a major role in what was commonly acknowledged to be a failed conference,[38] other factors were at work as well. For one, the escalation of the Vietnam War was by this time well under way.[39] Although the war was not yet a centrally divisive question,[40] particularly on the terrain of race and civil rights issues, it was prominent enough to reinforce growing divides between activists who believed that it was necessary to work with the Democratic party and those who thought that the party had proved itself to be untrustworthy and that it was necessary to go it alone.[41] By this time, it had also become apparent to everyone that the war was rapidly draining the time, energy, and resources of the administration away from questions of domestic reform, including both civil rights and the War on Poverty. This realization reinforced widespread feelings of frustration and disillusionment.[42]

The reverberating shock of the Watts riot further exacerbated these problems. Having taken both the Johnson administration and the Civil Rights movement completely off guard, Watts left each in a newly defensive and insecure position. Many Democratic politicians believed that Watts had made close association with the black movement a political liability. Consequently, they shifted to a more cautious posture on civil rights and related issues.[43] At the same time, Watts demoralized the Civil Rights movement by bluntly demonstrating how little contact it had with the urban ghetto, let alone leadership within it.[44] Consequently, just as movement activists were feeling an intensified sense of urgency regarding the need to find a way to address the problems of the ghetto, the national political climate was shifting in a more conservative direction, away from grand plans of domestic reform.

Radicalism and Reaction

During the same period that prominent social liberals such as Bayard Rustin were hoping for a convergence of the Civil Rights movement and the reformist wing of the Democratic party, other, more radical activists were coming to view this agenda with intense suspicion and hostility. Instead of seeing such a development as a promising opening toward positive social change, prominent activists associated with the New Left and Black Power movements believed that the Civil Rights movement was being coopted by liberal forces that stood opposed to anything but politics as usual—with, perhaps, a few token concessions thrown in to defuse demands for more serious political action. Consequently, by the time that Rustin published "From Protest to Politics" in 1965, his call for a commitment to "coalition politics" was greeted with widespread hostility in radical circles.[45] The dominant position among both white and black radicals was that it was futile to try to change the political system from within. Although some hope that it could be successfully pressured from without remained up through the mid-1960s, by 1967 the common call emanating from a wide variety of radical camps was for nothing less than "revolution"—a complete and transformative overturning of the established order in all realms of political, economic, and social life.

During 1965–1967, the white-dominated New Left, led by the Students for a Democratic Society (SDS), went through an extremely rapid ideological transformation as it rejected liberal politics and searched for a better alternative. What was needed, it was widely believed, was a systemic way of explaining why the country faced such seemingly intractable problems of racism and poverty at home, while being increasingly committed to a senseless and destructive war abroad. Such an explanation was rapidly developed: American liberalism, it was argued, represented a monolithic system of racist, capitalist imperialism, whose internal logic necessarily generated the problems wracking the nation.[46] With this basic ideology in place, the radicalization of New Left leaders produced by the escalation of the Vietnam War rapidly resulted in a revolutionary demand to destroy "the system" at all costs. Consequently, liberals of all stripes — but particularly the social liberals who had formerly been seen as important, if overly conservative, allies — were denounced as wolves in sheep's clothing, defenders of an evil system that could not be improved by merely reformist measures.

"Liberals," Stanley Aronowitz wrote in 1967:

> want to find a way to negotiate America out of the war in Vietnam . . . and out of racial "chaos" at home without surrendering white corporate power. The radical answer to liberalism is that it can't be done. American intervention abroad has solid economic and political roots in the corporate capitalist system and so does black oppression at home.[47]

Racial inequality was not, in this view, an internal contradiction of liberalism that had to be rooted out so that American society could at last realize its true potential. Rather, it was a necessary by-product of a capitalist, imperialist monolith that could not be eradicated without destroying the system itself. Similarly, the Vietnam War was not a mistake, but a logical necessity: the foreign equivalent of domestic racism. This understanding of the relationship between race and liberalism allowed the two key political issues of black liberation and the Vietnam War to be fused into a single problematic. As prominent New Left intellectual Staughton Lynd wrote in 1967, the movement had "redefined itself as a movement against racist capitalist imperialism at home and abroad."[48]

The New Left's shift in ideology and rhetoric was matched by an escalation of disruptive and increasingly violent actions. During 1968–1969, the New Left claimed responsibility for well over one hundred campus bombings, attempted bombings, and cases of arson nationwide, aiming at such diverse targets as Reserve Officers' Training Corps (ROTC) buildings, high schools, and electrical towers. Many young radicals, caught up in the thrall of revolutionary fantasies, outraged by the horrors of war abroad and the injustices of racism at home, shocked by the murders of Martin Luther King and presidential candidate Senator Robert Kennedy, and in awe of the revolutionary élan displayed by a new generation of black radicals (the Black Panther party in particular) came to glorify and romanticize violence as the only means capable of destroying racist, capitalist, imperialist "Amerika." Notably, this turn toward violence also embodied an important gender dimension, as many men—as well as some women—sought to embody the idealized image of the tough, fearless, macho revolutionary outlaw.[49]

The general public was repelled. Patriotic bumper stickers proliferated that summarized the widespread public disgust with anti-American radicalism of all stripes: "America: Love It or Leave It," they sneered. Class resentments fanned the flames of a growing conservative backlash, as working-class whites lashed back at the relatively elite college-educated radicals who were denouncing them as "racists" and "pigs." This dynamic reached an apotheosis at the 1968 Chicago Democratic National Convention, where middle-class protesters were shocked to find themselves brutally attacked by working-class policemen—often of more or less the same age—who, with the blessings of Mayor Richard Daley's administration, let loose with billy clubs and tear gas, backed up with the very visible threat of guns. As Americans watched the once proudly liberal Democratic party impotently presiding over a frighteningly violent political spectacle, many came to the conclusion that Democrats were incapable of governing themselves, let alone the nation.[50]

During the same period that the white New Left was developing its attack on liberalism, key forces of black protest were undergoing a parallel process of radicalization. This new movement in African-American politics was loosely organized around the concept of "black power," a highly controversial term that emerged suddenly onto the American political scene when Stokley Carmichael succeeded in making it the rallying cry of the Meredith March through Mississippi in 1966.[51] By 1967, what can be loosely referred to as the Black Power movement was widely seen as having eclipsed the Civil Rights movement, which remained stymied by the overwhelmingly difficult task of extending its operations out of the South to include the rest of the nation. Embraced by a wide variety of black activists and organizations, this new movement contained a variety of competing political philosophies and agendas.[52] Its dominant public image, however, was very much determined by its more radical, revolutionary wing, which, like the post-1966 New Left, was deeply hostile to all forms of liberalism.

Consequently, social liberals found themselves doubly attacked from the Left. Black Power advocates repeatedly attacked their ideas and practices as inherently reactionary and racially oppressive. In their well-known 1967 work, *Black Power: The Politics of Liberation in America*, Stokley Carmichael and Charles V. Hamilton denounced the entire concept of integration as "despicable," arguing that "it is based on complete acceptance of the fact that in order to have a decent house or education, black people must move into a white neighborhood or send their children to a white school. . . . 'integration' is a subterfuge for the maintenance of white supremacy." The Civil Rights movement's philosophy of nonviolence had "for the masses of black people . . . resulted in virtually nothing." The tactic of pursuing coalitions between blacks and like-minded liberals and parts of the labor movement was doomed to fail, as "at bottom, those groups accept the American system and want only—if at all—to make peripheral, marginal reforms in it. Such reforms are inadequate to rid the society of racism." Democratic social welfare programs typified the inadequacies of liberal reform. "Any federal program conceived with black people in mind is doomed if blacks do not control it," Carmichael and Hamilton argued. "It is our hope that the day may soon come when black people will reject federal funds because they have understood that these programs are geared to pacification rather than to genuine solutions."[53]

Black Power, however, was mild stuff compared to the inflammatory rhetoric that prominent movement figures such as Carmichael (whose radicalism quickly escalated following the publication of *Black Power*), H. Rap Brown, Huey Newton, Bobby Seale, and Eldridge Cleaver began to issue. "When you talk of Black Power," stated Carmichael in 1966, "you talk about bringing this country to its knees. When you talk of Black Power, you talk of building a movement that will smash everything Western civilization has created."[54] The following year, SNCC chairman H. Rap Brown stated that the anniversary of the Watts riot should be commemorated as the day that "the blacks of Watts picked up their guns to fight for their freedom. That was our Declaration of Independence, and we signed it with Molotov cocktails and rifles." During the Detroit riot of 1967—which left 43 dead, 7,000 arrested, 1,300 buildings destroyed, and 2,700 businesses looted—he threatened that "if America doesn't come around, we're going to burn it down." During the same year, Newton wrote: "Only with the power of the gun can the black masses halt the terror and brutality perpetuated against them by the armed racist power structure." Given the rapidly escalating number of ghetto riots during the time—43 in 1966, 164 in 1967, and 125 in 1968—such statements appeared to many to represent a real threat (or, to some radical elements, hope) of full-blown domestic insurrection.[55]

As in the case of the New Left, the national media focused heavily on a relatively small number of particularly telegenic individuals, anointing them as "movement leaders" and endlessly repeating their most shocking statements. In 1967, for example, *Time* magazine, in an article entitled "Civil Rights: The New Racism" (with the photo caption "Does Black Power . . . mean white blood?"), quoted CORE director Floyd McKissick as stating that "the greatest hypocrisy we have is the Statue of Liberty. We ought to break the young lady's legs and point her to Mississippi."[56] This media sensationalism created a negative dynamic within the movement, as it encouraged the growth of revolutionary fantasies and extremist tactics at the expense of more considerate—but less attention-getting—programs for political change. The resultant escalation of revolutionary posturing corresponded directly to a loss of political effectiveness at the organizational and local levels, where committed but less-prominent activists found themselves struggling with increasing internal divisions, external hostilities, and out-flowing resources.[57]

This situation further undermined political support for social liberalism, which was rapidly becoming linked in the public mind with what was widely understood as anti-American agitation and lawlessness. The War on Poverty in particular was stigmatized as a "black program" that was not only riddled with waste and abuse but encouraged antisocial behavior and violence.[58] As Weir notes, by the time of the 1967 congressional debates over reauthorization of the Office of Economic Opportunity (OEO), members of both parties "tried to link the poverty programs with urban riots, black militancy, and subversive political activity."[59] Representative Paul A. Fino, a Republican from New York, argued:

> [T]here is little doubt that the Office of Economic Opportunity has been at the bottom of much of the rioting and troublemaking which we have sadly witnessed in the past few years throughout this country. . . . [It] has hired muggers and criminals. It has subsidized revolution and social agitation. It has provided tax dollars for the dissemination of what [can] only be called—hard as it is to believe—Communist propaganda.[60]

Even more damaging to social liberals was the fact that such negative associations with violence, un-American agitation, and immorality were not simply pinned on particular programs, but were seen as part and parcel of the larger political world view that they were believed to embody. When Attorney

General Ramsey Clark criticized Chicago mayor Richard Daley's instructions to the police to "shoot to kill arsonists and shoot to maim looters" during the riots following King's murder, for example, scores of outraged citizens wrote furious letters of protest against what they saw as an unconscionable capitulation to mob violence.[61] As one resident of Columbus, Ohio, raged:

> It really makes one sick to think how hard our forefathers fought and strived to build the strongest and wealthiest Nation in the world, only to have a group of selfish cowards take over, and sell out the constitutional rights of the majority in order to appease the minority. Then to get on a national news network and tell the minority group in so many words its [*sic*] OK to riot, loot, steal, and burn down the country. . . . The Great Society is a very sick society. I only hope there [are a] few threads left by November for Mr. Nixon to rebuild the country we used to have.[62]

Such sentiments extended to what was widely seen as the insufficiently tough response to the massive antiwar protests of the period, which further reinforced a sense of social breakdown and government pusillanimity. A poll taken in the wake of the 1968 Democratic convention, for example, found that 71 percent of the public felt that the city's security measures had been justified, and 57 percent believed that the police and National Guard had not used excessive force.

The overall result was that social liberals suddenly found themselves in an increasingly isolated and politically tenuous position. While the radical Left subjected them to a constant barrage of highly publicized attacks, much of the rest of the country began to blame them for creating the conditions under which such agitation flourished. To a certain extent, this was not undeserved. Social liberals had promised more than they could deliver, raising the idealistic expectations of an influential minority of young white radicals, as well as the long-deferred hopes of millions of African Americans who had survived generations of racial oppression.

On the other hand, it was also true that social liberalism represented what by the mid-1960s had become the dominant understanding of what would be required to resolve the widely accepted conception of the American dilemma. The goals of ending poverty and racial discrimination had come to be regarded as necessary to the realization of American political values among a sizable and influential segment of the population. Yet, the force of the historical maelstrom that was unleashed in the late 1960s overwhelmed what had only recently seemed like a reasonable plan to build a new political coalition and move forward with a radically reformist domestic agenda. Consequently, social liberals themselves turned to a form of apocalyptic rhetoric that warned of a stark choice between continued reform and dangerous reaction.

The American Dilemma at the Breaking Point

In 1968, the Kerner Commission, organized by President Johnson to investigate the causes of the previous summer's massive riots in the ghettos of Newark and Detroit, opened its official report by asserting, "Our nation is moving toward two societies, one black, one white—separate and unequal." Racial divisions were rapidly deepening, the commission warned, and would continue to do so unless dramatic action was taken. Citing the institutional forces of white racism as the central cause of the destructive conditions of ghetto life, the commission depicted its call for an unprecedented program of social intervention to improve this situation as a moral responsibility and national imperative. "To pursue our present course," it warned, "will involve the continuing polarization of the American community and, ultimately, *the destruction of basic democratic values.*"[63]

This theme echoed across the battered social liberal coalition. America was at a crossroads, it was repeatedly stated. Promises made must be fulfilled. To turn back now would bring untold disaster. The democratic spirit of the nation was at stake. The old Myrdalian paradigm, it seemed, had been pushed to the breaking point. Either the American dilemma—now reformulated to demand not simply the end of formal discrimination, but the eradication of entrenched socioeconomic inequality—had to be resolved, or its contradictions would destroy the democratic spirit of the nation.

There is little question that this sense of urgency was primarily fueled by the riots. While social liberals generally condemned them as destructive outbursts of frustration likely to fuel a backlash of repressive reaction, they also portrayed them as an understandable response to a long history of racial oppression, legitimately raised hopes, and increasingly dashed expectations. Consequently, it was argued, the only way to stop the riots was to make good on the nation's long-deferred promise of liberal equality.

In "A Way Out of the Exploding Ghetto," published by the *New York Times* in 1967, Bayard Rustin wrote that if many in the previous generations of African Americans had, like most victims of systematic oppression, fatalistically acquiesced to their lot, the black youth of today weren't "having any":

They don't share the feeling that something must be wrong with them, that they are responsible for their own exclusion from this affluent society. The Civil Rights movement—in fact, the whole liberal trend beginning with John Kennedy's election—has told them otherwise.

Conservatives will undoubtedly seize the occasion for an attack on the Great Society, liberalism, the welfare state, and Lyndon Johnson. But the young Negroes are right: the promises made to them were good and necessary and long, long overdue. The youth were right to believe in them. The only trouble is that they were not fulfilled.

Prominent Republicans and Dixiecrats are demanding not that the promises be fulfilled, but that they be revoked. What they and the American people absolutely must understand now is that the promises cannot be revoked. They were not made to a handful of leaders in a White House drawing room; they were made to an entire generation, one not likely to forget or to forgive.

The ultimate decision that faced the country at this moment, Rustin concluded, was "whether we shall have a conscious and authentic democratic social revolution or more tragic and futile riots that tear our nation to shreds."[64]

In his 1968 writings, shortly before his assassination, Martin Luther King stressed his agreement with the conclusions of the Kerner report and proposed a massive, nonviolent campaign to pressure the federal government to act upon its recommendations.[65] Once again, the situation facing the nation was portrayed as a stark choice between transformation and destruction. If this campaign to provide jobs and income for the poor failed, King warned, "nonviolence will be discredited, and the country may be plunged into holocaust—a tragedy deepened by the awareness that it was avoidable." This threat was backed up by the specter of further riots, which were portrayed as the bitter fruit of promises unfulfilled:

> We have learned from bitter experience that our government does not correct a race problem until it is confronted directly and dramatically. We also know, as official Washington may not, that the flash point of Negro rage is close at hand. . . . there is no longer a choice now between nonviolence and riots. . . . I don't think America can stand another summer of Detroit-like riots without a development that could destroy the soul of the nation, and even the democratic possibilities of the nation.[66]

Despite such evocations of apocalyptic threat, social liberals portrayed themselves as representing a position of rationality and moderation that was in danger of being crushed between growing forces of extreme political polarization. In 1967, one of the editors of *Dissent* representatively lamented that in a crisis atmosphere where the violence of the urban ghetto seemed to merge with that of Vietnam, "political emotion bounces from far Right to far Left, with no room anywhere for the constructive analysis so desperately needed if American democracy is to survive in any viable condition."[67] During the same year, a group of ten congressmen issued a formal statement entitled "War, Riot, and Priorities," which argued:

> Our nation is in crisis. We fight a stalemated war 10,000 miles from our shores; there is no immediate prospect for peace. We face despair and disruption in our cities; there is no immediate prospect for solution. . . . The deprived, whether in Vietnam or the ghetto, cry out for redress and independence; but their call is not understood. . . . America, then, is threatened not only by overwhelming problems, but by the dangerous consequences of our response, a cycle of vigilantism and repression, in domestic and foreign policy alike, which may ultimately tear apart the soul of this nation.[68]

This sense of being at a crisis point, in which political polarization threatened to destroy the liberal center, was applied directly to the 1968 elections. In his 1968 book, *Beyond Civil Rights*, standing vice president and Democratic presidential candidate Hubert Humphrey wrote that "in 1968 there comes a crossroads: a dangerous election, a hazardous national choice":

> Are we going to move backward into separation and fear, into a society in which the races live in hostile enclaves, in which every man is continually conscious of his race, in which no man is safe from a mindless violence that may strike him solely because of his color? . . . Look at the seething cauldron of the cities, listen to the talk of white vigilantes and of black revolutionaries, watch the sale of guns and the making of firebombs, look at the flight of white people and the mounting anger of black people—*is that the way America ends, after all the dreams that mankind had for this nation?*

What was needed, Humphrey concluded, was "to complete the unfinished, peaceful American revolution." Once again, this demanded the resolution of the Myrdalian dilemma: "The struggle for equal opportunity in America," Humphrey claimed, citing the Civil Rights movement, "is the struggle for America's soul."[69]

The Implosion of Social Liberalism

Although the election of Richard Nixon as president of the United States in 1968 by no means entailed the sort of catastrophic shift to the right that Humphrey and others so direly intimated, it did represent a fundamental turning point in the evolution of American political life. In terms of electoral politics, it marked the beginning of the end of the New Deal coalition, signaling a partial realignment that would increasingly build the strength of what political analyst Kevin Phillips presciently described at the time as an "emerging Republican majority."[70] With regard to American liberalism more broadly, 1968 marked the implosion of a transformative liberal vision. Social liberals had challenged American democracy to resolve what was held to be its one great internal contradiction: the barriers that racial discrimination and entrenched poverty posed to the realization of individual potential for millions of American citizens. Judged by the terms posed by social liberals, the United States had lost this historic battle.

By 1965, after a decade of political mobilization, the Civil Rights movement had succeeded in having its expansive reformulation of the Myrdalian paradigm adopted by the president as the public position of the Democratic party. This development initially appeared to be fulfilling the prescription laid out by Rustin for a realignment of the Democratic party around a strong social liberal agenda. It quickly became apparent, however, that major obstacles stood in the way of translating social liberal goals into concrete policy outcomes. Rather than retreating from their stated position, however, social liberals responded to the increasingly polarized and crisis-ridden political atmosphere of the late 1960s by insisting that the nation had reached a critical turning point. It faced a stark choice, they insisted, between making good on its promise of eradicating racial inequities or losing the soul of its democratic tradition.

Although the dire predictions of such social liberals did not in any concrete sense come to pass—the wave of riots crested and died down, and governing institutions remained functioning and intact—something important had nonetheless occurred. Even if the form of American liberal democracy remained essentially unchanged, its cultural context was dramatically different. As long as something like social liberalism persisted as an important ideological force, the nation's claim to its own most central legitimating values stood under indictment. And, unlike the much more radical rejections of liberalism made by the New Left and Black Power movements, this indictment of the nation came not from the margins, but from what had become a substantial portion of the political mainstream. In this sense, an important current in American liberalism had turned against itself. Unable to resolve what had been nationally championed as its one great internal contradiction, social liberals had little choice but to move to the right or the left, withdraw into the politically protected world of the courts and bureaucracies, or stubbornly hang on in a state of self-accused impotence.

We've largely won the battle of ideas. We are in the implementation stage now.

—Kate O'Beirne, former vice president of government relations,

Heritage Foundation, and Washington editor of the National Review, 1998

8

The Conservative Movement

If 1968 was a year of crisis for social liberals, conservatives recognized it as a long-awaited moment of opportunity. With a few important exceptions (such as, most notably, the McCarthy era), conservatives had been in a relatively weak position since the triumph of the New Deal in the 1930s. Particularly in the heady days of liberal optimism during the early to mid-1960s, conservatives found themselves pushed to the margins of political influence, commonly dismissed as unfashionable and unimportant. By the late 1960s, however—with the ghettos burning, the New Left and Black Power movements preaching revolution, and social liberals reeling from their inability to make good on their promises of equalitarian reform—astute conservative strategists were devising the formula that would allow right-of-center forces to control the shape and direction of American politics for decades to come.

Racial politics was a key ingredient in this formula. In the realm of national electoral politics, race provided the most important means by which an increasingly conservative Republican party was able to dominate the Democrats by breaking up the New Deal coalition, capitalizing on the racially charged anger and resentment of lower- to middle-income whites. Race, in conjunction with other controversial sociocultural issues, such as feminism and gay rights, represented a primary factor that drove the development of an explicitly class-conscious movement against the left-liberalism of the 1960s among members of this primary demographic group. More broadly, race became the central issue cleavage that drove the basic left-of-center liberal commitment to using government power to reduce entrenched patterns of socioeconomic inequality to the margins of the mainstream political culture.

In 1968, the presidential campaign of Republican candidate Richard Nixon pioneered the use of race as a primary weapon of conservative electoral politics within the new context of a nation that had been profoundly changed (although by no means transformed) by the Civil Rights movement and its successful battle against Jim Crow. This new conservative approach avoided explicitly racist appeals, relying instead on carefully selected symbols, rhetorical pronouncements, and "code words" that appealed to white voters nervous about racial change without alienating moderates who had opposed Jim Crow segregation and discrimination. This formula proved to be extremely effective, helping Nixon to win the 1968 election by a narrow margin. Consequently, the national Republican party continued to use race as a primary means of recruiting formerly Democratic voters in the Nixon reelection campaign of 1972 and throughout the 1980s.

During this time, a new construction of race was developed that played a central role in promoting and legitimizing a newly ascendant conservative position. While linking up to long-standing conservative motifs, this new racial paradigm emerged out of a deliberate process of ideological innovation. In the Nixon campaign of 1968, race had been used in an opportunistic manner that was essentially divorced from any larger agenda or conservative philosophy. Beginning in the mid-1970s, however, neoconservative intellectuals developed a highly influential line of thought that, among other things, reinterpreted the meaning of race and its relationship to American liberalism. Like Nixon's "southern strategy," this new racial position rejected white supremacism and Jim Crow and embraced the basic antidiscrimination provisions of the Civil Rights acts of 1964 and 1965. Unlike the Nixon approach, however, it presented a coherent racial paradigm that spoke directly to the melded race and class divisions of the 1970s.

In a powerful reinvention of the traditional Myrdalian position, neoconservatives argued that policies such as affirmative action constituted a new form of "reverse discrimination" that, like its Jim Crow predecessors, represented an exceptional violation of basic principles of American liberalism. This, in turn, was held to be part and parcel of the larger corruption of liberal values caused by the excessive equalitarianism of the 1960s. Although this critique of equalitarianism extended beyond race to include attacks on feminism and what was seen as the overextension of the welfare state, it embodied a strong proscription against the broad social liberal goal of addressing issues of race and class inequality. This rejection of equalitarian politics was reinforced by the neoconservative insistence that racial equity had been achieved with the prohibition of de jure discrimination, as any remaining patterns of race or class inequality could be dismissed as a problem of lower-class culture or as an inevitable product of a competitive free-market order.

This neoconservative position would prove to be enormously influential over the course of the coming decades, having a direct impact on law, policy, and general political debate. As an ideological formulation, the success of this new paradigm was primarily attributable to the fact that it was firmly grounded in the widely resonant language of American liberalism. As former leftists or left-liberals who had migrated to the right, neoconservatives, unlike many other conservative factions, approached politics in a decidedly liberal mode. While echoing many old-line conservative stands against equalitarian values, the welfare state, and activist government, the liberal framing of neoconservative political thought made it much more acceptable to the political mainstream (and particularly to influential elites) than the anti–civil rights and, in some cases, antimodern traditionalism that had previously characterized conservative discourse on race and other, closely related equity issues.

In terms of practice, the enormous influence of the neoconservative position on race and the larger anti-equalitarianism of which it was a part was primarily the result of two factors. One was the exponential growth of a powerful new conservative "counterestablishment" of foundations, research institutes, media outfits, and advocacy groups dedicated to vaulting conservative ideas into a dominant position of political influence. This development was closely bound up with the rise of the neoconservative movement itself, which was intensely committed to mobilizing the financial, organizational, and intellectual resources needed to win the "war of ideas" against left-of-center liberalism. It was also heavily supported by the rise of the New Right and the new form of populist activism that it represented. While the mobilization of the New Right was strongly fueled by reactions against feminism, legalized abortion, gay rights, and the perceived erosion of traditional moral values, it also incorporated a strong element of white racial backlash, particularly among lower- to middle-income voters. As such, it bolstered the GOP attack on the New Deal coalition that had been pioneered by Nixon, while at the same time achieving a broad and highly organized conservative mobilization.[1] These developments pushed the Republican party further to the right, while placing it in a much stronger political position, both nationally and, increasingly, on the state and local levels. In combination, the revitalized conservative movement, new conservative establishment, and more conservative Republican party succeeded in pushing national political discourse dramatically to the right.

The foundations for this rightward shift were laid in the 1970s and cemented during the 1980s. The consequent conservative turn in the nation's political culture has been ongoing since that time. While this historic change cannot be attributed exclusively to race or any other single-factor explanation, race was the most important factor that allowed the national Republican party to break up the New Deal coalition. It was also the primary issue that enabled the larger conservative movement to relegate questions of socioeconomic equity to the margins of American politics. These developments have been particularly remarkable given that such inequality has grown substantially in the United States since the 1960s. To a significant extent, conservative policies have encouraged and exacerbated this larger trend. Nonetheless, forms of liberalism that advocate the use of government power to address socioeconomic inequity have remained moribund. While a number of important factors have contributed to this development, race has been the most influential in terms of sapping the support of lower- to middle-income whites away from any resurgent expression of liberal equalitarianism.

The Changing Racial Politics of the Nixon Administration

The bywords of the 1968 Nixon campaign were "law and order." Millions of ordinary Americans had been shocked and frightened by the events of that calamitous year: the slaughter of American forces by the North Vietnamese in the Tet offensive of January, the murder of Martin Luther King and consequent eruption of ghetto riots in April, the assassination of the widely revered senator and presidential candidate Robert F. Kennedy in June, and street fighting at the Chicago Democratic convention in August. Both the white Left and the radical wing of the Black Power movement had turned to a form of revolutionary politics that glorified violence and anti-American extremism. As the inflammatory pronouncements of their media-anointed leaders were continuously broadcast to a confused and increasingly angry public, Nixon's promise to restore social order and reassert the rule of law resonated widely.

While the many varieties of social disorder tended to blur together in the perceptions of the general public, the Nixon campaign was well aware that issues of race offered by far the most political leverage.[2] Nixon took careful note of the surprising degree of success that the presidential campaign of race-baiting Alabama governor George Wallace was experiencing among traditionally Democratic lower- to middle-class whites in both the South and North. The Wallace campaign was doing so well, in fact, that Nixon was concerned that it might cause him to lose the election by draining off too many voters who might otherwise be persuaded to vote Republican. Nixon was also aware, however, that while the 1964 Republican presidential contender, Barry Goldwater, had won five states in the Deep South, the widespread perception that he was a right-wing extremist had lost him the moderate Republican vote in the rest of the nation (excepting his home state of Arizona). Consequently, Nixon was determined to win as much of the white vote in the Deep South as he could without losing more moderate conservative voters in the border states and the rest of the nation.

The resultant racially driven campaign strategy marked a critical departure for the Republican party—and, consequently, for the nation at large. With the so-called southern strategy at its heart (engineered by Harry Dent, a former aide to the archconservative Senator Strom Thurmond of South Carolina), the Nixon campaign carefully crafted racial appeals capable of winning over unhappy white Democrats without invoking the sort of overt racism or segregationist nostalgia that would alienate moderates. The Nixon team understood that while most of the white electorate outside of the Deep South supported the principle of racial equality in the abstract, they drew the line at compensatory policies that would disrupt the racial composition of their schools or neighborhoods. In contrast to left-liberals who attacked this position as inherently racist and hypocritical, the message of the Nixon campaign was that it was reasonable and just. A Republican administration, the Nixon campaign reassured nervous whites, could be trusted to hold back the forces that threatened to impose integration on unwilling white communities.

Nixon won the election by a narrow margin, drawing 31.79 million votes (43.4 percent) to Senator Hubert Humphrey's 31.25 million (42.7 percent). Remarkably, Wallace won almost 9.9 million votes (13.5 percent) and carried the five Deep South states of Alabama, Mississippi, Arkansas, Georgia, and Louisiana. The fact that 70–80 percent of Wallace voters indicated that Nixon was their second choice reinforced Nixon's determination to draw more of this army of disaffected Democrats into the Republican fold come 1972.[3]

Given Nixon's concern with winning more of the Wallace vote, the fact that a raft of left-liberal domestic policy measures were nonetheless enacted during his first term in office was a testament to the continued strength of social ~~liberals in government~~, as well as an indication, in retrospect, of just how far to the right the nation has shifted since that time. The first Nixon administration pioneered federally mandated affirmative-action programs through such initiatives as the Philadelphia Plan, which sought to increase minority employment in the construction trades; "Eight-A" contracting requirements, which set aside fixed percentages of federal contracts for minority-owned businesses; and the establishment of the Office of Minority Business Enterprise, which provided assistance to minority businesses seeking to secure government contracts.[4] (While stemming in part from a genuine desire to promote "black capitalism" as a superior alternative to Democratic initiatives designed to support African-American economic advancement, Nixon was also pleased to promote programs that would drive a wedge between the key Democratic constituencies of labor and civil rights groups, which were deeply split on affirmative action.) At the same time, Nixon allowed the Department of Health, Education, and Welfare to push aggressively forward with school desegregation cases in the South, which were steadily building a body of law that could logically be extended to demand racial integration in public schools across the nation.

Nixon's key initiative in the area of social policy was equally remarkable. Daniel Patrick Moynihan—one of the initial architects of the War on Poverty and author of the infamous Moynihan report—had been hired as a key presidential advisor. Moynihan succeeded in convincing the president to support a guaranteed-income program dubbed the Family Assistance Plan. By today's standards a shocking expansion of the social safety net, this program would have established a national income floor for all families in the United States. (At that time, many left-liberal groups opposed it for not being generous enough.)[5] Nixon also signed into law a myriad of social welfare initiatives engineered by congressional Democrats, including a program to create temporary jobs in the ghettos, a subsidized-housing program, revenue sharing and block grants for cities, increased welfare payments, a major expansion of the food-stamp program, and a new Social Security program to aid the disabled.[6]

As these examples make clear, the first Nixon administration was not by any means following the conservative policy script as we know it today. One reason for this is quite simple: the now-familiar conservative domestic policy agenda did not exist at the time as a coherent set of ideas and policy prescriptions. Affirmative action was not yet held to equal reverse discrimination, and social welfare policies designed to help the poor were not yet portrayed as guaranteed to backfire and make things worse. "We just didn't have a new conventional wisdom—we accepted the paradigm of the Great

Society," explained former Nixon advisor Richard Nathan, considering this policy agenda in retrospect.[7] Particularly during the initial two years of the first Nixon administration, the shape of a new conservative alternative remained quite unclear.

During the early 1970s, however, a more sharply defined position began to appear. Its most prominent feature was an increasingly aggressive assault on the policy of busing to achieve racial integration in the public schools—which, by 1970, had emerged as the most controversial domestic issue facing the nation. Court-ordered remedies to proven histories of deliberate, state-sponsored discrimination were becoming more and more demanding, with school districts instructed to achieve actual integration, rather than simply instituting "freedom of choice" plans that ostensibly eliminated discrimination but in practice changed nothing.[8] Further, such remedies were rapidly being extended to the North and West, as civil rights lawyers succeeded in demonstrating that states in those regions had pursued segregationist measures that were just as effective—if less overt—than those in the South.[9]

Although a significant number of court-ordered desegregation plans were quietly implemented without undue racial strife (particularly in more rural areas), others were highly publicized disasters.[10] Overall, the national mood surrounding the issue was one of ugly and potentially explosive racial confrontation. White parents vowed massive resistance to what they regarded as a draconian plan to sacrifice their children's education and safety to a wrong-minded conception of racial justice. Black parents grew embittered over what they viewed as a racist attempt to continue to deny their children equal educational opportunities. Given that so much was at stake, fears and emotions ran high on both sides. Given, however, the greater numbers and power of the white majority, their concerns carried by far the most political weight.

Busing was only the most visible manifestation of a larger shift that had occurred in the nation's political culture. As Carmines and Stimson demonstrated, by 1972 racial issues had transformed the content and structure of American political beliefs. During the 1950s and early 1960s, the key issues that distinguished so-called liberals from conservatives centered around the social welfare policies of the New Deal. During that period, such attitudes had no correlation with issues of race. Beginning with the 1964 election, however, this pattern began to change. Race increasingly became the key issue that divided the left and right sides of the political spectrum and organized people's attitudes on a variety of other issues—including what were by then closely associated questions of social welfare policy. By 1972, this transformation was complete. Race was now the central issue cleavage in American political culture.[11]

A memo written by Patrick Buchanan—who at that time was working as a speechwriter for Vice President Spiro T. Agnew—to President Nixon in 1970 indicates that conservative strategists were aware of this sea change in public opinion. The busing controversy, Buchanan believed, was reversing the political momentum of civil rights issues:

> Where the Court in [the *Brown v. Board of Education* decision] in 1954 ruled at the crest of a national tide, their current rulings go against the grain of rising and angry public opinion. . . . The second era of Re-Construction [*sic*] is over; the ship of Integration is going down; it is not our ship; it belongs to national liberalism—and we cannot salvage it; and we ought not to be aboard. For the first time since 1954, the national Civil Rights community is going to sustain an up-and-down defeat. It may come now; it may come hard; it may be disguised and dragged out—but it can no longer be avoided.[12]

Nixon took note, ordering staffers to begin crafting a new policy position on school desegregation issues. As issued by the White House shortly thereafter, this position drew a sharp distinction between the de jure segregation of the Jim Crow South and the de facto segregation that existed in the rest of the nation. The first, Nixon held, had to be eliminated. The second, while "undesirable," should not "by itself be cause for federal enforcement actions."[13] Ignoring the fact that civil rights lawyers had provided meticulous evidence demonstrating the many means by which de facto segregation functioned just as effectively as its de jure counterpart, this position presaged the much more extensive conservative attack on civil rights policies that would emerge later by insisting that only the most baldly explicit forms of discrimination merited remedial government action.

Nixon followed through on this position by firing prominent liberals within the federal civil rights bureaucracy (most notably Leon Panetta, who had been serving as the director of HEW's Office of Civil Rights), while instructing others to make sure that everyone remaining toed the line. "I want you personally to jump Richardson and Justice and tell them to *Knock off this Crap*," stated a 1970 Nixon memo to high-ranking aide John Erlichman regarding those deemed too willing to support court-ordered busing decrees. "I hold them personally accountable to keep their left-wingers in step with my express policy—Do what the law requires and not *one bit more*."[14] By the end of the year, this newly aggressive conservative posture had been extended to other domestic policy arenas. The Family Assistance Plan, for example, was quietly dropped in conjunction with a general turn against remaining Great Society programs. "Flush Model Cities and Great Society," one memo instructed. "It's failed."[15]

The president's 1972 reelection campaign further publicized and extended this conservative turn as Nixon repeatedly stressed his opposition to busing and commitment to containing the rising costs of social welfare programs. He frequently voiced his support for the growing white reaction against affirmative action policies, despite the fact that it was his administration that had instituted them in the first place. Aided by the Democrats' internal disarray (which had only escalated with their selection of left-liberal George McGovern as their presidential nominee) and the attempted assassination of George Wallace (which left him paralyzed for life and unable to continue the race), this strategy succeeded in creating a landslide reelection victory for the president, who won every state but Massachusetts with almost 61 percent of the vote.[16]

Despite the consequent Watergate debacle, the 1972 campaign had set an important precedent for an increasingly conservative Republican party by demonstrating the leverage to be gained from divisive racial issues, particularly among formerly Democratic lower- to middle-class whites. The New Deal coalition could be broken up, and a critical group of swing voters gained, by carefully playing the new politics of race, as well as the controversial social issues with which it had become so closely associated. Still accepting some form of the welfare state and willing to enforce affirmative action policies (despite making rhetorical criticisms of them), however, the Nixon administration was not, by today's standards, strongly conservative. Developing domestic policy positions through more of an ad hoc process of political calculation than a defined conservative agenda, the Nixon administration only pointed the way toward a new form of racial conservatism. It remained for others to craft a more systematic position that included a coherent ideology and matching set of legal and policy prescriptions.

Neoconservatism and Its Legacy

By the beginning of the 1970s, it was clear that the social and political upheavals of the 1960s—particularly, although by no means exclusively, concerning issues of race—had instigated a serious reaction among a critical part of the American electorate. Given the political and cultural dominance of various strands of left-of-center liberalism during the postwar period, however, there was at that time no well-developed conservative position that could speak in a direct, coherent, and widely acceptable way to this newly emergent zeitgeist. Although a small band of intellectuals had laid the foundation for a new form of conservative political thought during the 1950s, their work predated the convulsive racial politics of the 1960s–1970s and could not speak to the new issues confronting the nation.[17] This was also true with regard to the several important sectors of conservative activism that had been established during the 1950s–1960s.[18] The rise of the neoconservative movement was the most important development that allowed the broader forces of political conservatism to develop a coherent position on race that would prove capable of successfully navigating the complex waters of white reaction, conservative principles, and discredited Jim Crowism.[19] (While the New Right, which will be discussed below, successfully mobilized forces of white reaction, it was much more oriented to political activism than to theory building and consequently did not develop a similarly well-articulated position on race.) Given the centrality of race to American domestic politics during this period, this represented a critical contribution to the growing conservative movement as a whole.

Important sectors of conservative activism during the 1950s–1960s had included the forces gathered around William F. Buckley's *National Review* (founded in 1955), the closely aligned Young Americans for Freedom (established in 1960) and American Conservative Union (established in 1964), and the more extremist John Birch Society (founded in 1958). All had opposed the passage of the Civil Rights Act of 1964 on the grounds that it represented an illegitimate extension of federal power into the private sector. Given that southern segregationists had been making this argument since the days of Reconstruction, it was difficult for what came to be known as the "Old Right" to draw a bright line between antistatism and white supremacism— or, at least, one that would be seen and understood as such by whites whose political identity had become bound up with their opposition to Jim Crow on what they understood to be the moral high ground of fundamental American political values.[20] The neoconservatives, in contrast, as northern intellectuals, former Leftists, and, commonly, Jews whose families had been victims of racial persecution themselves, had always been strongly opposed to any form of state-sanctioned discrimination and segregation. Consequently, they could not be accused of being simple (or simple-minded) racists nor antidemocratic elitists. This was very important in that it enabled others to embrace the neoconservatives' work without fear of suffering the stigma of a now-repudiated racial past.

Although not labeled as such at the time, the neoconservative movement dates back to the mid-1960s, when a loosely connected network of well-established academics, writers, editors, and publishers who had previously advocated left-of-center politics found common cause in their revulsion against the social liberalism and radical leftism of the era.[21] Originally, this network included such well-known figures as Edward Banfield, Daniel Bell, Nathan Glazer, and Seymour Martin Lipset (all Harvard professors), James Q. Wilson (a UCLA academic), Irving Kristol (editor of the important neoconservative publication *Public Interest*), Norman Podhoretz (editor of the other neoconservative flagship journal, *Commentary*, 1960–1985),[22] and Daniel Patrick Moynihan (member of the Kennedy, Johnson, Nixon, and Ford administrations and, later, senior U.S. senator from New York).[23] As shown by this partial listing of neoconservative leaders, the movement was distinguished by its high proportion of highly accomplished, intellectually sophisticated, politically savvy, and well-connected elites. Fervent believers in the power of ideas in political life, they possessed the intelligence and skills necessary to create a new corpus of conservative political thought.

Beginning in the early 1970s, neoconservative attacks on what was seen as a growing trend toward the dangerous overextension of civil rights policies began to appear regularly in *Public Interest* and *Commentary*.[24] In 1975, Nathan Glazer published the first major neoconservative work on racial issues, entitled *Affirmative Discrimination: Ethnic Inequality and Public Policy*. This influential book laid the groundwork for the new conservative position on race that would, in the course of the coming decade, be elaborated, extended, and endlessly reiterated by others.

According to Glazer, the Civil Rights Act of 1964 "could only be read as instituting into law Judge Harlan's famous dissent in *Plessy v. Ferguson*: 'Our Constitution is color-blind.'" Glazer based such historical claims on the (historically erroneous) proposition that American political values have always been rooted in a singular understanding of liberal equality. Race-conscious policies such as affirmative action had caused the nation to "abandon the first principle of a liberal society: that the individual and the individual's interests and good and welfare are the test of a good society." This, Glazer maintained, was "what was intended by the Constitution and the Civil Rights Act, and what most of the American people—in all the various racial and ethnic groups that make it up—believe." Consequently, he concluded, "it is now our task to work with the intellectual, judicial, and political institutions of the country to reestablish the simple and clear understanding that rights attach to the individual, not the group, and that public policy must be exercised without distinction of race, color, or national origin."[25]

Glazer's argument represented a brilliant inversion of the old Myrdalian position. In his formulation, Jim Crow and affirmative action were moral equivalents, as both violated the principle of color-blindness rooted in the American liberal tradition. By framing opposition to race-conscious policies designed to ameliorate the cumulative effects of generations of intense discrimination in the context of timeless liberal values, Glazer avoided any association with the history of white supremacism, while at the same time appropriating the widespread moral legitimacy associated with the Myrdalian position. Although Glazer's formulation rejected the tradition of conservative thought that had opposed the Civil Rights acts, mainstream conservatives quickly embraced it as their own. (While some right-wing groups continued to espouse traditional white supremacism, this placed them in a highly marginal position well outside the boundaries of mainstream political discourse.)[26] Presumably, this represented a pragmatic adaptation to the times, as the battle over Jim Crow had decisively ended.[27] In any event, Glazer's racial paradigm had a broad public appeal, as it was attractive both to mainstream conservatives and to others who, while not self-identified conservatives, were unhappy about the new course of American racial politics.

This racial paradigm was embedded in a larger critique of equalitarian politics that was similarly grounded in the language of American liberalism. While echoing larger conservative themes that had dominated the postwar period—including, most notably, a commitment to militant anti-Communism, free-market capitalism, traditional cultural values, and the rule of traditional elites—neoconservatives presented these precepts in a self-consciously liberal format.[28] Neoconservatives, as Himmelfarb would later explain in an ongoing debate on the conservative movement published in the *Public Interest* and *Commentary*, proudly placed themselves in "the tradition of liberal-democratic modernity" that prioritized the principles of "individual liberty, self-government, and equality of opportunity."[29] Although this insistence on liberal values alienated some factions of the hardcore Right,[30] it resonated strongly with the larger political culture. Consequently, it helped to propel the conservative movement forward as a whole, as it framed many traditional conservative ideas in ways that were newly appealing to a wide political audience.

Prominent neoconservatives warned that the equalitarianism that had developed in the 1960s threatened to destroy the foundations of American liberalism. In their view, these excessively equalitarian values were being promoted by a "New Class" of left-leaning professors, bureaucrats, Democrats, journalists, and their ilk who had formed a powerful "university-government-media complex." These New Class elites, they argued, were systematically promoting destructive government policies, undermining respect for American capitalism, and attacking traditional morality in pursuit of an equalitarian vision that was impossible to achieve and undesirable to pursue. Such an overcommitment to equality eroded social health and stability as it proliferated desires and demands that flew in the face of both nature and virtue. By insisting, for example, that women should be equal to men, or that government policies should assess racial equity in terms of group results rather than individual opportunities, the New Class was upsetting the natural balance of family life, violating the constitutional order, and promoting a widespread sense of socially destructive malcontent. Unless liberalism could be cleansed of such equalitarian commitments, the neoconservatives predicted, the entire social order would be in danger of collapse.[31]

In their critique of equalitarianism, the neoconservatives spoke directly to the newly intertwined race and class controversies of the 1970s. In 1970, Edward Banfield's *The Unheavenly City* dropped a bomb on the left-liberal sensibility of the time, arguing that the claim of a looming "urban crisis" that demanded dramatic government redress was nothing more than a self-fulfilling prophecy promoted by misguided upper middle-class do-gooders. Although it was true that there was a concentration of lower-class individuals in the central cities and that this group was disproportionately black, the overall historical trend was toward an unprecedented level of prosperity for urban dwellers. Poverty, Banfield argued, was primarily the result of lower-class cultural values, which instilled orientations toward fatalism, immediate gratification, antisocial conduct, cheap thrills and "action" (particularly for males), and an inability to work toward a more stable and productive future. There was little that government could do to change this culture, which typically evolved over the course of generations. Consequently, Banfield's number-one recommendation was to "avoid rhetoric tending to raise expectations to unreasonable and unrealizable levels" and to insist that "the individual," rather than "society" or "white racism," bears responsibility for the problems of poverty.[32] An immediate bestseller, *The Unheavenly City* went through twenty-two printings before being reissued in a slightly revised version in 1974.[33]

Unlike traditional conservatives, however, neoconservatives were not (at least initially) opposed to social welfare policies in general. In keeping with their left-of-center roots, neoconservatives supported basic New Deal reforms, rejecting only what they saw as a dangerous overreaching of the Great Society. As Aaron Wildavsky explained in a 1973 essay:

> In the past, the clients of the New Deal had been the temporarily depressed but relatively stable lower and middle classes, people

who were on the whole willing to work but who had been restrained by the economic situation. . . . Now, however, government policy was being designed to deal not with such people but
with the *severely* deprived, those who actually needed not merely
an opportunity but continuing, long-term assistance. No previous
government had ever attempted to do for this sector of the population—those whom Marx called the *lumpenproletariat*—what
the American government set out to do. Yet nobody knew *how* to
go about it, either.[34]

The attempt to provide effective government assistance to this "lumpenproletariat," neoconservatives believed, was doomed to fail: it was simply, in
Glazer's formulation, beyond "the limits of social policy." In such a context,
the "law of unintended consequences" inevitably took over, with money being thrown at programs that spun out of control and caused more harm than
good. The best response was instead to roll back the equalitarian impulse
that animated such policies, and thereby reduce expectations of government's capacities to a more reasonable level.[35]

During the 1980s, other conservative advocates radicalized the original
neoconservative position to claim that social welfare policies represented the
root cause of urban poverty and should therefore be abandoned completely.
George Gilder's *Wealth and Poverty* (1980) and Charles Murray's *Losing
Ground* (1984) were particularly influential in promoting this newly aggressive conservative position. Heavily funded and promoted by conservative
foundations and research institutes, both were "required reading" within the
circles of the Reagan administration and its "inside the beltway" supporters. Although not strictly neoconservatives per se, both Gilder and Murray
were supported by the neoconservative network, which quickly shifted its
stance to be essentially in line with their views. In this sense, the neoconservative movement laid the foundations for what would, during the 1980s,
blossom into a new and heavily promoted conservative discourse that combined an attack on race-conscious policies such as affirmative action with an
implicitly racialized attack on social welfare programs for the poor.

The New Right

Beginning in the early 1970s, the rightward shift in American political life was
greatly accelerated by the rise of the New Right. Organizationally, the New
Right consisted of a core group of conservative leaders who developed a new

strategy for political action and a network of organizations dedicated to promoting the conservative cause. Sociologically, the New Right tapped into the enormous wellspring of anger, frustration, and alienation that had developed among lower- to middle-class whites in reaction to the social and political changes of the 1960s—particularly, although by no means exclusively, with regard to race. Politically, it provided an ideal complement to the neoconservative movement in terms of promoting the larger conservative movement. While the neoconservatives were elites who were highly skilled at the development and promotion of ideas, leaders of the New Right were primarily seasoned political activists whose skills had been honed in the nascent conservative struggle of the 1960s.[36] By the early 1970s, they were prepared to launch a new stage of the conservative movement dedicated to organizing the millions of ordinary Americans who had become ripe for mobilization in the name of "traditional values" or "social conservatism."[37]

The core ideology of the New Right was not significantly different from that of the so-called Old Right, as both were similarly committed to anti-Communism, a minimally regulated free market, and traditional moral values.[38] The New Right, however, was new in several key respects. In terms of organizational development, it developed effective new tools, such as direct-mail solicitation, for cultivating donors, mobilizing the grassroots, and building organizations. In terms of ideology, it placed a new emphasis on the controversial social issues of the day, stoking the backlash against, most notably, feminism, legalized abortion, racial liberalism, gay rights, and secular humanism. In so doing, the New Right cultivated a newly aggressive form of "conservative populism" that blamed what it viewed as devastating social cancers on the pernicious values of the "liberal elite."[39]

Beginning in the mid-1970s, New Right activists launched a highly successful campaign to organize socially conservative white evangelical Protestants, who had traditionally shied away from activist politics. Members of this demographic group were ripe for mobilization, as they widely believed that their values and way of life were under attack from an aggressively secular and morally libertine culture. Hot-button issues for what would soon emerge as the religious Right included racial liberalism, school prayer, feminism, the Equal Rights Amendment (ERA), legalized abortion, the gay rights movement, and, perhaps most pivotally (at least in the short run), the 1978 threat by the Internal Revenue Service to revoke the tax-exempt status of independent Christian schools that did not take "affirmative steps to secure minority students."[40] New Right visionary Richard Viguerie reported that fellow New Right leaders Paul Weyrich and Howard Phillips "spent countless hours" with evangelical ministers such as Jerry Falwell, James Robison, and Pat Robertson, "urging them to get involved in conservative politics."[41] By the late 1970s, these and other conservative religious leaders had become convinced of the desirability of political action. Initially nurtured by the experienced activists of the New Right, they quickly developed the capacity to act as an independent political force.[42]

Many New Right activists deployed a highly class-conscious language to explain their goals, strategy, and constituency. One early essay by Paul Weyrich, one of the preeminent leaders of the movement, entitled "Blue Collar or Blue Blood? The New Right Compared with the Old Right," argued that prior to the 1970s, American conservatism had been primarily an upper-class phenomenon. Consequently, it had a highly intellectual orientation and was not adept at communicating with the average American. Similarly, it was not politically strategic nor good at generating media coverage. Weyrich critically noted that the Old Right had failed to build a lasting connection with the deep wellspring of working-class anticommunism that had been tapped by Senator Joseph McCarthy in the 1950s. The New Right, in contrast, had a largely "middle-class, blue-collar and ethnic" base and was dedicated to class-based mobilization—with class being understood in cultural, political, and economic terms.[43]

As New Right advocate Samuel Francis explained, this constituency—which he described as "Middle American Radicals," or "MARs"—was "less an objectively defined class than a subjectively distinguished temperament." It was, however, distinguished by several important demographic features:

> In the mid-1970s, MARs had a family income of three to thirteen thousand dollars. There was a strong presence among them of northern European ethnics. . . . MARs were nearly twice as common in the South as in the north-central states. They tended to have completed high school but not to have attended college . . . and were "significantly less likely to be professional or managerial workers" than to be "skilled or semi-skilled blue collar workers."

MARs, Francis argued, "form a class—not simply a middle class and not simply an economic category—that is in revolt against the dominant patterns and structures of American society." Through the vehicle of the New Right, their goal was "to become the dominant political class in the United States by displacing its current elite, dismantling its apparatus of power, and discrediting its political ideology."[44]

As Weyrich explained, the immediate priority of the New Right was to take action against "culturally destructive government policies." Although there were, in the view of the New Right, numerous examples of these—legalized abortion, court-ordered prohibitions against school prayer, and the pending ERA—the most egregious had to do with racial issues.[45] As another New Right advocate wrote in an important collection of essays, *The New Right Papers* (1982):

> Nothing has contributed more to white populist disillusionment than the breathtaking hypocrisy and condescending arrogance shown by the establishment over the race issue. Infuriated South Boston residents booed and threw tomatoes at Senator Edward Kennedy when he made a rare public appearance to defend the hated racial busing program. "We cannot have one set of laws for Mississippi and another set of laws for Massachusetts," Kennedy once said. But no Kennedy has ever had to experience the horrors of having himself or his children bused into the ghetto. The Kennedys of America have their own double standard: one set of rules for their own wealthy class, and another for the middle and working classes.[46]

Such charges of the racial hypocrisy of "limousine liberals" constituted a primary motif of the New Right. By articulating and mobilizing this white racial resentment, the New Right helped to produce a form of class consciousness that—in opposition to the traditional expectations of the Left—linked working-class interests to a larger conservative movement that was fundamentally opposed not simply to socialism and Communism, but also to left-of-center liberalism of any form.

While its hostility to all varieties of leftist politics was made plain, the positive relationship between the New Right and a larger tradition of political thought was not well articulated by its leaders. In this sense, it is unclear whether the New Right should be considered as having operated within the boundaries of a broadly defined liberal tradition. On the one hand, the political activities of the New Right operated very much within the established structure of interest groups, grassroots organizing, lobbying, and the Republican party. New Right advocates were committed to working within the established system and presented themselves as a responsible and balanced alternative to more extremist right-wing groups.[47] On the other hand, the primary political commitment of the New Right was to "traditional values," rather than restoring a more conservative understanding of the meaning of liberal principles, such as individual rights or limited government (as in the case of the neoconservatives). Because the energy and attention of the movement was so overwhelmingly directed toward rolling back left-liberal initiatives such as busing, legalized abortion, and the prohibition of school prayer, it is impossible to say what their program for positive action would have included. This is particularly true as leaders of the New Right were uninterested in articulating a foundational position that would specify the broader underlying theories, principles, and commitments of the movement.[48] Consequently, it is perhaps most accurate to say that while the New Right stayed within the established lines of liberal politics in terms of its day-to-day operations, it contained an ideological openness toward nonliberal alternatives that might, at least in theory, be willing to trump individual rights or other liberal principles in the name of the greater collective good.[49]

The New Conservative Establishment

During the 1970s, neoconservative and New Right leaders converged in a shared determination to build what Blumenthal aptly described as a new "conservative counter-establishment." In the view of these conservative activists, such well-known and powerful entities as Harvard University, the *New York Times*, the Ford Foundation, the Council on Foreign Relations, and the Brookings Institution constituted a "liberal establishment" that continually pushed American politics toward the dangers of extreme left-liberalism.[50] It was critical, they agreed, to build a network of conservative organizations capable of countering—and, eventually, supplanting—the negative influence of this liberal monolith. Over time, it was hoped, this conservative establishment would have the power to leverage a rightward shift in American politics and culture, particularly although not exclusively by means of a more purely and aggressively conservative Republican party.

Again, while there were important political and ideological differences between the neoconservatives and the New Right, they complemented one another well in terms of building a larger conservative movement. The neoconservatives, as well-connected elites skilled in the development and promotion of ideas, played a particularly important role in convincing other powerful actors that it was critical to establish an organizational structure capable of vaulting conservative ideas into the political spotlight. Neoconservative leaders—Irving Kristol in particular—launched a highly successful campaign to convince directors of conservative foundations, corporate executives, and wealthy conservative individuals of the importance of this goal.[51] At the same time, New Right leaders such as Richard Viguerie, Paul Weyrich, Jerry Falwell, and Phyllis Schlafly deployed their skills in direct-mail fundraising, church-based organizing, grassroots mobilization, and political networking to develop or expand many new conservative organizations.[52]

Critical social and economic changes had made the time ripe for such endeavors. A large-scale public reaction against the racial liberalism, social upheaval, and rapid cultural changes of the 1960s was well under way. By the early 1970s, it was also apparent that there had been a critical transformation in the structure of the economic opportunities and political constraints facing American business. The onset of a deep economic contraction in 1973 caused leading figures in the worlds of business, industry, and finance to conclude that newly intensified forces of economic globalization had rendered the Keynesian policies of the New Deal order obsolete. Keynesianism had, on the whole, worked well for many powerful American business concerns during the New Deal and postwar periods, when a rapidly expanding consumer economy was largely contained within national boundaries. Production, marketing, and consumption had, however, become more heavily internationalized since that time. This changed the structure of economic pressures, opportunities, and constraints in ways that reduced corporate leaders' commitment to the accord among business, government, and labor that had been forged during the New Deal. Business disillusionment with left-liberal politics further intensified in response to the dramatic expansion of environmental and consumer activism that occurred during the early 1970s. This activism successfully placed an unprecedented number of government regulations on American enterprise, which drove up the costs of doing business in an increasingly difficult economic environment. Many corporate leaders concluded that it was critical to shift national politics in a more conservative direction, at least on economic issues.[53]

Leaders of the neoconservative and New Right movements consequently joined forces with foundation directors, corporate executives, and wealthy individuals to build a new conservative establishment that most prominently included (1) conservative foundations, which underwrote much of the rest of the network; (2) research institutes (or, more colloquially, "think tanks"), which developed and promoted conservative ideas and policies; (3) advocacy groups, which engaged in grassroots mobilization and political lobbying; (4) media groups and conservative publications, which attacked the credibility of the mainstream media and provided alternative sources of news and information; (5) legal organizations, which cultivated conservative judges and lawyers and pursued litigation designed to further a conservative agenda; and (6) university programs and academic associations, which promoted conservative scholarship, teaching, and student activism.[54] The foundations for this new conservative establishment were laid in the 1970s. It gained direct access to national political power in the 1980s with the support of the Reagan administration, which drew many of its key policy proposals directly from this network. Having further expanded during the 1990s, it remains a formidable political force in the early twenty-first century.

Conservative Foundations

In the early 1970s, the executives of a number of traditionally conservative foundations redirected their programs toward the goal of reshaping the public policy agenda and constructing a network of conservative institutions, advocates, and scholars.[55] The largest and most important of these included the Lynde and Harry Bradley Foundation, Koch Family Foundations, Adolph Coors Foundation, John M. Olin Foundation, Scaife Family Foundations, and Smith Richardson Foundation.[56] Beginning in the mid-1970s, these and other like-minded conservative foundations channeled tens of millions of dollars annually into the various institutions of the conservative establishment (as they continue to do today). The volume of this conservative grant making increased exponentially over a short period of time: during 1977–1986, for example, the total contributions of the top twelve conservative foundations to various conservative causes increased by 330 percent.[57]

Although the full extent of conservative grant making during the 1970s–1980s is too extensive to be detailed here, the following figures provide a sense of its scope and uses. In 1973, Richard Mellon Scaife, heir to the Mellon oil fortune, assumed the chairmanship of the Sarah Scaife Foundation and began granting about $10 million a year ($42.2 million in 2004 dollars)[58] to conservative causes, providing the funds to start up more than two dozen new conservative organizations.[59] In 1983, the Olin Foundation possessed assets of more than $61.3 million ($115.2 million in 2004 dollars) and granted about $5 million ($9.4 million in 2004 dollars) to activist conservative institutions, including think tanks, university centers, advocacy groups, legal organizations, and conservative journals.[60] The Bradley Foundation became a major player in 1985, when the sale of the Allen-Bradley company to Rockwell International increased the assets of the foundation to $290 million (more than $504 million in 2004 dollars). It consequently directed millions of dollars to academic research and development programs in an effort to influence elite opinion and the policy process.[61] During 1986–1990, the libertarian Koch Family Foundations, which include the Charles G. Koch, David H. Koch, and Claude R. Lambe Charitable Foundations, contributed $6.5 million to the Cato Institute, $4.8 million to Citizens for a Sound Economy, and $2 million to the Institute for Humane Studies at George Mason University.[62]

Although these and other conservative foundations possessed significant assets during the 1970s–1980s, none would have made the list of the top ten most well-endowed foundations in the United States. Most conservative foundations would not have even ranked within the top fifty. They exerted (and continue to exert) a political influence that far exceeded their comparative size, however, due to the highly strategic and aggressively political nature of their grant making. While the grant making of mainstream and more politically left-liberal foundations overwhelmingly tends to be for specific, short-term projects, conservative funders have embraced a long-term strategy dedicated to building conservative institutions, promoting conservative ideas, and leveraging the policy process. Consequently, they tend to provide large grants for general operating support to conservative organizations, which provides them with the money necessary to sustain basic operations along with the flexibility to take advantage of opportunities for institutional advancement and political influence as they arise. Conservative foundations also invest heavily in conservative intellectuals, academics, writers, and policy analysts and provide generous financial assistance for promoting their work.[63]

Although there are important ideological differences among the most influential conservative foundations, they share a basic commitment to maximizing market freedoms, minimizing government regulation, promoting business interests, protecting individual property rights, and, in most cases, promoting traditional values. (Strongly libertarian foundations, such as, most notably, the Koch Family Foundations, would not support campaigns for traditional values deemed to interfere with individual and market freedoms.)[64] They have been fundamentally hostile to the welfare state and have heavily supported the network of conservative research institutes, writers, and advocacy groups that has engaged in a sustained attack on government entitlements for the poor since the 1970s. Conservative foundations have also been particularly concerned with rolling back affirmative action, which has been attacked using the neoconservative language of "reverse discrimination."[65]

Research Institutes

The research institutes—or, as they are often referred to, think tanks—of the conservative movement have played a pivotally important role in the manufacture and promotion of conservative ideas. As in the case of conservative foundations, these institutions differ from their more mainstream and politically moderate counterparts by virtue of their determination to achieve the greatest possible political leverage from their work. Organizations like the left-of-center Brookings Institution tend to produce more traditionally academic works that are accessible to only a small, highly specialized audience. They do not attempt to market and promote these products broadly nor think strategically about how to maximize their political effectiveness. Conservative think tanks, in contrast, produce work that is much more widely accessible and market and promote it to achieve the greatest possible political impact. As William Baroody, president of the American Enterprise Institute (AEI) during the late 1970s to early 1980s, explained:

> I make no bones about marketing. . . . We pay as much attention to the dissemination of the product as we do to the content. We're probably the first major think tank to get into the electronic media. We hire ghost writers for scholars to produce op-ed articles that are sent to the one hundred and one cooperating newspapers—three pieces every two weeks.[66]

The marketing and promotional operations of conservative think tanks such as AEI have grown considerably more aggressive and sophisticated since that time.

AEI and the Heritage Foundation emerged as the two most important conservative think tanks during the 1970s–1980s. Other important institutions included the Free Congress Research and Education Foundation, led by New Right luminary Paul Weyrich (who also founded the Heritage Foundation); the Cato Institute, established in 1977 to promote libertarian ideas; the Hoover Institution, the most traditionally academic of the conservative think tanks; and the Ethics and Public Policy Center, dedicated to defending the ethical importance of the unregulated corporation.[67] Founded in 1943, AEI was a fairly low-profile organization until 1977, when William Baroody, Jr., assumed the presidency. Under his leadership, AEI expanded from a staff of 18 and a budget of approximately $1 million in 1970 to a staff of 150 and a budget of more than $10 million in the early 1980s.[68] Although Baroody succeeded in making AEI highly influential, he incurred the wrath of two of its key funders, the Olin and Smith Richardson foundations, by hewing to what they saw as too moderate a position. In a dramatic example of the power of big money to affect the production of political ideas, Baroody was forced to resign in the ensuing financial crisis. Consequently, AEI shifted sharply to the right.[69]

AEI remained, however, far more moderate than the Heritage Foundation. Founded in 1973 by Paul Weyrich with $250,000 in seed money from Joseph Coors and Richard Scaife, by 1975 Heritage had a budget of more than $1 million ($3.48 million in 2004 dollars). By 1986, its budget had grown to $14 million (almost $24 million in 2004 dollars). Since the 1980s, Heritage has been widely considered to be the leading think tank of the New Right. Its leaders have been explicit regarding the nature of their commitment to the conservative cause. "We're not here to be some kind of Ph.D. committee giving equal time," stated Vice President Burton Hines in 1986. "Our role is to provide conservative public-policy makers with arguments to bolster our side." (Despite this stance, Heritage continues to get tax breaks as a "nonpartisan" organization.) By all accounts, Heritage has played this role extremely effectively, churning out a huge supply of books, monographs, newsletters, policy papers, and reviews on a wide variety of domestic and foreign policy issues and disseminating them to thousands of government officials, journalists, and academics. Extremely savvy at marketing its products, most Heritage work was designed to meet the "briefcase test": that is, it had to be written in such a way that its key points could be absorbed in the time it took to drive from Washington's National Airport to a congressional hearing— about twenty minutes.[70]

During the 1980s, conservative research institutes—most notably the Heritage Foundation, the Hudson Institute, and AEI—became leading advocates of conservative welfare reform.[71] The most influential product of this arm of the conservative establishment was Charles Murray's *Losing Ground*, which was underwritten by the Manhattan Institute for Policy Research, an economic policy organization whose motto is "Turning Intellect into Influence."[72] True to its creed, the Manhattan Institute aggressively marketed the book, sending 700 copies to journalists, politicians, and academics; hiring a public relations expert to turn the previously unknown author into a celebrity; and paying journalists $500 to $1,500 apiece to participate in a seminar on Murray and his thought.[73] This strategy proved to be extremely effective. *Losing Ground* was one of the bestsellers of the 1980s and played an enormously influential role in shifting public debate on welfare issues sharply to the right.[74]

The Heritage Foundation was particularly influential in promoting the conservative attack on affirmative action. Ten days after President Ronald Reagan assumed office, it issued a 3,000-page, 20-volume report entitled *Mandate for Leadership: Policy Management in a Conservative Administration* (commonly referred to as *Mandate I*), which detailed recommendations for virtually every federal agency, including those responsible for civil rights policy. This work, along with its later companion volume, *Mandate for Leadership II: Continuing the Conservative Revolution*, represented, according to one highly placed journalist, one of the most "widely circulated" documents in Washington during the early to mid-1980s.[75]

Mandate I and *Mandate II* presented an explicit plan for reshaping public discourse on civil rights issues:

For 20 years, the most important battle in the Civil Rights field has been for control of the language. . . . Americans and their laws oppose "discrimination," "segregation," and "racism"; they favor "equality," "opportunity," and "remedial action." The secret to victory, whether in court or in Congress, has been to control the definition of these terms.[76]

"The question," stated *Mandate I*, "boils down to a distinction between equality of opportunity and equality of results." Current policies, based on the latter, were promoting "reverse discrimination in job hiring and promotion, discriminatory awarding of government contracts, and quotas in medical and law school admissions." Consequently, the foundation recommended:

A new administration should base its Civil Rights policy on the notion that every person has an inherent right to obtain whatever economic or other rewards he (or she) has earned, by virtue of merit, and that it is inherently wrong to penalize those who have earned their reward by giving preferential treatment and benefits to those who have not.[77]

In 1981, President Reagan acted in accordance with this recommendation by appointing William Bradford Reynolds, an outspoken opponent of affirmative action and other race-conscious policies, to be assistant attorney general for civil rights.[78]

Advocacy Groups

The New Right and the closely affiliated Christian Right were particularly adept at building or expanding many important conservative advocacy groups during the 1970s–1980s. By 1981, a partial list of New Right advocacy organizations included the Conservative Caucus, which specialized in grassroots mobilization; the Committee for the Survival of a Free Congress, directed by Paul Weyrich; the National Conservative Political Action Committee (NCPAC), which provided technical expertise, training, and money to right-of-center candidates; the Republican Study Committee, which established a working network of conservative congressmen; the Senate Steering Committee, which coordinated the activities of conservative senators and representatives to stop "left-wing legislation"; the National Right to Work Committee, whose membership grew from 25,000 to more than 1.5 million during 1971–1981; the American Conservative Union, which engaged in lobbying and conservative broadcasting and publications; the Conservative Victory Fund, a newly professionalized conservative political action committee; the American Legislative Exchange Council, whose membership included 600 conservative state legislators; the National Pro-Life Action Committee; and Phyllis Schlafly's Stop ERA and Eagle Forum.[79] Important Christian Right organizations included the Moral Majority, Christian Voice, Religious Roundtable, National Christian Action Coalition, Focus on the Family, and the National Right to Life Committee.[80]

According to Viguerie, NCPAC and the Moral Majority represented the most potent forces of the New Right and Christian Right in the pivotal 1980 election. NCPAC "targeted six liberal senators for defeat—and saw four of them fall." The Moral Majority registered 2.5 million conservative Christians who were first-time voters. Aggressive efforts to persuade white evangelicals to vote for Reagan were highly successful: while 56 percent of this group had voted for Democrat Jimmy Carter in 1976 (versus 43 percent for Republican candidate Gerald Ford), 56 percent voted for Reagan in 1980 (while only 34 percent supported Carter). According to an ABC News/Lou Harris survey, "the white followers of the TV evangelical preachers gave Ronald Reagan two-thirds of his 10 point margin in the election."[81]

Conservative Media

Recognizing the importance of radio, television, and print media in shaping political discourse and public opinion, the conservative movement established its own media outlets, designed conservative public-affairs programming for public television and radio, promoted conservative commentators and pundits, and established media "watchdog" organizations to counter alleged "left-wing bias" and pressure the mainstream media to cover the Right's political and policy agendas. Again, these efforts were pioneered in the 1970s, consolidated in the 1980s, and expanded in the 1990s. They remain a powerful force in American political and cultural life in the first decade of the twenty-first century.[82]

During the 1970s–1980s, important conservative publications included the *National Review*, the conservative flagship journal founded by William F. Buckley back in 1955; the *National Interest*, published by Irving Kristol; the *Public Interest*, also published by Kristol; the neoconservative *Commentary*, edited by Norman Podhoretz; the *New Criterion*, a conservative art review founded in 1981 with the aid of the Olin Foundation; and the *American Spectator*, which would become a prime force in the anti-Clinton jihad of the 1990s. Conservative foundations such as, most notably, Olin, Smith Richardson, Bradley, and Scaife generously supported these and other conservative publications.[83]

National Empowerment Television (NET), established in 1991, has been an important outlet for the conservative movement.[84] Paul Weyrich, who originally sponsored the network through his Free Congress Foundation, described NET as the most exciting development of his twenty-five years of conservative political activism. Reaching more than 11 million homes by the early 1990s, NET ran such weekly programs as the "Cato Forum," which featured Cato Institute staff discussing the illegitimacy of taxation and government regulation; "Straight Talk," produced in conjunction with the Family Research Council; and "On Target with the National Rifle Association." In 1992, political commentator David Gergen credited NET with "the creation of a new politics in America" by virtue of its ability to mobilize core constituencies on issues ranging from immigration to tax policy to welfare reform.[85] Again, conservative foundations such as Scaife and Bradley provided generous funding for this enterprise.[86]

Conservative media watchdog organizations established during the 1970s–1980s included the Center for the Study of Popular Culture, the Center for Media and Public Affairs, Accuracy in Media, and the Media Research Center. Several of these organizations have been dedicated to attacking the alleged left-wing bias of public television (PBS). They have also worked with the Republican party and conservative think-tankers to cut funding for public television stations, with the long-term goal of privatizing the entire public broadcasting system. Over time, these assaults led PBS to expand its already substantial conservative public-affairs broadcasting. More broadly, they have helped to produce a climate in which mainstream journalists watch their step when it comes to commenting on conservative leaders, organizations, ideas, and issue campaigns.[87]

Legal Organizations

Legal organizations constitute yet another pillar of the conservative establishment. These include public interest law firms, which promote conservative legal change through litigation; professional associations, which bond conservative law students, lawyers, and judges into a common network; legal studies programs, which promote conservative theories of jurisprudence in elite law schools; and judicial education groups, which recruit federal judges to attend all-expenses-paid retreats to learn about conservative legal thought. According to Covington, the common purpose of these groups is "to overturn affirmative action, environmental regulations, rent control laws, and other government programs or statutes deemed inconsistent with the principles of economic liberty, freedom of contract or association, and private property." More broadly, their goal is to "remake legal theory and practice in ways more congenial to corporate or commercial interests."[88]

During the 1980s, prominent examples of legal advocacy groups included the Washington Legal Foundation and the Center for Individual Rights, which have been dedicated to rolling back affirmative action policies. The Federalist Society, founded by Yale Law School students in the early 1980s and heavily supported by conservative foundations, grew to be an extremely powerful professional association during the 1990s.[89] The "law and economics" method of jurisprudence, which uses economic models of efficiency and wealth maximization as the primary means of analyzing and producing law, has been heavily promoted in elite law schools and among the federal judiciary. By 1991, over 40 percent of federal judges had been provided with training on how to apply principles of economic analysis to law via all-expenses-paid seminars underwritten by conservative foundations and corporate funders.[90]

Higher Education

The conservative movement has also attempted to enlist the world of higher education in service of its cause. Seen as dens of leftist iniquity ever since the student rebellions of the 1960s, there has been a concerted effort to "take back" colleges and universities by, among other things, increasing the numbers of conservative professors and student activists, supporting and publicizing conservative scholarship, and launching high-profile attacks on the dangers of "political correctness" on campus. Tens of millions of dollars from conservative foundations have poured into the academy in pursuit of these goals, with the bulk of the money being directed toward such elite— and widely influential—campuses as the University of Chicago, George Mason University, Harvard, and Yale. Conservative foundations also supported the writing and dissemination of a series of influential books that attacked left-of-center professors and political thought in the academy. These include Allan Bloom's *The Closing of the American Mind* (1986); Charles J. Syke's *Profscam: Professors and the Demise of Higher Education* (1988); Roger Kimball's *Tenured Radicals: How Politics Corrupted Our Higher Education* (1990); and Dinesh D'Souza's *Illiberal Education* (1990).[91]

While this network of foundations, think tanks, advocacy groups, media, legal organizations, and higher-education initiatives institutionalized the conservative movement, the Republican party provided it with a direct conduit to government power. The presidential election of 1980 was pivotal in this regard. Movement conservatives had been deeply unhappy with the liberal governing record of Nixon and the middle-of-the-road moderation of Ford. Reagan, in contrast, had been a prominent hero of the movement since his successful run for California governor on an aggressively conservative platform in 1966. Consequently, movement activists mobilized to elect him president with an intensity unmatched since the Goldwater campaign of 1964. The 1980 campaign provided a test of the effectiveness of the new set of mobilizing tactics, fundraising operations, and political organizations that had been developed in the 1970s. In this process, the movement, the counter-establishment, and the campaign fused in an effort to inaugurate a new reign of conservative politics in the United States.

New Right activists hailed Reagan's 1980 victory as a historic reversal of their 1964 defeat. Howard Phillips of the Conservative Caucus announced that it represented "the greatest victory for conservatism since the American Revolution."[92] And, while many leading neoconservatives had maintained a vestigial tie to the Democratic party during the 1970s, they quickly shifted sharply to the right and become ardent Republicans. Reagan appointed numerous neoconservatives to leading positions in his administration. Many others moved into influential positions in conservative think tanks, which had a direct pipeline into the administration's policymaking apparatus. Although some factions of the larger conservative movement complained of their relatively limited access to the interconnected power centers of the conservative establishment and the Reagan administration (the "paleoconservatives"—that is, those of the staunchly old-school, anti–New Deal persuasion—in particular developed an ongoing feud with the neocons), overall, the nexus linking the conservative movement, the conservative establishment, and the Republican party had become strong, tight, and robust.

Crucially, however, neither the movement nor the establishment were dependent on the party for sustenance or inspiration. If the Republicans were not sufficiently conservative to meet the demands of various movement factions, conservative activists had established a lasting organizational structure with a secure funding base—and, in many cases, a dedicated political constituency—that was capable of putting pressure on the party without risking any serious loss of access. Having seen the conservative movement's importance in the 1980 election, the party establishment, while remaining wary of alienating moderates, understood that it could not be ignored. Consequently, when many activists were disappointed with the lack of progress on crucial planks of their political agenda (such as outlawing abortion or dismantling the welfare state), they retooled for the long haul by dedicating themselves to a continued conservative takeover of the Republican party, an intensified pursuit of government power at the local and state levels, and the development of additional tactics such as ballot initiatives and media campaigns. By institutionalizing itself through a self-sustaining set of increasingly sophisticated and diversified organizations, the conservative movement—despite the inevitable factionalism of such an intense and broad-based mobilization—had successfully established itself as a powerful, independent, and long-term force in American political life.

Race and Electoral Politics in the 1980s

A well-established literature attests to the central importance of race in the historic conservative turn of the 1980s.[93] Although the 1968 and 1972 Nixon presidential campaigns had established race as a potent Republican campaign tool, it had not played an important role in the 1976 election, which was dominated by the aftermath of the Watergate scandal. By 1980, this issue had receded, and the Republicans were poised to take to the next level the by-then time-tested strategy of using racial issues as the primary wedge to break lower- to middle-class whites out of the New Deal coalition. Whereas the Nixon administration had played racial politics on a relatively ad hoc basis, the Reagan campaign represented a self-conscious conservative crusade that flew the race-coded banner of "equality of opportunity" as its battle flag. Representing a promise to roll back what was seen by this critical group of swing voters as the Democratic party's special treatment of racial minorities—via reverse discrimination, welfare benefits, and so on—this new form of "conservative equalitarianism" succeeded in creating an alliance between two groups of voters who had formerly regarded their political interests as opposed: the wealthy and big business, on the one hand, and working-class whites, on the other.[94]

Despite the fact that the economic policies of the Reagan administration hurt Americans in the lower half of the income distribution, this coalition continued to hold throughout the 1980s. A 1992 congressional Budget Office report showed that during the course of that decade, the wealthiest 1 percent of the nation's population enjoyed a 60 percent increase in its after-tax income.

Meanwhile, middle-level incomes remained stagnant, and the lowest-paid fifth of American wage earners saw their incomes decrease by 10 percent—a development that particularly hurt the African-American population, who have always been disproportionately represented in that group.[95] Although some of these changes were the result of the profound macroeconomic restructuring that occurred during this period, a good deal of it must be attributed to Reagan era policies which, among other things, significantly cut taxes for the wealthy while increasing them for the lower to middle classes, reduced social welfare spending for the poor, and rolled back federal environmental and worker safety regulations in the interests of big business.[96]

Nonetheless, in 1984, even more white working-class voters left the Democratic party to vote for Reagan. Between the 1980 and 1984 elections, Democratic identification decreased 15 percent among blue-collar workers and 18 percent among high school graduates.[97] Greenberg identifies 1984 as the pivotal year in which Macomb County, Michigan—a heavily unionized, blue-collar area that had long been a Democratic stronghold—turned Republican, with two out of three voters choosing Reagan over Mondale, and nearly half of the seats in the state house going to Republicans. Race was the key issue driving this massive defection. Whites in Macomb County were struggling to maintain a middle-class standard of living. They blamed much of their predicament on Democratic catering to blacks through reverse discrimination and pouring tax dollars into what they viewed as the sinkhole of black Detroit. When the Mondale campaign attempted to address such voters' economic concerns by emphasizing the issue of "fairness," Macomb County whites rejected it out of hand as yet another instance of Democratic racial pandering.[98]

In 1988, the Bush campaign's infamous "Willie Horton" advertisements demonstrated the continued power of racial politics to move such voters into the Republican party. Viewed by campaign strategist Lee Atwater as the key to discrediting Democratic opponent Michael Dukakis, these sensational spots reported that Horton, an African-American male and convicted murderer, had raped a white woman and stabbed her white fiancé after being released from prison on a furlough program in Massachusetts—under the reign of Governor Dukakis. This deployment of incendiary racial stereotypes helped to discredit the Dukakis candidacy, while fueling the white tendency to blame African Americans and their left-of-center allies for all of the real and imagined ills of the nation.[99]

All of this is not to say that race was the only factor driving the conservative ascendancy of the Reagan–Bush I years. Of course, it was not. The mobilization of the religious Right in the late 1970s played an important role, and was driven more by a reaction to issues of gender and sexuality (most critically, abortion and gay rights) than by race. At the same time, the new competitive pressures caused by globalization drove the conservative turn among the forces of big business. Ideological developments such as supply-side economics played a leading role in legitimating new conservative economic policies and had only an indirect connection to race (which escalated antitax fervor among whites, but did not necessarily support the favor-the-rich logic of supply-side). More generally, conservatism also gained support from the reaction against the other disruptive social changes that had burst forth in the 1960s. While many of these, such as the movement to protect the rights of the criminally accused, were strongly linked to race, other extremely important ones, such as feminism and abortion, were not.

Nonetheless, issues of race provided the most leverage in the electoral arena, serving as the ideological axis that separated left- and right-of-center public opinion and political identification. While affecting the voting public at large, their most politically decisive impact was among lower- to middle-income whites. Within this demographic group, a pivotal number of formerly Democratic voters shifted their allegiance to an increasingly conservative Republican party. To a large extent, they blamed their increasing sense of economic and social insecurity on the Democratic embrace of racial liberalism. At the same time, racial liberals were widely reviled as hypocritical elitists who were pandering to black demands at the expense of white working people. With this development, the old social liberal goal of the 1960s was inverted: rather than forging a progressive race-class alliance, the Civil Rights movement had sparked the development of a newly potent form of race and class consciousness that fused white working- and middle-class identity with a racially driven rejection of left-liberal politics.

In terms of political discourse, this development found its most potent expression through the new racial paradigm developed by neoconservatives in the 1970s. By rejecting the traditional language of white supremacism and maintaining a commitment to a basic nondiscrimination principle, this position successfully divorced itself from the newly stigmatized legacy of the nation's racial past. At the same time, it appropriated the still-resonant cultural power of the postwar Myrdalian paradigm by arguing that racially equalitarian policies that went beyond simple nondiscrimination represented a dangerous violation of traditional liberal values. While linking up nicely to the code words of racially divisive Republican campaigns, this position was also embedded in a larger and more sophisticated structure of conservative political ideas. These could be systematically promoted through the new conservative establishment and, over time, translated into concrete legal reforms and policy initiatives. Grounded in a basic hostility toward what was viewed as the destructive equalitarianism of the 1960s, this new form of racially infused conservative politics successfully drove the traditional social equity commitments of left-of-center liberalism to the powerless margins of American politics.

CONCLUSION

The Impasse of Progressive Liberalism

The election of President Ronald Reagan in 1980 marked a sea change in American politics that set the country's primary direction for the next quarter-century. Most fundamentally, it established a new form of right-of-center liberalism as a powerful force in the nation's political life. Although the fortunes of the conservative movement would wax and wane over the next twenty-five years, overall it experienced remarkable consolidation and growth during this time. All of the cornerstones of the conservative ascendancy that were laid during the 1970s—the investment in conservative ideas, the construction of a conservative counterestablishment, the right-wing takeover of the Republican party, and the cultivation of a grassroots activist base—were strengthened during the 1990s, despite the concurrent fact of the first two-term Democratic presidency since the New Deal. The subsequent instatement of President George W. Bush in 2000 and the reaction to the terrorist attacks of September 11, 2001, have made the position of an even more aggressively right-wing movement even stronger.

Conversely, the fortunes of left-of-center liberalism have remained essentially moribund since the implosion of social liberalism in the late 1960s.

This is particularly true with regard to issues of socioeconomic equity, with regard to both race and the population more broadly. Although there has been substantial progress toward the goal of creating a society that is not only nondiscriminatory, but actively values racial and ethnic diversity and inclusion, this has not been accompanied by the development of any popular political understanding that considers broader questions of socioeconomic equity as vital to American democracy. At the same time, inequality has, despite the economic boom of the 1990s, continued to increase. While there are isolated constituencies that would support a revival of equalitarian politics, they have not to date been able to muster the strength necessary to have any significant impact on national political life.

Racial politics have played an important role in these developments. This was particularly true during the 1980s, when racial divisions were effectively manipulated for conservative advantage in national electoral politics and by fueling popular reaction against left-of-center liberalism. In a calculated response to these developments, the Democratic leadership of the 1990s worked assiduously to disassociate the party from negatively charged racial images, declaring that the party was "tough on crime," committed to "ending welfare as we know it," and so on. While this strategy played a useful role in the election and reelection of President Bill Clinton in 1992 and 1996, it was a reactive rather than creative approach that did nothing to establish a new progressive agenda for addressing the festering racial divisions and growing socioeconomic inequality of the nation. Subsequently, in the first decade of the twenty-first century, issues of racial inequality and socioeconomic equity more broadly have been largely ignored.

After almost four decades of more or less steady decline, the future of equalitarian liberalism in the United States appears uncertain at best. To a significant extent, the contemporary impasse of left-of-center liberalism can be attributed to broad contextual factors that are relatively unique to the current historical moment. Increased globalization of the economy has made the traditional left-liberal model of centralized government planning to promote social equity much more difficult to employ. The threat of terrorism has shifted attention away from domestic issues and created a climate that supports the stifling of political dissent. Political journalism has become much more sensational, encouraging the tendency to limit political knowledge to a highly superficial and constantly changing parade of pseudoscandals and soundbites. This shallow orientation to politics is strongly reinforced by an aggressive consumer culture that has no use for political projects that are not easily turned to profit or entertainment.

Despite the importance of such developments, the current impasse of equalitarian liberalism has deep historical roots. Most centrally, it stems from the difficulty of creating and sustaining political movements that possess both the desire and the capacity to tackle the intertwined problems of racial and class inequality.

Some particularly influential constructions of equalitarian liberalism, such as the anti-caste and postwar varieties, focused exclusively on the simple goal of establishing a national legal standard against racial discrimination in the major arenas of civic life. Viewed in retrospect, it is all too easy to condemn their advocates as naïve in their insistence that antidiscrimination laws would solve the racial problems of the nation. To do so, however, would be to underestimate the historical force of the norms and structures of white supremacy that they were confronting. If its legal achievements were rolled back, anti-caste liberalism nonetheless articulated a conception of human universalism and racial equity that was both radical and visionary for its time. Similarly, if postwar liberals set what would become a confounding precedent by equating the achievement of an antidiscrimination standard with the resolution of the American dilemma and the realization of liberal ideals, they also communicated the moral urgency of basic racial fairness with an effectiveness unmatched since the time of the first Reconstruction.

The political significance of such movements is underscored by the relatively weak and inconsistent position accorded to antidiscrimination principles by other important varieties of equalitarian liberalism, which stressed a class-based rather than a racially targeted agenda. If, for example, the Knights of Labor pursued an innovative and progressive strategy by attempting to reconfigure the meaning of race to promote solidarity between white and black, as well as native-born and immigrant workers, its lack of a principled commitment to nondiscrimination and legal equity meant that it had no compunction about vilifying the Chinese as an inferior race. (Notably, the KOL's rationalization of this characterization—that the Chinese served as the willing pawns of monopoly capital—provides an excellent illustration of how alternative conceptions of race, class, and civic equity are connected.) Alternately, while radical Populists such as Tom Watson of Georgia presented cogent—and politically powerful—arguments regarding the shared economic plight of white and black farmers, they remained loyal to an attenuated, but still sacrosanct, principle of white supremacy.

The failure of the labor and agrarian movements of the late nineteenth century to establish an enduring class-based coalition dedicated to ameliorating the socioeconomic inequities generated by corporate capitalism meant that the ensuing reforms of the Progressive Era took place in a political universe that had shrunk to accommodate a system of racial and class hierarchy even more restrictive and exclusionary than that of the preceding postbellum decades. The subsequent New Deal period experienced a resurgence of progressive labor politics and class-based reform, coupled with a new openness toward social democratic politics. However, the continued lockhold of conservative Democrats on the South constrained the progressive energies of New Deal reform and ensured that federal programs and policies would not challenge the reign of Jim Crow. Consequently, antiblack discrimination was built into many important federal programs and policies, including mortgage lending, unemployment, and Social Security.

The Civil Rights movement represented the most powerful political force dedicated to a simultaneous attack on both racial discrimination and socioeconomic inequality in the nation's history. The challenges that it faced in attempting to build a coalition capable of pursuing this agenda, however, proved overwhelming. Although movement activists consistently understood the problem of discrimination to be complex in character and national in scope, their everyday energies were consumed by the battle to overcome Jim Crow through the time of the passage of the Civil Rights acts of 1964 and 1965. Immediately following this historic achievement, an avalanche of socially dislocating events—including the eruption of ghetto riots, the escalation of the Vietnam War, the growing antiliberal radicalism of the New Left, the birth of the Black Power movement, and the intensification of white backlash—destroyed the forward momentum of the movement.

While it is impossible to precisely measure such cultural transformations, it may be reasonably argued that the rapidity and intensity of the rise and fall of the social liberal position developed by the Civil Rights movement was highly wrenching and left deep scars on the body politic. Certainly, this was a widespread perception at the time. Social liberals had taken the culturally resonant Myrdalian paradigm and revised it to claim that the democratic soul of the nation was at stake over the question of whether the country would make good on what had become a highly ambitious promise of equalitarian reform. Although the more literal interpretations of such warnings were certainly overblown—democratic institutions would continue to function, and the social liberal perspective was not shared (or even understood) by much of the nation—they represented an important turning point nonetheless. If postwar and social liberals had very different understandings of the nature of the relationship between race and American liberalism, they shared a belief that the cause of racial justice had a powerful claim on the conscience of the nation. The limitations of this perspective became painfully clear when the passage of historic antidiscrimination laws was followed by ghetto riots and white backlash, rather than by a renewed sense of common purpose forged by the achievement of equalitarian reform. Those who continued to equate racial equality with the establishment of a basic antidiscrimination standard were confronted with the fact that the realization of this goal had seemingly exacerbated, rather than resolved, the problems of racial division within American liberalism. Those who understood the problems of racial and class inequality as interconnected were faced with the reality that what they had thought would promote interracial unity and class solidarity had instead hardened the lines of both racial division and racially charged class division. Either way, the underlying faith that the nation shared a political ethos that encompassed a common understanding of the imperative of racial reform had been shattered.

In the mid-1970s, neoconservative intellectuals once again reformulated the postwar Myrdalian paradigm. In this incarnation, the liberal values of the nation were impeached by the existence of race-conscious policies, such as affirmative action, rather than by the continued existence of racial inequity per se. Invoking Justice Harlan's dissent in the *Plessy* case of 1896, the conservative movement adopted this position to insist that the Constitution had always been fundamentally committed to a color-blind principle that treated all individuals equally, regardless of race. Although affirmative action was arguably more in keeping with the broad logic of the anti-caste position in which Harlan's dissent was originally embedded, this argument had wide cultural and political resonance. It represented an important contribution to the growing conservative movement, whose racial politics had been formerly rooted in a now-illegitimate defense of segregation and discrimination and a loyalty to the white supremacist tradition. Framed in the common language of American liberalism and divorced from the explicit racism of the past, the neoconservative position on race helped to turn moderate opinion against race-conscious policies and advance the legal and political crusade to eliminate them.

During the same period, New Right activists worked to turn a widespread sense of grievance among lower- to middle-income whites into a powerful form of racially charged—and highly politicized—class identity. "Liberals," they charged—with some justification—were elitists who claimed the moral high ground on racial issues while exempting themselves from the social dislocations that their policies promoted. This sense of racial and class resentment merged with a larger reaction against both particular left-liberal positions (support for legalized abortion and the women's movement, a strict separation between church and state, and so on) and the general experience of rapid and often painful social change that had overtaken the country in the mid-1960s. By articulating and organizing this new form of white identity, conservative activists helped to build a powerful new coalition that united a significant proportion of working-class whites with traditional Republican elites, who had opposed the left-liberal trajectory of equalitarian reform since the New Deal.

This combination of neoconservative ideas and New Right organizing revitalized the larger conservative movement, which had been fighting an uphill battle for most of the several preceding decades. The ensuing institutionalization of the conservative movement through the building of a new conservative establishment, and the success of linking both with an increasingly conservative Republican party, laid the foundations for what would over time become the dominating force in American political life. While pursuing a broad, varied, and frequently self-contradictory agenda (e.g., promoting traditional and libertarian values at the same time), the conservative movement as a whole has remained consistently hostile to virtually all species of equalitarian reform. At the same time, inequality of wealth and income has increased steadily since the early 1970s (with the temporary exception of the late 1990s). Although changes resulting from economic globalization have to a significant extent contributed to this trend, it has also been the result of conservative policies that have weakened labor unions, prevented the maintenance of the real value of the minimum wage, blocked health-care reform, created a more regressive tax structure, and generally favored the interests of powerful corporations over average workers. By 2001, the wealthiest 1 percent of all U.S. households controlled over 33 percent of the national wealth, while the bottom 80 percent of households held only 16 percent. As has always been the case, inequality was even more sharply divided by race: in the same year, almost 31 percent of African-American households had zero or negative net worth, as opposed to just over 13 percent of white households.[1] Nonetheless, lower- to middle-income whites (particularly men) have continued to provide a crucial margin of support for conservative forces.

Culturally, conservative political ideas have become overwhelmingly dominant. Even the history of the Civil Rights movement has been largely rewritten to support the conservative crusade for color-blindness and against affirmative action. Even more problematically, any memory that the movement was in fact dedicated to building an interracial coalition committed to the joint pursuit of racial and class equity seems to have been completely erased from public consciousness. The fact that such a goal could have been conceived in terms of the fulfillment of American political ideals now seems virtually inconceivable. In part due to their own disillusionment and in part due to the force of historical events, left-of-center liberals have effectively ceded control of liberal discourse to an increasingly right-wing conservative movement. Conservatives, in turn, have successfully depicted such liberals as enemies of American values and their proposals for equitable reform as shell games designed to aid the undeserving (and, in the popular white imagination, largely black) poor at the expense of the hard-working (read: predominantly white) middle class. To be sure, the continued power of this perception can in some important respects be blamed on the historic failings of left-liberalism itself—including its naiveté regarding the complexity and tenacity of highly racialized forms of class inequality and its failure to think deeply or emphatically into the phenomenon of white working-class racial reaction. Left-liberals have also been dramatically out-organized by an increasingly powerful conservative establishment and out-gunned by a much more politically savvy GOP. More broadly, however, the accumulated weight of the nation's racial past has worked against them.

The future of equalitarian politics in the United States is at best uncertain. Reviving it will require the development of a larger motivating vision, a set of practical policy reforms capable of attracting broad political support, and an organizational structure with the muscle to get out both the message and the vote. Of these three elements, the first and the last are the most lacking. Although numerous proposed reforms can be ticked off that seem potentially workable and popular—health-care reform, curtailing "corporate welfare," increasing the earned income tax credit, and so on—they do not add up to a powerful political vision and are not connected to a dynamic political organization. The lessons of the past suggest that it is best to attempt to frame such a vision in the culturally resonant language of American liberalism. They also suggest, however, that promises of equalitarian reform are likely to be broken by the intertwined forces of race and class unless new ways can be found of creating and sustaining more unifying understandings of these primary political identities.

Notes

Introduction

1. This position can be traced back to Gunnar Myrdal's classic work, *An American Dilemma: The Negro Problem and Modern Democracy* (New York: Harper & Row, 1944), which posited a fundamental conflict between American liberalism and racial discrimination. Although Smith (1997) contests Myrdal's conception of a dominant liberal tradition, he similarly argues that "white supremacy and patriarchy are logically inconsistent with consensual liberal democratic principles." Rogers Smith, *Civic Ideals: Conflicting Understandings of Citizenship in U.S. History* (New Haven, CT: Yale University Press, 1997), 28.

2. Goldfield (1997), for example, posits that racial oppression is an integral part of a capitalist system. Michael Goldfield, *The Color of Politics: Race and the Mainsprings of American Politics* (New York: New Press, 1997). Smith (1997) briefly reviews and critiques other works that similarly argue that liberalism necessarily supports ascriptive ideologies of race and/or gender. See Smith, *Civic Ideals*, 28–30.

3. See, for example, Rogers Smith, "Liberalism and Racism: The Problem of Analyzing Traditions," and Carol Nackenoff, "Gendered Citizenship: Alternative Narratives of Political Incorporation in the United States, 1875–1925," both in David R. Er-

icson and Louisa Bertch Green, eds., *The Liberal Tradition in American Politics: Reassessing the Legacy of American Liberalism* (New York: Routledge, 1999), chaps. 1, 7.

There are some important exceptions to this rule. Gerstle (2001) argues that American liberals combined elements of what he terms "civic" and "racial" nationalism throughout most of the twentieth century. Gary Gerstle, *American Crucible: Race and Nation in the Twentieth Century* (Princeton, NJ: Princeton University Press, 2001). More controversially, Ericson (2001) argues that both the proponents and opponents of slavery shared an essentially liberal political framework during antebellum debates on abolition. David F. Ericson, *The Debate over Slavery: Antislavery and Proslavery Liberalism in Antebellum America* (New York: New York University Press, 2001).

Although not addressing the United States, the seminal work of Uday S. Mehta (1990, 1999) provides an elegant theoretical formulation and compelling historical analysis of the capacity of liberalism to both justify and oppose systematic political exclusion and subordination. See Uday S. Mehta, "Liberal Strategies of Exclusion," *Politics and Society* 18 (1990): 427–454; and Mehta, *Liberalism and Empire: A Study in Nineteenth-Century British Liberal Thought* (Chicago: University of Chicago Press, 1999).

4. For general theories of culture and discourse that do not specifically consider the issue of liberalism but support this approach, see Charles Taylor, "Interpretation and the Sciences of Man," in Paul Rabinow and William M. Sullivan, eds., *Interpretive Social Science: A Second Look* (Berkeley: University of California Press, 1987), esp. 55–62; Clifford Geertz, *The Interpretation of Cultures: Selected Essays* (New York: Basic, 1973), chap. 1; and John Comaroff and Jean Comaroff, *Ethnography and the Historical Imagination* (Boulder, CO: Westview, 1992), chap. 1.

5. This conception of liberalism is indebted to the work of J. David Greenstone. See, in particular, Greenstone, "Political Culture and American Political Development: Liberty, Union, and the Liberal Bipolarity," *Studies in American Political Development* 1 (1986): 1–49. Greenstone, however, asserted a fundamental "bipolarity" of American liberalism, as opposed to the radically plastic conception presented in this book.

6. Within the social sciences, historians have been particularly interested in documenting alternatives to liberalism in the United States ever since the New Left scholars of the 1960s attacked the then-dominant "consensus" school developed by Hartz (1955) and others in the 1950s. Louis Hartz, *The Liberal Tradition in American Politics* (New York: Harcourt Brace Jovanovich, 1983 [1955]). As Brinkley (1994) notes, however, this work was much more interested in exploring radical alternatives to liberalism than in understanding American right-wing traditions. Although historical work on conservative and right-wing politics has taken off since the mid-1990s, the majority of it focuses on mainstream conservatism, which typically speaks in a liberal idiom (see chap. 8, n. 18). In recent decades, however, right-wing politics in the United States has contained an important strain of religious fundamentalism that rejects not simply liberal but modernist values. See Alan Brinkley, "The Problem of

American Conservatism," *American Historical Review* 99, no. 2 (Apr. 1994): esp. 423–429.

During the 1980s, interest in civic republicanism, which was widely seen as an important historical alternative to liberalism, was particularly strong. Rogers (1992) provides a useful, if rather hostile, review of the several sets of historical literatures that focus on issues of republican politics. Although there is no agreement as to the precise definition and appropriate periodization of republicanism in the United States, it has been established as a culturally important set of politically distinctive ideas, particularly during the eighteenth century. See Daniel T. Rogers, "Republicanism: The Career of a Concept," *Journal of American History* 79, no. 1 (June 1992): 11–38.

7. The central work of the consensus school of American historiography, which claimed that the national political culture had historically been almost monolithically liberal, is Hartz, *The Liberal Tradition in American Politics*. Smith (1997) provides a useful review of the classic literature on American liberalism (focusing on the work of Tocqueville, Myrdal, and Hartz) and more recent critiques of it (Smith, *Civic Ideals*, 14–30).

8. As Rogers (1992) explains, the majority of early American historians accept Wood's (1969) claim that the popular republicanism of the colonial era was superseded by the liberalism of the early national period (Gordon S. Wood, *The Creation of the American Republic, 1776–1787* [New York: Norton, 1969]). The literature on "labor republicanism," however, posits the existence of a new iteration of the republican tradition through the course of the nineteenth century (and, in some cases, beyond). See Rogers, "Republicanism," 19–31.

As discussed in chapter 3, my view is that that while the producer republicanism of the nineteenth-century labor and agrarian movements pointed beyond the boundaries of liberalism, its base of popular support remained rooted in the basic categories of liberal politics. In this sense it was similar to the Civil Rights movement, which also used the language of American liberalism to evoke visions of social justice and solidarity that were more organically connected to radical Christianity than to secular liberalism.

9. James Oakes's review of Eric Foner's *The Story of American Freedom* (New York: Norton, 1998) provides a succinct defense of this claim based on a reading of this historically sweeping work by a preeminent American historian. Oakes critically notes that while "for a quarter of a century American historians have been tripping over themselves to find an alternative (radical *or* reactionary) to the dominant 'liberal' tradition," Foner's work demonstrates that America's great progressive social movements were in fact "fought on the terrain established by bourgeois ideology's competing conceptions of freedom"—i.e., liberalism. In keeping with the analysis presented in this book, Oakes argues that Foner "is able to show that liberalism is more a language of dissent than of consensus. . . . it is a shared political language that lays the groundwork for fundamental and enduring debate." James Oakes, "Radical Liberals, Liberal Radicals: The Dissenting Tradition in American Political Culture," *Reviews in American History* 27, no. 3 (1999): 503–511.

10. Particularly compelling explorations of the historically embedded and socially contingent nature of race include Barbara Jeanne Fields, "Slavery, Race and Ideology in the United States of America," *New Left Review*, no. 181 (1990): 95–118; Evelyn Brooks Higginbotham, "African-American Women's History and the Metalanguage of Race," *Signs: Journal of Women in Culture and Society* 17 (1992): 251–274; Thomas C. Holt, *The Problem of Race in the 21st Century* (Cambridge, MA: Harvard University Press, 2000); and Michael Omi and Howard Winant, *Racial Formation in the United States: From the 1960s to the 1990s*, 2d ed. (New York: Routledge, 1994).

11. For an outstanding examination of the changing construction of whiteness in American history, see Matthew Frye Jacobson, *Whiteness of a Different Color: European Immigrants and the Alchemy of Race* (Cambridge, MA: Harvard University Press, 1998). Other notable works on this subject include James R. Barrett and David Roediger, "Inbetween Peoples: Race, Nationality, and the 'New Immigrant' Working Class," *Journal of American Ethnic History* 16, no. 3 (Spring 1997): 3–45; Karen Brodkin, *How Jews Became White Folks and What That Says about Race in America* (New Brunswick, NJ: Rutgers University Press, 1998); Grace Elizabeth Hale, *Making Whiteness: The Culture of Segregation in the South, 1890–1940* (New York: Pantheon, 1998); Ian F. Haney Lopez, *White by Law: The Legal Construction of Race* (New York: New York University Press, 1998); and David Roediger, *The Wages of Whiteness: Race and the Making of the American Working Class* (New York: Verso, 1991).

12. For an excellent examination of a particularly important manifestation of this larger issue, see Martin Gilens, *Why Americans Hate Welfare: Race, Media, and the Politics of Antipoverty Policy* (Chicago: University of Chicago Press, 1999).

13. The literature on American exceptionalism has been organized around the question originally posed by Werner Sombart in his 1906 work, *Why Is There No Socialism in the United States?* (White Plains, NY: International Arts and Sciences Press, 1976 [1906]). As Foner (1984) notes, this literature is built upon the assumption that "under capitalism, the working class will develop class consciousness, expressed in unions and a labor or socialist party, and that consequently the failure of either to emerge must be the result of some outside interference." Eric Foner, "Why Is There No Socialism in the United States?" *History Workshop* 17 (Spring 1984): 73–74. A good collection of essays on this subject is provided by Jean Heffer and Jeanine Rovet, eds., *Why Is There No Socialism in the United States?* (Paris: Ecoles des Hautes Etudes en Sciences Sociales, 1988).

14. On the social construction of class, see Gareth Stedman Jones, *Languages of Class: Studies in English Working Class History, 1832–1982* (New York: Cambridge University Press, 1983), esp. the introduction and chap. 3. An interesting poststructuralist feminist critique of Stedman Jones is provided by Joan W. Scott, "On Language, Gender, and Working Class History," *International Labor and Working Class History* 31 (Spring 1987): 1–13. For a helpful essay that places that Stedman Jones–Scott debate within a larger theoretical context, see William H. Sewell, Jr., "Toward a Post-Materialist Rhetoric for Labor History," in Lernard R. Berlanstein, ed., *Rethinking Labor History* (Urbana: University of Illinois Press, 1993), 15–38.

15. For an outstanding example of how constructivist theories of political economy can be fruitfully applied to the study of American political development, see Gerald Berk, *Alternative Tracks: The Constitution of American Industrial Order, 1865–1917* (Baltimore, MD: Johns Hopkins University Press, 1994).

16. Sean Wilentz, "America's Lost Equalitarian Tradition," *Daedalus* 131, no. 1 (Winter 2002): 66–80.

17. J. David Greenstone described this tradition as "reform liberalism." See Greenstone, *The Lincoln Persuasion: Remaking American Liberalism* (Princeton, NJ: Princeton University Press, 1993), esp. 59–63.

18. A classic expression of this view is found in William Graham Sumner, *What the Social Classes Owe Each Other* (Caldwell, ID: Caxton, 1995 [1883]). Sumner's influence in American political culture is contextualized in Richard Hofstadter, *Social Darwinism in American Thought* (Boston: Beacon, 1992 [1944]). Although contemporary anti-equalitarianism is significantly less harsh and uncompromising than its nineteenth-century counterpart, it represents a similar celebration of the virtues of unbridled individualism, competition, and ostensibly free markets, as well as hostility toward socially minded regulation and redistribution.

19. On the traditional black commitment to both racial and socioeconomic equity, see Dona Cooper Hamilton and Charles V. Hamilton, *The Dual Agenda: Race and Social Welfare Policies of Civil Rights Organizations* (New York: Columbia University Press, 1997). On the relationship between black political thought and American liberalism more generally, see Michael C. Dawson, *Black Visions: The Roots of Contemporary African-American Political Ideologies* (Chicago: University of Chicago Press, 2001), chap. 6.

20. In their leading synthesis of 1960s historiography, Isserman and Kazin (2000) argue that the Civil Rights movement inspired a tremendous expansion of grassroots organizing and new mass movements, ranging from the expansion of the American Civil Liberties Union and the Sierra Club to the mobilization of the United Farm Workers and the development of the modern feminist movement. Maurice Isserman and Michael Kazin, *America Divided: The Civil War of the 1960s* (New York: Oxford University Press, 2000), 119–123.

Chapter I

1. C. Vann Woodward, "*Plessy v. Ferguson*: The Birth of Jim Crow," *American Heritage* 15 (1964): 103.

2. For an alternative interpretation of the Harlan dissent, see Andrew Kull, *The Color-Blind Constitution* (Cambridge, MA: Harvard University Press, 1992), chap. 7.

3. Eric Foner, *Politics and Ideology in the Age of the Civil War* (New York: Oxford University Press, 1980), chap. 6. The issue of land redistribution had first arisen during the Civil War, when a minority of abolitionists and Radical Republicans had seen it as a logical component of the goal of emancipation, and a majority of Republicans

had viewed it as a potentially effective war measure against the South. It continued to be debated during the years following the war, both in conjunction with the question of the role of the Freedmen's Bureau and in the form of proposed congressional legislation, and remained "very much a live political issue" up until the autumn of 1867 (ibid., chap. 7).

4. Of these two, Stevens was by far the more forceful advocate. Other prominent supporters of land redistribution included George Julian, Wendell Phillips, and Benjamin F. Butler. It was also endorsed by the American Anti-Slavery Society (ibid., 134, 142).

5. Charles Sumner, *The Works of Charles Sumner*, vol. 11 (Boston: Lee & Shepard, 1875), 124–136.

6. Ibid., 368.

7. U.S. Congress, House, 40th Cong., 2d sess., *Congressional Globe*, vol. 38, pt. 1 (1867), 205.

8. Eric Foner, "Rights and the Constitution in Black Life during the Civil War and Reconstruction," *Journal of American History* 74 (1974): 863–883; David Montgomery, *The American Civil War and the Meanings of Freedom* (New York: Oxford University Press, 1987); Leon F. Litwack, *Been in the Storm So Long: The Aftermath of Slavery* (New York: Vintage, 1979), 399–408.

9. Quote altered to conform to standard English. Cited in Foner, "Rights and the Constitution in Black Life during the Civil War and Reconstruction," 871.

10. Quoted without alteration from letter reprinted in Ira Berlin, Steven Hahn, Steven F. Miller, Joseph P. Reidy, and Leslie S. Rowland, "The Terrain of Freedom: The Struggle over the Meaning of Free Labor in the U.S. South," *History Workshop* 22 (1986): 127–128.

11. On the conservative shift in mainstream black politics, see Eric Foner, "Black Reconstruction Leaders at the Grass Roots," in Leon Litwack and August Meier, eds., *Black Leaders of the Nineteenth Century* (Chicago: University of Illinois Press, 1988), 229. On the resurgence of black nationalism following the collapse of Reconstruction, see Alphonso Pinkney, *Red, Black, and Green: Black Nationalism in the United States* (New York: Cambridge University Press, 1976), chap. 2. On the labor and agrarian movements of the late nineteenth century, see chaps. 3–4.

12. This interpretation draws from Foner, *Politics and Ideology in the Age of the Civil War*, 128–149; and Foner, *Reconstruction: America's Unfinished Revolution, 1863–1877* (New York: Harper & Row, 1988), 153–170, 235–237.

13. Eric Foner, *Free Soil, Free Labor, Free Men: The Ideology of the Republican Party before the Civil War* (New York: Oxford University Press, 1970).

14. See also Eric Foner, *Politics and Ideology in the Age of the Civil War*, and David Montgomery, *Beyond Equality: Labor and the Radical Republicans, 1862–1872* (New York: Knopf, 1967).

15. Foner, *Reconstruction*, 512–513; Montgomery, *Beyond Equality*, 7; Alan Trachtenberg, *The Incorporation of America: Culture and Society in the Gilded Age* (New York: Hill and Wang, 1982), 73–74.

16. Foner, *Reconstruction*, chaps. 3, 10; Montgomery, *Beyond Equality*.

17. Foner, *Reconstruction*, 512–518.

18. Sidney Fine, *Laissez Faire and the General-Welfare State: A Study of Conflict in American Thought, 1865–1901* (Ann Arbor: University of Michigan Press, 1956); Hofstadter, *Social Darwinism in American Thought*.

19. Foner, *Politics and Ideology in the Age of the Civil War*, 66.

20. Philip S. Foner, *Organized Labor and the Black Worker, 1619–1973* (New York: Praeger, 1974); Sumner Eliot Matison, "The Labor Movement and the Negro during Reconstruction," *Journal of Negro History* 33 (1945): 426–468.

21. Foner, *Free Soil, Free Labor, Free Men*, 104–105.

22. My interpretation of the arguments made both for and against the civil rights bill is based on a content analysis of the entire set of congressional debates as recorded in U.S. Congress, Senate, 41st Cong., 2d sess., *Congressional Globe*, vol. 42, pts. 4 and 6 (1870); U.S. Congress, Senate, 42d Cong., 1st sess., *Congressional Globe*, vol. 44, pts. 1 and 2 (1871); U.S. Congress, House and Senate, 42d Cong., 2d sess., *Congressional Globe*, vol. 45, pts. 2 and 6 (1872); U.S. Congress, House and Senate, 43d Cong., 1st sess., *Congressional Record*, vol. 2, pts. 1 and 6 (1873–1874); U.S. Congress, House and Senate, 43d Cong., 2d sess., *Congressional Record*, vol. 3, pts. 2 and 3 (1875); Alfred Avins, ed., *The Reconstruction Amendments' Debates* (Richmond: Virginia Commission on Constitutional Government, 1976); and Irving J. Sloan, ed., *American Landmark Legislation*, vol. 1 (Dobbs Ferry, NY: Oceana, 1976). (The latter two references are important supplements to the former, as the indexes to the *Globe* and *Record* are both incomplete.) In addition to analyzing the entire record in terms of broad themes and recurrent categories, the statements of each congressman who participated in the debates, as indexed in Avins, *The Reconstruction Amendments' Debates*, 745–764, were all examined individually.

Out of the 147 individuals indexed, 91 said enough to allow at least a partial analysis of their general ideological orientation. Of these, 35 were in favor of the bill, 54 were against it, and 2 had unclear positions which changed over time. Thirty-three were senators (17 Republicans, 3 Union Republicans, 13 Democrats), and 58 were representatives (27 Republicans, 1 Union Republican, 29 Democrats, 1 Conservative). Seven were black, 84 white. Thirty-one different states were represented (out of a total of 37 at that time).

23. Charles Sumner, *The Works of Charles Sumner*, vol. 14 (Boston: Lee & Shepard, 1883), 412; Sumner, *The Works of Charles Sumner*, vol. 15 (Boston: Lee & Shepard, 1883), 288.

24. *Congressional Record*, vol. 2, pt. 4 (1874), 3451.

25. *Congressional Record*, vol. 3, pt. 2 (1875), 1004.

26. Sloan, *American Landmark Legislation*, 307. See also the remarks of Rep. Julius C. Burrows (R, MI) (Avins, *The Reconstruction Amendments' Debates*, 728); Rep. E. Rockwood Hoar (R, MA) (*Congressional Record*, vol. 3, pt. 2 [1875], 979); and Rep. Charles G. Williams (R, WI) (ibid., 1002).

27. African-American representatives were first seated in the federal Congress fol-

lowing the enactment of the Fifteenth Amendment in 1870. (Although John Willis Menard was the first black man to be elected to the U.S. Congress in 1868, he was not allowed to take his seat following a governmental decision that it was "too early" to admit a Negro to Congress. Annjennette Sophie McFarlin, *Black Congressional Reconstruction Orators and Their Orations, 1869–1879* [Metuchen, NJ: Scarecrow, 1976], 177.) Between 1870 and 1877, during the 41st to the 44th Congresses, a total of sixteen black men served in the Congress, fourteen in the House and two in the Senate. The height of black representation during this period was reached during the 43d and 44th Congresses (1873–1877), following the elections of 1872 and 1874, which placed first seven and then eight black men in the Congress (for a total of twelve congressmen). These Congresses set a record that would not be surpassed until the commencement of the 91st Congress in 1969. Maurine Christopher, *Black Americans in Congress* (New York: Crowell, 1976), 309–311.

28. *Congressional Record*, vol. 3, pt. 2 (1875), 959.

29. Ibid., 957; emphasis added.

30. Ibid., 945.

31. On the general issue of race, see also the remarks of Rep. Julius C. Burrows (R, MI) (ibid., 1000), Rep. Benjamin W. Harris (R, MA) (ibid., 958), Rep. Barbour Lewis (R, TN) (ibid., 998), Sen. Roscoe Conkling (Union Republican, NY) (Avins, *The Reconstruction Amendments' Debates*, 675), Sen. George F. Edmunds (R, VT) (ibid., 647), Sen. John Sherman (R, OH) (ibid., 614), Rep. Chester B. Darrall (R, LA) (*Congressional Record*, vol. 2, pt. 6 [1873–1874], 478), Sen. Frederick T. Frelinghuysen (R, NJ) (*Congressional Record*, vol. 2, pt. 4 [1874], 3453), and Rep. William J. Purman (R, FL) (*Congressional Record*, vol. 2, pt. 1 [1874], 425).

32. Senator Daniel D. Pratt of Indiana in Sloan, *American Landmark Legislation*, 284. See also the remarks of Representative Richard H. Cain (R, SC) (*Congressional Record*, vol. 2, pt. 1 [1874], 902; and Rep. Joseph H. Rainey (R, SC) (Avins, *The Reconstruction Amendments' Debates*, 658), both black Republicans from South Carolina.

33. Avins, *The Reconstruction Amendments' Debates*, 609.

34. Ibid., 610.

35. Sloan, *American Landmark Legislation*, 284.

36. Ibid., 306–307.

37. *Congressional Record*, vol. 2, pt. 1 (1874), 425.

38. Sloan, *American Landmark Legislation*, 295.

39. For an excellent biography of Sumner, see David Donald, *Charles Sumner and the Rights of Man* (New York: Knopf, 1970).

40. This was also an important theme of black politics during Reconstruction. Foner, "Rights and the Constitution in Black Life," 872–873.

41. Sumner, *The Works of Charles Sumner*, vol. 14, 375.

42. Ibid., 425. See also the remarks of Rep. Barbour Lewis (R, TN) (*Congressional Record*, vol. 3, pt. 2 [1875], 998); Rep. Ellis H. Roberts (R, NY) (Sloan, *American Landmark Legislation*, 354); and Sen. Timothy O. Howe (R, WI) (ibid., 306).

43. Legal scholars have devoted extensive attention to the question of the original meaning of the Fourteenth Amendment. For a succinct review of this literature, see William E. Nelson, *The Fourteenth Amendment: From Political Principle to Judicial Doctrine* (Cambridge, MA: Harvard University Press, 1988), 1–7. Within this literature, the work of Robert J. Kaczorowski, "Revolutionary Constitutionalism in the Era of the Civil War and Reconstruction," *New York University Law Review* 61 (1986): 863–940; and Harold M. Hyman and William M. Wiecek, *Equal Justice under Law: Constitutional Development, 1835–1875* (New York: Harper & Row, 1982), comes closest to the view presented here. (Both stress that a sizable bloc of Radical Republicans held that the Reconstruction amendments had nationalized the rights of citizenship and given the federal government the power to enforce those rights in both the public and private sectors.) Neither, however, frames their analysis in terms of an anti-caste principle per se.

44. See the remarks of Sen. Frederick T. Frelinghuysen (R, NJ) (*Congressional Record*, vol. 2, pt. 4 [1874], 3453–3454); Rep. Robert B. Elliott (R, SC) (ibid., 711; *Congressional Record*, vol. 2, pt. 1 [1874], 407); Rep. William J. Purman (R, FL) (*Congressional Record*, ibid., 423); Sen. George F. Edmunds (R, VT) (*Congressional Record*, vol. 3, pt. 3 [1875], 1869); Sen. James L. Alcorn (R, MS) (Avins, *The Reconstruction Amendments' Debates*, 690); Sen. Oliver P. Morton (R, IN) (ibid., 683); Rep. Benjamin W. Harris (R, MA) (Sloan, *American Landmark Legislation*, 346); Sen. Henry R. Pease (R, MS) (ibid., 308); Sen. Daniel D. Pratt (R, IN) (ibid., 284); Rep. Joseph H. Rainey (R, SC) (ibid., 244–245); and Rep. James T. Rapier (R, AL) (McFarlin, *Black Congressional Reconstruction Orators*, 262).

45. Sumner, *The Works of Charles Sumner*, vol. 14, 424.

46. *Congressional Record*, vol. 3, pt. 2 (1875), 1002.

47. Avins, *The Reconstruction Amendments' Debates*, 614.

48. *Congressional Record*, vol. 2, pt. 4 (1874), 3454.

49. Avins, *The Reconstruction Amendments' Debates*, 722–723.

50. Sloan, *American Landmark Legislation*, 302. See also the remarks of Sen. Frelinghuysen in the *Congressional Record*, vol. 2, pt. 4 (1874), 3451; Sen. Oliver P. Morton of Indiana in Avins, *The Reconstruction Amendments' Debates*, 588; and Rep. Lynch in *Congressional Record*, vol. 3, pt. 2 (1875), 943.

51. Avins, *The Reconstruction Amendments' Debates*, 683.

52. *Congressional Record*, vol. 3, pt. 3 (1875), 1870.

53. For a supporting analysis, see Hyman and Wiecek, *Equal Justice under Law*, 507.

54. See, for example, the remarks of Sen. Wilson (R, MA) (Avins, *The Reconstruction Amendments' Debates*, 608); and Sen. Morton (R, IN) (ibid., 683).

55. Ibid., 664.

56. See, for example, the remarks of Rep. William H. Stowell (R, VA) (ibid., 665) and those of Sen. Frelinghuysen (ibid., 674).

57. The Radical and Stalwart factions were responsible for the passage of the Civil Rights Act of 1875 and were the primary supporters of the anti-caste position outside of the black community. While Radical support was a matter of ideological commitment, that of the Stalwarts was strategic, as they believed that "waving the bloody

shirt" (i.e., inflaming the sectional passions of the Civil War) represented the best means of retaining Republican control of the South. See William Gillette, *Retreat from Reconstruction, 1869–1879* (Baton Rouge: Louisiana State University Press, 1979), esp. 202–203; Michael Perman, *The Road to Redemption: Southern Politics, 1869–1879* (Chapel Hill: University of North Carolina Press, 1984); and Montgomery, *Beyond Equality*, 359.

58. 109 U.S. 3 (1883).

59. Philip B. Kurland and Gerhard Casper, eds., *Landmark Briefs and Arguments of the Supreme Court of the United States: Constitutional Law*, vol. 8 (Arlington, VA: University Publications of America, 1975), 317.

60. Ibid., 315.

61. Ibid., 315–316.

62. Ibid., 314.

63. Ibid., 351; emphases in original.

64. Ibid., 343, 352.

65. 109 U.S. 3 (1883).

66. Ibid., emphasis in original.

67. Woodward, "*Plessy v. Ferguson*," 103.

68. Michael J. Horan, "Political Economy and Sociological Theory as Influences upon Judicial Policy-Making: The *Civil Rights Cases* of 1883," *American Journal of Legal History* 16 (1972): 73.

69. Woodward, "*Plessy v. Ferguson*," 103.

70. U.S. Congress, Senate, 48th Cong., 1st sess., *Congressional Record*, vol. 15, pt. 1 (1883), 135.

71. Stanley P. Hirshson, *Farewell to the Bloody Shirt: Northern Republicans and the Southern Negro, 1877–1893* (Bloomington: Indiana University Press, 1962), 104–105.

72. Valeria W. Weaver, "The Failure of Civil Rights 1875–1883 and Its Repercussions," *Journal of Negro History* 54 (1969): 371–372.

73. David W. Blight, *Beyond the Battlefield* (Amherst: University of Massachusetts Press, 2002), 95; Philip S. Foner, *The History of the Labor Movement in the United States*, vol. 2 (New York: International Publishers, 1955), 392–403; Alphonso Pinkney, *Red, Black, and Green: Black Nationalism in the United States* (New York: Cambridge University Press, 1976), 30–31.

74. Thomas R. Frazier, *Afro-American History: Primary Sources* (New York: Harcourt, Brace & World, 1970), 189–190.

75. In 1886, the well-known black newspaper the *New York Freeman* had described the Brotherhood of Liberty as "a large organization of representative influential men (in Baltimore), with the purpose of furthering the interest of colored citizens and securing and maintaining their rights under the Constitution of the United States." Notably, the paper reported that the keynote address at the Brotherhood's annual meeting strongly endorsed both the action of the Knights of Labor at its 1886 Richmond convention, as well as the cause of the labor movement in general (see chap. 4).

76. Brotherhood of Liberty, *Justice and Jurisprudence: An Inquiry Concerning the*

Constitutional Limitations of the Thirteenth, Fourteenth, and Fifteenth Amendments (Philadelphia: Lippincott, 1889), 149, 161.

77. Ibid., 168, 159, emphasis in original.

78. Kurland and Casper, *Landmark Briefs and Arguments*, vol. 13, 58–60, 41, emphasis in original.

79. Ibid., 47–48.

80. Ibid., 38–39; emphases in original.

81. Ibid., 61.

82. Clint Bolick, "Discriminating Liberals," *New York Times* (May 6, 1996), A13. See also Terry Eastland, *Ending Affirmative Action: The Case for Colorblind Justice* (New York: Basic, 1996), 28.

83. William Bradford Reynolds, "Individualism vs. Group Rights: The Legacy of *Brown*," *Yale Law Journal* 93 (1984), 1005. See also William Bradford Reynolds, "The Reagan Administration and Civil Rights: Winning the War against Discrimination," *University of Illinois Law Review* 1986 (1986): 1001–1023.

84. For a similar argument, see T. Alexander Aleinikoff, "Re-Reading Justice Harlan's Dissent in *Plessy v. Ferguson*: Freedom, Antiracism, and Citizenship," *University of Illinois Law Review* 1992 (1992): 961–978. For a theoretical elaboration of how an anti-caste principle might be relevant to contemporary jurisprudence, see Cass Sunstein, "The Anticaste Principle," *Michigan Law Review* 92 (1994): 2140.

Chapter 2

1. The term *Darwinian liberalism* is used to connote the close association between the laissez-faire and social Darwinist ideologies of the late nineteenth century. This is not meant to suggest, of course, that the work of Charles Darwin would itself support such a position.

2. This is but one instance of a much-larger historical phenomenon. See Mehta, *Liberalism and Empire*, for an important argument that places the issue of the compatibility between liberalism and systems of ascriptive hierarchy within a broader theoretical and historical context.

3. *Congressional Record*, vol. 2, pt. 6 (1874), 4.

4. *Congressional Record*, vol. 3, pt. 2 (1875), 984.

5. Richardson (2001) alternatively argues that opposition to the Civil Rights Act of 1875 was based on the claim that it violated the free labor presumption that social standing should be determined by individual economic achievement. While she makes a convincing case that this perspective was important among many moderate Republicans, this chapter argues that the more politically important position held that blacks and whites could never coexist on a level of social equality due to the natural inequality of the races. See Heather Cox Richardson, *The Death of Reconstruction: Race, Labor, and Politics in the Post–Civil War North, 1865–1901* (Cambridge, MA: Harvard University Press, 2001), chap. 4.

6. *Congressional Record*, vol. 3, pt. 3 (1875), 119.

7. Avins, *The Reconstruction Amendments' Debates*, 664.

8. *Congressional Record*, vol. 3, pt. 2 (1875), 949. See also the remarks of Rep. Hiram P. Bell (D, GA) (*Congressional Record*, vol. 2, pt. 6 [1874], 3); Sen. Francis P. Blair, Jr. (D, MO) (Avins, *The Reconstruction Amendments' Debates*, 632, 644); Rep. Alyett Hanes Buckner (D, MO) (ibid., 666); Rep. Michael C. Kerr (D, ND) (ibid., 605); Sen. Thomas M. Norwood (D, GA) (ibid., 608); and Rep. Henry D. McHenry (D, KY) (*Congressional Globe*, vol. 45, pt. 6 [1872], 219).

9. *Congressional Record*, vol. 2, pt. 6 (1874), 3.

10. Ibid., 4. See also the remarks of Sen. Thomas F. Bayard (D, DE) (*Congressional Record*, vol. 3, pt. 3 [1875], 105); Rep. Charles D. Eldredge (D, WI) (*Congressional Record*, vol. 3, pt. 2 [1875], 983); Rep. John J. Davis (D, WV) (*Congressional Record*, vol. 2, pt. 6 [1874], 481); Rep. John M. Glover (D, MO) (*Congressional Record*, vol. 2, pt. 6 [1874], 4); Rep. William M. Robbins (D, NC) (*Congressional Record*, vol. 2, pt. 1 [1874], 898–900); Rep. Milton I. Southard (D, OH) (*Congressional Record*, vol. 2, pt. 6 [1874], 2); Rep. Henry D. McHenry (D, KY) (*Congressional Globe*, vol. 45, pt. 6 [1872], 218); and Sen. Eli Saulsbury (D, DE) (Avins, *The Reconstruction Amendments' Debates*, 593).

11. *Congressional Globe*, vol. 45, pt. 6 (1872), 370.

12. *Congressional Record*, vol. 2, pt. 6 (1874), 3. See also the remarks of Rep. Milton J. Durham (D, KY) (*Congressional Record*, vol. 2, pt. 1 [1874], 406); Rep. Simeon B. Chittenden (R, NY) (*Congressional Record*, vol. 3, pt. 2 [1875], 982); and Rep. James C. Harper (Cons., NC) (*Congressional Globe*, vol. 45, pt. 6 [1872], 371).

13. Avins, *The Reconstruction Amendments' Debates*, 624–625.

14. *Congressional Record*, vol. 3, pt. 2 (1875), 949. See also the remarks of Sen. Thomas F. Bayard (D, DE) (*Congressional Record*, vol. 3, pt. 3 [1875], 104–105); Sen. William T. Hamilton (D, MD) (ibid., 114); Rep. John B. Storm (D, PA) (*Congressional Record*, vol. 3, pt. 2 [1875], 951); Rep. John J. Davis (D, WV) (*Congressional Record*, vol. 2, pt. 6 [1874], 481); Rep. Milton I. Southard (D, OH) (ibid., 2); Rep. James C. Harper (Cons., NC) (*Congressional Globe*, vol. 45, pt. 6 [1872], 372); Sen. Lot M. Morrill (R, ME) (Avins, *The Reconstruction Amendments' Debates*, 590); and Sen. Allen G. Thurman (D, OH) (Sloan, *American Landmark Legislation*, 20).

15. Avins, *The Reconstruction Amendments' Debates*, 627.

16. Ibid., 642.

17. *Congressional Record*, vol. 2, pt. 1 (1874), 428.

18. *Congressional Record*, vol. 3, pt. 3 (1875), 1866.

19. *Congressional Globe*, vol. 45, pt. 6 (1872), 218.

20. *Congressional Record*, vol. 2, pt. 6 (1874), 4.

21. *Congressional Record*, vol. 3, pt. 2 (1875), 984.

22. *Congressional Record*, vol. 3, pt. 3 (1875), 157.

23. *Congressional Record*, vol. 2, pt. 1 (1874), 428.

24. *Congressional Record*, vol. 3, pt. 3 (1875), 104–105.

25. See the remarks of Sen. Allen G. Thurman (D, OH) (*Congressional Globe*, vol. 45, pt. 6 [1872], 25–30).

26. See the remarks of Rep. William M. Robbins (D, NC) (*Congressional Record*, vol. 2, pt. 1 [1874], 897–903).

27. For the descriptions of the voting patterns from which these figures were drawn, see Alfred Avins, "The Civil Rights Act of 1875: Some Reflected Light on the Fourteenth Amendment and Public Accommodations," *Columbia Law Review* 66, no. 5 (1966): 912; Alfred Avins, "Racial Segregation in Public Accommodations: Some Reflected Light on the Fourteenth Amendment from the Civil Rights Act of 1875," *Western Reserve Law Review* 18 (1967): 1279; and Sloan, *American Landmark Legislation*, 232.

28. William Gillette, *Retreat from Reconstruction, 1869–1879* (Baton Rouge: Louisiana State University Press, 1979), 205.

29. Foner, *Reconstruction*, 525–527.

30. James S. Pike, *The Prostrate State: South Carolina under Negro Government* (New York: Appleton, 1874). On the influence of Pike's work, see Foner, *Reconstruction*, 525–526; and John G. Sproat, *"The Best Men": Liberal Reformers in the Gilded Age* (Chicago: University of Chicago Press, 1982), 35–36.

31. Pike, *The Prostrate State*, 67.

32. Ibid., 48, 12.

33. Ibid., 67, 83.

34. Ibid.

35. Ibid., 83–84 , 277, 279.

36. Foner, *Reconstruction*, 526.

37. *New York Times*, May 26, 1874, 4.

38. *New York Times*, Nov. 16, 1874, 4.

39. George M. Frederickson, *The Black Image in the White Mind: The Debate on Afro-American Character and Destiny, 1817–1914* (Middletown, CT: Wesleyan University Press, 1971), 198–199; Joel Williamson, *The Crucible of Race: Black-White Relations in the American South since Emancipation* (New York: Oxford University Press, 1984), 83.

40. Stephen Skowronek, *Building a New American State: The Expansion of National Administrative Capacities, 1877–1920* (New York: Cambridge University Press, 1982), 44.

41. Wade Hampton, "Ought the Negro to Be Disenfranchised? Ought He to Have Been Enfranchised?" *North American Review* 128 (1879): 240–241. Hampton subsequently published another article devoted exclusively to a vigorous endorsement of the description of Reconstruction provided by *The Prostrate State*. See Hampton, "What Negro Supremacy Means," *Forum* 5 (1888): 383–395.

42. C. Vann Woodward, *Origins of the New South, 1877–1913* (Baton Rouge: Louisiana State University Press, [1951] 1971), 148, 151.

43. Frederickson, *The Black Image in the White Mind*, 203.

44. Joel Chandler Harris, ed., *Joel Chandler Harris' Life of Henry W. Grady, including His Writings and Speeches: A Memorial Volume* (New York: Haskell House, [1890] 1972), 101.

45. Quoted in Allen W. Trelease, *White Terror: The Ku Klux Klan Conspiracy and Southern Reconstruction* (New York: Harper & Row, 1971), xxxvii–xxxviii.

46. Ibid., xv.

47. Litwack, *Been in the Storm So Long*, 260. See also Trelease, *White Terror*, xxxvii–xxxviii.

48. John A. Carpenter, "Atrocities in the Reconstruction Period," *Journal of Negro History* 47 (1962): 240.

49. While working as a federal judge, Tourgee participated in the federal prosecution of the Ku Klux Klan during the early 1870s. Later, he and another attorney represented Homer Plessy in *Plessy v. Ferguson*, writing the briefs cited in chapter 1. The standard biography of Tourgee is Otto H. Olsen, *Carpetbagger's Crusade: The Life of Albion Winegar Tourgee* (Baltimore, MD: Johns Hopkins University Press, 1965).

50. Albion W. Tourgee, *The Invisible Empire* (New York: Fords, Howard, & Hulbert, 1879), 496–497; emphasis added.

51. Ibid., 498.

52. Walter L. Fleming, *Documents relating to Reconstruction* (Morgantown, WV: n.p., 1907), 339–340.

53. Tourgee, *The Invisible Empire*, 503.

54. Fleming, *Documents relating to Reconstruction*, no. 1.

55. Ibid.

56. The best account of racial and political terrorism in the South during this period remains Trelease, *White Terror*. See also Foner, *Reconstruction*, chap. 9; Gillette, *Retreat from Reconstruction*, chap. 2; Vernon Lane Wharton, "The Revolution of 1875," in Kenneth M. Stampp and Leon F. Litwack, eds., *Reconstruction: An Anthology of Revisionist Writings* (Baton Rouge: Louisiana State University Press, 1969); Barry A. Crouch, "A Spirit of Lawlessness: White Violence, Texas Blacks, 1865–1868," *Journal of Social History* 18 (1984): 217–232; and Billy D. Ledbetter, "White Texans' Attitudes toward the Political Equality of Negroes, 1865–1870," *Phylon* 40 (1979): 253–263. The most important primary source is U.S. Congress, 42d Cong., 2d. sess., Joint Select Committee to Inquire into the Condition of Affairs in the Late Insurrectionary States, *Report of the Joint Select Committee to Inquire into the Condition of Affairs in the Late Insurrectionary States* (13 vols., 1872). Convened by the U.S. Congress in 1871 in conjunction with the passage of the Enforcement Acts—which were designed to, and temporarily succeeded in, breaking the back of terrorist organizations in the South—this committee conducted one of the largest governmental investigations ever undertaken up to that time.

57. Foner, *Reconstruction*, 425, 430–433; Trelease, *White Terror*, xii, xlvii, 62, 114.

58. 83 U.S. (16 Wall.) 36 (1873).

59. Ibid.

60. 109 U.S. 3 (1883).

61. Ibid.

62. The majority opinion did not explicitly express the white supremacist ideology that had been such a prominent feature of congressional debates. Although it cannot be known with certainty why this was the case, it seems likely that the reason was that the Court was at this time dominated by moderate-to-conservative Republicans who were not inclined to take the more hard-line white supremacist position, which was strongly associated with the Democratic party. With the exception of Justice Stephen J. Field, all of the members of the Court were Republicans — including Chief Justice Bradley, who had been appointed by President Ulysses S. Grant in 1870, and firmly supported the Thirteenth and Fourteenth amendments at the time of their passage. See Alan F. Westin, "The Case of the Prejudiced Doorkeeper," in John A. Garraty, ed., *Quarrels That Have Shaped the Constitution* (New York: Harper & Row, 1962), 137.

63. Horan, "Political Economy and Sociological Theory as Influences upon Judicial Policy-Making," 73; Hirshson, *Farewell to the Bloody Shirt*, 103.

64. "The End of the Civil Rights Bill," *Nation* 37 (1883): 326.

65. Ibid. Although the Civil Rights Act was enforced by some state and federal courts during the time that it was in effect, the relevant case history indicates that this editorial view was widely shared by lawyers, judges, and the general (white) public during both Reconstruction and its aftermath. See John Hope Franklin, "The Enforcement of the Civil Rights Act of 1875," *Prologue* 6 (1974): 225–235. Riegal's (1984) analysis of the forty known racial segregation cases heard in the lower federal courts during 1865–1896 found not only that "the federal courts from Reconstruction onward consistently and frequently decreed Jim Crow segregation to be constitutional and consistent with the laws of the land," but also that "many federal judges held that the 'separate but equal' doctrine was even consistent with the Civil Rights Act of 1875 during its lifetime" (20, 32). The key rationale supporting this view was the claim that to prohibit racial discrimination was an illegitimate attempt to enforce social equality, which was antithetical to the principle of equal citizenship rights. Stephen J. Riegal, "The Persistent Career of Jim Crow: Lower Federal Courts and the 'Separate but Equal' Doctrine, 1865–1896," *American Journal of Legal History* 28 (1984): 17–40.

66. Woodward, "*Plessy v. Ferguson.*"

67. Similarly, Riegal, "The Persistent Career of Jim Crow," argues that "the Supreme Court's adoption of the 'separate but equal' doctrine in *Plessy v. Ferguson* was not a turning point or point of departure in the legal history of race relations, as many commentators have suggested. It was rather an affirmation of the dominant legal concept of equal rights in public accommodations in the federal courts all across the country after the Civil War" (39).

68. 163 U.S. 537 (1896).

69. Bolick (1996) claims that *Plessy* "marked a crucial and disastrous turning point, away from the principles of civil rights and in favor of a regime in which fundamen-

tal rights were subordinated to racist social engineering." Clint Bolick, *The Affirmative Action Fraud: Can We Restore the American Civil Rights Vision?* (Washington, DC: Cato Institute, 1996), 33. See also Eastland, *Ending Affirmative Action*, 27.

70. John S. Wise, "The Constitutional View of the Race Question," *Ohio Law Bulletin* 48 (1903): 718.

71. Dos Passos, who lived from 1844 to 1917, was a leading practitioner of banking, corporate, and financial law and was active in the formation of large business amalgamations, including the "sugar trust," American Thread Company, and many others. Dos Passos was also the author of *A Treatise on the Law of Stock Brokers and Stock Exchanges*, a two-volume work first published in 1882 and reprinted in a second edition in 1905 (*Who Was Who in America*, vol. 1: *1897–1942* [Chicago, IL: Marquis, 1942], 334; *Dictionary of American Biography*, vol. v [New York: Scribner's, 1930], 388–389).

72. John R. Dos Passos, "The Negro Question," *Yale Law Journal* 12 (1903): 468–470.

73. Ibid., 472.

74. Charles Wallace Collins, "The Fourteenth Amendment and the Negro Race Question," *American Law Review* 45 (1911): 855–856.

75. Ibid., 853.

Chapter 3

1. The body of literature commonly referred to as "new labor history" contains extensive discussions of producer republicanism. See, in particular, David Montgomery, "Labor and the Republic in Industrial America: 1860–1920," *Le Movement Social* 3 (1980): 201–215; and Sean Wilentz, "Against Exceptionalism: Class Consciousness and the American Labor Movement, 1790–1920," *International Labor and Working Class History* 26 (Fall 1984): 1–24. For a dated, but still useful, review of this literature, see David Brody, "The Old Labor History and the New: In Search of an American Working Class," *Labor History* 20 (1979): 111–126. A good recent, if critical, review which situates this literature within the larger examination of American republicanism is provided by Rodgers, "Republicanism."

2. Recent research has demonstrated that this vision of the cooperative commonwealth was rooted in certain practical schemes for economic reform. Both in the United States and Europe, "for almost a century, cooperation was corporate capitalism's twin, its shadow, its progressive alternative." Daniel T. Rogers, *Atlantic Crossings: Social Politics in a Progressive Age* (Cambridge, MA: Harvard University Press, 1998), 326. In Britain, for example, membership in cooperative stores grew from 350,000 in 1873 to 1.7 million in 1900. During the same period in France, producers' cooperatives flourished in the small shop and building trades. In Germany, cooperative loan associations were common. Other cooperative enterprises also existed in Italy, Denmark, Ireland, and Belgium. While cooperative arrangements in the United States were relatively weak, this was the result of cultural and political, rather than

purely economic factors. Ibid., 327–343. For a detailed study of the U.S. case, see Berk, *Alternative Tracks*.

3. This raises the question of whether producer republicanism can legitimately be considered to be a variant of American liberalism at all. The answer to this is ambiguous, as it depends on what part of the movement is stressed. On the one hand, many leaders and intellectuals were strongly interested in transcending competitive capitalism, which would make it a nonliberal alternative. On the other hand, its millions of rank-and-file supporters appeared to have been much more concerned with practical reforms, such as the institution of the eight-hour day. Both spoke the familiar language of American liberalism, making repeated references to the Constitution, the Declaration of Independence, and so on. Neither were anticapitalist in the traditional Marxian sense. Consequently, this book places producer republicanism at the outer edge of the American liberal tradition, as an ideological position that worked within it while at the same time imagining something beyond it. (This characterization also holds true for the social liberalism of the Civil Rights movement. See chap. 6.)

4. Important works on the Knights of Labor include Leon Fink, *Workingmen's Democracy: The Knights of Labor and American Politics* (Chicago: University of Illinois Press, 1983); Richard Jules Oestreicher, *Solidarity and Fragmentation: Working People and Class Consciousness in Detroit, 1875–1900* (Chicago: University of Illinois Press, 1986); Peter Rachleff, *Black Labor in Richmond, 1865–1890* (Urbana: University of Illinois Press, 1989); and Kim Voss, *The Making of American Exceptionalism: The Knights of Labor and Class Formation in the Nineteenth Century* (Ithaca, NY: Cornell University Press, 1993).

5. The analysis of Populism presented in this and the following chapter rely heavily on Gerald H. Gaither, *Blacks and the Populist Revolt: Ballots and Bigotry in the "New South"* (University: University of Alabama Press, 1977); Lawrence C. Goodwyn, *The Populist Moment: A Short History of the Agrarian Revolt in America* (New York: Oxford University Press, 1978); Robert C. McMath, Jr., *American Populism: A Social History, 1877–1898* (New York: Hill and Wang, 1993); Bruce Palmer, *"Man over Money": The Southern Populist Critique of American Capitalism* (Chapel Hill: University of North Carolina Press, 1980); C. Vann Woodward, *Tom Watson: Agrarian Rebel* (New York: Oxford University Press, [1938] 1963); and Woodward, *Origins of the New South, 1877–1913* (Baton Rouge: Louisiana State University Press, [1951] 1971).

6. Prior to the advent of the new labor history, the fact that this understanding of class does not fit a traditional Marxian schema and that producer republicanism sought to modify, rather than overthrow, capitalism caused many scholars to dismiss this important part of American labor history as an incipient but inchoate form of pre-Marxian consciousness. Such interpretations, however, obscured more than they revealed. For a good overview of the scholarly debate surrounding the KOL on this issue, see Voss, *The Making of American Exceptionalism*, 85–89. For a parallel discussion of the Populists, see McMath, *American Populism*, 9–17.

7. As Omi and Winant (1994) explain, the concept of "ethnicity," as developed in the United States during the 1920s–1930s, represented a challenge to the then widely accepted belief that "race" accurately identified biological differences among different social groups. Omi and Winant, *Racial Formation in the United States*, 14–15. Yet, as Jacobson (1998) argues, the distinction between the "black" and "white" races developed into a harder binary in conjunction with the shift of various European immigrant groups from racial to ethnic status. Jacobson, *Whiteness of a Different Color*, chap. 8. Consequently, we are left with a historical legacy that considers ethnic groups to be culturally and/or religiously based and racial groups to be, if not biologically distinct (a notion that has been widely discredited even in popular discourse), nonetheless comparatively much more different from one another than ethnic groups. Race, in other words, continues to function as a social marker of profound difference despite the fact that the belief in biological difference that once supported it has been largely abandoned.

8. Although Indians, or Native Americans, occupied a critically important position in the racial lexicon of late nineteenth-century America, they were not seen as a part of the producing classes, or even of the citizenry more broadly.

9. Foner, *Organized Labor and the Black Worker*, 47.

10. Jonathan E. Garlock, "A Structural Analysis of the Knights of Labor: A Prolegomenon to the History of the Producing Classes" (unpublished Ph.D. dissertation, University of Rochester, 1974), 1–4.

11. Trachtenberg, *The Incorporation of America*, 80–99.

12. George E. McNeill, *The Labor Movement: The Problem of Today* (Boston: Bridgman, 1887), 485. According to McNeill, this declaration was "the embodiment of the measures of the organized labor movement from 1825 to the present time" and "the same in scope, and nearly the same in language, as that adopted by the National Labor Congress of 1874." Ibid., 483.

13. McNeill also served as president of the Eight-Hour League, state secretary of the Sovereigns of Industry, and president of the International Labor Union of America. He was an active public speaker and editor or associate editor of the *New York Labor Standard, Fall River Labor Standard, Paterson Labor Standard*, and *Paterson Home Journal*. Ibid., 612.

14. Ibid., 459.

15. Ibid., 456, 465–466.

16. Fink, *Workingmen's Democracy*, 912.

17. Foner, *Organized Labor and the Black Worker*, 48.

18. This statement, drawn from the larger statement entitled "What We Are Here For," can be consistently found on the front page of the paper throughout 1883. See also John Swinton, *Striking for Life: Labor's Side of the Labor Question; the Right of the Workingman to a Fair Living* ([n.p.]: American Manufacturing and Publishing, 1894), 370. A biographical sketch of Swinton can be found in McNeill, *The Labor Movement*, 613–614.

19. See, for example, McNeill, *The Labor Movement*, 464, 495. Good secondary source examinations of the importance of constitutionalism in republican thought can be found in Leon Fink, "Labor, Liberty, and the Law: Trade Unionism and the Problem of the American Constitutional Order," *Journal of American History* 74 (1987): 904–925; and William E. Forbath, "The Ambiguities of Free Labor: Labor and the Law in the Gilded Age," *Wisconsin Law Review* 1985, no. 4 (1985): 767–817.

20. McNeill, *The Labor Movement*, 462–463.

21. Voss, *The Making of American Exceptionalism*, 82–83.

22. Fink, *Workingmen's Democracy*, 26–31.

23. Voss, *The Making of American Exceptionalism*, 83.

24. McNeill, *The Labor Movement*, 508–509.

25. Ibid., chap. 21. See also William E. Barns, ed., *The Labor Problem: Plain Questions and Practical Answers* (New York: Harper & Brothers, 1886), chaps. 1, 9; David Dudley Field, "Industrial Cooperation," *North American Review* 140 (1885): 411–420; and S. M. Jelley, *The Voice of Labor* (Chicago: Gehman, 1887), chap. 17.

26. Henry D. Lloyd, "Lords of Industry," *North American Review* 138 (1884): 552.

27. McNeill, *The Labor Movement*, 485.

28. Gutman and Berlin (1987) estimate that during the 1880s, African Americans and European immigrants and their children made up three-fourths of the industrial labor force. Herbert Gutman and Ira Berlin, "Class Composition and the Development of the American Working Class, 1840–1890," in Ira Berlin, ed., *Power and Culture* (New York: Pantheon, 1987), 380–395.

29. Fink, *Workingmen's Democracy*, xii.

30. Gender inclusiveness was also important. Levine (1984) reports that in 1887 an estimated 55,000 women belonged to the order. This figure represented approximately 10 percent of the Knights' total membership, and was just under the percentage of women in the work force generally. During the 1880s, the KOL chartered more than 400 LAs that included women. Two-thirds of these were "ladies locals"; the rest were mixed assemblies of men and women. Susan Levine, *Labor's True Woman: Carpet Weavers, Industrialization, and Labor Reform in the Gilded Age* (Philadelphia: Temple University Press, 1984), 106. (See, in general, chap. 5 of this work for a detailed discussion of the role of women in the KOL.)

31. Voss (1993) estimates that in 1887, one-half of the 40,275 Knights in New Jersey were immigrants, while nationwide 10 percent were African American. Voss, *The Making of American Exceptionalism*, 81, 129.

32. "In the nation, at large, from 1889 to 1899, on the average, one person was lynched every other day, and two out of three were black. . . . In the 1930s, lynching declined significantly. Still, between 1889 and 1946, a year widely accepted as marking the end of the era of lynching, almost 4,000 black men, women, and children had been mobbed to their deaths." Williamson, *The Crucible of Race*, 117–118. Williamson provides a stomach-turning description of lynching and other forms of racial violence in chapter 6 of this work.

33. See, in general, Hirshson, *Farewell to the Bloody Shirt*.

34. Woodward, *Origins of the New South*, 51.

35. Ibid., 49, 114.

36. Numerous primary sources attest to the importance that KOL organizers attached both to recruiting blacks into the union and to overcoming white prejudice in order to achieve interracial unity. For a useful collection of such citations, see Philip S. Foner, "Documents: The Knights of Labor," *Journal of Negro History* 53 (1968): 70–77. For an excellent secondary source discussion of this issue, see Sidney H. Kessler, "The Organization of Negroes in the Knights of Labor," *Journal of Negro History* 37 (1952): 248–276.

37. Bernard Bailyn, *The Ideological Origins of the American Revolution* (Cambridge, MA: Harvard University Press, [1967] 1992), 232–235; Roediger, *The Wages of Whiteness*, pt. 2.

38. The seminal work on this subject is Roediger, *The Wages of Whiteness*.

39. Rachleff, *Black Labor in Richmond*, 5.

40. Roediger (1991) argues that during the 1840s, the terms *white slavery* and *wage slavery* were interchangeable and effectively served to exclude all but white men from the solidaristic ranks of the oppressed republican worker. As the national controversy over African chattel slavery heated up, however, and the association between "slavery" and "blackness" became more pronounced, white labor advocates backed away from both terms and took up the banner of free labor instead. In the changed context of the postbellum period, however, the concept of wage slavery reemerged as a critique of the emptiness of the promise that the demise of chattel slavery would be sufficient to establish a regime of truly free labor. Roediger, *The Wages of Whiteness*, chap. 4.

41. Swinton, *Striking for Life*, 1–2. For a short description of Swinton's role in the labor movement, see Frank T. Reuter, "John Swinton's Paper," *Labor History* 1 (1960): 298–307.

42. Rachleff, *Black Labor in Richmond*, 139. For other primary sources, see Jelley, *The Voice of Labor*, 347; McNeill, *The Labor Movement*, 463–465, 495; William Godwin Moody, "Workingmen's Grievances," *North American Review* 138 (1884): 509; and Mullen as quoted in Fink, *Workingmen's Democracy*, 159.

43. S. B. Elkins, "The Labor Crisis," *North American Review* 142 (1866): 610.

44. Labor Publishing Company, ed., *Labor: Its Rights and Wrongs* (Washington, DC: Labor Publishing, 1886), 212–213.

45. Rachleff, *Black Labor in Richmond*, 119.

46. McNeill, *The Labor Movement*, 461.

47. Terence V. Powderly, *Thirty Years of Labor* (Columbus, OH: Excelsior, 1890), 657.

48. The most extensive examination of the relationship between black political and cultural life and the republican labor movement is found in Rachleff, *Black Labor in Richmond*. For a general survey and literature review of the history of the relationship between the labor movement and African-American workers between the time

of the Civil War and the establishment of the CIO, see Eric Arneson, "Following the Color Line of Labor: Black Workers and the Labor Movement before 1930," *Radical History* 55 (1993): 53–87.

49. The editor of the *New York Freeman* during this period was T. Thomas Fortune, a prominent black intellectual, journalist, and political activist during the late nineteenth and early twentieth centuries. Fortune was an avid supporter of the KOL during the early to mid-1880s and regularly wrote editorials urging blacks to join its cause. His book *Black and White: Land, Labor, and Politics in the South* (New York: Forde, Howard, & Hulburt, 1884) is a fascinating and underexamined example of the intersection between black and republican political thought during this period.

50. "Industrial Slavery in the South," *New York Freeman*, Dec. 25, 1886.

51. Kenneth Kann, "The Knights of Labor and the Southern Black Worker," *Labor History* 18 (1977): 51.

52. Foner, *History of the Labor Movement in the United States*, vol. 2, 68–69.

53. Rachleff, *Black Labor in Richmond*, 123.

54. Kessler, "The Organization of Negroes in the Knights of Labor," 256–272; Foner, *Organized Labor and the Black Worker*, 49; Kann, "The Knights of Labor and the Southern Black Worker," 54. See also, in general, Melton Alona McLaurin, *The Knights of Labor in the South* (Westport, CT: Greenwood, 1978), chap. 7.

55. John Higham, "Origins of Immigration Restriction, 1882–1897: A Social Analysis," *Mississippi Valley Historical Review* 39 (1952): 78, 180.

56. Oestreicher, *Solidarity and Fragmentation*, 32.

57. John Higham, *Strangers in the Land: Patterns of American Nativism, 1860–1925*, 2d ed. (New Brunswick, NJ: Rutgers University Press, [1955] 1988), 46–48.

58. Ibid., 11.

59. McNeill, *The Labor Movement*, 467.

60. Quoted in ibid., 421.

61. Fink, *Workingmen's Democracy*, 185.

62. Oestreicher, *Solidarity and Fragmentation*, 115–116.

63. Foner, *The History of the Labor Movement in the United States*, vol. 2, 58; Catharine Collomp, "Unions, Civics, and National Identity: Organized Labor's Reaction to Immigration, 1881–1897," *Labor History* 29 (1988): 464; Voss, *The Making of American Exceptionalism*, 162.

64. Foner, *The History of the Labor Movement in the United States*, vol. 2, 58–59; Herbert Hill, "Anti-Oriental Agitation and the Rise of Working-Class Racism," *Society* 10, no. 2 (1973): 46. There were a few notable exceptions to this general pattern. Henry George, for example, denounced the anti-Chinese movement as an unnecessary distraction for the labor movement and attributed its influence in California to opportunistic demagogues. Henry George, "The Kearney Agitation in California," *Popular Science Monthly* 17 (1880): 433–453. Such misgivings did not, however, appear to be widespread among whites. The general pattern among blacks was significantly different: while most accepted the negative stereotyping of the Chinese, particularly to-

ward the end of the century, there was nevertheless a widespread belief that it was wrong to systematically discriminate against them and a general opposition to the Chinese Restriction Act. David J. Hellwig, "Black Reactions to Chinese Immigration and the Anti-Chinese Movement: 1850–1910," *Amerasia* 6, no. 2 (1979): 25–44.

65. John Swinton, *The New Issue: The Chinese-American Question* (New York: American News Company, 1870), 6, 13.

66. McNeill, *The Labor Movement*, 431–432, 438.

67. Ibid., 437. According to Hutton and Reed (1995), "the image of Chinese as slaves comes from the coolie trade of the 1840s," when plantation owners in Latin America and the West Indies worked with pirates, Chinese brokers, and shippers to abduct people to make up for the reduced slave population effected by the recent ban on the African slave trade. Frankie Hutton and Barbara Straus Reed, eds., *Outsiders in Nineteenth Century Press History: Multicultural Perspectives* (Bowling Green, OH: Bowling Green State University Popular Press, 1995), 99.

68. John H. Durst, "The Exclusion of the Chinese," *North American Review* 139 (1884): 257–272.

69. Hill, "Anti-Oriental Agitation," 45–46.

70. Quoted in McNeill, *The Labor Movement*, 441.

71. Alexander Saxton, *The Indispensable Enemy: Labor and the Anti-Chinese Movement in California* (Berkeley: University of California Press, 1971). Also helpful is Stuart Creighton Miller, *The Unwelcome Immigrant: The American Image of the Chinese, 1785–1882* (Berkeley: University of California Press, 1969); Carlos A. Schwantes, "Protest in a Promised Land: Unemployment, Disinheritance, and the Origin of Labor Militancy in the Pacific Northwest, 1885–1886," *Western Historical Quarterly* 13 (1982): 373–390; and Hill, "Anti-Oriental Agitation," 43–54.

72. Saxton, *The Indispensable Enemy*, 7, 11, 210.

73. Lee (2003) documents that Terence Powderly, who was at this time leader of the KOL, served as U.S. commissioner-general of immigration from 1898 to 1902. Although she does not discuss the Knights or his former connection to the organization, she notes that Powderly was a strong labor advocate dedicated to helping white workers by restricting the influx of immigrants who might take their jobs. Powderly was particularly zealous on the issue of Chinese and Japanese immigration, which he continued to describe in highly racist terms as a threat to "American values and civilization." This suggests that Powderly—and, presumably, other labor advocates as well—believed deeply in the anti-Chinese rhetoric that they espoused. Erika Lee, *At America's Gates: Chinese Immigration during the Exclusion Era, 1882–1943* (Chapel Hill: University of North Carolina Press, 2003), 64–67.

74. Goodwyn, *The Populist Moment*, 297.

75. Ibid., viii; McMath, *American Populism*, chap. 1.

76. Jack Abramowitz, "The Negro in the Populist Movement," *Journal of Negro History* 38, no. 3 (July 1953): 257; Woodward, *Origins of the New South*, 192.

77. Gaither, *Blacks and the Populist Revolt*, 3–4.

78. Thomas E. Watson, *People's Party Campaign Book, 1892: Not a Revolt, It Is a Revolution* (Washington, DC: National Watchman, 1892 [microfilm]), 123–124.

79. Woodward ([1951] 1971) describes the "national headquarters of the Alliance at Washington" as "a great powerhouse of doctrine, sending pulsations through the most obscure backwoods suballiance." He additionally notes that the *National Economist* "had a tremendous influence." Woodward, *Origins of the New South*, 194.

80. "The Origin and Results of Monopoly," *National Economist* (Apr. 29, 1889): 66–67. See also Watson, *People's Party Campaign Book*.

81. James A. Weaver, *A Call to Action* (New York: Arno, [1892] 1974), 132, 135, 102–103.

82. Agrarian activists associated with the Farmers' Alliance and the Populist movement were also committed to the cooperative project. As Goodwyn (1978) documents, the more radical branches of the Farmers' Alliance, dedicated to the vision of the cooperative commonwealth, worked assiduously to establish a cooperative system of agriculture credit, distribution, and exchange during the late 1880s and early 1890s. This cooperative drive succeeded both in recruiting "huge numbers of farmers in the South and West" and laying the foundations for the budding "movement culture" of Populism. Goodwyn, *The Populist Moment*, 66.

83. Woodward, *Origins of the New South*, 93–96, 179, 235.

84. People's Party of the United States, National Executive Committee, *The People's Party and the Present Political Contest* (n.p., 1896), 13–14.

85. Watson, *People's Party Campaign Book*, 15, 22–23.

86. Goodwyn, *The Populist Moment*, 169, 187; Woodward, *Origins of the New South*, 200–201, 242–254, 322–323; Gaither, *Blacks and the Populist Revolt*, xvi.

87. Public Opinion Company, "The Farmers' Alliance" (*Farmer's Advocate* quote contained in reprinted article originally published by the *Minneapolis Times*), *Public Opinion* 10, no. 8 (Nov. 29, 1890): 170. See also Public Opinion Company, "The Farmers' Alliance" and "The Alliance and the Federal Election Bill," *Public Opinion* 10, no. 10 (Dec. 13, 1890): 217–221; N. A. Dunning, *The Farmers Alliance History and Agricultural Digest* (Washington, DC: Alliance Publishing, 1891), sec. 2, chap. 6; "How It Is in Texas" and "Act! Act! In the Living Present," *People's Party Paper* (Apr. 28, 1892), 3–4; "A Nefarious Scheme," *People's Party Paper* (May 1, 1892), 7; W. Scott Morgan, *History of the Wheel and Alliance, and the Impending Revolution* (St. Louis, MO: Woodward, 1891), 713–720; Thomas E. Watson, "The Negro Question in the South," *Arena* 6 (1892): 548; and Watson, *People's Party Campaign Book*.

88. Morgan, *History of the Wheel and Alliance*, 727.

89. Dunning, *The Farmers Alliance History and Agricultural Digest*, 253.

90. Gaither, *Blacks and the Populist Revolt*, 67–68.

91. The only way to avoid the problem of forming a strong interracial alliance in a region that was steeped in a culture of white supremacy was to eliminate the black vote through disfranchisement. Those who had the means to do this, however, were those who held the reins of political power—the very Conservative Democrats

whom the Populists were organized to overthrow. Without first gaining power themselves, the Populists could not control the terms of black disfranchisement and therefore risked becoming disfranchised themselves.

92. Woodward, *Origins of the New South*, 257.

93. Abramowitz, "The Negro in the Populist Movement," 266–267; Alex Mathews Arnett, *The Populist Movement in Georgia* (New York: Longmans, Green, 1922), 132, 144; Palmer, *"Man over Money,"* 52–53, 195–196; William R. Gnatz, "The Negro and the Populist Movement in the South" (unpublished Ph.D. dissertation, University of Chicago, Department of History, 1961), 39, 56; Goodwyn, *The Populist Moment*, 215; Woodward, *Tom Watson*, chaps. 9–14.

94. Watson, *People's Party Campaign Book*; C. Vann Woodward, "Tom Watson and the Negro in Agrarian Politics," *Journal of Southern History* 4 (1938): 17; Woodward, *Tom Watson*, 210–211.

95. Goodwyn, *The Populist Moment*, 189.

96. Thomas E. Watson, "The Negro Question in the South," *Arena* 6 (1892): 548. See also "One-Horse Farmers," *People's Party Paper* (Aug. 25, 1892), 5; and "Watson at Sparta," ibid. (Sept. 2, 1892), 1–5.

97. For further discussion of the Australian ballot, see chap. 4, p. 117.

98. Woodward, "Tom Watson and the Negro," 17–18.

99. Woodward, *Tom Watson*, 224–225.

100. Ibid., 225.

101. Ibid., 251, 256.

102. Abramowitz, "The Negro in the Populist Movement," 286.

103. "The Democrats Frightened and Threatening to Go on the War-Path," *People's Party Paper* (Apr. 2, 1892), 1.

104. "Nigger!" *People's Party Paper* (Aug. 6, 1892), 7.

105. Watson, "The Negro Question in the South," 541.

106. Quoted in Palmer, *"Man over Money,"* 59.

107. Ibid., 56–58.

108. Gaither, *Blacks and the Populist Revolt*, 70; Goodwyn, *The Populist Moment*, 191.

109. Woodward, "Tom Watson and the Negro," 21.

110. Abramowitz, "The Negro in the Populist Movement," 273.

111. Woodward, *Tom Watson*, 19–21; Abramowitz, "The Negro in the Populist Movement," 275.

112. Woodward, *Tom Watson*, 21.

Chapter 4

1. The rapidity of this transformation of dominant racial categories was a remarkable historical occurrence. The classic work on the subject is Higham, *Strangers in the Land*. Essentially, this work characterizes this development as part of a larger historical pattern in which nativist anxieties waxed and waned in correspondence to

societal strain. See also John Higham, "Integrating America: The Problem of Assimilation in the Nineteenth Century," *Journal of American Ethnic History* 1 (1981): 7–25.

2. Philip S. Foner, *History of the Labor Movement in the United States, vol. 1: From Colonial Times to the Founding of the American Federation of Labor* (New York: International Publishers, 1947), 464.

3. Gabriel Kolko, *Railroads and Regulation, 1877–1916* (New York: Norton, 1965), 12; Dorothy Ross, *The Origins of American Social Science* (New York: Cambridge University Press, 1991), 100–101.

4. Trachtenberg, *The Incorporation of America*, 40–41; Foner, *History of the Labor Movement in the United States*, vol. 1, 464–474.

5. Richard Slotkin, *The Fatal Environment: The Myth of the Frontier in the Age of Industrialization, 1800–1890* (New York: Atheneum, 1985), 478–479. See, in general, chap. 19.

6. J. A. Dacus, *Annals of the Great Strikes* (St. Louis, MO: Scammell, 1877), 310.

7. Quoted in Robert V. Bruce, *1877: Year of Violence* (Chicago: Quadrangle, 1970), 225–226.

8. Godkin was widely considered by his contemporaries to be, in the words of William James, "the towering influence in all thought concerning public affairs" during the period 1865–1899, with an indirect influence "more pervasive than that of any other writer of the generation, for he influenced other writers who never quoted him, and determined the whole current of discussion." Quoted in George Henry Payne, *History of Journalism in the United States* (New York: Appleton, 1926), 348. Although the *Nation*'s circulation never exceeded 12,000 during this period, historians have generally upheld James's estimation of its influence, which was directly attributable to Godkin's editorship. See, for example, Frank Luther Mott, *A History of American Magazines, 1865–1885* (Cambridge, MA: Harvard University Press, 1957), 338–339.

9. "The Late Riots," *Nation* 25 (Aug. 2, 1877), 68–69 (emphasis added). See also Slotkin, *The Fatal Environment*, chap. 18, for an excellent discussion of how the Great Strike contributed to the racialization of the radical working class.

10. Mott, *A History of American Magazines*, 124–125; Kolko, *Railroads and Regulation*, 13.

11. Ross, *Origins of American Social Science*, 57–58.

12. While the leading proponents of this conservative position were largely found within the elite strata of businessmen, academics, journalists, lawyers, and so on, each of those groups also contained a sizable, and usually growing, current of more-progressive, oppositional thought. Consequently, while the general pattern of political beliefs during this period can be strongly correlated with class position, it can by no means be reduced to it. Ibid., chap. 4.

13. Ibid., 94.

14. "The Gospel of Wealth" (originally, simply "Wealth") first appeared in the *North American Review* 148 (June 1889): 653–664. Like the *Nation*, the *North American Re-*

view "had an influence out of proportion with its relatively modest circulation figures." Reaching its height of influence in the 1880s (despite a circulation of only 17,000 in 1889), it "filled its pages with the names of the world's great and with a swirling clash of opinion about the problems of the new industrial society rising in America." Alan and Barbara Nourie, *American Mass-Market Magazines* (Westport, CT: Greenwood, 1990), 333–335.

15. Fine, *Laissez Faire and the General-Welfare State*, chaps. 2–5; Hofstadter, *Social Darwinism in American Thought*, chaps. 2–3.

16. Caudill (1989) writes that "The Gospel of Wealth," which drew directly on Darwin and Spencer, "set the tone for the period" with its argument "in support of a natural aristocracy to run the economy." Edward Caudill, *Darwinism in the Press: The Evolution of an Idea* (Hillsdale, NJ: Erlbaum, 1989), 73. Similarly, Fine (1956) argues that it represented the epitome of the exceptionally influential blend of social Darwinism and laissez-faire economics which dominated the political thought of the business community—particularly among industrial capitalists—during that time. Fine, *Laissez Faire*, chap. 4.

17. Edward C. Kirkland, ed., *The Gospel of Wealth and Other Timely Essays* (Cambridge, MA: Harvard University Press, 1962), 17–18.

18. Ross, *Origins of American Social Science*, 86.

19. Albert Galloway Keller and Maurice R. Davie, eds., *Essays of William Graham Sumner*, vol. 2 (New Haven, CT: Yale University Press, 1934), 95. The essay quoted, "The Challenge of Facts," was originally titled "Socialism" and written sometime during the 1880s.

20. Although Carnegie believed that the wealthy had a duty to ameliorate the harsh realities of the law of competition by using their fortunes to create public libraries, parks, museums, and other institutions for the common good, he had no regard for the more democratic proposition that the management of the public interest should not be entrusted to the wealthy.

21. Keller and Davie, *Essays of William Graham Sumner*, 110.

22. Kirkland, *Gospel of Wealth*, 14.

23. Keller and Davie, *Essays of William Graham Sumner*, 105–106.

24. Sumner as quoted in Hofstadter, *Social Darwinism in American Thought*, 58; Kirkland, *Gospel of Wealth*, 17.

25. Keller and Davie, *Essays of William Graham Sumner*, 114, 106, 119–120.

26. The 1880s witnessed more than 10,000 strikes and lockouts. Trachtenberg, *The Incorporation of America*, 89.

27. Richard Oestreicher, "A Note of Knights of Labor Membership Statistics," *Labor History* 25 (1984): 106.

28. For an excellent general history of the Haymarket Affair, see Paul Avrich, *The Haymarket Tragedy* (Princeton, NJ: Princeton University Press, 1984). For an analysis of the discourse surrounding the Haymarket Affair which parallels the interpretation presented here, see Carl Smith, *Urban Disorder and the Shape of Belief: The*

Great Chicago Fire, the Haymarket Bomb, and the Model Town of Pullman (Chicago: University of Chicago Press, 1995), chap. 8.

29. "Anarchy as a Blood Disease," *Age of Steel*, July 31, 1886, p. 5.

30. Quoted in Public Opinion Company, "The Red Flag in America," *Public Opinion* 1, no. 5 (May 15, 1886): 82.

31. Ibid., 81.

32. Fred Woodrow, "The Race Element in Social Trouble," in William E. Barns, ed., *The Labor Problem: Plain Questions and Practical Answers* (New York: Harper & Brothers, 1886): 311–312. See also "Thoughts on the Labor Problem," *Age of Steel*, May 29, 1886, p. 7; "Side-Lights on the Labor Problem: Agitation and Agitators," ibid., Sept. 11, 1886, p. 8; and "Light on the Labor Question," ibid., Dec. 4, 1886, pp. 9–10.

33. "Disrating the Foreign Element," *Age of Steel*, Aug. 7, 1886, p. 9.

34. Quoted in Public Opinion Company, "The Red Flag in America," 84. See also S. B. Elkins, "Symposium: The Labor Crisis," *North American Review* 142 (1886): 607–616.

35. George Frederic Parsons, "The Labor Question," *Atlantic Monthly* 58 (1886): 97–113.

36. Henry Clews, "The Labor Crisis," *North American Review* 142 (1886): 598–599.

37. Rufus Hatch, "The Labor Crisis," *North American Review* 142 (1886): 605–606.

38. Oestreicher, "A Note of Knights of Labor Membership Statistics," 106.

39. Although many historians have long believed that the Haymarket Affair was one of the key factors which sent the Knights into a state of rapid decline, explanations of precisely why this was the case remain somewhat murky. At the same time, arguments continue over whether other factors were ultimately more important. For a review of contending explanations, see Voss, *The Making of American Exceptionalism*, 11, 185–189.

40. Higham, *Strangers in the Land*, 52–55, 137–138; Avrich, *The Haymarket Tragedy*, chap. 15.

41. Oestreicher, *Solidarity and Fragmentation*, chap. 6; Voss, *The Making of American Exceptionalism*, chap. 7.

42. Compare, for example, the Knights of Labor's *Record of the Proceedings of the Tenth Regular Session of the General Assembly*, vol. 4 (n.p., 1886 [microfilm]), 10–11, to the statement by the Chicago newspaper the *Knights of Labor*, quoted in Avrich, *The Haymarket Tragedy*, 22.

43. Hartmut Keil, "The Impact of Haymarket on German-American Radicalism," *International Labor and Working Class History* 29 (1986): 16–27. For a similar argument applied to a somewhat later period, see John J. Bukowczyk, "The Transformation of Working-Class Ethnicity: Corporate Control, Americanization, and the Polish Immigrant Middle Class in Bayonne, New Jersey, 1915–1925," *Labor History* 25 (1984): 53–82.

44. See, in particular, Oestreicher, *Solidarity and Fragmentation*, chap. 6. The contemporaneous comments of the immigrant press are also suggestive in this regard

(see, for example, Public Opinion Company, "The Red Flag in America"). This issue is difficult to research thoroughly, however, as it would require being able to read the non–English-language immigrant press.

45. Higham, *Strangers in the Land*, 53–54. See also Avrich, *The Haymarket Tragedy*, chap. 15; and Henry David, *The History of the Haymarket Affair* (New York: Russell & Russell, [1936] 1958), chap. 24.

46. Weiss (1970) suggests, but does not really develop, such a connection in a short article that surveys racist thought during the Gilded Age. Richard Weiss, "Racism in the Era of Industrialization," in Gary B. Nash and Richard Weiss, eds., *The Great Fear: Race in the Mind of America* (New York: Holt, Rinehart and Winston, 1970), 121–143.

47. Labor historians have generally paid extremely little attention to the South. Consequently, the history of the labor movement in that region is often considered inconsequential. As McLaurin (1978) demonstrates, however, the South represented a very important region for the KOL. By mid-1886, the union had gained a foothold in every major southern industry and was particularly strong in mining, textiles, lumber, and construction. It had a strong base in the major southern cities of Richmond, Raleigh, Durham, Atlanta, and Birmingham and was growing in small towns and rural areas. Overall, in fact, the Knights believed that it would be able to establish as strong a presence in the South as in any other part of the country. McLaurin, *The Knights of Labor in the South*, 3–6, 51.

48. Quotations from Foner, *History of the Labor Movement in the United States*, 71.

49. For a complete transcript of Ferrell's and Powderly's remarks, see Knights of Labor, *Record of the Proceedings of the Tenth Regular Session of the General Assembly*, vol. 4 (n.p., 1886 [microfilm]), 7–12. The convention is also retrospectively discussed by Powderly in his *Thirty Years of Labor* (Columbus, OH: Excelsior, 1890), 651–662.

50. Powderly, *Thirty Years of Labor*, 654–655.

51. For an excellent collection of contemporary newspaper citations, see "Knights of Labor and the Color Line," *Public Opinion* 2, no. 27 (Oct. 16, 1886): 1–5. Notably, the Republican press offered substantial support for District 49, often arguing that the Ferrell incident should have the beneficial effect of dramatizing the seriousness of the race issue in the South. The *Brooklyn Times*, for example, wrote that it "was a well-merited rebuke to the pig-headed Southern prejudice against the negro" and "ought to be something of an eye-opener to the Northern members of the order" (ibid., 2).

52. "Knights of Labor and the Color Line," 1, 4.

53. Powderly, *Thirty Years of Labor*, 656.

54. Ibid., 658–659.

55. Foner, *Organized Labor and the Black Worker*, 55–56.

56. Rachleff, *Black Labor in Richmond*, chap. 11.

57. McLaurin, *The Knights of Labor in the South*, 144.

58. This wave of labor repression culminated in the murderous suppression of a sugarcane-workers strike in Louisiana in 1887. See McLaurin, *The Knights of Labor in the South*, 140–145.

59. Foner, *Organized Labor and the Black Worker*, chap. 4; McLaurin, *The Knights of Labor in the South*, chaps. 7, 9. McLaurin (1978) concludes that "internecine fighting, together with racial prejudice and the intransigence of management, contributed most to the decline of the order" (*The Knights of Labor in the South*, 187).

60. Charles Kendall Adams, "Contemporary Life and Thought in the United States," *Contemporary Review* 52 (1887): 731–733.

61. Samuel Rezneck, "Patterns of Thought and Action in an American Depression, 1882–1886," *American Historical Review* 61 (1955): 307.

62. Richardson (2001) argues that northern antiblack prejudice also intensified as the popular white image of the black worker became tarred by the charge of socialism. See Richardson, *The Death of Reconstruction*, chap. 6.

63. During this period, lynching became ritualized as a horrific spectator sport, with African Americans being routinely tortured and killed before appreciative crowds of "hundreds and sometimes thousands of spectators," who commonly took specially commissioned "excursion" trains out to the murder site. Williamson, *The Crucible of Race*, 185–187. For the connection between lynching, as well as other forms of racial violence and oppression, and the campaign to defeat Populism, see Woodward, *Origins of the New South*, chaps. 9, 12, 13.

64. Gerald H. Gaither, *Blacks and the Populist Revolt: Ballots and Bigotry in the "New South"* (University: University of Alabama Press, 1977), xvi. For the classic analysis of Populism, which first developed this position, see Woodward, *Origins of the New South*, chaps. 9, 10, 12. The leading alternative argument is presented in Lawrence C. Goodwyn, *The Populist Moment* (New York: Oxford University Press, 1978), which emphasizes the importance of nonracial issues of political strategy.

65. The free-silver issue hinged on the belief that had grown popular among debtors, farmers, laborers, and others deeply affected by the economic contractions of the 1870s–1890s that their problems stemmed from the establishment of the gold standard in 1873 and that the free coinage of silver would alleviate them. While this was not an accurate analysis, the cause of free silver was a very important issue at the time. It was, however, the least radical of the southern Populist demands. Goodwyn, *The Populist Moment*, 16–18; Woodward, *Origins of the New South*, 280–281.

66. Gaither, *Blacks and the Populist Revolt*, xii.

67. Abramowitz, "The Negro in the Populist Movement," 286.

68. Woodward, *Tom Watson*, 222.

69. Quoted in ibid., 238.

70. Gaither, *Blacks and the Populist Revolt*, 134. Although bribery was certainly an important factor, Gnatz (1961) argues that "the tendency of Negroes to be bought by money or strong drink has been overplayed by white observers of the nineties as well as by later commentators. Contemporary Negro estimates place the corrupted portion of the Negro voting population at less than ten percent." William R. Gnatz, "The Negro and the Populist Movement in the South" (unpublished Ph.D. dissertation, University of Chicago, Department of History, 1961), 130.

71. Gaither, *Blacks and the Populist Revolt*, 100.

72. Alex Mathews Arnett, *The Populist Movement in Georgia* (New York: Longmans, Green, 1922), 150–151; Gaither, *Blacks and the Populist Revolt*, xvii, 99–101; Woodward, *Tom Watson*, 241, 269–270. There is a dearth of reliable information about the shape of black political opinion during this period; consequently, estimates of the degree of black support for the People's party vary considerably (compare, for example, Gnatz, "The Negro and the Populist Movement in the South," chap. 4, and Barton C. Shaw, *The Wool-Hat Boys: Georgia's Populist Party* [Baton Rouge: Louisiana State University Press, 1984], chap. 5).

73. Gaither, *Blacks and the Populist Revolt*, 99.

74. Woodward, *Tom Watson*, 269.

75. Gaither, *Blacks and the Populist Revolt*, chap. 6; Woodward, *Origins of the New South*, 259–278; Woodward, *Tom Watson*, 241–277.

76. Woodward, *Origins of the New South*, 282.

77. See Woodward, *Tom Watson*, chap. 17; Goodwyn, *The Populist Moment*, chap. 8; and Palmer, *"Man over Money,"* chap. 12.

78. Kousser (1974) tabulates that the overall decline in voter turnout in the South following suffrage restriction averaged 37 percent, with an average decline of 26 percent among white voters and 62 percent among blacks. Similarly, Woodward (1971 [1951]) reports that white voter registration in Louisiana declined from 164,088 in 1897 to 91,716 in 1904 in the wake of suffrage restriction, while black voter registration declined from 130,344 to 1,342 during the same years. J. Morgan Kousser, *The Shaping of Southern Politics: Suffrage Restriction and the Establishment of the One-Party South, 1880–1910* (New Haven, CT: Yale University Press, 1974), 241–242; Woodward, *Origins of the New South*, 342–343.

79. V. O. Key, Jr., *Southern Politics in State and Nation* (Knoxville: University of Tennessee Press, [1949] 1977), 8–9; Woodward, *Origins of the New South*, 347–348; Kousser, *The Shaping of Southern Politics*, 260–261. As Tindall (1967) notes, the difference between the demagogic politics of men such as "Pitchfork" Ben Tillman, Cole Blease, and James Vardaman, who appealed to the racial, class, and religious prejudices of lower-class southern whites, and the more overtly conservative politics of other southern Democratic elites, was purely a matter of style rather than substance. George B. Tindall, *The Emergence of the New South, 1913–1945* (Baton Rouge: Louisiana State University Press, 1967), 20–21.

80. Woodward (1966) notes that the "origin of the term 'Jim Crow' . . . is lost in obscurity. Thomas D. Rice wrote a song and dance called 'Jim Crow' in 1832, and the term had become an adjective by 1838. The first example of 'Jim Crow law' listed by the *Dictionary of American English* is dated 1904." The expression was used by writers in the 1890s whom Woodward quotes in his book. Woodward, *The Strange Career of Jim Crow*, 7.

81. John W. Cell, *The Highest Stage of White Supremacy: The Origins of Segregation in South Africa and the American South* (New York: Cambridge University Press, 1982), 233–234.

82. Ibid., 3; Williamson, *The Crucible of Race*, 253–255. See also, in general, C. Vann Woodward, *The Strange Career of Jim Crow*, 2nd rev. ed. (New York: Oxford University Press, [1955] 1966).

83. E. E. Schattschneider, *The Semisovereign People: A Realist's View of Democracy in America* (Hinsdale, IL: Dryden, [1960] 1975), 76–83.

84. "By 1898, the AFL had 278,016 members, a little more than a third of the Knights' peak membership. In the next six years it grew six-fold to over 1 million and almost doubled again by 1914." J. David Greenstone, *Labor in American Politics* (Chicago: University of Chicago Press, [1969] 1977), 24.

85. Although the AFL, which was established in 1886, had begun with a quasi-Marxian commitment to the solidarity of labor, this had completely eroded by the turn of the century. Victoria Hattam, *Labor Visions and State Power: The Origins of Business Unionism in the United States* (Princeton, NJ: Princeton University Press, 1993), 137–139.

86. See, in general, Gwendolyn Mink, *Old Labor and New Immigrants in American Political Development: Union, Party, and State, 1875–1920* (Ithaca, NY: Cornell University Press, 1986). Mink argues that racism undercut class solidarity and that the AFL institutionalized this development with the establishment of a powerful form of conservative, exclusionary trade unionism. While I agree with this position, my purpose is to analyze the development of racial paradigms that Mink essentially takes for granted (e.g., the racialization of Southern and Eastern European immigrants), connecting these to larger patterns of political identity and discourse.

87. Foner, *The History of the Labor Movement in the United States*, vol. 2, 361–362. See also Catharine Collomp, "Unions, Civics, and National Identity: Organized Labor's Reaction to Immigration, 1881–1897," *Labor History* 29 (1988): 450–474.

88. Herbert Hill, "In the Age of Gompers and After: Racial Practices of Organized Labor," *New Politics* 4 (1965): 39–40.

89. Bernard Mandel, "Samuel Gompers and the Negro Workers, 1886–1914," *Journal of Negro History* 40 (1955): 53

90. For an exceptionally lucid discussion of voluntarism, see Greenstone, *Labor in American Politics*, 25–29.

91. The AFL was willing to make exceptions, however, in the case of women and children. As voluntarist theory did not view them as free and independent citizens to begin with, the rationale was that government regulation would not interfere with their right to freedom of contract as it would in the case of adult males. Ibid., 26–27.

92. The fact that the racial fragmentation of working-class politics involved divisions both between the "old" and "new" European immigrant groups and between white and black Americans should not be misinterpreted to mean that the cultural and structural barriers confronting the new immigrants were equivalent to those faced by African Americans. The racial animus directed against blacks was more virulent, monolithic, and resistant to change, and their social position was more unfavorable. In 1900, for example, approximately 90 percent of the total black population

lived in the South, which was characterized by an exceptionally oppressive social, political, and economic system organized around the principle of white supremacy.
Further, as Lieberson (1980) documents, while the socioeconomic position of blacks
in the North stood in a position of rough parity with that of the new immigrant
groups in 1900, it declined steadily throughout the course of the twentieth century,
even as the black percentage of the population in that region rose and the socioeconomic standing of new immigrant groups improved. The best explanation for these
developments is not that these immigrants were more industrious, but that blacks
experienced much more severe discrimination from the old and the new European
groups combined. Stanley Lieberson, *A Piece of the Pie: Blacks and White Immigrants
since 1880* (Berkeley: University of California Press, 1980), chaps. 10–12.

93. Andrew Dawson, "The Parameters of Craft Consciousness: The Social Outlook
of the Skilled Worker, 1890–1920," in Dirk Hoerder, ed., *American Labor and Immigration History, 1877–1920s: Recent European Research* (Chicago: University of Illinois
Press, 1983), 149.

94. Herbert Hill, "In the Age of Gompers and After: Racial Practices of Organized
Labor," *New Politics* 4 (1965): 37–38. For a detailed analysis of the economic position
of blacks during this period, see W. E. Burghardt Du Bois, ed., *The Negro Artisan: A
Social Study* (Atlanta, GA: Atlanta University Press, 1902); and W. E. Burghardt Du
Bois and A. G. Dill, eds., *The Negro American Artisan* (Atlanta, GA: Atlanta Univer-
sity Press, 1912).

95. Walter Dean Burnham, "The Changing Shape of the American Political Universe," *American Political Science Review* 59 (1965): 7–28; Burnham, *Critical Elections
and the Mainsprings of American Politics* (New York: Norton, 1970); Burnham, "Theory and Voting Research: Some Reflections on Converse's 'Change in the American
Electorate,'" *American Political Science Review* 68 (1974): 1002–1023. See also Schattschneider, *The Semisovereign People*, chap. 5.

96. Philip E. Converse, "Comment on Burnham's 'Theory and Voting Research,'"
American Political Science Review 68 (1974): 1024–1027; Jerrold G. Rusk, "The Effect
of the Australian Ballot Reform on Split-Ticket Voting: 1876–1908," *American Political Science Review* 64 (1970): 1220–1238; Rusk, "Comment: The American Electoral
Universe: Speculation and Evidence," *American Political Science Review* 68 (1974):
1028–1049.

97. Walter Dean Burnham, *The Current Crisis in American Politics* (New York: Oxford University Press, 1982), 142.

98. R. Jeffrey Lustig, *Corporate Liberalism: The Origins of Modern American Political Theory, 1890–1920* (Berkeley: University of California Press, 1982); Berk, *Alternative Tracks*; Mink, *Old Labor and New Immigrants*; Goodwyn, *The Populist Moment*,
pt. 3; and Mike Davis, *Prisoners of the American Dream: Politics and Economy in the
History of the US Working Class* (New York: Verso, 1986), pt. 1.

Chapter 5

1. Jacobson (1998) makes a similar point, arguing that the development of a new black-white binary during the 1930s–1940s was caused in part by the era's new attention to civil rights issues. See Jacobson, *Whiteness of a Different Color*, chap. 8.

2. Harvard Sitkoff, *A New Deal for Blacks: The Emergence of Civil Rights as a National Issue*, vol. 1: *The Depression Decade* (New York: Oxford University Press, 1978), 95–101.

3. Carl N. Degler, *In Search of Human Nature: The Decline and Revival of Darwinism in American Social Thought* (New York: Oxford University Press, 1991), pt. 2.

4. Woodward, *The Strange Career of Jim Crow*, 128; Doug McAdam, *Political Process and the Development of Black Insurgency, 1930–1970* (Chicago: University of Chicago Press, 1982), 81; Gerald N. Rosenberg, *The Hollow Hope: Can Courts Bring about Social Change?* (Chicago: University of Chicago Press, 1991), 157–160.

5. For a detailed examination of the relationship between black civil rights issues and the Cold War, see Mary L. Dudziak, *Cold War Civil Rights: Race and the Image of American Democracy* (Princeton, NJ: Princeton University Press, 2000).

6. Gunnar Myrdal, *An American Dilemma: The Negro Problem and Modern Democracy* (New York: Harper & Row, 1944), vliii, 21, 13; emphases added.

7. Walter A. Jackson, *Gunnar Myrdal and America's Conscience: Social Engineering and Racial Liberalism, 1938–1987* (Chapel Hill: University of North Carolina Press, 1990), 242.

8. Arthur Schlesinger, Jr., *The Vital Center: The Politics of Freedom* (Boston: Houghton Mifflin, 1949), 190. See also Peter J. Kellogg, "Civil Rights Consciousness in the 1940s," *Historian* 42 (1979): 31.

9. Alonzo L. Hamby, *Beyond the New Deal: Harry S. Truman and American Liberalism* (New York: Columbia University Press, 1973), 188–189; U.S. President's Committee on Civil Rights, *To Secure These Rights: The Report of the President's Committee on Civil Rights* (New York: Simon and Schuster, 1947); Sitkoff, *A New Deal for Blacks*.

10. U.S. President's Committee on Civil Rights, *To Secure These Rights*, 139–141; emphasis in original.

11. Quoted in Jackson, *Gunnar Myrdal and America's Conscience*, 277.

12. James R. Newman, "Examination of Freedom," *New Republic* (Nov. 17, 1947), 24–28, quoted in Hamby, *Beyond the New Deal*, 189.

13. In contrast, radical activists associated with the Communist party (CPUSA), which reached its height of influence during this period, explicitly emphasized the importance of combating racism. Their efforts, however, were directed toward the larger goal of building working-class solidarity and were therefore also quite different from the postwar liberal goal of eliminating racial discrimination from an otherwise individualistic social order.

14. Richard H. Pells, *Radical Visions and American Dreams: Culture and Social Thought in the Depression Years* (Middletown, CT: Wesleyan University Press, 1973),

89–95, 300–303. See also Ira Katznelson, "Was the Great Society a Lost Opportunity?" in Steve Fraser and Gary Gerstle, eds., *The Rise and Fall of the New Deal Order* (Princeton, NJ: Princeton University Press, 1989), 185–211; and Nelson Lichtenstein, "From Corporatism to Collective Bargaining: Organized Labor and the Eclipse of Social Democracy in the Postwar Era," in ibid., 122–152.

15. Theda Skocpol, "The Legacies of New Deal Liberalism," in Douglas MacLean and Claudia Mills, eds., *Liberalism Reconsidered* (Totowa, NJ: Rowman and Allenheld, 1983), 90–96; Katznelson, "Was the Great Society a Lost Opportunity?" 193; Margaret Weir, "The Federal Government and Unemployment: The Frustration of Policy Innovation from the New Deal to the Great Society," in Margaret Weir, Ann Shola Orloff, and Theda Skocpol, eds., *The Politics of Social Policy in the United States* (Princeton, NJ: Princeton University Press, 1988), 158–160; Weir, *Politics and Jobs: The Boundaries of Employment Policy in the United States* (Princeton, NJ: Princeton University Press, 1992), 48–49.

16. As Lichtenstein (1989) points out, the success of such a campaign would have required the same sort of federal backing that would (eventually) be given to the Civil Rights movement; without such support, the determined opposition of the white elite—which, of course, had a tremendous economic interest in maintaining a nonunionized, low-wage labor force—was simply too formidable to be overcome. Lichtenstein, "From Corporatism to Collective Bargaining," 134–136.

17. Hamby, *Beyond the New Deal*, chaps. 6–12.

18. Alan Brinkley, "The New Deal and the Idea of the State," in Fraser and Gerstle, eds., *The Rise and Fall of the New Deal Order*, 109.

19. Here, "poor" is defined as a before-tax family income of under $4,000 in 1960 dollars; "middle class" as an income of $6,000–14,999 measured similarly. Dwight MacDonald, "Our Invisible Poor," *New Yorker* 38 (Jan. 19, 1963), 110.

20. Thomas J. Sugrue, *The Origins of the Urban Crisis: Race and Inequality in Postwar Detroit* (Princeton, NJ: Princeton University Press, 1996), 126, 144.

21. This is not, of course, the full picture: the number of black males employed in middle-class occupations, for example, increased from 9.6 percent in 1940 to 24 percent in 1960, while the proportion of those holding semiskilled blue-collar jobs increased from 12.7 percent to 26.6 percent. By 1960, consequently, the proportion of black men working in lower-class positions had decreased substantially from its level of 78.1 percent in 1940. It still remained, however, at the quite high level of 50.7 percent. (Here, "middle-class" occupations are defined as white-collar jobs, as well as craftsmen and foremen positions; "working class" refers to semiskilled operatives; and "lower class" refers to service workers, farm workers, and unskilled laborers.) The overall black unemployment rate increased from 5.9 percent in 1948 to 10.2 percent in 1960, while the rate for black teenagers aged 16–19 rose from 16.5 percent in 1954 to 24.4 percent in 1960. (Corresponding rates for white unemployment were 3.5 percent in 1948 and 4.9 percent in 1960; for white teenagers, 12.1 percent in 1954 and 13.4 percent in 1960.) William Julius Wilson, *The Declining Significance of Race: Blacks*

and Changing American Institutions, 2d ed. (Chicago: University of Chicago Press, 1980), 127–129, 90–91.

22. See, in general, Katznelson, "Was the Great Society a Lost Opportunity?" and Lichtenstein, "From Corporatism to Collective Bargaining."

23. The average weekly earnings of production or nonsupervisory workers as a percentage of autoworkers' average weekly earnings, for example, fell from 76.3 percent in 1947 to 64.5 percent in 1960 for those employed in miscellaneous manufacturing industries, and from 71.2 percent to 49 percent for those employed in the apparel industry. These divisions widened even more dramatically after 1965, so that by 1983 they had fallen to 50.6 percent and 38.2 percent, respectively. Meanwhile, in the retail trades, the corresponding figures had fallen from 53.1 percent in 1950, to 50.1 percent in 1960, to 32.6 percent in 1983. Lichtenstein, "From Corporatism to Collective Bargaining," 140–145.

24. Gerstle (1994) presents a similar, if much more fine-grained, analysis of the evolution of American liberalism from the 1920s to the 1940s. Gary Gerstle, "The Protean Character of American Liberalism," *American Historical Review* 99, no. 4 (Oct. 1994): 1043–1073.

25. Theda Skocpol, "The Limits of the New Deal System and the Roots of Contemporary Welfare Dilemmas," in Weir, Orloff, and Skocpol, eds., *The Politics of Social Policy in the United States*, chap. 8. See also Hamby, *Beyond the New Deal*, 277–281; Brinkley, "The New Deal and the Idea of the State"; Katznelson, "Was the Great Society a Lost Opportunity?"; Weir, "The Federal Government and Unemployment"; Weir, *Politics and Jobs*, chap. 2.

26. For an analysis of the critical importance of race in the development of New Deal era social welfare programs and their consequent discriminatory structure, see Robert C. Lieberman, *Shifting the Color Line: Race and the American Welfare State* (Cambridge, MA: Harvard University Press, 1998); and Michael K. Brown, *Race, Money, and the American Welfare State* (Ithaca, NY: Cornell University Press, 1999), chaps. 1–5.

27. St. Clair Drake and Horace Cayton, *Black Metropolis: A Study of Negro Life in a Northern City*, rev. ed. (New York: Harcourt, Brace & World, [1945] 1970), 1: xlvi–xlvii.

28. Sugrue, *The Origins of the Urban Crisis*, chap. 4.

29. Racial discrimination on the part of labor unions also constituted a serious problem. By the time of the AFL-CIO merger in 1955, the CIO had largely lost its original initiative to fight against the traditionally conservative and discriminatory practices of the older organization. Consequently, while there was tremendous variation among different unions, much of organized labor either tolerated or pursued racially discriminatory policies. As Herbert Hill, labor secretary of the NAACP, subsequently documented, racially discriminatory practices such as (1) the exclusion of black workers from union membership and apprenticeship training programs; (2) the maintenance of segregated union locals within a larger system of white power and control; and (3) the construction of separate racial seniority lines in collective bar-

gaining agreements subsequently persisted in a variety of unions across the country throughout the 1950s and early 1960s. Herbert Hill, "Racism within Organized Labor: A Report of Five Years of the AFL-CIO, 1955–1960," *Journal of Negro Education* 30 (1961): 109–118; Sumner M. Rosen, "The CIO Era, 1935–55," in John H. Bracey, Jr., August Meier, and Elliott Rudwick, eds., *Black Workers and Organized Labor* (Belmont, CA: Wadsworth, 1971), 170–184.

30. "Whereas before 1940 no racial or ethnic group in American history had ever experienced an isolation index above 60%, by 1970 this level was normal for blacks in large American cities. . . . Not only was the segregation of European ethnic groups lower, it was also temporary. Whereas Europeans' isolation indices began to drop shortly after 1920, the spatial isolation characteristic of blacks had become a permanent feature of the residential structure of large American cities by 1940." Douglas S. Massey and Nancy A. Denton, *American Apartheid: Segregation and the Making of the Underclass* (Cambridge, MA: Harvard University Press, 1993), 57.

31. Sugrue, *Origins of the Urban Crisis*, 262.

32. Massey and Denton, *American Apartheid*, 44.

33. Ibid., 45–46.

34. Ibid., 51–53.

35. Arnold Hirsch, *Making the Second Ghetto: Race and Housing in Chicago, 1940–1960* (Cambridge: Cambridge University Press, 1983), 262–263. The Robert Taylor homes were built during 1960–1962—before the enactment of the Great Society programs on which they are commonly blamed. Universally regarded as an urban disaster, 23 of the original 28 units were demolished by the Daley administration during 1998–2003 with funding from the federal HOPE VI grant. The five remaining buildings are slated to be closed by 2005. See Pam Belluck, "Razing the Slums to Rescue the Residents," *New York Times* (Sept. 6, 1998), on the Web at http://www.personal.psu .edu/faculty/r/x/rxj9/hdfs597f/housing.html (Jan. 2005); and Chicago Housing Authority Web site, "Robert Taylor Homes," http://thecha.org/housingdev/robert_ taylor.html (Jan. 2005).

36. Hirsh, *Making the Second Ghetto*, 41, 74–78. See also Sugrue, *The Origins of the Urban Crisis*, pt. 3; and Arnold Hirsch, "Massive Resistance in the Urban North: Trumbull Park, Chicago, 1953–1966," *Journal of American History* 82, no. 2 (Sept. 1995): 522–550.

37. Sugrue, *Origins of the Urban Crisis*, 188. Wilson (1987) argues that the exodus of more affluent residents has significantly damaged ghetto neighborhoods. William Julius Wilson, *The Truly Disadvantaged: The Inner City, the Underclass, and Public Policy* (Chicago: University of Chicago Press, 1987).

38. Sugrue, *Origins of the Urban Crisis*, 261–262.

39. From the late 1920s through the late 1960s, the Southern and Eastern European immigrants of the late nineteenth century and their descendants were strongly aligned with the Democratic party, which brought them into the political mainstream and promoted policies that helped working-class people like themselves. They were strong supporters of the New Deal and active participants in the newly revital-

ized labor movement of the 1930s–1940s. See Nelson Lichtenstein, "The Making of the Postwar Working Class: Cultural Pluralism and Social Structure in World War II," *Historian* 51 (1988): 42–63.

40. Sugrue, *Origins of the Urban Crisis*, represents the definitive work on this issue. A shorter version of the argument presented in that book is available in Sugrue, "Crabgrass-Roots Politics: Race, Rights, and the Reaction against Liberalism in the Urban North, 1940–1964," *Journal of American History* 82, no. 2 (Sept. 1995): 551–578. Other important works on this topic include Hirsch, *Making the Second Ghetto*, chap. 6; and Hirsch, "Massive Resistance in the Urban North."

41. Historical work documenting the precise processes through which this transformation from race to ethnicity occurred is still in its infancy. Jacobson (1998) provides the most detailed account, but does not claim to present comprehensive causal analysis. (Jacobson, *Whiteness of a Different Color*, 5–7, 201–202, 274–280.) For a case study of this transformation, see Brodkin, *How Jews Became White Folks*.

42. Hirsch, *Making the Second Ghetto*, 186–187.

43. In Chicago, notes Hirsch (1983), "Nowhere was a single ethnic group fighting for its own homogeneous neighborhood or nationality." Ibid.

44. Ibid., 216.

45. Ibid., 207–209.

46. This description, of course, focuses solely on domestic concerns. Postwar liberalism was also strongly committed to containing Soviet expansion, being fiercely anti-Communist both at home and abroad.

Chapter 6

1. As Hamilton and Hamilton (1997) document, this agenda followed what was in fact the true tradition of the Civil Rights movement, including such venerable organizations as the National Association for the Advancement of Colored People (NAACP) and the National Urban League (NUL), since at least the 1930s: a "dual agenda" that was equally committed to the realization of progressive civil rights and social welfare policies. Hamilton and Hamilton, *The Dual Agenda*.

2. Although Stein (1998) does not address her argument specifically to the politics of the Civil Rights movement, her analysis supports the claim that such problems were in fact of critical importance during the 1950s and 1960s. Judith Stein, *Running Steel, Running America: Race, Economic Policy, and the Decline of Liberalism* (Chapel Hill: University of North Carolina Press, 1998).

3. Highly focused on issues of race and class, the Civil Rights movement had no comparable analysis of the importance of gender oppression. Further, its day-to-day operations were characterized by a patriarchal model of organization and leadership, which, among other things, prevented women from occupying titled leadership positions within the movement. Although Ella Baker was an exception to the rule, she too chafed at the sexism of the Southern Christian Leadership Conference

(SCLC) in particular. See Joanne Grant, *Ella Baker: Freedom Bound* (New York: Wiley, 1999). Nonetheless, as Barnett (2000) documents, women did play a very important role in the movement as "bridge leaders," connecting the formal leadership with the movement's mass base. Bernice McNair Barnett, *Sisters in Struggle: Invisible Black Women in the Civil Rights Movement, 1945–1970* (New York: Routledge, 2000).

4. Civil rights historian Hugh Davis Graham (1992), for example, writes that while "the movement for black civil rights was originally driven by liberalism's classic theory of individual rights and nondiscrimination," by the late 1960s it was "moving away from the NAACP's historic model of a 'color-blind' Constitution." Hugh Davis Graham, *Civil Rights and the Presidency: Race and Gender in American Politics, 1960–1972* (New York: Oxford University Press, 1992), 4.

5. In his path-breaking analysis of the development of the Civil Rights movement, McAdam (1982) describes this sense of empowerment as "cognitive liberation" and argues that it is just as important to the development of social movements as is a confluence of enabling structural factors. With regard to the Civil Rights movement, McAdam attributes the development of cognitive liberation to the way in which new structural conditions encouraged relatively positive responses on the part of the federal government to black political activism during the New Deal and early postwar periods. His analysis is incomplete, however, in that it fails to consider the central importance of issues of racial consciousness in this regard. Doug McAdam, *Political Process and the Development of Black Insurgency, 1930–1970* (Chicago: University of Chicago Press, 1982), 111–112.

6. This claim parallels Dawson's (1994) argument that the historical experience of African Americans since the time of Reconstruction has caused them to forge an exceptionally strong connection between their "political beliefs and actions as *individuals*" and "their perceptions of racial *group* interests." Michael Dawson, *Behind the Mule: Race and Class in African-American Politics* (Princeton, NJ: Princeton University Press, 1994), 45 (emphases in original).

7. This term was not new in the larger context of African-American history; it had been, most notably, widely used in conjunction with the Harlem Renaissance of the 1920s. See, for example, Nathan Irvin Huggins, *Harlem Renaissance* (New York: Oxford University Press, 1971), chap. 2.

8. Aldon D. Morris, *The Origins of the Civil Rights Movement: Black Communities Organizing for Change* (New York: Free Press, 1984), 106.

9. James Melvin Washington, ed., *A Testament of Hope: The Essential Writings of Martin Luther King, Jr.* (New York: Harper & Row, 1986), 76.

10. Martin Luther King, Jr., *Stride toward Freedom: The Montgomery Story* (New York: Harper & Row, 1958), 190. See also Washington, ed., *A Testament of Hope*, 85–86, 96, 101, 108, 137, and 145–146.

11. For a discussion of the formation, structure, philosophy, and activities of the SCLC from the time of its organization in 1957 through 1963, see Morris, *The Origins of the Civil Rights Movement*, esp. chaps. 4–5. For a history of the Civil Rights

movement that focuses on King and the SCLC, see David J. Garrow, *Bearing the Cross: Martin Luther King, Jr., and the Southern Christian Leadership Conference* (New York: Vintage, 1988).

12. Morris, *The Origins of the Civil Rights Movement*, 106.

13. D'Emilio (2003) provides a detailed biography of Rustin that examines his profound, if largely behind-the-scenes, influence on King. See John D'Emilio, *Lost Prophet: The Life and Times of Bayard Rustin* (New York: Free Press, 2003), esp. chap. 11.

14. Bayard Rustin, "Getting On with the White Folks," *Liberation* 1 (1956), 7, 9.

15. Morris, *The Origins of the Civil Rights Movement*, 96–99.

16. William R. Beardslee, *The Way Out Must Lead In: Life Histories in the Civil Rights Movement* (Atlanta, GA: Emory University Center for Research in Social Change, 1977), 60.

17. Clayborne Carson, David J. Garrow, Gerald Gill, Vincent Harding, and Darlene Clark Hine, eds., *The Eyes on the Prize Civil Rights Reader: Documents, Speeches, and Firsthand Accounts from the Black Freedom Struggle, 1954–1990* (New York: Penguin, 1991), 143.

18. Peter B. Levy, ed., *Documentary History of the Modern Civil Rights Movement* (New York: Greenwood, 1992), 98. See also Pat Watters, *Down to Now: Reflections on the Southern Civil Rights Movement* (New York: Pantheon, 1971); and Beardslee, *The Way Out Must Lead In*, chap. 12.

19. Watters, *Down to Now*, 198–199.

20. Charlotte Devree, "The Young Negro Rebels," *Harper's* 223 (1961): 135.

21. Editorial, "Integration Leaders Examine Lessons of Birmingham," *Liberation* 8, no. 4 (1963): 4. See also John O. Killens, "Explanation of the 'Black Psyche,'" *New York Times Magazine* (June 7, 1964), 37ff., reprinted in Francis L. Broderick and August Meier, *Negro Protest Thought in the Twentieth Century* (New York: Bobbs-Merrill, 1965), 348–357.

22. Beardslee, *The Way Out Must Lead In*, 121. See also Killens, "Explanation of the 'Black Psyche.'"

23. Broderick and Meier, *Negro Protest Thought in the Twentieth Century*, 318.

24. "Man of the Year: Never Again Where He Was," *Time* 83, no. 1 (Jan. 3, 1964), 26.

25. Harold R. Isaacs, "Integration and the Negro Mood," *Commentary* (Dec. 1962), 488–489, 497. See McAdam, *Political Process and the Development of Black Insurgency*, for an analysis of the key historical factors that enabled African Americans to achieve an unprecedented degree of political power at this time.

26. For a philosophical analysis of this broad democratic vision focusing on the central concept of "freedom," see Richard H. King, *Civil Rights and the Idea of Freedom* (New York: Oxford University Press, 1992).

27. Levy, *Documentary History of the Modern Civil Rights Movement*, 73.

28. King, *Stride toward Freedom*, 219–220. See also King's 1963 essay, "The Ethical Demands for Integration," in Washington, ed., *A Testament of Hope*, 117–125.

29. See, for example, Watters, *Down to Now*, 84, 109; and Beardslee, *The Way Out Must Lead In*, 81.

30. Levy, *Documentary History of the Modern Civil Rights Movement*, 73.

31. Watters, *Down to Now*, 236. See also the comments of John Lewis, as quoted in ibid., 24; and of King, as recorded in Washington, ed., *A Testament of Hope*, 207.

32. Carson et al., *The Eyes on the Prize Civil Rights Reader*, 121.

33. James Baldwin, "A Negro Assays the Negro Mood," *New York Times Magazine* (Mar. 11, 1961), 25ff. See also John Lewis, " . . . A Serious Revolution," *Liberation* 8, no. 7 (1963): 8; and *New York Times* (Aug. 26, 1961), 20.

34. Washington, ed., *A Testament of Hope*, 160–161.

35. Quoted in Sally Belfrage, *Freedom Summer* (New York: Viking, 1965), 7–8.

36. Bayard Rustin, *Down the Line: The Collected Writings of Bayard Rustin* (Chicago: Quadrangle, 1971), 94.

37. Ibid., 95. For further evidence of the deep commitment of Rustin and other movement leaders to macroeconomic reform during the early 1960s, see Hamilton and Hamilton, *The Dual Agenda*, 122–135.

38. King, *Stride toward Freedom*, 202–204. See also King's 1961 speech to the Fourth Constitutional Convention of the AFL-CIO, reprinted in Philip S. Foner, Ronald L. Lewis, and Robert Cvornyek, eds., *The Black Worker since the AFL-CIO Merger, 1955–1980*, vol. 8: *The Black Worker: A Documentary History from Colonial Times to the Present* (Philadelphia: Temple University Press, 1984), 184–188; and King's 1962 article "If the Negro Wins, Labor Wins," reprinted in Washington, ed., *A Testament of Hope*, 201–207.

39. See Rustin as quoted in Paul Goodman, *Seeds of Liberation* (New York: Braziller, 1964), 317; and Martin Luther King, Jr., *Why We Can't Wait* (New York: Mentor, 1964), chap. 1.

40. Goodman, *Seeds of Liberation*, 317–318, 323.

41. Paula F. Pfeffer, *A. Philip Randolph: Pioneer of the Civil Rights Movement* (Baton Rouge: Louisiana State University Press, 1990), 246.

42. Ibid., chap. 7.

43. Ibid., 255.

44. Bayard Rustin, "The Meaning of the March on Washington," *Liberation* 8, no. 8 (1963): 11–13.

45. Martin Luther King, Jr., "The Case against Tokenism," *New York Times Magazine* (Aug. 5, 1962), 11, 53. See also Washington, ed., *A Testament of Hope*, 104.

46. "Nation Is Warned on Negro Status," *New York Times* (Dec. 3 1961), 62. See also the remarks of Whitney Young to the national conference of the NUL in Damon Stetson, "Action Is Urged by Urban League: Injustice to Negro in Both North and South Is Cited," *New York Times* (Sept. 6, 1962), 21; and James Farmer of CORE in Murray Illson, "Cruelty in South Is Laid to Police: CORE Chief Says Greenwood Used Dogs on Negroes," *New York Times* (Apr. 7, 1963), 57.

47. "Negro Is Said to Face 'Hidden' Prejudice," *New York Times* (Sept. 7, 1961), 18.

48. Stetson, "Action Is Urged by Urban League," 21.

49. Foner et al., *The Black Worker since the AFL-CIO Merger*, 79.

50. King, *Why We Can't Wait*, 24. See also the comments of Jack Greenberg in Jack Greenberg, "An NAACP Lawyer Answers Some Questions," *New York Times Magazine* (Aug. 18, 1963), 16ff.; Loren Miller, "Freedom Now—But What Then?" *The Nation* (June 29, 1963), 539–542; Whitney Young in Theodore Jones, "Urban League Expanding to Fight Negro 'Despair,'" *New York Times* (Apr. 10, 1964), 20; Leslie W. Dunbar, executive director of the Southern Regional Council, in Claude Sitton, "Since the School Decree: Decade of Racial Ferment," *New York Times* (Mar. 18, 1964), 24; and the report on a White House meeting among King (SCLC), Wilkins (NAACP), Young (NUL), and Farmer (CORE) in Jack Raymond, "Johnson Is Hopeful House Will Debate Rights This Month," *New York Times* (Jan. 19, 1964), 1, 42.

51. Martin Arnold, "Negroes Here Held More Upset over Jobs Than Segregation," *New York Times* (June 18, 1963), 22.

52. Foner et al., *The Black Worker since the AFL-CIO Merger*, 80.

53. King, *Why We Can't Wait*, 129–130.

54. M. S. Handler, "White and Negro Clash at Parley: Bryn Mawr and Haverford Hear Debate on Rights," *New York Times* (Feb. 9, 1964), 51.

55. Foner et al., *The Black Worker since the AFL-CIO Merger*, 80.

56. Whitney Young, *To Be Equal* (New York: McGraw-Hill, 1964), 84.

57. Foner et al., *The Black Worker since the AFL-CIO Merger*, 80. See also King, *Why We Can't Wait*, 138.

58. See King, *Why We Can't Wait*, 141–142; and Randolph (1963) in Foner et al., *The Black Worker since the AFL-CIO Merger*, 81.

59. Nancy J. Weiss, *Whitney M. Young, Jr., and the Struggle for Civil Rights* (Princeton, NJ: Princeton University Press, 1989), 152; Young, *To Be Equal*, 26–33.

60. Gertrude Samuels, "Five Angry Men Speak Their Minds," *New York Times Magazine* (May 17, 1964), 14ff.

61. King, *Why We Can't Wait*, 136–140.

62. Weiss, *Whitney M. Young, Jr., and the Struggle for Civil Rights*, 150.

63. Foner et al., *The Black Worker since the AFL-CIO Merger*, 315.

64. "Mrs. King Asks Help for Poorer Negroes," *New York Times* (Mar. 12, 1962), 40.

65. Loren Miller, "Farewell to Liberals: A Negro View," *Nation* 195 (1962): 237.

66. See also the comments of Young in his speech to the Ninetieth Annual Conference on Social Welfare, as reported in Emma Harrison, "'Better' Rights for Negro Urged: Urban League Official Calls Equality No Compensation," *New York Times* (May 21, 1963), 22; and in Whitney M. Young, Jr., and Kyle Haselden, "Should There Be 'Compensation' for Negroes?" *New York Times Magazine* (Oct. 4, 1963), 43ff.

67. King, *Why We Can't Wait*, 134–135.

68. See comments of Roy Wilkins, as reported in Harrison, "'Better Rights for Negro Urged,'" 22; Loren Miller, "Farewell to Liberals: A Negro View," *The Nation* 195 (1962): 235–238; Loren Miller, "Freedom Now—But What Then?" *The Nation* 196

(June 29, 1963): 539–542; Jack Greenberg, "An NAACP Lawyer Answers Some Questions"; and James Farmer in "What Next? Five Negro Leaders Reply," *New York Times Magazine* (Sept. 29, 1963), 27ff.

69. Foner et al., *The Black Worker since the AFL-CIO Merger*, 81.

70. M. S. Handler, "Rustin Sees Losses," *New York Times* (Dec. 2, 1963), 1.

71. Murray Friedman, "The White Liberal's Retreat," *Atlantic* 211, no. 1 (1963): 44.

72. Charles B. Turner, Jr., "The Black Man's Burden: The White Liberal," *Dissent* 10 (1963): 215–216.

73. Stephen B. Oates, *Let the Trumpet Sound: The Life of Martin Luther King, Jr.* (New York: Mentor, 1982), 247–248.

74. "How Whites Feel about Negroes: A Painful American Dilemma," *Newsweek* (Oct. 2, 1963), 44–57.

75. Indeed, in July 1964, pollster Lou Harris found that 61 percent of urban white working-class ethnics (e.g., Poles, Hungarians, Slovaks, Italians) believed that blacks were "getting a better break than their own fathers and grandfathers received as immigrant outsiders," while "two out of every three feel that most Negroes want to take jobs held by whites." Theodore H. White, "Backlash," *Life* (Oct. 16, 1964), 100ff.

76. Louis Harris, "The 'Backlash' Issue," *Newsweek* 64 (July 13, 1964), 27.

77. Charles Silberman, *Crisis in Black and White* (New York: Random House, 1964), 10.

78. David Danzig, "Rightists, Racists, and Separatists: A White Bloc in the Making?" *Commentary* (Aug. 1964), 32. See also Sumner M. Rosen, "Liberals and Reality: A Response to Gus Tyler," *Liberation* 8, no. 12 (1964): 25ff.

79. Emphasis in original in first part of quote; emphasis added in second part. David Danzig, "The Meaning of Negro Strategy," *Commentary* (Feb. 1964), 42–44.

80. Emphasis in original. Norman Podhoretz, James Baldwin, Nathan Glazer, Sidney Hook, and Gunnar Myrdal, "Liberalism and the Negro: A Round-Table Discussion," *Commentary* (Mar. 1964), 25–26.

81. "The Negro Movement: Where Shall It Go Now?" *Dissent* 11 (1964): 282.

82. Emphasis in original in second quote, added in third. Ibid., 283–284, 289.

83. Ibid., 282–285.

84. Danzig, "The Meaning of Negro Strategy," 46. See also Turner, "The Black Man's Burden," 219.

Chapter 7

1. The term *social liberalism* is here used to refer to the variety of liberalism inspired by the Civil Rights movement and temporarily embraced by the national Democratic party under the Johnson administration. As described in the previous chapter, this position was characterized by its commitment to the dual agenda of ending both poverty and racial discrimination. Although Civil Rights movement leaders were strongly influenced by social democratic ideas, within the U.S. context

these continued to be expressed within the broad confines of an essentially liberal, as opposed to socialist, tradition. The term *social liberalism*, however, is intended to signal its affinity with what in Western Europe would be referred to as *social democracy*.

2. Bayard Rustin, "From Protest to Politics: The Future of the Civil Rights Movement," *Commentary* 39, no. 2 (1965), 25.

3. Ibid., 30, 25.

4. For a summary discussion of the key provisions of the 1964 Civil Rights Act, see *Revolution in Civil Rights*, 4th ed. (Washington, DC: Congressional Quarterly, 1968), 62–67.

5. Rustin, "From Protest to Politics," 30. Civil rights were commonly understood to have been the pivotal issue in the 1964 elections. Republican presidential candidate Barry Goldwater—one of the eight nonsouthern senators who had voted against the Civil Rights Act of 1964—went down to a crushing defeat, carrying only his home state of Arizona and five states in the heart of the Deep South (Alabama, Georgia, Louisiana, Mississippi, and South Carolina). Johnson, meanwhile, won 61 percent of the popular vote and forty-four states, carrying the traditional Republican constituencies of white Protestants, suburbanites, midwestern farmers, and Wall Street businesspeople. At the same time, in the congressional elections, fourteen of the thirty-four Republican representatives who had voted against the Civil Rights Act were defeated (eleven northerners and three southerners), as were the two Republican senators running for office who had similarly voted against it (Goldwater of Arizona and Mechem of New Mexico, who was up for reelection). James L. Sundquist, *Dynamics of the Party System: Alignment and Realignment of Political Parties in the United States* (Washington, DC: Brookings, 1983), 357; Allen J. Matusow, *The Unraveling of America: A History of Liberalism in the 1960s* (New York: Harper Torchbooks, 1986), 15; *Congress and the Nation*, vol. 2: *1965–1968* (Washington, DC: Congressional Quarterly, 1968), 61.

6. Rustin, "From Protest to Politics," 28–30.

7. The full text of Johnson's speech is reprinted in Lee Rainwater and William L. Yancey, *The Moynihan Report and the Politics of Controversy* (Cambridge, MA: MIT Press, 1967), 125–132.

8. Ibid., 125.

9. Ibid., 131–132.

10. "President's Michigan Speech on 'Great Society,'" *Congressional Quarterly Almanac: 1964* (Washington, DC: Congressional Quarterly, 1965), 874.

11. Ibid., 126.

12. Adam Yarmolinsky, who served as deputy director of the President's Task Force on the War on Poverty in 1964, for example, explained: "The crisis of the Northern ghetto was simply not foreseen in anything like its present critical character by the draftsmen of the [War on Poverty] program. . . . Negro poverty was thought about and talked about largely in the geographical context of the Deep South." James L. Sundquist, ed., *On Fighting Poverty: Perspectives from Experience* (New York: Basic,

1969), 42, 49. Similarly, Ramsey Clark (assistant and deputy attorney general, 1961–1967; attorney general, 1968–1969) stated in 1968 that up until the fall of 1965, "we had looked at the civil rights problem basically as a Southern problem." Transcript, Ramsey Clark oral history interview, Lyndon Baines Johnson Library, Austin, Texas (hereafter LBJL), 7.

13. Piven and Cloward (1971, 1974) alternatively argue that the War on Poverty was in fact a strategic ploy on the part of the Democratic party designed to secure the black urban vote and to quell disorder in the cities. In agreement with other scholars such as Brauer (1982) and Weir (1992), however, I believe that they are simply wrong on this point and that there is no solid evidence to support their claim. Frances Fox Piven and Richard A. Cloward, *Regulating the Poor: The Functions of Public Welfare* (New York: Vintage, 1971), chap. 9; Piven and Cloward, *The Politics of Turmoil: Essays on Poverty, Race, and the Urban Crisis* (New York: Pantheon, 1974), pt. 4; Carl M. Brauer, "Kennedy, Johnson, and the War on Poverty," *Journal of American History* 69 (1982), 98–119; Weir, *Politics and Jobs*, 84. For a helpful discussion of this controversy, see Michael B. Katz, *The Undeserving Poor: From the War on Poverty to the War on Welfare* (New York: Pantheon, 1989), 81–88.

14. Rainwater and Yancey, *The Moynihan Report and the Politics of Controversy*, 126.

15. Johnson pointed out that while black and white unemployment rates had been roughly the same in 1930, by 1965, blacks were twice as likely to be unemployed. Similarly, the unemployment rate among experienced black workers had reached 29 percent by 1963. During 1949–1959, the income of black men relative to white men declined; during 1952–1963, the comparative median income of black families dropped from 57 to 53 percent. At the same time, de facto segregation in the urban North was steadily increasing. Rainwater and Yancey, *The Moynihan Report and the Politics of Controversy*, 127–128.

16. Ibid., 128–130.

17. The Moynihan report had provided the most immediate basis for the Howard speech, which, at Johnson's directive, had been drafted by Moynihan and presidential assistant Richard N. Goodwin the day before its delivery. Ibid., 4, 32.

18. Ibid., 4, 18, 188–189.

19. For a good primary source statement that was used to advocate the passage of the Economic Opportunity Act of 1964, see "The Problem of Poverty in America," in U.S. Congress, House, Committee on Education and Labor, *Economic Opportunity Act of 1964: Hearings before the Subcommittee on the War on Poverty Program*, 88th Cong., 2d sess. (1964), 31–61. Particularly good secondary source discussions of the War on Poverty include Katz, *The Undeserving Poor*, chap. 3; and James T. Patterson, *America's Struggle against Poverty, 1900–1980* (Cambridge, MA: Harvard University Press, 1981), chap. 8. A valuable article which falls into the grey area between primary and secondary sources is Adam Yarmolinsky's "The Beginnings of OEO," in Sundquist, *On Fighting Poverty*, chap. 2.

20. The key provisions of the Economic Opportunity Act of 1964 were as follows: Title I established the Job Corps, federally assisted state and local job-training pro-

grams for young adults, and the Work-Study Program. Title II established the (soon to be infamous) Community Action Program and federally assisted state and local adult education services. Title III established a loan program for low-income rural families; Title IV established one for small businesses. Title V provided additional funding for an established work-training program for Aid to Families with Dependent Children (AFDC) recipients. Title VI established the Office of Economic Opportunity (OEO) and the Volunteers in Service to America (VISTA) program. Title VII exempted individual payments made under the poverty program from being counted as income when determining need levels for public assistance. *Congressional Quarterly Almanac: 1964* (Washington, DC: Congressional Quarterly, 1964), 210–212.

21. Good collections of relevant primary source essays from the social democratic perspective include Jeremy Larner and Irving Howe, eds., *Poverty: Views from the Left* (New York: Morrow, 1965); and Ben B. Seligman, ed., *Poverty as a Public Issue* (New York: Free Press, 1965). For a good secondary source discussion of the Civil Rights movement's perspective on poverty issues, see Thomas F. Jackson, "The State, the Movement, and the Urban Poor: The War on Poverty and Political Mobilization in the 1960s," in Michael B. Katz, ed., *The "Underclass" Debate: Views from History* (Princeton, NJ: Princeton University Press, 1993).

22. Sundquist, *On Fighting Poverty*, 42. In concrete terms, the president's original request for the first year of the program was a relatively paltry (given his stated ambitions) $965 million. Of this, Congress granted just under $950 million. *Congressional Quarterly Almanac: 1964*, 208.

23. Daniel P. Moynihan, *Maximum Feasible Misunderstanding: Community Action and the War on Poverty* (New York: Free Press, 1969), 28–29.

24. The above two paragraphs draw from Katz, *The Undeserving Poor*; Moynihan, *Maximum Feasible Misunderstanding*; and Patterson, *America's Struggle against Poverty*.

25. Seligman, ed., *Poverty as a Public Issue*, 5–6.

26. OEO allocations during 1965–1970 averaged $1.7 billion per year, or about 1.5 percent of the federal budget. If all of this money had been distributed directly to the poor as income, each poor person in the country would have received about $60 per year. Patterson, *America's Struggle against Poverty*, 151.

27. A. Philip Randolph Institute, "A 'Freedom Budget' for All Americans" (New York: A. Philip Randolph Institute, Oct. 1966). Reprinted in U.S. Congress, Senate, Subcommittee on Executive Reorganization, Committee on Government Operations, *Federal Role in Urban Affairs*, pt. 9, 89th Cong., 2d sess. (1966), 1893–1992.

28. Pfeffer, *A. Philip Randolph*, 286–290.

29. The controversy over the Moynihan report reverberated for decades. Wilson's (1987) criticism that this controversy "had the effect of curtailing serious research on minority problems in the inner city for over a decade," for example, generated enormous national attention and renewed conflict. Reed and Bond (1991) subsequently denounced "Moynihan's racist, scurrilously misogynist 1965 report" and "the canard—legitimized by William Julius Wilson's black imprimatur—that the left was

responsible for the backlash against antipoverty policy because of its refusal to confront the issue of social pathology." Wilson, *The Truly Disadvantaged*, 4; Adolph Reed, Jr., and Julian Bond, "Equality: Why We Can't Wait," *Nation* 253 (Dec. 9, 1991): 733–734.

30. Moynihan, along with Sargent Shriver, Adam Yarmolinsky, and James Sundquist, was centrally responsible for developing the legislative proposals of the War on Poverty. Rainwater and Yancey, *The Moynihan Report and the Politics of Controversy*, 19.

31. Ibid., 3–4, 26–29.

32. For a more recent, complementary analysis, see Daryl Michael Scott, *Contempt and Pity: Social Policy and the Image of the Damaged Black Psyche, 1880–1996* (Chapel Hill: University of North Carolina Press, 1997), 150–159.

33. Rainwater and Yancey, *The Moynihan Report and the Politics of Controversy*, 141–142, 375–377.

34. Ibid., 67, 192, 61–71, 143, 157, 172.

35. Ibid., 197–198, 220, 411.

36. Ibid., 200, 202, 410.

37. Ibid., chap. 12. For the official report of the conference, see White House Conference, "To Fulfill These Rights," *Report of the White House Conference "To Fulfill These Rights"* (Washington, DC: Government Printing Office, 1966).

38. SNCC, which was rapidly radicalizing during this time, formally withdrew from the conference in May 1966. In an obvious reference to the Moynihan report, SNCC's formal withdrawal statement charged that the conference represented an attempt "to shift responsibility for the degrading position in which blacks now find themselves away from the oppressors to the oppressed." Claybourne Carson, *In Struggle: SNCC and the Black Awakening of the 1960s* (Cambridge, MA: Harvard University Press, 1981), 204.

39. In January 1965, American involvement in Vietnam consisted of 20,000 military advisors. The Vietcong were winning, however, so the United States initiated air attacks on North Vietnam in February. When this proved insufficient, combat troops were sent in March. Subsequently, in July, troops were increased to 125,000, and the ground war officially began. By the end of 1965, paying for the war in Vietnam had added $4.7 billion to the 1966 budget, and expenditures for fiscal 1967 were projected at $10.5 billion. By January 1966, more than 400,000 American troops were in Vietnam. Matusow, *The Unraveling of America*, 154–156; Rainwater and Yancey, *The Moynihan Report and the Politics of Controversy*, 204.

40. Floyd McKissick introduced a resolution at the White House conference urging an end to the Vietnam War, but it was voted down by a ten-to-one margin. The reason for this was not that so many conference delegates supported the war, but rather because they knew that both the labor movement and the administration did, and they did not want to cause unnecessary rifts. Rainwater and Yancey, *The Moynihan Report and the Politics of Controversy*, 283.

41. The event that had done the most to establish this rift was the Democratic

party's refusal to officially recognize the Mississippi Freedom Democratic party at the party's convention in Atlantic City in August 1964.

42. Rainwater and Yancey, *The Moynihan Report and the Politics of Controversy*, 203–204, 283–284.

43. Matusow, *The Unraveling of America*, 214.

44. Rainwater and Yancey, *The Moynihan Report and the Politics of Controversy*, 193.

45. See, for example, Staughton Lynd, "Coalition Politics or Nonviolent Revolution?" *Liberation* 10, no. 4 (1965): 18–21; Ronald Radosh, "From Protest to Black Power: The Failure of Coalition Politics," in Marvin E. Gettleman and David Mermelstein, eds., *The Great Society Reader: The Failure of American Liberalism* (New York: Vintage, 1966), 278–293; and Stokley Carmichael and Charles V. Hamilton, *Black Power: The Politics of Liberation in America* (New York: Vintage, 1967), chap. 3. See also D'Emilio (2003) for a detailed examination of "From Protest to Politics" and the strength and influence of the Left's reaction against it (D'Emilio, *Lost Prophet*, chap. 17).

46. Staughton Lynd, "Radical Politics and Nonviolent Revolution," *Liberation* 11, no. 2 (1966): 13–19.

47. Stanley Aronowitz, "White Radicals and Black Revolt," *Liberation* 12, no. 5 (1967): 12.

48. Staughton Lynd, "Resistance: From Mood to Strategy," *Liberation* 12, no. 8 (1967): 41.

49. For a provocative analysis of the importance of cultural images of masculinity in the development of the New Left, see Alice Echols, "'We Gotta Get Out of This Place': Notes toward a Remapping of the Sixties," *Socialist Review* 22, no. 2 (Apr. 1992): 9–33.

50. For an excellent analysis of the 1968 Democratic convention, see David Farber, *Chicago '68* (Chicago: University of Chicago Press, 1988).

51. The Meredith March occurred when James Meredith, who had single-handedly integrated the University of Mississippi in 1962, embarked on a 220-mile walk from Memphis to Jackson to demonstrate to Mississippi blacks that it was safe for them to travel to vote. After getting only twenty-eight miles out of Memphis, however, Meredith was shot. Consequently, Martin Luther King, Floyd McKissick (president of CORE), and Stokley Carmichael went to Mississippi to continue the march. After more violence and arrests, Carmichael made national headlines by repeatedly shouting, "We want black power!" to an assembled crowd and generating an enthusiastic response. Matusow, *The Unraveling of America*, 354–355.

52. The Black Power movement primarily consisted of three wings: pluralist, culturalist, and revolutionary. Generally speaking, the pluralist wing of the movement was dedicated to building strong, independent black communities and political organizations that, being free from white influence or control, would be capable of pursuing black interests without undue compromise. The culturalist wing prioritized the importance of developing an empowered African-American cultural identity, one which emphasized its uniqueness from—and superiority to—white (or, more

broadly, Western) traditions and values. Finally, the revolutionary wing sought to join the African-American struggle for freedom to a larger movement of Third World peoples dedicated to destroying both the United States and the larger system of Western racist, capitalist imperialism of which it was a part. William L. Van Deburg, *New Day in Babylon: The Black Power Movement and American Culture, 1965–1975* (Chicago: University of Chicago Press, 1992), chap. 4.

53. Carmichael and Hamilton, *Black Power*, 54, 50–51, 60–61, 183.

54. Quoted in Carson, *In Struggle*, 221.

55. Matusow, *The Unraveling of America*, 327, 363, 365, 368, 396.

56. "Civil Rights: The New Racism," *Time* (July 1, 1966), 11.

57. Todd Gitlin, *The Whole World Is Watching: Mass Media in the Making and Unmaking of the New Left* (Berkeley: University of California Press, 1980), 162–163; Carson, *In Struggle*, 224–230.

58. The perception that the War on Poverty became disproportionately targeted on blacks was an accurate reflection of how these programs evolved after 1964. Weir (1992) notes that "by 1966 over half the individuals involved in poverty programs were members of racial minorities." In addition, the perception that the poverty programs were encouraging violence, while impossible to prove, was plausible. Button (1978) found, for example, that the riots did, if only in the short run, produce increased federal funding: OEO funds per poor family in Los Angeles, for instance, "increased more than six-fold in the year following the Watts outbursts." The critical point, however, is that the conservative view refused to consider the ways in which preexisting conditions affected these developments. Weir, *Politics and Jobs*, 84; James W. Button, *Black Violence: Political Impact of the 1960s Riots* (Princeton, NJ: Princeton University Press, 1978), 31.

59. Weir, *Politics and Jobs*, 88.

60. U.S. Congress, House and Senate, 90th Cong., 1st sess., *Congressional Record*, vol. 113, pt. 23 (1967), 31812.

61. See, in general, Personal Papers of Ramsey Clark, LBJL.

62. Letter from Louis A. Chapin to Ramsey Clark, Apr. 21, 1968, Personal Papers of Ramsey Clark, Box 68, "Loose Material—Letters (2 of 2)," LBJL.

63. National Advisory Commission on Civil Disorders, *The Kerner Report: The 1968 Report of the National Advisory Commission on Civil Disorders* (New York: Pantheon, [1968] 1988), 1–2; emphasis added.

64. Bayard Rustin, *Down the Line: The Collected Writings of Bayard Rustin* (Chicago: Quadrangle, 1971), 184–186. For similar statements, see ibid., 153, 178, 212, 231, 241.

65. This later became known as the Poor People's Campaign. Occurring soon after King's assassination, this demonstration brought thousands of people to Washington, DC, to live in a shantytown designed to house them until such time as their demands (such as for public jobs and a guaranteed annual income) were met. Quickly degenerating into chaos due to, among other things, poor planning and torrential rains, the campaign proved to be utterly ineffective, if not embarrassing—all in all, an ignominious end to the era of massive civil rights demonstrations.

66. Washington, ed., *A Testament of Hope*, 64–69.

67. Jeremy Larner, "Initiation for Whitey: Notes on Poverty and Riot," *Dissent* 14 (1967): 691.

68. Phillip Burton et al., "War, Riot, and Priorities: A Statement by Ten Congressmen," *Dissent* 14 (1967): 527.

69. Hubert H. Humphrey, *Beyond Civil Rights: A New Day of Equality* (New York: Random House, 1968), 9–10 (emphasis added), 187, 192–193.

70. Kevin P. Phillips, *The Emerging Republican Majority* (New Rochelle, NY: Arlington House, 1969).

Chapter 8

1. While these developments rested on the foundation that had been laid by the "Old Right" activists of the 1950s–1960s, they represented a vital new infusion of energy and resources into the larger conservative movement, which propelled its subsequent political ascendance.

2. See in particular Thomas Byrne Edsall and Mary D. Edsall, *Chain Reaction: The Impact of Race, Rights, and Taxes on American Politics* (New York: Norton, 1991), chap. 4; and Dan T. Carter, *From George Wallace to Newt Gingrich: Race in the Conservative Counterrevolution, 1963–1994* (Baton Rouge: Louisiana State University Press, 1996), chap. 2.

3. Edsall and Edsall, *Chain Reaction*, 79; Carter, *From George Wallace to Newt Gingrich*, 18.

4. Edsall and Edsall, *Chain Reaction*, 86.

5. For an exhaustive, if highly partisan, examination of the birth and death of the Family Assistance program, see Daniel P. Moynihan, *The Politics of a Guaranteed Income: The Nixon Administration and the Family Assistance Plan* (New York: Random House, 1973).

6. A. James Reichley, *Conservatives in an Age of Change: The Nixon and Ford Administrations* (Washington, DC: Brookings Institution, 1981), chap. 8, 409; Nicholas Lemann, "The Unfinished War, Part II," *Atlantic Monthly* (Jan. 1989), on the Web at www.theAtlantic.com/atlantic/election/connection/poverty/lemannf2.htm (2000), p. 25 (of 29).

7. Quoted in Lemann, "The Unfinished War, Part II," 18s.

8. The key case in this regard was *Swann v. Charlotte-Mecklenburg Board of Education* (402 U.S. 28, 1971) in which the Supreme Court ruled unanimously that busing constituted a reasonable remedy to school segregation.

9. See Gary Orfield, *Must We Bus? Segregated Schools and National Policy* (Washington, DC: Brookings Institution, 1978).

10. Boston is the most famous such case. See Ronald P. Formisano, *Boston against Busing: Race, Class, and Ethnicity in the 1960s and 1970s* (Chapel Hill: University of North Carolina Press, 1991).

11. Edward G. Carmines and James A. Stimson, *Issue Evolution: Race and the Transformation of American Politics* (Princeton, NJ: Princeton University Press, 1989), chap. 5.

12. Quoted in Reichley, *Conservatives in an Age of Change*, 190.

13. Ibid., 191.

14. Quoted in Edsall and Edsall, *Chain Reaction*, 89 (emphases in original).

15. Lemann, "The Unfinished War, Part II," 28.

16. Reichley, *Conservatives in an Age of Change*, 232.

17. On the intellectual foundations of the postwar conservative movement, see George H. Nash, *The Conservative Intellectual Movement in America since 1945* (Wilmington, DE: Intercollegiate Studies Institute, 1996).

18. General overviews of the development of the postwar conservative movement include William C. Berman, *America's Right Turn: From Nixon to Clinton*, 2d ed. (Baltimore, MD: Johns Hopkins University Press, 1998); Sara Diamond, *Roads to Dominion: Right-Wing Movements and Political Power in the United States* (New York: Guilford, 1995); Paul Gottfried, *The Conservative Movement*, rev. ed. (New York: Twayne, 1993); Jerome L. Himmelstein, *To the Right: The Transformation of American Conservatism* (Berkeley: University of California Press, 1990); Godfrey Hodgson, *The World Turned Right Side Up: A History of the Conservative Ascendancy in America* (New York: Houghton Mifflin, 1996); and Nash, *The Conservative Intellectual Movement in America since 1945*.

Increased historical attention has recently been devoted to building a better understanding of the early roots of the contemporary conservative movement, particularly during the early 1960s. Notable works include John A. Andrew III, *The Other Side of the Sixties: Young Americans for Freedom and the Rise of Conservative Politics* (New Brunswick, NJ: Rutgers University Press, 1997); Mary C. Brennan, *Turning Right in the Sixties: The Conservative Capture of the GOP* (Chapel Hill: University of North Carolina Press, 1995); Rebecca Klatch, *A Generation Divided: The New Left, the New Right, and the 1960s* (Berkeley: University of California Press, 1999); Lisa McGirr, *Suburban Warriors: The Origins of the New American Right* (Princeton, NJ: Princeton University Press, 2001); Gregory L. Schneider, *Cadres for Conservatism: Young Americans for Freedom and the Rise of the Contemporary Right* (New York: New York University Press, 1999); and Jonathan M. Schoenwald, *A Time for Choosing: The Rise of Modern American Conservatism* (New York: Oxford University Press, 2001).

19. See Peter Steinfels, *The Neoconservatives: The Men Who Are Changing America's Politics* (New York: Simon and Schuster, 1979); Gary Dorrien, *The Neoconservative Mind: Politics, Culture, and the War of Ideology* (Philadelphia: Temple University Press, 1993); Gary Dorrien, "Inventing an American Conservatism: The Neoconservative Episode," in Amy Ansell, ed., *Unraveling the Right: The New Conservatism in American Thought and Politics* (Boulder, CO: Westview, 1998), chap. 3; and Gottfried, *The Conservative Movement*, chap. 4.

20. Andrew, *The Other Side of the Sixties*, 208–210; Hodgson, *The World Turned Right Side Up*, 63–68; McGirr, *Suburban Warriors*, 182–185.

21. The term *neoconservative* first appeared in 1972, when leading social democratic writer and activist Michael Harrington coined it as a means of identifying and critiquing the rightward shift of many of his former colleagues on the Left. Although at first resented and rejected by those so labeled, by the end of the decade they had embraced the term and made it their own—in large part because they had become increasingly willing to renounce their political roots and openly champion a new conservative agenda. Dorrien, "Inventing an American Conservatism," 60.

22. These two journals published the bulk of early neoconservative writing. The *Public Interest* was cofounded by Bell and Kristol in 1965 to take a hard look at Great Society programs. *Commentary* was transformed by Norman Podhoretz from an obscure left-liberal publication of the early 1960s to an aggressively conservative journal "read and discussed by the president, his advisers, and foreign heads of government" in the 1980s. Gottfried, *The Conservative Movement*, 83.

23. Bell and Moynihan later disassociated themselves from the movement when it lurched significantly further to the right during the 1980s.

24. Examples include Elliot Abrams, "The Quota Commission," *Commentary* (Oct. 1972): 54–57; Nathan Glazer, "Is Busing Necessary?" *Commentary* (Mar. 1972), 39–52; and Ben Wattenburg and Richard Scammon, "Black Progress and Liberal Rhetoric," *Commentary* (Apr. 1973), 35–44.

25. Nathan Glazer, *Affirmative Discrimination: Ethnic Inequality and Public Policy* (Cambridge, MA: Harvard University Press [1975] 1987), 43–44, 220–221. Glazer later repudiated many of his former views on racial issues, stating that the failure of American society to open up more fully to African Americans after the passage of the Civil Rights acts of 1964 and 1965 demonstrates that the principles of individualistic liberalism that worked to assimilate other racial and ethnic groups do not work equally well in their case. See Nathan Glazer, *We Are All Multiculturalists Now* (Cambridge, MA: Harvard University Press, 1997).

26. Diamond (1995) provides a detailed examination of the activities of politically marginal, but increasingly violent, right-wing racist groups during the 1980s and 1990s (Diamond, *Roads to Dominion*, chap. 11). See also Chip Berlet and Matthew N. Lyons, *Right-Wing Populism in America: Too Close for Comfort* (New York: Guilford, 2000), chap. 13.

27. It is difficult to find either primary or secondary source discussions of how conservatives justified shifting their views on civil rights issues so quickly. Presumably, their traditional opposition to antidiscrimination law—and not infrequent advocacy of white supremacy—had become such a political embarrassment that they subsequently avoided any in-depth consideration of it.

28. Dorrien, "Inventing an American Conservatism," 62; Berman, *America's Right Turn*, 85–88.

29. Dan Himmelfarb, "Conservative Splits," reprinted in Gregory L. Scheider, ed., *Conservatism in America since 1930: A Reader* (New York: New York University Press, 2003), 388. This essay responded to Stephen J. Tonsor's extremely interesting paleoconservative attack on neoconservatism, "Why I Am Not a Neoconservative," origi-

nally published in the *National Review* in 1986 and reprinted in the same volume (chap. 33).

30. Neoconservatives clashed with several groups of conservatives: antistate absolutists who opposed any and all manifestations of the welfare state, isolationists who rejected the goal of American leadership in the world, and moral traditionalists who espoused a sweeping rejection of modernity. During the 1980s, these cleavages shifted somewhat, as the neoconservatives moved further to the right to join the larger conservative crusade to eliminate social welfare subsidies to the poor (most notably, the AFDC program, which would be ended in 1995). At the same time, however, as the neoconservative movement grew more powerful with the support of the Reagan administration, some conservatives resented its comparative political success, particularly with regard to its newfound dominance of established conservative institutions such as the American Enterprise Institute (AEI).

31. Steinfels, *The Neoconservatives*, chaps. 8–9.

32. Edward C. Banfield, *The Unheavenly City: The Nature and Future of Our Urban Crisis* (Boston: Little, Brown, 1970), 245.

33. Edward C. Banfield, *The Unheavenly City Revisited* (Boston: Little, Brown, 1974).

34. Aaron Wildavsley, "Government and the People," *Commentary* (Aug. 1973): 26. Thirty years of empirical research on the effectiveness of antipoverty programs that target the poorest and most dysfunctional families has proven Wildavsky's assessment to be essentially correct. Although some evaluations have found dramatic effects for particular programs, these have been limited to small numbers of individuals, and the effects have not always been lasting. See Robert G. St. Pierre and Jean I. Layzer, "Improving the Life Chances of Children in Poverty: Assumptions and What We Have Learned," *Society for Research in Child Development Social Policy Report* 12, no. 4 (1998): 1–25.

35. Nathan Glazer, "The Limits of Social Policy," *Commentary* 52, no. 3 (Sept. 1971): 51–58. See also Wildavsky, "Government and the People," 25–32. For a critical assessment of Wildavsky's claims concerning the Great Society, see Steinfels, *The Neoconservatives*, 221–224.

36. Key leaders of the New Right included Richard Viguerie, who pioneered the enormously successful tactic of direct-mail fundraising; Paul Weyrich, head of the Committee for the Survival of a Free Congress and Coalitions for America; John Terry Dolan, director of the National Conservative Political Action Committee; and Phyllis Schlafly, who spearheaded campaigns against the Equal Rights Amendment and gay rights.

37. Important primary source materials on the New Right include Richard A. Viguerie, *The New Right: We're Ready to Lead* (Falls Church, VA: Viguerie, 1981); and Robert A. Whitaker, *The New Right Papers* (New York: St. Martin's, 1982).

38. Himmelstein, *To the Right*, 80–94.

39. Ibid.

40. Hodgson, *The World Turned Right Side Up*, 166–178.

41. Viguerie, *The New Right*, 53.

42. Duane M. Oldfield, *The Right and the Righteous: The Christian Right Confronts the Republican Party* (Lanham, MD: Rowman & Littlefield, 1996), 100–102.

43. Paul M. Weyrich, "Blue Collar or Blue Blood? The New Right Compared with the Old Right," in Whitaker, *The New Right Papers*, 48–62; quote cited on p. 52.

44. Samuel Francis, "Message from MARs: The Social Politics of the New Right," in Whitaker, *The New Right Papers*, 64–83; and in Schneider, *Conservatism in America since 1930*, chap. 29. Francis's analysis of the MARs demographic was based on his reading of Donald I. Warren, *The Radical Center: Middle Americans and the Politics of Alienation* (Notre Dame, IN: University of Notre Dame, 1976), 23–29.

45. Weyrich, "Blue Collar or Blue Blood?" in Whitaker, *The New Right Papers*, 53. Weyrich cites "racial hiring quotas and busing" as primary examples of such policies.

46. Robert J. Hoy, "Lid on a Boiling Pot," in Whitaker, *The New Right Papers*, 98.

47. Hoy, for example, warns that "white racist political activity will grow in the years ahead unless the frustration it symptomizes can be directed into regular political channels." Ibid., 99.

48. Gottfried, *The Conservative Movement*, 111.

49. Fleming (1982), for example, wrote in *The New Right Papers* that "society is composed not of individuals, but families" and that "no civil right is absolute." Similarly, he argued that "the land, the home, and the church—not the marketplace—are the only proper foundations for a healthy society." Such views would presumably place him outside of even a broadly defined liberal tradition (Thomas Fleming, "Old Rights and the New Right," in Whitaker, *The New Right Papers*, 180–200). Fleming was not a leader of the New Right, however, and his essay was not typical of the movement as a whole. See Gottfried, *The Conservative Movement*, 111–112.

50. Sidney Blumenthal, *The Rise of the Counter-Establishment: From Conservative Ideology to Political Power* (New York: Times Books, 1986), 4.

51. James A. Smith, *The Idea Brokers: Think Tanks and the Rise of the New Policy Elite* (New York: Free Press, 1991), 180–181.

52. A detailed primary source description of this process is provided by Viguerie, *The New Right*.

53. Himmelstein, *To the Right*, chap. 5. See also Thomas Byrne Edsall, *The New Politics of Inequality* (New York: Norton, 1984); and Thomas Ferguson and Joel Rogers, *Right Turn: The Decline of the Democrats and the Future of American Politics* (New York: Hill and Wang, 1986).

54. This list is adopted from Sally Covington, *Moving a Public Policy Agenda: The Strategic Philanthropy of Conservative Foundations* (Washington, DC: National Committee for Responsive Philanthropy [NCRP], 1997).

55. Smith, *The Idea Brokers*, 181.

56. See Covington, *Moving a Public Policy Agenda*; and People for the American Way (PFAW), *Buying a Movement: Right-Wing Foundations and American Politics* (Washington, DC: PFAW, 1996).

57. Smith, *The Idea Brokers*, 35.

58. Currency conversion rate of 1 to 4.22 for 1973 to 2004 dollars provided by the

Federal Reserve Bank of Minneapolis consumer price index (CPI) calculator on its Web site at http://woodrow.mpls.frb.fed.us/research/data/us/calc/ (May 2004).

59. Covington, *Moving a Public Policy Agenda*, 35.

60. Blumenthal, *Rise of the Counter-Establishment*, 66.

61. PFAW, *Buying a Movement*, 16.

62. Ibid., 17–18.

63. Covington, *Moving a Public Policy Agenda*.

64. Different foundations support different factions of the conservative movement. As Heritage Foundation president Ed Feulner commented in 1992, "If you are a neo-conservative, your first call would be Bradley. If you are a traditional conservative, Scaife. And if you are a libertarian, the first call is the Koch family." NCRP, *$1 Billion for Ideas: Conservative Think Tanks in the 1990s* (Washington, DC: NCRP, 1999), 33.

65. Covington, *Moving a Public Policy Agenda*; Jean Stefancic and Richard Delgado, *No Mercy: How Conservative Think Tanks and Foundatations Changed America's Social Agenda* (Philadelphia: Temple University Press, 1996), chaps. 4–5; PFAW, *Buying a Movement*, 27–30.

66. Quoted in Covington, *Moving a Public Policy Agenda*, 20.

67. Ibid., 13–18.

68. Smith, *The Idea Brokers*, 179.

69. Gregg Easterbrook, "Ideas Move Nations," *Atlantic Monthly* (Jan. 1986), 70–71; Covington, *Moving a Public Policy Agenda*, 15.

70. Easterbrook, "Ideas Move Nations," 72–73; Covington, *Moving a Public Policy Agenda*, 13–15; Stefanic and Delgado, *No Mercy*, 53.

71. Stefancic and Delgado, *No Mercy*, 90.

72. Manhattan Institute Web site: www.manhattan-institute.org (2004).

73. Eric Alternman, "The 'Right' Books and Big Ideas," *Nation* (Nov. 22, 1999), on the Web at www.thenation.com/docprint.mhtml?i=19991122&s=alterman2 (2004), p. 3 (of 6).

74. Smith, *The Idea Brokers*, 192.

75. Easterbrook, "Ideas Move Nations," 72.

76. Heritage Foundation, *Mandate for Leadership: Policy Management in a Conservative Administration* (Washington, DC: Heritage Foundation, 1981), 155. Similarly, Robert R. Detlefsen wrote in a 1985 issue of the *Cato Journal* (published by the conservative think tank the Cato Institute) that "the challenge that has faced the [Reagan] administration is not simply one of modifying one or two arguably wrong-headed policies, but of displacing an entire way of thinking about Civil Rights." Detlefsen, "Civil Rights, the Courts, and the Reagan Justice Department," *Cato Journal* 4, no. 3 (Winter 1985): 94.

77. Heritage Foundation, *Mandate for Leadership*, 447–448.

78. Stefancic and Delgado (1996) document that "virtually every conservative and even some mainstream think tanks and foundations have played important roles" in the ongoing attack on affirmative action (Stefancic and Delgado, *No Mercy*, 45). This activity has had a profound effect. Gamson and Modigliani (1987) demonstrate

that from the late 1960s to the late 1980s, the way in which affirmative action was most commonly framed in the mainstream media shifted from the widely acceptable concept of "remedial action" to the negatively charged "reverse discrimination." The most important reason that this shift occurred, they believe, was that the reverse-discrimination frame was heavily promoted by conservative journals, think tanks, and advocacy organizations, as well as by the Reagan administration. William A. Gamson and A. Modigliani, "The Changing Culture of Affirmative Action," in Richard D. Braungart, ed., *Research in Political Sociology*, vol. 3 (Greenwich, CT: JAI, 1987), 163–166.

79. Viguerie, *The New Right*, 25–26, 100–103.

80. Although a good number of such Christian Right organizations were defunct or moribund by the end of the 1980s, the Christian Coalition, which proved to be an even more effective political force, was established in 1989. Oldfield, *The Right and the Righteous*, 188–191.

81. Viguerie, *The New Right*, 8, 28.

82. For an in-depth examination of how conservative foundations and think tanks have successfully used the media to shift political debate to the right, see Trudy Lieberman, *Slanting the Story: The Forces That Shape the News* (New York: New Press, 2000).

83. Covington, *Moving a Public Policy Agenda*, 22; PFAW, *Buying a Movement*, 11–12.

84. The expansion of Fox News as a de facto advocate of conservative politics has since made it the most important media outlet for the movement. The rapid expansion and widespread popularity of conservative talk radio since the late 1980s has also been extremely important.

85. Covington, *Moving a Public Policy Agenda*, 16.

86. PFAW, *Buying a Movement*, 11.

87. Covington, *Moving a Public Policy Agenda*, 22–23; PFAW, *Buying a Movement*, 12.

88. Covington, *Moving a Public Policy Agenda*, 23.

89. People for the American Way Foundation, *The Federalist Society: From Obscurity to Power* (Washington, DC: People for the American Way, 2001).

90. Covington, *Moving a Public Policy Agenda*, 9, 24; Karen M. Paget, "Lessons of Right-Wing Philanthropy," *American Prospect* 9, no. 40 (Sept. 1, 1998): 91.

91. Covington, *Moving a Public Policy Agenda*, 11–12; see also PFAW, *Buying a Movement*, 27–34.

92. Quoted in Diamond, *Roads to Dominion*, 210.

93. See, for example, Amy Elizabeth Ansell, *New Right, New Racism: Race and Reaction in the United States and Britain* (New York: New York University Press, 1997); Dan T. Carter, *The Politics of Rage: George Wallace, the Origins of the New Conservatism, and the Transformation of American Politics* (New York: Simon & Schuster, 1995); Carmines and Stimson, *Issue Evolution*; Edsall and Edsall, *Chain Reaction*; Jonathan Rieder, *Carnarsie: The Jews and Italians of Brooklyn against Liberalism* (Cambridge, MA: Harvard University Press, 1985); Stanley B. Greenberg, *Middle*

Class Dreams: The Politics and Power of the American Majority (New York: Times Books, 1995); Sugrue, *The Origins of the Urban Crisis*; and Jill S. Quadrango, *The Color of Welfare: How Racism Undermined the War on Poverty* (New York: Oxford University Press, 1994). Although these books present different arguments, all agree on the central importance of race in the conservative turn.

94. Edsall and Edsall, *Chain Reaction*, chap. 7.
95. Carter, *From George Wallace to Newt Gingrich*, 63.
96. Edsall and Edsall, *Chain Reaction*, chap. 8.
97. Ibid., 170–173.
98. Greenberg, *Middle Class Dreams*, 23–44.
99. Carter, *From George Wallace to Newt Gingrich*, 72–80.

Conclusion

1. Lawrence Mishel, Jared Bernstein, and Sylvia Allegretto, *The State of Working America, 2004/2005* (Ithaca, NY: Cornell University Press, 2005), 1–17.

Index

American dilemma (*continued*)
   as reformulated by the neoconservatives, 192, 201–202, 221, 227
   as reformulated by social liberalism, 168, 171, 185–188, 226
   rejection of concept of the, 161
   See also An American Dilemma; Democratic party, twentieth century; Myrdal, Gunnar
American Enterprise Institute (AEI), 212–213, 282 n. 30
American exceptionalism, 7, 234 n. 13
American Federation of Labor (AFL)
   and the CIO, 127
   and constriction of American liberal politics, 97, 113, 118
   growth and membership of the, 115, 261
   and protective legislative for women and children, 261 n. 91
   racial exclusion and the, 115–116, 261 n. 85, 261 n. 86
American Indians, 58, 101–102, 104
American Jewish Committee, 161
American Jewish Congress, 153
American Legislative Exchange Council, 215
American liberalism
   boundaries of, 5, 233 n. 6, 247 n. 3
   centrality of race to the development of, 9–14, 51, 64
   Civil Rights movement and the boundaries of, 159, 233 n. 8
   definition of, 5
   New Right and the boundaries of, 207–208, 283 n. 49
   plasticity of, 4–9, 232 n. 3, 233 n. 9, 241 n. 2
   producer republicanism and the boundaries of, 62, 69–70, 233 n. 8
   and racial equity, 3–4, 51
   turning points in development of, 11–14, 223–229
   See also anti-caste liberalism; conservative movement; Darwinian liberalism; neoconservative movement; postwar liberalism; producer republicanism; social liberalism
An American Dilemma, 121, 124, 125, 231 n. 1

anarchism
   and alternatives to liberalism in America, 5
   and the Haymarket Affair, 103, 106
   as a sign of racial inferiority, 103
Anglo-Saxons, 37, 59, 79, 92, 96, 103, 104, 110
anti-caste liberalism
   and the Civil Rights Act of 1875, 22–29
   economic conservatism of, 12, 16, 22, 34–35, 122
   and the Fourteenth Amendment, 16, 25–33, 41–43, 54–55, 239 n. 43
   and human universalism, 16, 23–29, 61, 225
   political commitments of, 11–12, 15–17
   political marginalization of, 29–33, 54–57, 61, 65
   and the Reconstruction amendments, 11, 23, 25–34
   and the Thirteenth Amendment, 16, 25–26, 30–33, 55
anti-communism
   and the conservative movement, 202, 205, 206, 207
   and postwar liberalism, 122, 126, 128, 267 n. 46
   and reaction against the War on Poverty, 183
   See also communism
Aronowitz, Stanley, 180
Atwater, Lee, 220
Australian ballot system, 90, 117
automation. *See* deindustrialization

Baker, Ella, 149, 267–268 n. 3
Baldwin, James, 149, 162
Banfield, Edward, 201, 203
Baroody, William, 212
Bayard, Thomas F., 44
Bell, Daniel, 201, 281 n. 22, 281 n. 23
Bell, Hiram P., 40
Bevel, James, 145
Bill of Rights for the Disadvantaged, 157
John Birch Society, 200
Birmingham, Alabama, 152, 153, 165, 170, 258 n. 47
Black Panther party, 181

black politics
    and black congressmen during Recon-
        struction, 237–238 n. 27
    and black nationalism, 5, 19
    and Chinese exclusion, 252 n. 64
    and the Civil Rights Act of 1875, 23, 32
    and the Knights of Labor, 76–77,
        240 n. 75, 249 n. 31
    and the Populist movement, 90, 92–93,
        259 n. 70
    postwar increase in national power of,
        123–124, 135
    relationship of individual and group
        identity in, 141, 268 n. 6
    and support for land redistribution, 12,
        18–19
    and support for socioeconomic equity,
        10, 150, 155, 267 n. 1
    See also Black Power movement; Civil
        Rights movement; New Negro
Black Power movement
    on American liberalism, 179, 182–183,
        188
    media sensationalism and the, 183, 194
    origins of the, 181, 277 n. 51
    primary wings of the, 194, 277–278 n. 52
    reaction against the, 168, 183–184, 191, 226
    See also black politics
Bloom, Allan, 217
Bolick, Clint, 34
Boutwell, George, S., 24
Bradley Foundation, 210, 216, 284 n. 64
Brookings Institution, 211
Brown, H. Rap, 182
Brown v. Board of Education, 198
Bryan, William Jennings, 97, 113
Buchanan, Patrick, 198
Buckley, William F., 200, 215
Buckner, Aylett Hanes, 42, 43
Burnham, Walter Dean, 117. *See also* elec-
    tion of 1896
Bush, George, 220
Bush, George W., 223
busing. *See* school desegregation

Cain, Richard H., 23
capitalism. *See* free markets

Carmichael, Stokley, 181, 182, 277 n. 51
Carnegie, Andrew
    and the Gilded Age, 66, 256 n. 20
    and the Gospel of Wealth, 95, 100–102,
        256 n. 16
Carter, Jimmy, 215
caste
    anti-caste liberal conception of, 11–12, 16,
        26–27, 33–34
    late nineteenth-century system of, 71
    white southern endorsement of, 52
Cato Institute, 210, 212, 216, 284 n. 76
Center for Individual Rights, 217
Center for Media and Public Affairs, 216
Center for the Study of Popular Culture,
    216
Chicago, Illinois, 103, 131, 133, 135, 136. *See also*
    Democratic party, twentieth century
Chinese Exclusion Act of 1882, 70–71,
    81–82, 252 n. 64. *See also* Knights of
    Labor
Christian Coalition, 285 n. 80
Christian Voice, 215
Citizens for a Sound Economy, 210
Civil Rights Act of 1875
    anti-caste liberals and the, 16, 22–31
    Civil Rights Cases and the, 55–57
    Darwinian liberals and the, 33–46, 241 n. 5
    enforcement of the, 245 n. 65
Civil Rights Act of 1964
    effects of the, 131, 170
    and the evolution of the Civil Rights
        movement, 139, 140, 161, 226
    neoconservative interpretation of the,
        192, 201, 281 n. 25
    opposition to the, 273 n. 5
    passage of the, 154
    social liberalism and the, 173
Civil Rights Act of 1965, 139, 170, 192, 226,
    281 n. 25
Civil Rights Cases, 29–32, 55–56
Civil Rights movement
    and the black church, 144–145
    and Christian radicalism, 148–149,
        33 n. 8
    conservative reinterpretation of history
        of the, 141, 228, 268 n. 4

attack on social welfare programs, 196, 197, 199, 204, 219, 282 n. 30

business support for the, 209, 211, 221

growth and development of the, 13, 169, 191–194, 223–224, 227–229, 279 n. 1

and growth of socioeconomic inequality, 194, 219–220, 224, 228

moral traditionalism and the, 193, 202, 205, 207, 211, 228, 282 n. 30

and the war of ideas, 191, 193

See also conservative establishment; neo-conservatives; New Right; race; Republican party, twentieth century

Conservative Victory Fund, 215

Constitution

anti-caste constitutionalism, 11, 15–17, 23–34, 40

Civil Rights movement and the, 147, 268 n. 4

conservative movement and the, 201, 227

Darwinian liberalism and the, 38–42

producer republicans and the, 68, 71, 85, 93, 108, 247 n. 3

white nationalism and the, 53

See also Fifteenth Amendment; Fourteenth Amendment; Reconstruction amendments; Thirteenth Amendment

cooperative commonwealth, 62, 69–70, 246–247 n. 2, 252 n. 82

Adolph Coors Foundation, 210

Coors, Joseph, 212

corporate capitalism, late nineteenth century, 117

development of, 19, 64–65

producer republican attack on, 12, 62, 83, 86, 225

crop lien system, 84

Dacus, J. A., 98

Daley, Richard, 181, 184

Danzig, David, 161–162, 164

Darwinian liberalism

and the New South, 49–51

political commitments of, 12, 37–38, 69, 241 n. 1

political strength of, 46–49, 54, 61, 65, 113, 119, 121

and reaction against the labor movement, 95–96, 100–102, 106

and reaction against Reconstruction, 46–49

and the Reconstruction amendments, 38–45, 54–59

Declaration of Independence

anti-caste liberal conception of the, 23–25, 33, 67–68

Black Power movement's invocation of the, 182

producer republicanism and the, 67, 71, 85, 247 n. 3

deindustrialization

and black unemployment, 129, 131–132, 134, 138, 155

Civil Rights movement's understanding of, 140, 150–154, 156, 163–164

in the postwar period, 129–130, 136, 138

Democratic party, late nineteenth century

Conservative Democrats in the, 49–50, 88, 92, 96, 110, 114–115, 260 n. 79

and the People's party, 87, 91, 253–254 n. 91

and producer republicanism, 65

and racial terrorism, 54, 87–88, 93, 96–97, 112

and white supremacy, 17, 45, 49, 72, 87–88, 110, 245 n. 62

Democratic party, twentieth century

and the black vote, 124

and Chicago 1968 Democratic National Convention, 168, 181, 184, 194

and the Civil Rights movement, 157, 167, 169–179, 188

and the Clinton administration, 223, 224

and the Popular Front, 128

and postwar liberalism, 121

and social liberalism, 13, 167, 169–171

southern wing of the, 115, 126, 127, 128, 170, 171, 186

support for civil rights legislation, 125–126

white working-class defection from the, 219–221, 228–229

See also Great Society; Howard University speech; War on Poverty

laissez-faire
  and American liberalism, 6
  and anti-caste liberalism, 16, 21–22
  and the *Civil Rights Cases*, 55
  and Darwinian liberalism, 37, 46–47, 54,
    65, 95, 241 n. 1, 256 n. 16
  and the free labor ideology, 19–21, 64
  and New South, 50
  and Republican opposition to the labor
    movement, 72
land redistribution, 16–19, 21, 34–35,
    235–236 n. 3, 236 n. 4
law of competition, 95, 101
Lawson, James, 147, 148
Lee, Fitzhugh, 107
Lewis, John, 146, 163
liberalism. *See* American liberalism
Liberation, 142, 143
Lipset, Seymour Martin, 201
Lloyd, Henry Demarest, 69–70
Lynch, John Roy, 23
Lynd, Staughton, 180

Manhattan Institute for Policy Research, 213
March on Washington (MOW), 153–154,
    163, 165
McCarthy, Joseph, 191, 206
McHenry, Henry D., 42
McKissick, Floyd, 178, 277 n. 51
McNeill, George E., 66–70, 76, 79, 81
Media Research Center, 216
Meredith, James, 277 n. 51
Meredith March, 181, 277 n. 51
Miller, Loren, 158
Mondale, Walter, 220
monopoly capital, 62, 68, 73, 81–83, 85
Montgomery, Alabama, 142
Montgomery bus boycott, 139
Moral Majority, 215
Morgan, W. Scott, 87
Morton, Oliver P., 27
Moynihan, Daniel Patrick
  and the Family Assistance Plan, 196
  and the neoconservative movement, 201,
    281 n. 23
  and the War on Poverty, 276 n. 30
  See also Moynihan report

Moynihan report, 176–178, 196, 274 n. 17,
    275–276 n. 29, 276 n. 38
Mullen, Willian H., 75
Murry, Charles, 204, 213
Myrdal, Gunnar, 121, 124–125, 149, 162,
    231 n. 1
Myrdalian paradigm. *See* American
    dilemma

Nation
  and the Civil Rights movement, 158, 178
  influence in late nineteenth-century of
    the, 255–256 n. 14
  and reaction against the labor move-
    ment, 99
  and reaction against Reconstruction, 48, 56
National Association for the Advancement
    of Colored People (NAACP)
  King speech to the, 142
  and the March on Washington, 153
  politics of the, 156, 158, 267 n. 1, 268 n. 4
National Catholic Conference for Interra-
    cial Justice, 153
National Christian Action Coalition, 215
National Conservative Policy Action Com-
    mittee (NCPAC), 214, 215, 282 n. 36
National Council of Churches, 153
National Empowerment Television, 216
National Pro-Life Action Committee, 215
National Review, 191, 215
National Rifle Association, 216
National Right to Work Committee, 214
National Urban League (NUL), 131, 153, 157,
    267 n. 1
Native Americans. *See* American Indians
Negro American Labor Council (NALC),
    153, 157
neoconservative movement
  attack on 1960s equalitarianism, 192–193,
    202–204
  and the conservative establishment,
    208–209
  and the New Right, 14, 193, 205, 208–209,
    228
  origins of term, 281 n. 21
  political thought of the, 13, 201–204, 207,
    221, 282 n. 30

and fusion, 86, 113

growth and development of the, 62–64, 73, 83–84, 253–254 n. 91

political thought of the, 62–64, 84–86, 252 n. 82

support for white supremacy by the, 88, 92–93, 225

and western regional politics, 73, 83, 84, 86, 87

See also People's party

postwar economic boom, 127, 128, 135, 175

postwar liberalism

antidiscrimination commitment of, 13, 121–123, 126, 137–139, 225

compared with social liberalism, 173–174

and expectations of civil rights legislation, 123, 131, 134, 138, 140, 226–227

and rejection of class-based politics, 13, 122–123, 126–130, 137–138

white working-class reaction against, 134–138

Powderly, Terence, 76, 79, 105, 107–108, 252 n. 73

Pratt, Daniel D., 24

producer republicanism

and American liberalism, 233 n. 8, 247 n. 3

defeat of, 93, 97, 113, 118–119

politics of, 12, 62–65, 84–85

See also Knights of Labor; Populist movement

producing classes, 12, 63, 70

Progressive Era, 13, 97, 118, 225–226

progressive liberalism, 123, 223–225, 229

Progressive reform movement, 113, 114, 117–119

Public Interest, 201, 202, 281 n. 22

Purnam, William J., 24

race

alternative conceptions of, 6–8

anti-caste understanding of, 23–25, 27–29, 33

and the conservative movement, 194, 205, 213–214, 219–222, 224, 281 n. 27, 284 n. 76

historically variable constructions of, 7, 78–79, 248 n. 7, 254–255 n. 1

impact on American liberalism, 4, 7, 9–14, 119

and late nineteenth-century regional politics, 72–72

and marginalization of progressive liberalism, 192, 225–229

neoconservative construction of, 192–193, 200–202, 227

postwar reconfiguration of, 122, 126, 136

producer republicanism and, 63, 70–71, 250 n. 40, 259 n. 62

and white rejection of liberal equalitarianism, 194, 197–198, 219–224, 228–229

See also ethnicity; immigrants, South and Eastern European

racial terrorism

and Conservative Democrats, 49

and creation of postwar ghetto, 133

and the Enforcement Acts, 244 n. 56

lynching and, 71, 110, 249–250 n. 32, 259 n. 63

and white nationalism, 38, 53–54, 57

See also Democratic party, late nineteenth century

Radical Republicans

and anti-caste liberalism, 11, 22–29, 239 n. 43, 239–240 n. 57

decline of the, 29, 46, 72

and laissez-faire, 19–22

and land redistribution, 17–19

and reaction to Reconstruction, 46, 52

Rainey, Joseph H., 23

Randolph, A. Philip, 153–156, 158, 176

Reagan, Ronald

and election of 1980, 215, 219, 220, 223

and election of 1984, 220

Reagan administration

civil rights issues and the, 34, 213–214, 284 n. 76, 284–285 n. 78

neoconservatives and the, 218, 282 n. 30

social and economic policies of the, 204, 209, 219–220

Reagon, Bernice, 144

Reconstruction

American liberalism and, 11, 121, 125, 225

anti-caste liberalism and, 15–17

collapse of, 29, 61, 65, 71–72, 100, 127

Compromise of 1877, 29, 31, 49, 65, 97

Darwinian liberalism during, 37–38

Smith, Edwin B., 30
Smith, J. Ambler, 43
Smith Richardson Foundation, 212, 215–216
social democracy
    and the Civil Rights movement, 139, 150,
        157, 163–165, 175, 272–273 n. 1
    and critique of neoconservatism, 281 n. 21
    definition of, 126
    and the labor movement, 127, 129
    and the New Deal, 13, 122, 126–128, 138,
        226
    postwar liberal rejection of, 122, 126–130
    in Western Europe, 118
social equality
    Civil Rights movement's support for, 152
    Darwinian liberal opposition to, 12,
        39–40, 44–46, 56, 58, 61, 241 n. 5
    and enforcement of the Civil Rights Act
        of 1875, 245 n. 65
    and the Knights of Labor, 108
    Populist opposition to, 88, 92–93
socialism
    and American liberalism, 5
    and the Civil Rights movement, 151,
        273 n. 1
    Darwinian liberal attack on, 95–96,
        101–102, 105, 109–110
    as mark of racial inferiority, 96, 104,
        259 n. 62
social liberalism
    and coalition politics, 167, 169–171, 173,
        184–185
    and commitment to ending poverty and
        racial discrimination, 167, 170–177, 193
    conservative attacks on, 177, 183–184
    definition of, 272–273 n. 1
    implosion of, 13, 167–169, 188–191, 223,
        226–227
    left-of-center attacks on, 178–183
    and warnings of democratic collapse,
        168, 185–189
    See also Civil Rights movement; Democ-
        ratic party, twentieth century; Great
        Society; War on Poverty
social science
    and the attack on biological racism,
        123–124

and support for Darwinian liberalism,
    100, 101
and the War on Poverty, 175
solid South, 97, 113–115. See also white su-
    premacy
Southard, Milton I., 39
Southern Christian Leadership Conference
    (SCLC), 142, 145, 149, 153, 170,
    267–268 n. 3
Soviet Union, 124, 128, 130
Spencer, Herbert, 100, 256 n. 16
Stalwarts, 20, 29
Stevens, Thaddeus, 17–18
Stone, W. W., 81, 82
Stop ERA, 215, 282 n. 36
Stride toward Freedom, 142, 147, 151
Student Nonviolent Coordinating Com-
    mittee (SNCC)
    and the Black Power movement, 182
    and the Civil Rights movement, 147, 149,
        153
    and Freedom Summer, 150
    and the transformation of black con-
        sciousness, 144, 145, 146
Students for a Democratic Society (SDS),
    180. See also New Left
suburbanization, 132, 134, 159
Sumner, Charles, 17–18, 22, 25–26, 41
Sumner, William Graham, 100–102
Sundquist, James, 276 n. 30
Swinton, John, 67, 74, 81
Syke, Charles J., 217

Taft-Hartley Act, 128
talk radio, 285 n. 84
Thirteenth Amendment, 16, 25–26, 30–33,
    52, 55, 245 n. 62
Thurman, Allen G., 42
Thurman, Strom, 195
To Secure These Rights, 125, 126
Tourgee, Albion W., 32–33, 52, 53, 244 n. 49
Truman, Harry S., 125–126, 128
Trumbull, Lyman, 41
Turner, Henry M., 32

United Auto Workers (UAW), 153
urban renewal, 133, 136. See also ghetto

Veterans Administration (VA), 132, 133
Vickers, George, 41
Vietnam War
    Civil Rights movement and the, 276 n. 40
    domestic turmoil and the, 13, 187
    escalation of the, 168, 176, 178, 194, 226,
        276 n. 39
    New Left's understanding of the, 180
Viguerie, Richard, 205, 208, 215, 282 n. 36
Voting Rights Act of 1965. *See* Civil Rights
    Act of 1965

wage slavery, 67, 73–76, 82
Walker, James C., 32–33
Wallace, George, 160–161, 195, 199
Wallace, Henry, 128
Walls, Josiah T., 27
War on Poverty
    architects of the, 196, 276 n. 30
    originating views of the, 172–175,
        273 n. 12, 274 n. 13
    reaction against the, 183, 278 n. 58
    spending on the, 168, 176, 275 n. 22
    Vietnam War and the, 179
    See also Economic Opportunity Act of
        1964; Office of Economic Opportunity
Washington, Mrs., 146
Washington Legal Foundation, 217
Watergate, 199, 219
Watson, Tom, 89–93, 110–113, 152, 225
Watts riot of 1965
    Black Power movement's reaction to the,
        182
    imagery of the, 133
    political effects of the, 130, 168
    social liberal reaction to the, 177, 179,
        278 n. 58
Weaver, James, 85
Weyrich, Paul
    and institutions of the New Right, 212,
        214, 216
    and the mobilization of the New Right,
        205, 208, 282 n. 36
    on the politics of the New Right, 206
white backlash
    against the New Left, 181
    and the growth of the New Right, 193

    in 1964, 160–161
    in the late 1960s, 13, 135, 168, 226
white ethnics
    anti-black perspectives of, 136–138
    class identity of, 136–138
    and reaction against postwar liberalism,
        122, 134–138
    socioeconomic status of, 136
    origins of category, 135–136
white liberals
    and conflict with Civil Rights movement,
        13, 140–141, 158–163, 167
white nationalism, 5, 6, 40, 51–54, 57
white supremacy
    American liberalism and, 12, 37–38, 46,
        51, 225, 231 n. 1
    Black Power movement's understanding
        of, 182
    Civil Rights movement's opposition to,
        141
    and Darwinian liberalism, 12, 37–40,
        44–46, 61, 245 n. 62
    and late nineteenth-century American
        political culture, 71–72, 93
    neoconservative rejection of, 192, 200,
        221, 227
    Populist support for, 88, 92–93, 225
    and the South, 49–51, 113–115, 127
    and white nationalism, 51–54
Why We Can't Wait, 155, 156, 157, 158
Wilkins, Roy, 158, 174
Williams, Charles G., 26
Wilson, Henry, 23
Wilson, James Falconer, 31–32
women's liberation. *See* feminism
Woodward, C. Vann, 90–91, 93
World War I, 123
World War II, 121, 124, 127

Yarmolinksy, Adam, 273 n. 11, 276 n. 30
Young, Whitney
    on affirmative action, 157, 158
    on black politics and democratic reform,
        156
    and the Howard University speech, 174, 178
    on the limits of anti-discrimination law,
        154–155